BEING HUMAN . . . BECOMING HUMAN

HELMUT THIELICKE

Being Human... *Becoming Human*

AN ESSAY IN CHRISTIAN ANTHROPOLOGY

TRANSLATED BY GEOFFREY W. BROMILEY

DOUBLEDAY & COMPANY, INC.

GARDEN CITY, NEW YORK

1984

Library of Congress Cataloging in Publication Data

Thielicke, Helmut, 1908–
Being human . . . becoming human.

Translation of: Mensch sein–Mensch werden.
Includes bibliographical references and indexes.
1. Man (Christian theology)   I. Title.
BT701.2.T4813   1984   233
Library of Congress Catalog Card Number 77-12880
ISBN 0-385-12492-9
English translation copyright © 1984 by Doubleday & Company, Inc.
and William Collins Sons & Co., Ltd.
This book was originally published in German as
Mensch Sein–Mensch Werden.
Entwurf einer christlichen Anthropologie, © R. Piper & Co. Verlag,
München, 1976.
All biblical selections are from the Revised Standard Version of the Bible.
Excerpt from *The Family Reunion* by T. S. Eliot,
copyright 1949 by T. S. Eliot;
copyright renewed 1967 by Esme Valerie Eliot.
Reprinted by permission of Harcourt Brace Jovanovich, Inc.
and Faber and Faber Ltd. Publishers.

First Edition

To the Lenoir-Rhyne College in Hickory, North Carolina, as a Token of Gratitude for the Conferring of the Honorary Degree of Doctor of Letters on the Author

The last continent unknown to humanity is humanity itself.
Edgar Morin, *Das Rätsel des Humanen*

What a web of contradictions humans are! They are the most indigestible morsel in a system. They are the snag in all that is true and false. They embarrass both naturalists and the orthodox. . . . We are dealing here with a chaos that is harder to fathom than that of the poets.
Pierre Bayle, *Réponse aux questions d'un Provincial*, 1702

No psychiatrist or psychotherapist—or even logotherapist—can tell sick people what the meaning is, only that life has a meaning, and that it has this in every condition and circumstance, thanks to the possibility of finding meaning in suffering.
Viktor E. Frankl, *Der Mensch auf der Suche nach Sinn*

> What ambush lies beyond the heather
> And behind the Standing Stones? . . .
> And behind the smiling moon?
> And what is being done to us?
> And what are we, and what are we doing?
> To each and all of these questions
> There is no conceivable answer.
> We have suffered far more than a personal loss—
> We have lost our way in the dark.
T. S. Eliot, *The Family Reunion*

Those who have to live a "why" can almost always tolerate a "how."
Nietzsche

The ground of things is far off and deep, very deep; who can find it out?
Ecclesiastes 7:24

Contents

Translator's Preface

During the past two decades Helmut Thielicke of Hamburg has established a solid reputation as an ethicist and theologian. His many volumes of *Theological Ethics*, which have been partly translated into English, provide a carefully constructed theological foundation for ethical inquiry, followed by detailed discussions of right action in such varied fields as politics, medicine, aesthetics, law, and sexuality. In the three volumes of the *Evangelical Faith*, which are all available in translation, he works over the primary themes of Christian doctrine, beginning with the noetic problems posed by contemporary hermeneutics, then following a broadly trinitarian schema, and at every point entering into discussion with leading thinkers both ancient and modern, both sacred and secular.

Thielicke, however, has never been an ivory-tower theologian. Indeed, he first became more widely known in the United States not for his academic work but for his sermons, in which, as an opponent of Hitlerism who was unavoidably implicated in the sufferings it caused, he spoke with such relevance and power to the generation of the Second World War and its aftermath. Even during his many years as a professor at Hamburg, although primarily devoted to his scholarly tasks, he never ceased to maintain an active interest in the church's ministry and mission. With his ethical concerns he has been plunged into discussion of all the leading and pressing issues of the day. Medical problems have led him to a consideration of death, as in his work *The Doctor as Judge*, and later in the more comprehensive treatment of all the issues of dying in his *Living with Death*. His continuing concern for mission in our highly secularized modern society has brought him into dialogue with contemporary intellectual movements, as in his little book *The Hidden Question of God*.

The present "essay in anthropology" is intended as a more popular piece of the same kind, although much larger and more sharply focused. It is not written in academic style with bulky bibliographies and elaborate footnotes. Ranging over a wide area of human themes, Thielicke here allies his extensive learning with a deep concern for humanity and a desire to communicate his faith in a relevant idiom and context. Without obtruding, yet also without surrendering his own Christian commitment, he takes up a topic that is of universal and enduring interest and deals with it in all its most important dimensions. Readers who are already familiar with the author's writings will catch many echoes here of what they have heard elsewhere. Nevertheless, they will still find the book valuable, partly because it presents these older materials in a different context, and partly because it assembles them now in a comprehensive form. For those who have not yet made Thielicke's acquaintance it offers an admirable starting point, the more so if they do not come with any developed theological knowledge or even with any initial Christian conviction. For in all its directness and simplicity it has also all the range and depth of Thielicke's more academic work and it forces us to come to grips with the most profound and elemental issues.

In the translation an attempt has been made to balance the required fidelity to the original text with sufficient latitude to make possible an idiomatic English that will serve the author's purpose of reaching a wider audience. In a few passages that use examples either from German sources or from books not so readily accessible to English-speaking readers, some slight abridgment has been thought permissible. Along the same lines some quotations, especially from German works, have been given in shorter, indirect form, although always with the references (where supplied) for closer consultation. So far as possible English equivalents have been given for works identified in the notes, but readers should be aware that the English rendering of the author's own *Theological Ethics* did not reproduce every passage in the original, so that in some instances only the German reference will be found.

Except, perhaps, in an introductory sense, a translation is not intended for those who want to do more detailed studies of an author's thought. By its very nature, however, this "essay in anthropology" is not meant for specialists with more restricted academic interests but for all thoughtful people who are concerned about humanity and would like to make some sense of human nature, history, and destiny. Not all such people have either the time or the opportunity for delving into large works in other languages, and it is with the hope of making such a work more readily available, and thus helping in part to meet the desire for meaning, that the present rendering of Thielicke's wide-ranging and thought-provoking essay is offered.

Pasadena, Lent, 1982

BEING HUMAN . . . BECOMING HUMAN

Understanding with the Reader

Anthropology has to do with everything human, and what does not come under this rubric? As Erich Fromm says, not just neurology and psychology but many other disciplines must be integrated if we are to achieve a science of humanity. In fact, all the disciplines and all spheres of life—art and economics, thought and speech, the irrational and ecstatic—have a human reference.

In anthropology, then, it is less a matter of selection and more a matter of finding the perspective that will give a view of the whole.

Perspective means two things.

First, it distinguishes between objects that are closer to me and those that are more distant. It thus rules out the equality of purely statistical statement.

Second, and closely related, it relates objects to the viewpoint of the observer and thus ensures an element of subjectivity.

Applying perspective to the theme of humanity can only mean addressing what is important to me, what is interesting to me (in the sense of inter-esse), and what is relevant to my age. I write neither for the year 1890 nor the year 2010. I should like to stress this subjective, or confessional, element.

But does not this mean writing such a book mainly for myself? Why, then, expect readers?

A consciously subjective starting point of this kind—which must not be irrational, of course, but use scientific data and rational arguments—can be a fruitful basis for dialogue with contemporaries. I am thinking of a conversation in which experts and interested amateurs gather around a table (or fireplace) and raise matters of ultimate concern. Then all must make their own confession. No one can indulge in mere generalities that the others can share in and agree to with indifference. Each one will listen to all the rest and let them have their say. And in this listening, what is said will have a power of maieutic release. Those who listen will feel that they are being questioned.

Along these lines I want to have my own say—though it is not just my own product but has arisen under the pressure of experiences, in life's fulfillments and failures, in contact with friends and foes, in conflicts and hours of peace. I want readers who will be patient enough to let me have my say and who will perhaps be inclined to let it release their own say, or at least help to stimulate it.

My concern in all this is the common search for identity. We speak as those who suffer from a common loss of this or as those who think they have found a path and a goal. As my calling demands, I have in view especially young people of student age.

In a book that deals with the center of life, readers are continually confronted by certain basic questions that I will explore and have been trying to answer for decades, often with debatable success. This insistence on my own problems of thought is undoubtedly a sign of the subjectivity of my attempt. But how can we write about humanity without exposing the marks that the vicissitudes of our own life have left on us? Superiority and aloofness would be a swindle here. To the hard chips left by my own stonebreaking belong problems that are often culpably overlooked by many theologians, namely, the autonomous working of historical processes that threatens to swallow up our freedom, or the search for identity that has harassed and will harass the younger generation in the seventies and eighties.

Although I am not concerned in any chapter to disavow theologians, I want to avoid technical jargon and speak to open-minded contemporaries as I usually do in oral discussion. It has needed no special courage to speak at a more popular level and thus to break step with my respected colleagues. Guest professorships in Anglo-Saxon countries and the corresponding lectures have helped me gradually to give flesh and blood to this kind of style (though "Made in Germany" still betrays itself at times, and perhaps ought to do so). At any rate, I have nothing against the style or against illustrations and anecdotes if they give vividness and clarity. On the contrary, I find it sterile when theologians write only for other theologians and think they prove their expertise in this way.

The only courage required is that of being a dilettante. In anthropology we constantly meet with themes in which we cannot all be experts: the humanities and sciences, philosophy and medicine, and the like. Hence we have to cross boundaries that are full of traps, although, as Paul Tillich once said, frontiers are also places that yield abundant knowledge. *One* concern I must admit to the reader. Among the many things I have had to leave out is a chapter on the typical human characteristic of humor. But I have already written a book on this, and warming this up would have been difficult and done little credit to humor itself.

I should like to mention a couple of technicalities in closing.

My *Theological Ethics* deals with anthropology too, and if I often refer to this in footnotes (and to other books of my own), this is not because of any arrogant assumption that they are particularly valuable or indispensable. It is because I have to abbreviate a good deal in the present volume, and sometimes merely hint at things. Thus it helps to pacify my conscience when I can point the reader to what I have thought and said about many of these problems elsewhere.

These references are the more necessary because I have kept quotations and bibliography to a minimum here. In the past, once begun, a gigantic apparatus would immediately develop. But this book is meant to be readable. Experts will know on what authorities I rely or with whom I am in debate.

Finally, I must thank those who have assisted me, especially with the indexes and proofreading: Uwe Böschemeyer in Hamburg and Reinhard Gilster in Bremen. My former assistant Siegfried Scharrer deserves special mention for scrutinizing the manuscript and making valuable criticisms and suggestions. Not last or least of all I am grateful to my wife for supervising the publication.

A. HUMANITY—
AN OPEN QUESTION

I. THE QUESTION WHAT HUMANITY IS CANNOT BE ANSWERED OBJECTIVELY

There is hardly an industrial or New Year's political address that does not say in some way that people are the real issue, not tariffs or wages or social reforms—at least not as separate measures, only for the sake of people. In both East and West everybody speaks about positive humanism, about the humanizing of the penal codes, abortion, bureaucracy, the care of the elderly. But what is meant by people? What view of humanity is normative?

Though it sounded macabre coming from his lips, Stalin gave us food for thought when in an appeal to industry he said that in the period of reconstruction, technology is decisive, but that many people are wrong when they construe this mechanically, as though all that were needed is a great multiplication of machines, for technology cannot be divorced from the people that set it in motion; without people it is dead. There is need then, he continued, to lay emphasis on those who have mastered technology. We must cherish all capable and informed officials and foster their development; distribute and organize people properly in the process of production; arrange wages in such a way that they will give security to the decisive members of the production team and inspire them to improve their qualifications. The final point of this concern for people was to create a large army of cadres for technical production.

What is the picture of humanity that the speaker has in view here? People are no longer distinguished from the technological process but integrated into it. They are given key positions among the tools of technology. Then a further distinction is made according to the degree of qualifications.

If we are right, then, humanity is not given the dignity of being an end in itself in Immanuel Kant's sense but is a means to the end of production even if a means of uniquely high rank. There is here no infinite worth of the human soul, no privilege that differentiates humanity from things, no according of a qualitative distinction. People are significant only as they are useful in the process of production or in society.

But does not this raise at once the question of the limit of their value? When people get old or sick or incompetent or mentally ill, do they not lose every chance of qualifying? If there is no qualitative distinction in value, the only criterion is that of social or technical utilizability—from the cradle to the grave. But if we take this path, we have to tread it to the end. The next step in this direction follows with dreadful ineluctability.

Once utilizability achieves the rank of a criterion, the question arises when and where its limit is reached. The line may be fixed differently. It may be marked by the incarceration of hopelessly hardened criminals or the institutionalizing of the insane and asocial elements or in other ways, but it has to be drawn somewhere. Behind this frontier the idea of those who are not fit to live gains credence.

Whether this idea establishes itself does not depend on cynicism or other traits of character. On good grounds I do not believe that definitely criminal instincts drove the Nazis to eliminate the mentally ill and persecute the Jews. In many people idealism and a readiness for self-denial were motives in this dreadful business, perverted though these might have been. What triggered them and set rolling the apocalyptic drama of mass murder was not the subjective disposition of the murderer but their table of anthropological values. For if humanity is defined by its utilizability, the diagnosis of unfitness to live follows as night follows day. It is not dependent at all on traits of character. One moment a person like Reinhard Heydrich can be listening to a Mozart quartet and the next sending the thugs of the SS on a bloody hunt. The anthropological principle carries with it every other implication. And the rigor with which it does so is almost like the ineluctability of a natural law.

When we see this from the examples provided by history in our own time, we are confronted by a whole list of questions.

First is that of the alternative to the antihuman thesis of utilizability, of the basis on which to ascribe unconditional, independent, and sacrosanct value to human existence. Is it really enough simply to proclaim or postulate value of this kind? Such declarations would certainly be accompanied by the suspicion that under the shock of the thesis of utilizability and its historical consequences one is simply taking refuge in its antithesis and thus saying: Only if human life is unconditionally sacred and humanity is made the measure of all things are we protected against its being made a thing or tool and thus consigned to the scrap heap, as machines are when they wear out and are no longer of use. For if the statement that human life is unconditional and an end in itself is a mere product of anxiety, it can hardly be credible. But if it is to be credible, what basis is there for it? Without a basis, there can be no credibility! Undoubtedly it is not enough merely to appeal to the Western Christian tradition, within which the thesis of personal unconditionality has a firm place. For it might well be—and no doubt is—that we have lost the presuppositions of this tradition and its table of values. And how can we retain the conclusions if we have lost the premises?

Let us assume that Christianity normally shared the estimation of the person as an unconditional entity that is not at our disposal. How does this affect human destiny when we are secularized? Is it possible that the motor of this humane tradition will be shut off but the wheels will keep up the momentum of human impulse for a time, though ever more slowly, until things come to a complete stop? But stopping means farewell to the unconditionality of the person. It means giving the person a purely instrumental rank, reducing it to utilizability—or?

Reflection on this question is the axis of the deliberations that follow. I believe that this is a primary and decisive issue.

If we want to make it clear that the reasons for viewing human existence as unconditional are theological, it is not enough simply to say this. Our task is, so far as possible, to give intelligible reasons for saying it. By its very nature the Christian faith, which represents these reasons, cannot be demonstrated. We deny this faith and are guilty of epistemological naiveté if we try to base a proof of humanity on a proof of God. But we can do something else. We can consider how far the question of God—as a question—arises within anthropology.[1]

We thus proceed on the heuristic assumption that this question of God does not rest simply on dogmatic assertions—a dominant clerical ideology—but has its basis in real experiences and necessarily arises (as a question, not with an appended answer) when we penetrate into the deeper dimensions of existence.

Those who are acquainted with religious discussion from the time of the Enlightenment, from our emergence from culpable immaturity (Kant), will realize that theology has become increasingly linked with anthropology and to a large extent—to its own loss—been integrated into it. The more, since René Descartes, we have been aware of our own ego and sought autonomy, the more we have ceased to be passengers on the good ship Tradition, accepting the itinerary and the order of boarding as things that are self-evident. Instead, we have questioned the validity of traditional values and investigated their binding force. For those who regard themselves as liberated, the question thus takes the sharper form: What do these values mean for me? Can I recognize traditional norms as maxims for my own will instead of finding in them an autocratic authority and thus abnegating responsibility and delegating this to authoritative courts? But if this is so—and who would not wish it!—then the question of God comes also into the zone of doubt and has to be investigated. The questions now are: How relevant is God to me? Where does God come in? What is his relation to the realities of my own life? A heaven that is a mere hereafter remote from our here and now is no longer of any interest. It has no validity and is a mere assertion carried on the conveyor belt of tradition from generation to generation. Rightly, then, we may leave it to angels and the birds!

But there are other problems on the list as well. Reflection on how to inquire into human nature is among them. For it is clear that humans cannot be investigated just like inanimate objects, plants, and animals. If we treat them thus and establish certain objectifiable characteristics, our statements may well be true. But they do not hit the real truth of humanity. They put the essence of humanity in the twilight of exchangeability. According to this view, as Norbert Wiener has wittily pointed out, we are merely featherless bipeds. One cannot say that this description is incorrect, but it grotesquely misses the point of real humanity. What can be said about us from the standpoint of objective phenomenology does not get at our essential being. But the qualities by which our essential nature may be characterized are not subject to objective control. Freedom and responsibility are among such qualities. In education and penal law and the intimate sphere of marriage, in all human relations, and even in the organization of society, we count upon the presence or at least the possibility of freedom and responsibility. Without them there can be no trust, and without trust, human life becomes a process ruled by force and matter. There can no longer be demands or expectations, i.e., trust. Others are simply the object of calculable reactions: a truly apocalyptic and inhuman vision!

II. PROBLEMS IN SCIENTIFIC ANTHROPOLOGIES[2]

The essential facts constituting humanity do not submit to the methods of investigation applied by natural science to inanimate objects. This is why scientific attempts to project a picture of humanity based on its own presuppositions are unsatisfying. One might illustrate this from Jacques Monod's effort to arrive at the essence of humanity by way of molecular biology. The a priori probability that among all possible events in the universe one special event—human development—should take place, is very small. That we are human is a lucky chance. We are the product of an accident, gypsies on the edge of the universe. Evolution with its leaps replaces the Creator. We are projected into being by chance with neither goal nor destiny.

Apart from the question whether this theory is correct—we shall not presume to judge this—the question arises what image of humanity Monod presents here. Does not anthropology degenerate in his case into a mere physics of living matter? Does he not offer us a truly shadowy picture, or, better, a white wall on which something intangible and unrecognizable is depicted in weak contours? Where in all this is our real life, the relationship of I and Thou, the question of norms and values by which we may orient ourselves, the readiness for decision? On this view, where does initiative come from? as Salvador de Madariaga y Rojo rightly asks. What place is there for the end and the energy of will which cannot be equated with energy in general but which drives evolution forward? What is the source of the choice and perseverance that produced the Sistine Chapel and the *Ninth Symphony*? But this is the true secret of human life. And on the thematic horizon of Monod it can never become the subject of the question put to humanity. Strictly this means that humanity itself is left out of consideration.

In the same way the "new" anthropology of Edgar Morin seems to me to come up against the same frontier. The author suffers from the illusion that the essence of humanity is objectifiable and can be described by assembling empirical data. Since previous traditional views and beliefs have now lost their cogency, one must seek a new and comprehensive science of humanity. This universal anthropology is reached by relating the individual disciplines, e.g., the theory of information, cybernetics, research into the brain and behavior, ecology, et cetera.

I believe it is basically a mistake to think that the essence of humanity can be reached by adding up various empirical aspects. The present book tries to achieve a radically different anthropological conception by drawing out convictions about humanity from other than scientific sources—perhaps a well-considered or less well-considered world view, or religious conviction, or contemporary traditions, or direct human experience, or what have you. This given certainty about what constitutes humanity forms the framework for all that is experienced by way of empirical detail. I interpret the individual facts in the light of this a priori scheme.

Probably it would be justifiable to take Monod as an example of the same procedure. Molecular biology is not the basis of his theory that human life is an accident and we are gypsies on the edge of the universe. This conviction precedes the empirical components of his view of humanity. He shared with his friend Albert Camus the conviction that ours is an absurd Sisyphus existence and the findings of molecular biology simply seem to provide confirmatory indications.[3]

No one has shown more impressively than Kant in his *Critique of Practical Reason* how impossible it is to treat humans as things and then investigate them in objectifying fashion. In this book Kant specifically finds the uniqueness of humanity in something that cannot be grasped noetically, namely, freedom.

Why cannot freedom be objectified? To attempt it is to presuppose a gap in the system of causally determined processes where a cause does not automatically produce an effect but the nexus is broken and a human resolve, instead of being an effect, is a first cause. But if it is possible to find such a gap, I can triumphantly exclaim that I have captured the moment of freedom, the moment that has no cause, the moment in which the human I is not an effect of the causal nexus but is itself a cause, so that I can speak of its self-determination or autonomy.

III. THE INTERFACE OF FREEDOM
AND NECESSITY AS THE MYSTERY
OF HUMAN EXISTENCE

Why is it not possible to discover freedom as a gap of this kind in causality? Kant offers both an epistemological and an empirical reason.

Epistemologically, causality is for him a category operative in the act of understanding. In simple terms, what he is saying is that I am forced to see the objects of experience as effects and then as causes of new effects. An uncaused event is inconceivable. It is beyond the competence of my noetic process to perceive any break in the causal nexus at the gap of freedom. Freedom is not a sure thing for me within the theoretical knowledge that relates to objects. I know it nonobjectively as I experience in my conscience the summons of the categorical imperative and am under responsibility to comply with it. As the practical Logos says to my conscience: "Thou shalt," I cannot argue that I am deterministically impelled by causal necessity and hence cannot do what I would. To the "Thou shalt" corresponds the certainty of "Thou canst." The sphere of freedom is assigned by this summons.

Hence I attain the certainty of freedom in the nonobjectifiable realm of the moral I. According to Kant, even theoretical reason knows something of this freedom, but again nonobjectifiably, for if reason were to say that all its conclusions are determined, e.g., by the functions of the brain, it could not conceive of anything unconditional. Truth, then, could make no claim, and it would be plunged into "an abyss of skepticism." The certainty that reason can freely choose—i.e., choose truth—is thus an analytical principle of purely speculative reason. Thus knowledge of freedom in the sphere of theoretical experience is not based on the self-objectification of the reason within which it can observe itself and discover the gap of freedom in its deductions. No, this knowledge of freedom, too, arises, as it were, as a spontaneous and nonobjectifiable self-certainty of reason.

Alongside this epistemological reason why I cannot demonstrate freedom in theoretical analysis there is in Kant an empirical observation pointing in the same direction. Assuming it were possible to have such profound insight into human thinking that even the slightest impulse toward this was known to us and that we knew all the external influences to which it was exposed, we might be able to predict human conduct with the same certainty astronomers have when calculating eclipses of the sun and moon. The impossibility of doing this and the inhuman nature of the vision show us that the factor of freedom is overlooked. We do despite to human nature when we treat people as calculable objects and rule out their freedom. And, we might add, history constantly deals blows to such predictions and calculations as human freedom does what is incalculable. Prognosticators are always making fools of themselves.

Kant adds a further thought that is highly typical. Even if we ventured the hypothesis that human conduct can be calculated and acts can be predicted like eclipses, we should still have to maintain that humans are free. This sounds perverse and even absurd. Nevertheless, from what has been said we can see what Kant meant. Even if I see myself subject to the stringency of necessary processes and encounter the "Thou shalt" under this compulsion, I still know that I am responsible. An alcoholic who beats his wife and children and smashes his furniture when drunk will have a moral as well as a physical hangover when sobriety returns. He cannot simply say that his father was an alcoholic and he is a victim of heredity and thus excused. Except by way of self-protection he can hardly plead that an "it" took over. He will have to admit that "he" did it. He will be aware of his responsibility, his freedom.

Kant, then, relates responsibility to the fact that people are not things notwithstanding the reality of the law of causality. At a first glance this may sound abstract. Yet it is in tune with experiences familiar to all of us. I am reminded of a kleptomaniac who wrote me from prison. Though he knew that he was under an irresistible urge, his conscience pricked him and he was fighting self-contempt. Without having read Kant, he told me that a kind of impulse took over and he could not leave the "silver spoon" alone. Yet he could not be satisfied that an "it" outside the self was acting here. He could not escape the fact that it was he himself. (Kant alludes to kleptomania in exactly the same terms.)

In my experience no one has tried to explain this union of freedom and necessity so profoundly as Martin Luther in his work against Erasmus, *The Bondage of the Will.* Here what Kant calls necessity is predestination. Luther's question is, "How I can assume that on the one hand I stand under the ineluctability of divine foreordination and yet be responsible on the other, so that I cannot say that because of this foreordination God is responsible for my mistakes?"

To solve this problem, Luther makes a very typical distinction between coercion (*coactio*) and necessity (*necessitas*). Coercion is an external constraint, as when a policeman hauls off a helpless drunk to the police station. The drunk has no say in this and takes no part in the procedure. The initiative lies wholly outside him; the policeman is the one who acts. The drunk can say later that the policeman dragged him off to the cells. But can I accuse God in this way of condemning me to do what is morally wrong? Not so, thinks Luther. For the ineluctability under which I stand in this regard has the character of necessity. It is because I am fallen and alienated that without saving grace I can only go astray. The guilt for this can be imputed to no one but myself. I myself am the subject of the action. I have thus claimed in freedom this necessity under which I stand.

Those who think this is theological quibbling should learn from Johann Wolfgang von Goethe as well as Kant. Goethe in his *Urworte Orphisch* says of the "daimon" that it is the "stamped form that vitally unfolds itself." The impressed entelechy of our nature actualizes itself in a necessary drive that does not contradict the freedom of the process of self-actualization. We have to become what we are, and our will is only a willing because we have to (Ananke). Here again I have to say "I" to me and my acts because it is I myself who am in the process of self-actualization. In this sense freedom and necessity are not in contradiction.

IV. HERMENEUTICAL CONCLUSION: HUMANITY CANNOT BE "GRASPED" BUT ONLY "UNDERSTOOD"

Why have we felt impelled to raise this problem of freedom at the very outset? We have had to do so to deal with a methodological problem that cannot be evaded if we are to deal with the theme of anthropology. If freedom is an essential mark of human existence, its nature cannot be grasped objectively, according to the method rightly used with things, e.g., in physics or biology. Freedom is not a subject of knowledge in this sense. I know it only nonobjectively. It is known only in direct experience of the self. Trusting this, I can trust the activity of reason that gives me knowledge of the subjects of experience.

From the time of Dilthey one may thus say rightly that we can only "understand" and not "explain" human beings and history. To explain is to deduce causally. Inexplicable freedom resists this. Hence a normative element in human nature does so. "To understand" is something different from "to explain."

In Dilthey's usage understanding means knowing the personal life of another only on the specific condition of having the same personal structure of being. Only because I myself have a responsible relation to the practical logos and the meaning of my existence can I understand others in a corresponding relation. Only for this reason, e.g., am I affected by the boredom or emptiness or failure or success of others. For this reason I understand that this other being is called upon exactly as I am to grasp his or her destiny, and with the same risk of failure. The possibility of understanding arises by reason of the solidarity that binds us together in the same life-agenda. In one of his earlier books on an older and unknown inland China, Paul Claudel offers a fine commentary on this problem when he defines *connaissance* by breaking it down into *con* and *naissance*, i.e., being born together as similar beings on the same earth. This provides the analogy that is essential to understanding.

In his work on the development of hermeneutics Dilthey describes this solidarity psychologically as "the power of congenial fellow-feeling" and therefore as what Friedrich Schleiermacher calls "divinatory understanding." The ability to understand rests on relationship or analogy between those who understand and those who are understood, between expositors and authors, enhanced by entering into the authors' lives and constant study.

In Dilthey the idea of congeniality is undoubtedly the psychological superstructure of a basic anthropological fact, namely, that expositors and authors are in solidarity as bearers of personal life. They meet as people who might grasp or miss one another, who face the alternative of self-actualization or alienation, who are marked both by the gift and fear of freedom. "If the eye were not sunny, it could never see the sun"; in this saying Goethe touches on the law of analogy that underlies the possibility of understanding.

People cannot be explained but only understood—this is the first principle of anthropology. But it includes the point that I first need to understand myself if I am to understand others. I cannot speak seriously about the guilt of others (or regard them as guilty) if I do not face my own ambiguity and weakness. Jesus had this in mind, did he not, when he told us to think about the beam in our own eye before worrying about the splinter in someone else's.

But how do I come to understand myself?

Certainly not by focusing on myself with the aid of self-analysis! Certainly not by contemplating my own navel! We can know ourselves, as Goethe said in one of his autobiographical works, only as we know the world in us and ourselves in the world. Every object, properly observed, opens up a new organ in us. As we encounter others, mirrors are put at our disposal in which we can see into ourselves more clearly. We thus come to know ourselves only by activity, for it is thus that we move out and affect the world and are affected by it. Thus somewhere in *Wilhelm Meisters Lehrjahre* Goethe says that when we learn to know people we ask what they are doing and how and in what order, and our interest in them is decided for life by the answers to these questions. Along similar lines Goethe says in his prose proverbs that we never learn to know ourselves by self-contemplation but by action. When we try to do our duty, we find out what is in us. Goethe scoffs at the sterile attempt to get behind the wings of our own being by self-analysis. The blinded soul lives autochthonically and autodidactically. It should test itself and find out to its vexation that it is failing at every point. And in *Torquato Tasso* Antonio thinks it good to focus on himself only if it is useful, but it is not, for we know ourselves only in humanity, and life teaches us what this is. Similarly Dilthey thinks we can never know ourselves directly but only in encounter with history. This is the human sphere—the analogue that we can approach with understanding in order to know ourselves. We know ourselves only in history, not in introspection. Basically we all seek ourselves in history.

More essential than establishing where we find ourselves when we want to understand ourselves is the negative indicating where we cannot find ourselves, namely, in direct introspection, in a curving in upon the self. That this path is absurd and sterile is not just a result of experience. That it prevents self-understanding is related to the very basis of our being.

A depth psychologist who had his starting point originally with Sigmund Freud, the logotherapist Viktor E. Frankl, stated this with all the clarity one could wish for when he said that we are not here to observe ourselves but with knowledge and love to give ourselves. Being summoned to give ourselves, to act for . . . , we can in fact understand ourselves only when we do this deliberately, experiencing ourselves in love, self-sacrifice, the search for meaning, activity, a concern of constant striving. Introspective curving in upon the self produces only a distorted view of humanity.

To sum up, self-understanding does not come with the contemplative act of immersion in the self but only with an outward movement, with action in the world and the encounter with history. Self-knowledge does not come directly by preoccupation with the self but indirectly and by a detour. Why this is so is explained by the fact that we are never "objects" of knowledge, not even of self-knowledge. When we say that people cannot be explained but only understood, this means that only free beings can understand free beings. This being so, we understand ourselves as we understand others. Goethe pregnantly expresses this dialectical relation between knowing the world and the self when he says that we can know ourselves only as we know the world in us and ourselves in the world. The world is a macrocosmic reflection of me and I am a microcosm of the world. The inner and the outer are thus analogous. I receive self-awareness by encounter with the world. I know the world only as I know myself. This is particularly true of the world of history, which as the human sphere is my direct analogue.

V. HISTORY AND MYTH
AS AIDS IN UNDERSTANDING

We have now been given an important hint as to the method to be employed in an anthropology.

The truth that people can only be understood and not explained applies specifically to history as what we have called the human sphere. In relation to history, too, I cannot document myself as an object. As a historical being I am constantly included in my understanding of history. And if we have said that we experience ourselves only by the detour of encounter with history, the opposite is true that we experience history only by the detour of self-understanding. In this dialectic may be seen what is usually called the hermeneutical circle. The way I see myself—either as a spiritual being, as in Georg Wilhelm Friedrich Hegel, or as one that is conditioned materially by economics, as in Karl Marx—is certainly influenced by the course of history, whether world history (Hegel) or modern history in the form of the early capitalist class-conflict (Marx). In the form of a reaction the self-understanding provoked and shaped by the impact of history then achieves the rank of a category that leads to a new and methodologically sharper look at history, fixing the perspective and acting as a criterion for the selection and evaluation of the historical data. There will always be an active prejudgment of this kind, dictated by the understanding of the self, so that in principle the understanding of history can never be "presuppositionless."

That this is so is not a liability that might cause historians to look enviously at the exact natural sciences on the ground that these can more easily postulate freedom from presuppositions. If historians were to try to break free from the presuppositions of their self-awareness, they would no longer be viewing human history but a degenerated form of pseudo-nature, which is not history. No, it lies in the nature of the case that historians should not emancipate themselves from these presuppositions of their self-awareness and pre-understanding. Only as bearers of freedom can they understand history as the sphere of freedom. But freedom is not abstract choice; it is commitment to something. When we call ourselves free, we recognize, for example, our ability to pursue a goal, to actualize ourselves, to grasp our destiny. What we thus know as our nature and goal inevitably affects the way we view and interpret other people and history as a whole.

Discerning in this way that as historical beings we always bring ourselves to the understanding of history, we come up afresh against the nonobjective and nonobjectifiable element to which our discussion of the problem of freedom led us.

It is for this reason that Nikolai Berdyaev in his book on history presents myth as a deeper reconstruction of life. Myth grasps a di-

mension of human life that is inaccessible to objective study. We
cannot conceive of an exclusively objective history because there is a
need for mystification, a longing for worlds beyond secretly directing
things. The very elemental reason for this is that the subjects are included in the history they seek to know and are thus forced to feel
and disclose the historical in themselves. As Goethe said, they know
the world only in themselves and themselves only in the world. Berdyaev makes exactly the same point when he says that penetrating
the depths of the ages means penetrating the depths of the self. History, then, presents itself from within, not from without, which
means by recollection of the basis, goal, and meaning of our own existence.

As myth seeks to express the depth-dimension of history,[4] it forms
an element in all historical interpretation. In myth, thinks Leopold
Ziegler, we do not have invented history but interpreted history. It is
thus a fatal habit of thought to pose the alternative of poetic myth
and sober history. This is a false alternative because the understanding subjects share nonobjectively in historical understanding.
Since these subjects, being human, are concerned to actualize meaning, and meaning relates to the totality of being, in all historical understanding of details a preliminary attempt is made to grasp the
whole of history and its meaning. But this attempt cannot possibly
be based on an objective recording of the facts, as though the course
of these revealed movement toward some final goal. Postulating such
a goal has its basis in decisions that are taken as the subjects seek
and presuppose meaning.

There is no investigation of human existence and its history in the
sense of objective science (for all the detailed things that might be
said about people along these lines). Human existence as a whole is
subject to the hermeneutical law of understanding. But this need not
lead philosophical and theological anthropologists to think that they
are of less worth and do not belong among their more scientific colleagues. They can show with epistemological rigor—and hence
scientifically—why human existence has to be disclosed by way of understanding rather than explanation. We comprehend the incomprehensibility of human existence.

This statement is the tangent at which anthropology touches the
circle of science. Mathematicians for the same reason need not capit-
ulate with pained resignation when they say that squaring a circle is
geometrically impossible. For they can prove why it is impossible.

They thus uphold the sovereignty of their discipline even in areas where they have to admit that they cannot do things. Even more pregnantly, we might say that there are reasons why they may not even want to do them.

In exactly the same sense Kant explains the incomprehensibility of humanity by that of its basic quality, namely, freedom. In his *Grundlegung zur Metaphysik der Sitten* he thus says that while we do not comprehend the practical unconditioned necessity of the moral imperative, we do comprehend its incomprehensibility, which is all that can be fairly asked of a philosophy that pushes to the limit of human reason in principles.

Taking the line we do, we thus come up against the nonobjective sphere that refuses to be grasped objectively. We can understand humanity and its history only in a venture. We derive the courage to make this venture from a realization that the secret of humanity is our own secret, and this identity forces us to put our question. We cannot break free from the presuppositions that lead to this question —for we ourselves are the presupposition—but we can at least ask what are the premises that control us.

B. HUMANITY—
AN INSECURE QUESTION

I. THE PROBLEMATIC NATURE OF HUMANITY AS A THEME OF ANTHROPOLOGY

Before we take up our question, we need to discuss another matter. We have tried to explain why humanity is itself a question and also why this is a peculiar question distinct from more strictly scientific questions and thus demanding peculiar methods if it is to be answered. But we have not so far considered why the problem of our humanity is treated with such intensity today.

We find that almost all the faculties are concerned about this theme. Philosophers and theologians are professionally interested—I need only recall the great works of Arnold Gehlen and Emil Brunner.[1] But scientists, too, are putting the anthropological question,[2] and so are doctors in the context of psychosomatic medicine, organ transplants, and euthanasia.[3] For sociology Peter Berger explicitly raises the question of the view of humanity.[4] As for psychotherapy and psychiatry, Viktor Frankl, in reaction to Freud, does the same thing in almost all his publications. Heinrich Henkel and Richard Lange[5] represent the same concern in law. The list could easily be extended. Thus the many studies of humanity and technology, of whether we are existentially mature enough for our physical and biological resources, should not be forgotten.

What has caused this surprising focus on the anthropological question? Is there a new human self-awareness that proudly vaunts itself and proclaims its privileges in face of the inanimate world and the animal kingdom? Often we might almost believe this when in appeals and discussions and national anniversaries and all kinds of celebrations we are monotonously assured that people are the issue. But this widespread modern slogan really indicates, not human self-awareness, but a rapidly increasing uncertainty. I might venture the rather daring statement that whenever humanity is made a theme, the crisis of humanity is brought to expression. It is perhaps a sign of this that the question of humanity is usually accompanied by that of basic human rights. But these are acutely and flagrantly at issue in times when humanity and its rights are under severe threat. To see this it will be worth our while to take a few examples.

a. Symptoms of Insecurity—Natural and Human Rights

Hesiod might be called the creator of ancient natural law with its protective function. But for this rhapsodist of Ascra, who tried to put us under the patronage of a cosmic order of being, the harmony of the Homeric age had been shattered. He himself experienced this crisis and expressed it in his bucolic didactic poem *Works and Days*. The tragic reason for writing this poem was provided by his quarrelsome and indolent brother, who squandered their patrimony, harassed him with constant unreasonable demands, and had no hesitation about bribing judges. The conflict between right and brutal force into which Hesiod is plunged is for him a paradigm of the world situation in general and especially the human situation. History as he sees it is a process in which the battle between might and right becomes increasingly sharper as gift-consuming lords can more and more exploit the privileges of their positions of power. Whereas the first golden age begins under the rule of Cronos, there will be no right or happiness in the finale of history, for Aidos (reverence) and Nemesis (the sense of right) have hidden themselves and left the earth, returning to the gods on Olympus. They have left only endless suffering and discord to humanity. Hence Hesiod begins to ask whether there is any basic order in the universe by which perverted positive law should be measured. Such an order is not made by us. Timelessly valid, it stands above us and thus characterizes our nature and goal.

What seems to be important in all this is that for Hesiod the question of the sustaining form of human existence arises out of awareness of its falsification. The question of right is posed by longing for liberation from wrong. It is because the structure is tottering and falling that its foundations are sought.

Something of the same may be seen in the development of international law. Here again the basis of humanity is at issue, this time in its form as a collection of nations. The call for international law is heard when chaos replaces uniting and sustaining order, especially when the pluralism of ideologies drives from view everything that brings together. A world in such a condition is an inhuman world abandoned to self-destruction. It is worth noting that the call for international law was heard particularly when an attempt was made to deal legally with the inhumanity of the Nazi regime. The principle of no punishment without law threatened to call in question the judicial competence of the Nuremberg trials. There was in fact no legal code in which genocide, euthanasia, and pogroms were forbidden. The imagination of earlier lawgivers had not been sufficient to dream up the dreadful possibilities of mass destruction initiated by national socialism. Did this mean that the Nazi criminals were legally innocent and could not be punished? Was there no positive law to which their judges could appeal with the claim that they had broken it? This legal problem raised the question whether there were not eternal unwritten laws—the very laws to which Sophocles' Antigone appealed—that would make a competent verdict possible.

In fact, the prosecution in this case did argue that certain basic laws that protect humanity were in force when the crimes were committed—because they are always valid. At issue are the axioms of humanity, transgressions of which are "crimes against humanity." This was the very slogan on which the Nuremberg court based its competence to impose punishment. The trials undoubtedly raised some questions. The triumph and bias of victory helped to force Dike (justice) to conceal her face or at least occasionally close her eyes. Nevertheless, the principle that there are timeless norms cannot be shaken.

But this is not the decisive point in the present context. Our real concern is with the conditions under which the idea arose that there have to be these eternal unwritten laws, or axioms of humanity. The uncertainty of a vague and chaotic state, in which all values slip, provided these conditions. The American prosecutor Robert H. Jackson formulated them in a classical statement when he said that international law must develop case by case, and it constantly marches forward at the cost of those who ignore it and discover their error too late.

This statement has the ring of antiquity. It reminds us of the dark background of Attic tragedy. Why does Oedipus have to be guilty of patricide and incest? Does it make sense that the tragic hero unsuspectingly, and therefore innocently even in his guilt, transgresses eternal ordinances and violates both his father and mother? It does in fact make sense, for in breaking the ordinances Oedipus enables the ordinances to avenge the transgression and thus to manifest themselves in so doing. Prior to their violation, the ordinances were, as it were, concealed; they had not come into the zone of awareness. But now they leave the state of incubation and become virulent. The order of being must be provoked to be able to react and thus to be manifest in its reaction. Humanity and human law become a question only when there is a mortal assault upon humanity and its world.

This leads to a third slogan: the proclamation of human rights. This, too, takes place only the moment they are threatened and insecure. This moment usually comes when the tension between the individual need for freedom and the claim of the state to sovereignty becomes intolerable, and the pressure produces reflection on what is right for humanity. It is no wonder, then, that the proclamation of human rights came with the liquidation of the inhuman system of the Third Reich. The United Nations made a basic statement of this kind on December 10, 1948, publishing a whole list of social rights, such as the right to work, to just pay, and to personal freedom. In 1950 member states of the Council of Europe promulgated a selection of these statements as "fundamental rights."

Here again we have confirmation of our prior observation that human rights as to what is "due" us can be formulated only on the basis of what we "are." Only a prior realization of our human nature opens up the possibility of defining our rights. But does this realization really come first? Does it not come later, as a consequence of forgetfulness, unawareness, or even betrayal? The question of what we are and what we are due arises only when what is self-evident is driven out by uncertainty and something that had ruled only as a kind of instinctive taboo in the unconscious has to be expressly stated and proclaimed. Reflection on natural, human, and basic rights usually comes only as a kind of defensive measure protecting against violations. Perhaps this defensive motive underlies all anthropological concern and all humanism. The human question is a product of human insecurity.

The same observation applies to our own days. Wherever racial conflicts rage, or apartheid problems exist, or the rights of minorities are contested, the basic question of what constitutes humanity is posed. Those who engage in conversations in South Africa and do not confine themselves to the banalities of everyday life find themselves suddenly plunged into the fundamental questions of anthropology. These take here the specific form of the constitutive character of race and the extent to which it creates distinction and difference in worth. If one says that race has constitutive significance for the quality of humanity, being more than accidental in character, then it is natural to demand that both individuals and groups have a right to racial identity. The priority of race does in fact fix my identity. And if it is legitimate to protect individual identity by human rights, racial identity will be seen to be covered by the same rights. They can thus be invoked in favor of a policy of apartheid.

Those who have some awareness of the intellectual climate in those areas can feel almost physically the insecurity behind these anthropological theses. An almost insoluble problem—the mingling of various races with the minority in control—demands in ideological justification a theory of humanity that will even use pseudobiblical arguments. (Ham, Noah's son, who is cursed and condemned to slavery, is the ancestor of the North African, Arab, and Canaanite nations, Genesis 9:20 ff.) The question what we are, or what we are supposed to be on certain ideological postulates, is a product of insecurity under the pressure of what seems to be a politically insoluble situation.

b. Three Humblings:
Copernicus, Darwin, Freud

The anthropological question arises in the same way in science. Sigmund Freud referred to the three great humblings to which humanity has been subjected in the modern age. Copernicus was responsible for the first when he showed that the earth and humanity are not the center of the universe. He forced upon us the startling insight that we are an insignificant marginal phenomenon, mere dust set on a particle of dust. Darwin brought the second humbling when with his theory of evolution he demonstrated our animal ancestry. This seemed to demand the conclusion that we are no longer privileged as compared with the animal kingdom, that we no longer enjoy the prerogative of divine likeness, but that we have to regard ourselves as higher animals. The third humbling was effected by Freud himself. For he had made it plain to us that from the root up we are not under the control of the self and its will but of a complex of subconscious impulses.

The men responsible for these three humblings were all three afraid to make their revolutionary insights public. What they feared was not so much the inquisition—including that of public opinion— as the philosophical impact of their views, the shattering of humanity's understanding of itself. Thus Copernicus in the preface to his main work says that he withheld his discovery for four decades. In fact, his work was published only in 1543, the year of his death, though he had known the facts as early as 1507. Darwin, too, hesitated for two decades before publishing his findings, and he admitted to his friends that he felt as though he had committed a murder. Nor was it without sorrow that he confessed that his researches had made him color-blind to the things of faith. In a letter to his wife, who was trying to restore what he had lost, he said that when he was dead, she should know that he had often kissed her words and wept over them. And when Freud's ship docked in New York and the crowds welcomed the prophet of psychoanalysis, he asked those with him whether people realized he was bringing them the plague. Even if this is not to be regarded as a serious judgment on his life's work, the irony of the statement shows that Freud was not unaware of the darker side of his discovery.

In all three cases we have a relativizing of humanity. The privileges seem to be buried that had been reflected in earlier enthusiastic descriptions of human existence: divine likeness, autonomy, unconditionality, its state as an end in itself.

The impact of Darwin is typical. At first people were fascinated by the continuity with animals and the analogy to them. This was the revolutionary aspect that shook existing humanism to its foundations. It seemed directed against all forms of self-understanding that stressed humanity's special place in the cosmos, and particularly against the biblical story of creation and the supranatural origin of humanity recounted in it.

In contrast, contemporary biologists, e.g., Adolf Portmann and Joachim Illies, are again trying to bring out the qualitative distinction of the human even at the biological level. If appearances do not deceive, this tendency has developed because humanity sees itself threatened and misunderstood at the very center when it is viewed only from a genetic standpoint and seen only as the tip of the pyramid of living things. How can personal essence—with reason and conscience—be regarded only as something that is different in degree and not as totally distinct qualitatively, as hitherto? And what would be the consequences of such a view?

If humans are understood in analogy to animals, for good or ill the laws of nature have to be applied to history, and the principle of oppression, the instinct of aggression, and the right of the strong have to be described as natural, and divested of moral relevance. If, as in the critical theory of the Frankfurt school, spirit is reabsorbed into nature, history loses its point. It is no longer the zone in which the human self pits itself against nature. The naturalizing of history forces us to vacate the kingdom of values and truth (and this not merely in the sense of timeless ontic essences as in the metaphysics of Plato and Aristotle). "There is no eternal kingdom of values," said —at least the earlier—Horkheimer in his attempt to reabsorb history into nature. (It may be noted that he made this statement in a lofty dialectic, not in crude naturalism, but this need not concern us in the present context.)

To take up our main thread, the naturalizing of the human ethos necessarily avenges itself. Since we have only reduced instincts, we have to look around for values and norms to guide us instead of impulses, and we thus expose ourselves to the world of culture. But this positive effect of deficiency of instinct is accompanied by a very destructive possibility. Unlike animals, we no longer have restraining instinctual mechanisms to protect our fellow-humans against us. We destroy one another. And as our culture produces technology, technology includes sophisticated weaponry. The remnants of restrictive instinct are lost when remote weapons make killing anonymous and impersonal. If aggression and the desire to hunt and destroy are not restrained by anything specifically human, humanity is delivered up to self-destruction. Goethe's ironical comparative, that humans are more animal than animals, makes reference to this possibility. I will refrain from showing how the thesis of continuity between humans and animals affects our understanding of sex and leads to the loss of the more human qualities (love and fellowship) in this area. Only when we are aware of the special character of humanity may we focus also on analogies to the animal kingdom. Our house certainly has an animal cellar as well as the main rooms of personality. To have elucidated this afresh is not the least service rendered by Konrad Lorenz.

The impact of Freud, which we shall discuss later, has been similar to that of Darwin. If we are directed by impulses of the libido in the subconscious, values and norms and orientations to meaning seem to be just projections established in an imaginary zone of the superego. This thesis is thus an attack on the foundations of personality. We shall deal with the implications of this in another context. Freud's fellow citizen and contemporary in Vienna, the satirist Karl Kraus, sums them up in the statement that psychoanalysis is the sickness for which it thinks it is the remedy. Freud sees extremely well what repressing sex involves, but he never even asks what repressing the spirit involves, says Karl Jaspers, and he describes in this way the assault on personality.

Here again the insecurity that is triggered about humanity raises the counterquestion as to the basis of our human essence and whether this can be defined in such a way as to be related to the power of the spirit and to norms and values instead of simply "producing" these as a superstructure. One may already see important signs that out of the ruins of humanity there is a return to its true form and an effort to devise a psychology and psychotherapy that will recognize human primacy. Many weighty authors might be quoted in this regard. I will mention only Viktor E. Frankl with his logotherapy and the American psychoanalyst Karl Menninger with his concern to show—again—that sin is not just the expression of a complex but a personal reality.[6]

We mention all this to show how insecurity as to what humanity is constantly gives rise in some way to the question of humanity and the motive power of the human spirit. Precisely when humanity is called in question it raises the question of humanity.

II. INSECURITY AND THIN ICE

It would be as well to pursue this line a little further and examine the reasons for insecurity that characterize our own age in respect to our present question. If it is true that the question of the essence of humanity arises when this essence is obscured, that it is human alienation that triggers the counterquestion of human uniqueness and authenticity, then there can never be a timeless or supratemporal anthropology. We can approach the human phenomenon only as we orient ourselves to the special questions of an age and the special situations that raise them. In this sense anthropology is a matter of perspective. The standpoint of the observer determines the view.

a. The Longing for Emancipation

Emancipation or liberation has become an attractive and programmatic word in our day. It denotes a return from the loss of self and heteronomous distortion. It thus implies the question, What is the true being to which we are to return? Here again, then, the crisis triggers the inquiry.

The model situation that determines the decisive features of the later and present-day concept of emancipation is provided by Roman law. Here the term denotes the legal release of a grown-up son from his father's authority. It can also be applied to the manumission of slaves. Today, symbolically, it embraces liberation from nature, from the (almost natural) constraint of social relations, and finally from suprahuman forces.

Emancipation is thus a synonym of responsible adulthood. In it, even theonomy is regarded as a special kind of heteronomy. (Whether this equation is correct will be examined later.) Thus in a class-society, according to Marx, people are oppressed not merely by the structure—owners treat the lower classes merely as objects to be exploited—but also by ideology, the dispensing of the opium of religion. Thus emancipation as a return to the true self can come only as religion as well as the class-society is abolished. Religion is an illusory sun that revolves around us as long as we do not revolve around ourselves. The goal of emancipation is that we should revolve around ourselves and thus be self-determining subjects, no matter whether what is in view is individual autonomy or the liberation of repressed groups such as the American blacks or women deprived of equal rights.

Fëdor Dostoevski gives a classical description of the hope and crisis of this drive for emancipation in his chapter on the Grand Inquisitor in The Brothers Karamazov. Like all those who are motivated by hate-love, the Grand Inquisitor has a thorough knowledge of the human heart. He knows its elemental longing for self-determination. But he resists this because he knows, or thinks he knows, that we are not ready for it, and as victims of our rebounding longing will be delivered up to the much more dreadful domination of substitute gods and new and worse forms of alienation. When Jesus comes back to the earth, therefore, he tells him why he has had to deny us the freedom of the children of God that Jesus proclaimed, and why he has had to set us under the rule—and protection—of the ecclesiastical institution.

Nothing is more tempting, he says, than freedom of conscience, but nothing is more burdensome. Instead of having a fixed law handed down from the past, people now have to make their own decisions as to what is good and bad, with only the example of their Leader as a guide. But have you not considered that they will finally reject your example and truth and repudiate every obligation if you lay upon them such a terrible burden as freedom of choice?

For those who are free there is no more constant or tormenting concern than to find a being to worship . . . a being to whom they may hand over as quickly as possible the gift of freedom with which they were unhappily born. But such a being can take over their freedom only if it satisfies their conscience. They will worship you if you give them bread, for nothing is less contested than bread, but if someone else at the same time gets power over their conscience they will leave the bread and follow that one. For the secret of human existence is not just living but living for a purpose. If people have no idea of the purpose for which they live, they do not want to live any longer and prefer self-destruction to remaining on earth, no matter how much bread there is around them.

In the light of this searching commentary one might perhaps say that the drive for emancipation derives from a crisis situation and in the course of its fulfillment triggers a new crisis situation. In their different ways, both phases of the crisis raise the human question.

The first situation consists of the real or supposed domination of powers—despotisms and clerical and ideological inquisitions—that misuse people as the instruments and objects of their will and thus bring about self-alienation. This oppression produces the ideal of adults freely fulfilling themselves. The description of what this true humanity is forms the answer to the first question regarding humanity.

But if the first crisis is overcome by emancipation, we are at once delivered up to a second one, i.e., confrontation with the terror of freedom: a freedom that, in extreme form, according to Jean-Paul Sartre, has not just to choose between right and wrong, but primarily to determine what right and wrong are, thus posing an impossible burden. Our passionate concern, then, is to find someone or something new to worship, to dedicate ourselves to, delegating the overpowering burden of responsibility. And if the gods have vanished from the earth and cannot be brought back, this makes no difference, for we will bow down to idols and pander to ideologies. For elementary though bread may be, and ready though we may be to sing the tune of those who give it to us to eat, even more urgent is the need to be committed to a purpose for which it is worth our while to live. Bread can only enable us to live on and vegetate. Awareness that vegetating does not meet life's demands but leaves us defective raises afresh the question of what we have to be truly to fulfill ourselves. If the freedom of emancipation is the first stage on the way to the self, if it enables us to lift up our heads a little above the water of alienation, the next moment a negative and a positive insight are communicated to us.

The negative insight is that freedom is as little a mere freedom of choice as it is a power that leads automatically to self-fulfillment. Freedom on its own can lead only to the vegetating that does not achieve the self-fulfillment sought in emancipation. The positive insight is that we have to lay hold upon ourselves and move toward a goal. We are subjects as we wanted to be by emancipation only if we actualize in adult responsibility what we ought to be and know to be our purpose. If freedom distinguishes us from animals, it is not just because we have escaped the constraint of instincts and can thus do what we want but because we can and will become what we ought to be.

The need to inquire into what we ought to be, however, implies the further need to commit ourselves to the who or what by which this is decided, or in whom or what the final purpose or meaning resides. This can only mean finding out about that which controls us instead of being controlled by us. We ourselves fix our goals in the penultimate sphere, but meaning as the ultimate goal is beyond our control.

Strictly, then, the imperative is not "Become what you should be," but "Become what you are." This expresses the truth that being is given me as a goal of my becoming. I have not chosen myself in that into which I am thrust. The situation in the resultant inquiry might be described thus. Freedom compels me to ask about my purpose and destiny. The talents that I am given—from bread to intellectual gifts—demand that I ask not merely "how" to use them but "to what end." But this involves the question of my commitment, of my obligation to values and norms and goals, which is from the very first

outside my own control. Thus freedom and commitment are not opposed to one another; they demand one another.

Dostoevski's Grand Inquisitor offers terrifying analyses of this relation (terrifying because they cannot be met by arguments but only
by a nevertheless, in faith). The thrust of emancipatory freedom toward commitment to a new power is so elemental that it can put
even the hunger for bread in the shade. You may give them bread
and they will sing to your tune, but let an ideological tyranny claim
their conscience, offering itself as a surrogate for the power that
demands commitment, and they will leave you to follow the power
that takes over the burden of the uncommitted conscience. Even
painful chains are better to them than freedom in a vacuum. This is
how inescapable is the need for commitment. And this explains the
vulnerability of emancipated people to self-fabricated idols that play
the role of pseudo-ends and substitute masters. Ideologies figure
among these idols. They are commandos behind the lines of our
conscience, guiding its decisions and thus robbing it of responsibility
for itself. The evil of the situation is that those who cast off the old
tyrannies do not notice that they are subjecting themselves to new
lords. They suffer from the illusion that they want to do what they
are forced to do and are themselves the subjects of what the idols really suggest to them.

Here again, then, there are many different forms and degrees of insecurity that raise the question of essential humanity. It can be from
the very first a perverted question and may then produce a perverted
answer. But the question has to be put in some way when humanity
sees itself called in question. The need to ask about ourselves has an
indelible character.

b. Rendezvous with the Self: Crisis of Identity

Sören Kierkegaard can say that there is a "sickness unto death"
that comes to expression in two forms of despair: the despair of
wanting to be oneself and the despair of not wanting to be oneself.
The question who I am or not, and why I am as I am and not otherwise, conceals the deeper question of humanity itself, namely, how I
can accept myself as I am. To put this in focus, one might formulate
it thusly: How does it stand with my identity, its loss and regaining?
We shall adopt Kierkegaard's division in what follows.

DESPERATE WANTING TO BE ONESELF

Loss of the I and the Sickness of Self-Forgetting

In his biography the psychiatrist Alfred E. Hoche tells of the superintendent of a public park who saw that a visitor was behaving strangely. When he addressed him and had had some conversation with him, he finally put the polite question, "Who are you?" "If only you could tell me!" was the answer. In fact the man was no other than Arthur Schopenhauer.

Augustine in his *Tractate on John* put the riddle of the self as follows: "What is so much thine as thyself, and what is so little thine as thyself?" Underlying the question, "Who am I?" is the further question, "Is my I really mine?" How far does it really belong to me so that I control it? Must I accept what I am when I am not even asked whether I want to be what I am or to live as such? (An adolescent once put this difficult question to me.) Do I have to be what I am? If we eavesdrop in our own day, this question, "Who am I?" is an unmistakable and universal symptom of our insecurity about the self. But this crisis of identity finds less expression in the variation, "Do I have to be what I am?" than in the other variant, "How can I find myself and become what I am?"

There can be no doubt what contemporary groupings trigger this question about the self. The slogans of a society oriented to consumption, success, and affluence express the fact that I am condemned to play a certain part. I am held down by social structures that make me a mere executive, functionary, and channel, so that I am the object and transitional stage of an alien will and suprapersonal pressures.

The Marxist view finds this alienation especially in our role as objects of exploitation. In reality, however, it extends far beyond the mere economic sphere. It occurs in all social systems, whether controlled or free, totalitarian or democratic. The greater the organization of society and the economy, the more unmistakable is the interpendence of all phenomena, the autonomy of processes, and the onward movement to which not merely the individual wheels but even the great figures of world history are subject. To the overwhelming force of the apparatus corresponds the anonymity of individuals, their position of servitude to the process, and hence the alienation that binds them to forces other than themselves and does not allow them to be themselves.

If technology provides the means to subdue the earth and to cultivate and humanize nature, these means have long since become too much for the sorcerer's apprentice—ourselves. We can more easily summon up the spirits than bend them to our will.

This change in the situation may be seen in the changed concept of utopia, which we shall discuss in a later chapter on the belief in progress. Whereas we once saw utopia as the goal of history—a world of justice with neither hunger nor class conflict—we are now eaten up by a concern to control the means that will enable us to achieve the goal. For these means threaten to control us instead of our controlling them. They make us vulnerable to an automatic process that may be seen at various points. At any rate, we cannot feel that with the help of these means we are achieving self-fulfillment and leaving our mark on the earth: "The trace of our earthly days will not perish for aeons." No, we threaten to become mere instruments and transitional stages of processes that do not initiate with us and are thus testimonies to our alienation.

Perhaps the call for an extension of freedom is more deeply grounded than in the mere desire for indolent comfort or work-shyness. Its true motive might be the wish to be left alone so that we can come to ourselves and work against our alienation. Our vocational life as the place of our social activity binds us to the alienating forces, the assembly line being only an extreme symbol of this, no more. Is not freedom, then, an area at our own disposal in which we can come to ourselves and become what we are? But do we not have to know first who we are so as to know whom to address? And supposing we are no longer there and are no longer ourselves? Is not a degree of depersonalization and anonymity conceivable in which we are mere dwellings from which the self has long since departed? Might not the sad diagnosis that most people do not know what to do with their freedom, because they do not know what to do with *themselves*, bear witness to this departure from the self?

Perhaps another pointer in the same direction is that our recreation usually takes the form of dissipation rather than concentration, that it is subject to centrifugal rather than centripetal thrusts. Blaise Pascal at least thinks so when in his *Pensées* he says that the simple cause of our unhappiness is that we cannot sit still in a room. To be alone can be a terrifying thing, creating great anxiety, if we encounter no one. The only option then is to dispel the vacuum, to go headlong into pleasures, to fill the void with imports.

Once I have lost my I, my identity, it is dangerous for me to knock at my own door and to be frustrated by signs of absence. Loss of identity provides a *chance* to raise the counterquestion of myself and of humanity in general, but there is no *guarantee* that the question will in fact be pursued.

The question can fade out or be suppressed. Herbert Marcuse thinks he sees how this can happen. In place of the antagonism between the individual and society that Freud presupposed, he finds in the new welfare states an indentification of individuals with their kin and a principle of reality controlled by society. Thus determined, individuals feel at home in society with pathetic complacency. They have adjusted to it. They have done so, Marcuse thinks, because humans—again in opposition to Freud—are not constant bundles of impulses independent of time and place but plastic constructs that can be molded. Hence society can pervert them, pulling down their psychological structure, impoverishing them, rendering them impotent, fitting them into society as representatives of its principle of reality. It can integrate and accept them, alienating them by adjustment.

When this happens, we are no longer dealing with people who are aware of themselves and striving after autonomy, but with castrates, lemures, mini-humans, homunculi.

When people are sick in this way, Marcuse cannot see them curing themselves. The degenerate state of social castrates does not produce of itself the question of authentic humanity and its goal. The initiative for regeneration and liberation must be seized by those in whom the image of authentic humanity still lives and who can free it by altering the social structure that has deformed it. This is why Marcuse appeals to students rather than to saturated workers who are now incapable of action. This is why he became the chief ideologist and father figure of the student rebellion in the sixties.

But did he who could see our plight really have a picture of authentic humanity? Did he really trigger the counterquestion?

One might suppose that this question did in fact become virulent in him. But the picture to which it points and with which it can be answered remained vague and contourless. Marcuse merely describes future technological developments in society and changes in productive capacity, concluding that these will produce a new humanity—

but what kind of new humanity? Work will be kept to a minimum and freedom raised to the maximum. Hence aggressive instincts that have been constantly aroused by repression will wither away, as will also Judaeo-Christian morality and the immanent asceticism of Max Weber. New people will thus emerge with a good conscience who do not have to merit life but can really enjoy it. When this reprogramming becomes possible, supported by biology, earlier instincts and demands will no longer be operative. What remains of them can be sublimated in sport or building cities. The urge to destroy can be magnificently worked out in the reconstruction of towns and the reversal of the horrors of violent industrialization and the destruction of nature.

We need not discuss here how far this harmonious utopian society will be peopled by stupidly happy lemures, by truncated homunculi who can be neither Romeo nor Juliet, and among whom no Shakespeare can find any source for drama. Instead, only one question interests me, and I confess that it is inspired by theology.

The question is, Do we have anything at all here about the ontological status of this new humanity and its nature? The new people are simply depicted as a function of emergent social conditions. They occur only as the shadow of what will occur in society. They are simply a filling for the free spaces made available by the automatizing of production. That is all.

This exclusive relation of humanity to social conditions presents it as plastic material that can be molded and remolded by forces emanating from the changing circumstances of production. The awaited question of humanity can thus be put only as the question of these circumstances of production is put, and inferences are drawn from it regarding the changing picture of humanity as this is functionally dependent on those circumstances.

The once famous statement of Jacob Moleschott that "we are what we eat" has now been changed into "we are what we produce." One might say that the basic question of anthropology is missed. Neither "God" (the God of Christianity or Plato) nor "man" (in the sense of Protagoras) is the measure of all things. Material structures constitute this measure. No wonder that the new people of Marcuse are shadowy and docetic with no fixed contours. Marcuse's coming society is a shadowy realm of things and people are shadows haunting it. They are not even Charon the ferryman holding the rudder. Again we have the impression of lemures—a mythical, not a historical picture.

In view of this, is it surprising that the advocates of social change who are nurtured on such ideologies have no answer when they are asked to say not only what they are against but also and especially what they are really for, what form of humanity they have in mind? The unreality of the absurd picture presented cannot produce a real utopia. Hence the newly awakened sense of the importance of the social structure for the state of humanity puts us on a false track, insofar as it does not advance the thesis of a humanizing of this structure (for which an independent picture of humanity would be needed), but takes this structure to be a kind of demiurge that will create the coming humanity.

The "sickness unto death" that Kierkegaard mentions and Marcuse also has in view, though without overcoming it, covers a third form of the present crisis of identity. This is not just wanting or not wanting to be oneself but a despairing lack of awareness of being a self at all.

This self-forgetting of adjusted and comfortably dominated people is perhaps what Marcuse meant when he said that the identification of the individual with society is the collective sickness of our age. It is a state in which the question of the self is eliminated, the husk of the self is emptied, and no one is at home to visitors. It is a state in which humanity does not exist even as the object of a question.

The despair that Kierkegaard sees behind this self-forgetting cannot be understood psychologically as a mood of despair. Where the subject of grief—the lost I—is not even the object of a question, one cannot grieve over it. This kind of despair—what Kierkegaard calls inauthentic despair—is not something that can be recorded emotionally. It is the existential anxiety described by both Kierkegaard and Martin Heidegger. It lies behind the I, and forms the source of a process in which I repress the hopeless question of the self. It can have an impact in this unobjective, latent sense. Those afflicted by it do not anxiously run around, perhaps shrieking and in panic. They may work hard. They may be constantly engaged in productive activity. But this is simply an active form of repression. The anxiety may not be detected as a psychological state, let alone openly recognized. Self-forgetting as a sickness unto death belongs to the nonobjective zone to which we referred earlier.

The Identity Crisis in Literature

That the problem of identity is the existential question of our age and testifies to the hunt for the lost I finds a multiple echo in literature. In French existentialism it may be seen especially in the question of how we can escape the bondage of being pinned down from outside. In Sartre, others around me tie me down by gazing at me and laying on me expectations that make me docile and wrest control from me. An even more powerful force than the external world in depriving me of free self-determination is my past and the past of my *polis*, whose suprapersonal power seeks to control me.

Jean Anouilh, for example, describes a man who was shot in the head and suffered total loss of memory. Losing his past, he lost his identity. For—in a dreadful way—I "am" my past. To achieve the self, one needs a life without gaps. Laying bare the past is laying bare the self. Anouilh's character seems almost to enjoy having no past and no identity, like those who forget themselves in our own day. For to live without the past is to be freed from its liabilities, to be, as it were, without debts. Those who have no past are like astronauts in space. No wonder that the man resists the concern of those around him to identify him, to impose on him once again the liabilities of his past. He fears the shock that the astronaut experiences when he returns to the earth's field of gravity and is bowed down by what is now his unaccustomed weight.

The anxiety of having to be oneself again does not express itself only negatively. The man without memory will not just return to the old self but have a new self. He can begin afresh and freely make of himself what he wills. He will forge his own identity and not inherit it as a product of his past. Thus he does not return to his parents' house, even though they recognize and identify him. He has himself adopted by strangers so as to be a blank page on which he can begin new writing.

Things are much the same in Sartre's *Flies*. When Orestes returns home, he enters a city afflicted by the curse of regicide. His mother Clytemnestra has murdered the returning Agamemnon with the help of her lover Aegisthus. The avenging goddesses—the "flies"—take over the city and affix the curse of the evil deed to it. The life of the *polis* stands under the shadow of the dreadful event. Orestes does not want to identify himself with this crippling guilt. He refuses to be pinned to the cross of a past that grasps him suprapersonally and fixes identity with the guilt upon him. Thus the key to the play is the cry that escapes him, and that is also a proclamation: "I am my freedom." He does not say, "I *have* freedom," but, "I *am* freedom." Freedom is no less than my very essence and self. I am not the object and product of a past—a past for which I am not responsible but which grips me suprapersonally. I am the subject of a future that I myself fashion. *I* determine who I am—I and no one else am the author of my own self. Thus he goes among the Furies (the keepers of the past), seeking space for an open and unburdened future. But into what time and place does he go? Will not the very next moment be the first phase of a process in which he adds a new past and is thus exposed to liabilities and fixations? Will not the crisis of identity inevitably become a chronic illness in this way? Those who know Sartre will note that this is the weak spot in his doctrine of freedom.

Theologians can only observe with astonishment how the Pauline doctrine of justification by faith and the dialectic of law and gospel are reflected in these conceptions of identity. The law nails me to my past. It seeks to define me by what is behind me, by what I have done. It makes my past the mark of my identity. The gospel, however, enables me to view myself as a new creature for whom old things have passed away. The bond that represents my past, according to Colossians, has been canceled and nailed to the cross. In redemption I am no longer tied to my past but achieve a new future. A new identity is given me. But what is here a gift imparted by Christ —not something at my own disposal—is in Sartre and Anouilh the content of a titanic act, a demonstration of human autonomy.

Who is right? Nowhere do the Christian and the secular views of identity collide more basically and decisively than here, where they stand on the horizon of my temporality and set me before the alternative whether I am governed by my past or my future, and who or what has the power to free me from the one and open up to me the other.

For Max Frisch the problem of identity is lifelong. The goal he envisions can be defined only dialectically (in the novel *Stiller*). On the one hand, he attacks the images we have of people and then pin to them. Such images threaten to become fetishes that are to be rejected, just as we reject attempts to depict God. On the other hand, he attacks the facelessness of the modern world manifested in the superfluity of alienated images. Frisch has some acquaintance with the self-forgetting that is riveted to appearance and has lost the true self—our own and that of others. The same insight may be found in

Peter Handke's *Die Stunde der wahren Empfindung* when the reporter Gregor Keuschnig tries to rediscover his lost identity. He is waiting for the hour of true experience when he will be rid of feelings controlled by others and thoughts fixed in advance. He wants to discover feeling afresh and experience the moment of subjective truth when he comes to himself and is himself. According to Frisch, only the strictest asceticism—repudiation of the image that others pin on us and the pinning of self-manufactured images on others—can liberate us for an open encounter. If we are to experience our own identity in encounter, we must first be ready not to go by predetermined images of ourselves or others but to be open on both sides. In readiness for encounter of this kind I first become a nobody. Only by giving myself my chosen identity can I make the leap into a different being.

But is this kind of openness ever really achieved? The novel *Mein Name sei Gantenbein* by Frisch seems to expose the crisis of the identity won in this way. At its heart is a man who has had a certain experience but cannot integrate it into his consciousness or harmonize it with his person. He is thus looking around for models of situations into which he can fit himself (and them into him). He calls them stories that fit his life. He thus examines the stories of various people and in the end only that of Gantenbein fits his own experience. He thus concludes: "My name is Gantenbein."

We have here a desperate—if humorous—search for identity. As its theme-song we might take the little verse:

> We all of us well know
> What folk we ought to be,
> And while it is not so
> No perfect peace we see.

But is there really any such thing as an open encounter in which the nobody dies and becomes a somebody, finding identity, as promised in *Stiller?* The stories examined in *Gantenbein* are not those of real people whom he meets openly and is thus ready to accept. He himself is the criterion whether they can be "relevant" for him. Hence he does not stand in an area of open encounter. He makes a selection and asks whether the stories fit his own situation. Is this possible without a self-image, a fixed point around which the stories of others revolve like planets around a sun? (I have such a self-image, even if I only say negatively who or what does not fit in with me and thus threatens my identity. In this sense Françoise Sagan in *Bonjour tristesse* demands the freedom "to decide how I want to be myself—I cannot just say 'to be myself,' for I was only dough that could be molded—but the freedom to reject a particular mold.") Throughout his work Frisch has several subsidiary themes. A great deal is expressed in vague dialectic, so that readers are prevented from tying the author to specific theses. Yet one might well ask whether Frisch in *Gantenbein* does justice to the postulates of *Stiller*, namely, that those who move into unconditional encounter and hope to find themselves in it must be prepared to accept others even in opposition to fixed images they might previously have had of them; and if they achieve self-certainty in such encounter and become "somebody," they must accept themselves even in opposition to fixed images they might previously have had of themselves. Is there this twofold openness in *Gantenbein?* Does not the hero of this novel have a fixed idea in advance who he is, and does he not examine the stories of others only to see if they fit in with this? If they do, can he make them his own story and give a new name, e.g., Gantenbein, to his identity as thus elucidated?

It is not by accident that I speak of an identity that is elucidated. When I said that his identity was already fixed when he surveyed the stories of others, this was true only with some reservations. His identity is still developing in the early stages. He is trying to feel it out with the help of the stories. He wants an "Aha" experience when he lights on the right story: "Aha, there I am; I recognize myself there." Who he is, is fixed in advance, but he himself does not yet know it. He has to come to know it. The encounters make no difference ontically, but they do make some difference noetically.

Is he really ready, then, to accept others as well as himself unconditionally? Do we not have here what Kierkegaard had in mind when he spoke of the despair of trying to be oneself, of desperately being in search of one's own image?

Perhaps one might say that the individual seeking identity in Frisch shows some similarity to what Goethe calls the entelechy. What is meant is that human beings are active centers or self-grounded personal organisms. Identity is found by encounter with other entelechies (as in Goethe's *Elective Affinities*). If, however, personality is differently understood, other crises of identity occur.

One may see this from Friedrich Georg Jünger's novel *Der erste*

Gang. The background here is the monstrous process of change initiated by World War I. Many who suffered in it, especially on the
eastern front, find their identity melted down. As the world from
which they come perishes, so do they. The present is a strong dividing line between a closed past and an unimaginable future. They
thus feel that their identity is taken from them with their familiar
world. The places where they grew up, the education they were
given, the symbols they honored—in short, all that shaped them and
formed their roots, has gone, has lost its validity and substance. The
identity of a self-contained selfhood is brought under critical scrutiny
by a kind of cleavage of consciousness. On the one hand, time falls
into a conservatory sphere filled with personal memories that arrest
the past. On the other, it is filled with a dynamic that carries them
along and cannot be stopped, dissolving the past and pointing to a
future in which what is swept aside cannot be located, and against
which they struggle without a lodging-place.

Here the crisis of identity does not result merely from the rift between what is going and what is coming, between named and solid
recollection and anonymous hope, but more from the homelessness
and rootlessness to which we are condemned with the liquidation of
our past. Home and place are a part of human identity. We are not
merely self-resting entelechies. We have our being in that which sustains us, in the times and places that shape us, in the values that direct us, in the symbols to which we look up, in the people who accompany us, in the history that we live, in the houses in which we
dwell. Losing all these, we lose ourselves. The line between past and
present that is violently drawn by the melting process of war is also a
line dividing the I that drags out a shadowy existence and the world
that abandons it. But since this world belongs to the I and helps to
constitute its selfhood, the I leaves itself behind and experiences the
fear of lost identity.

In spite of all the differences between Sartre, Anouilh, and Frisch,
in every form of the identity crisis we find a problem that we shall
later see to be decisive in anthropology, namely, that of relation. All
identity crises arise through the disturbance of a basic relation of existence. This may be the relation to a past which holds us and by
which we do not want to be determined. It may be the relation to
someone else helping or hindering us in discovery of the self. It may
be the relation to what we have experienced as our world only to find
our selfhood perishing with it. Those who ask about their identity,

about the congruence of their being with what they ought to be, unconsciously or deliberately put the question of what sustains their life. This being so, we shall see what significance the question of God, of the ultimate relation of life has for the understanding of our identity.

DESPERATE NOT WANTING TO BE ONESELF

Tacit Overcoming of Individuality
(Mysticism, Romanticism)

According to Kierkegaard, there corresponds to the desperate effort to be oneself the opposite and equally passionate tendency to transcend the limits of one's identity, to escape oneself and be someone else. The personal I or identity is not native to that which bears the human face, as though we were furnished with identity from the outset and could keep it intact through stages of humanity that are hostile to the individual and collectively oriented. The sharply contoured individual I that is aware of its particularity occurs only relatively late in human history. Many factors were needed—social conditions, such as the division of work, religious developments, such as the sense of immediacy to God, and many more—to produce the self that is conscious of its autonomy and qualified for independent rights and duties.

If outwardly delimited, inexchangeable, and unique individuality in this sense is an achievement sustained by the fervor of humanity, it still forms a painful boundary. I am only who I am. The potentiality of my I has been actualized. But this means that I *have* to be who I am. I must accept it.

The process of the development of the I that is at issue here can be described only dialectically. On the one hand, I *may* be who I am. I *may* achieve congruence with my latent image. On the other hand, I resist being chained to this I. I desperately do not want to be myself. We can think of impulses that control this house of the I and that I cannot evade because I cannot evade myself. What dope addicts or criminals have not cursed themselves and their nature!

The desire to transcend the limits of selfhood need not be a despairing one. It may express itself in pantheistic union with the universe. Even if we leave the religious world and confine ourselves to that of culture, we can see this kind of tendency in romanticism. When the youthful Schleiermacher calls religion contemplation of the universe and a feeling for it, he is expressing this union of the limited I with the universe, the broadening out into a cosmic sense that finds in the individual I a compendium of humanity, a microcosmic reflection of the universe. This expansion of the I in the sense of the one and all (*hen kai pan*) is closely related, even in formulation, to the absorption in the universe that Goethe hymns in his *Werther* when he tells how Werther, lying in the grass by a brook, feels very close even to the worms and flies, sensing the movement of universal love that sustains us in eternal rapture, and wishing that this could be the mirror of his soul, and his soul the mirror of the infinite God.

The universe the mirror of the soul and the soul the mirror of the universe, all things resting in the soul and the soul in all things—here individuality is dissolved, or, better, in moments of extreme joy it can dissolve itself. Of course, these are only exceptional moments in processes that lead back to development of the I and force us to accept its fetters again. Goethe's Werther as well as Schleiermacher realizes how ecstatic and exceptional these moments are. What is experienced cannot be expressed either in image or speech. Both must be renounced, and those who know unity or identity with the universe are destroyed in the moments they do so: "When the soul speaks, alas, it speaks no more," Schiller can say. Speech is possible only later, when the wonder of union has passed and there is temporal distance. The moment of experience knows no speech. For this reason the ecstasy of rapture, the transcending of identity can be spoken of only in recollection.

Speech as an Extension of Individuality

Speech occurs only as communication between those who are apart. If we were not different, we should not speak to one another. The partial elimination of individuality in relationships, as in many older married couples who know each other's reactions and have learned about one another all that can be known, removes the need for the bridge of speech and may produce long silences. This may be a caricature of speechless union, but caricatures have much to tell us. And what may be seen here is a basic quality of speech. It links those who are apart. We *have* to express ourselves because individuality prevents the inner being from being perceived without this outward movement. Speech, then, is possible only where there is distance in space or time. This is why historians usually say of events of their own time that it is too early to speak about them. (What is said by contemporaries, e.g., those present at a battle or revolution, is not speech in the full sense but verbal liberation.)

The thesis that speech occurs at a distance indicates two things. First, the medium of speech increases in significance as individualization develops (not merely that of individuals, but that of pluralistically specialized groups). Second, speech is progressively reduced to silence as individuality bursts its frontiers and achieves identification with the universe. For this reason, in Schleiermacher's *Speeches on Religion*, even the words of Holy Scripture are only later rationalizations of an elemental experience. They are mere stones in a mausoleum of religion, embalmings of an experience that is no longer a living one when it passes into speech.

The speaking in tongues (glossolalia), which is so common in charismatic movements today, points in the same direction. In an ecstatic mystical union believers find themselves so taken out of themselves and their finitude, and so fully set in union with God, that normal speech fails and they utter sounds of joy and bliss that only God can understand. If there is to be an understanding with others and the overcoming of the distance that separates them, an interpreter must step forth and put the speechlessness of ecstasy into intelligent speech to make communication possible (cf. 1 Corinthians 14).

In thus expanding our individuality, speech also ensures our individuality. It means that none of us can be a self-enclosed monad with no window, but all of us are posited for others, for co-humanity.

As an aid to identity, speech has, of course, a dark reverse side. It can carry with it a threat to identity. Schiller's saying, "When the soul speaks, alas, it speaks no more," indicates this threat. The soul or true self is no longer healthy and complete when it goes into the exile of speech. The initial stages of direct and elemental experience, e.g., unbroken ecstasy, leave the soul intact, manifest its basis, that in which it has its being and ecstatic entry, and release it from all that estranges. This is what Schleiermacher has in view when he speaks of the I entering ecstatically into contemplation of the universe and feeling for it, and in this way coming to its true self. This union with the universe is authentic identity. But it is notably beyond speech. Once the *kairos* of identity is caught in speech, it has gone and the unity has been shattered. What is put in concepts is already recollection and no longer the moment with its fullness. Speech as a herbarium contains life that is no longer lived. As we have said, it is the idiom of distance. This distance is either a presupposition (the distinction of individuals between whom it establishes communication) or a consequence (e.g., when it imprisons something originally vital in concept).

This burdensome side of speech, its possible threat to identity, is particularly felt in the modern period. In face of its assault we might fall victim to a new kind of speechlessness deriving from overuse, from inability to handle its wealth. This secondary speechlessness is to be distinguished from the original speechlessness that precedes speech. The latter is healthy, the former a type of decadence.

Hugo von Hofmannsthal first spoke about this new speechlessness, which derives from the threat to identity and necessarily affects the author in particular, when he said in his famous *Letter to Lord Chandos* (1902) that he had lost the ability to think or speak coherently. He experienced an inexplicable discomfort in even saying such words as spirit, soul, and body. The abstract terms needed to make evaluations were moldy on his lips. His spirit was forcing him to see all things with uncanny closeness, viewing humans and their acts as though looking at a piece of his skin through a microscope. He was no longer content to see them in the usual way. They all split up into parts, and then into more parts, which concepts could not encompass. Individual words became staring eyes—constant whirlwinds leading nowhere. The real being atomized by speech is maintained, as it were, only in silent things and manifested in silent encounters with them, such creatures as dogs and rats and beetles and crooked apple trees and moss-covered stones being more significant than the most beautiful lover on the happiest of nights. It seems we can enter into a new relation to things when we begin to think with the heart. But when the special magic fades, he cannot express it. He can as little say in rational words what the harmony of the cosmos is, or how it is felt, as he can describe the inner movements of his entrails or the pulsing of his blood.

Peter Handke in his *Stunde der wahren Empfindung* speaks similarly of this speechless being that does not cause alienation but brings us to our true selves. For in this hour the hero of his novel, Keuschnig, finds in a park in Paris a chestnut leaf, a bit of a pocket mirror, and a child's hair clasp. And he too, fleeing from alien feelings and preconceived thoughts and clichés, presses on through what is spoiled by speech to real experience, finding a first hint of it in these things which are so banal and insignificant, which cannot be put into concepts, which are on a plane that is below that of speech.

Hofmannsthal, of course, did not want to say that silence is the final state. Chandos, in the letter to Francis Bacon dated 1605, is simply saying that he must be silent in the speech that is *now* at his command. But he longs for a more expressive speech which he does not as yet know, for the speech in which he might think as well as write is neither Latin, English, Italian, nor Spanish, but a totally unknown language in which silent things speak to him and in which, perhaps, he will one day have to answer in the grave to an unknown judge.[7]

How is it that Hofmannsthal rejects speech in this way and reverts to speechlessness? He is struck by the falsity of speech, or, better, by the fact that it has become false. But what is this falsity, and why have our words begun to act like a slow poison?

By nature speech ought to contain the reality it expresses. As Hans-Joachim Mähl rightly says, there was an original unity of person, expression, and object. But this has been shattered. The claim of speech to contain the intended reality is no longer met in our speech. Why not? Do we stammer? Are we defective in speech? Is our grammar faulty? Not at all! The reason we renounce speech is because of its changed nature. In the words and concepts that we use, earlier interpretations of being are accumulated. But these are not ours—at any rate not initially—so that we pass false words as forgers do their coins. We constantly hand out notes that are not covered. This is why Hofmannsthal speaks as he does of empty words that are moldy on his lips. For when we open our mouths, ten thousand of the dead always speak. Thus words get in the way of things instead of having and expressing reality. Chatter has engulfed the world. Words, words! They have only to open their wings and centuries drop out, as Gottfried Benn puts it.

This is why speech embarrasses authors. It no longer seems to have the power to express. Within it one no longer seems able to achieve the "true sound" on which everything depends, according to Hofmannsthal, because it indicates the discovery of identity. Along the lines of Bertolt Brecht and Gottfried Benn, perhaps the very alienation of speech, its cunning dressing up of things, can help us not just to swallow the usual empty clichés but to choke on something that will shock us and make us wrestle with it. Thus the ardent is reduced to the everyday, the lofty to the banal; Benn brings odd words and expression into his poems to cause the block, to prevent the uplifting reactions which are usually evoked by poems but which do not hear the "true sound" but simply the warmed-up experiences of others that were once authentic but are now merely preserved in language. There are more rather than fewer than the "five difficulties in writing (and speaking) the truth" with which Bertolt Brecht dealt.

To sum up, speech is shown to be contradictory and many-sided once we ask what significance it has for self-discovery or how it can serve to drive us to despair and strip us of our identity.

It helps toward self-discovery inasmuch as it makes possible communication with others and thus frees our humanity for co-humanity. But it also works against self-discovery, as our excursus on Hofmannsthal has indicated, because it is burdened with the past—it is dated—and is thus out of contact with our own reality, getting in its way and becoming a series of empty clichés.

This situation may be welcome to us if we despairingly do not want to be ourselves. For it enables us to evade authentic selfhood and the "true sound" by losing ourselves in the experiences and interpretations of others. The formal virtuosity of speech—e.g., in a poet or journalist—can sometimes conceal the complete lack of any real identity. Imitation of earlier forms of expression and styles can superficially seem to be original when in truth there is nothing at all original. But the same depletion of speech that can lead to a flight from the self can also force us into a new search for the self, whether by accepting the burden of silence (like Lord Chandos) so as not to come under the dominion of the alienated word, or by seeking new forms of expression (like Brecht), or by waiting for a new and, as it were, eschatological miracle of speech (like Hofmannsthal).

Merging into Others
and Attempts to Break Free from Bodily Individuality
(in Daily Life, Poetry, Art, and the Carnival)

No matter whether I despairingly seek to be myself or ecstatically try to transcend my identity in some union, I do not feel my uniqueness to be merely a gain but also experience it as a liability, as the burden of being chained to identity. "We are all slaves of the self," says Siegfried Lenz in his *Feuerschiff*, "caught like insects in amber, crucified on this one life, and forced to smuggle in the experience of others through the portcullis of the I." "Often we cannot stand ourselves but hang heavily round our own necks," thinks Erich Kästner. No wonder that the excessive coverings of the same I that surround us and limit our perspective can plunge us into the despair, not, or not only, of wanting to be ourselves, but of wanting to be different, to exchange our identities. For Schopenhauer it is death that frees us from the uniqueness of individuality. For individuality is not the innermost core of our being but is to be thought of instead as a perversion of it. Our true, original freedom returns in death. Death restores our first integrity. When death is seen in this way, we renounce the desire to live and really want to die. Prolongation of the person is of no significance. The longed-for liberation from limited identity is achieved. In Joseph Conrad's novel *Lord Jim*, the merchant, adventurer, entomologist and sage achieves his wish and becomes someone else, escaping from the chains of his given identity. We want to *be* in different ways. The beautiful butterfly finds a small bit of dirt and is content to sit on it, but human beings are not prepared to do this. They want to be in one way and then in another. They want to be saints and they want to be devils, and as often as they open their eyes they see themselves as very fine people—finer than they can ever be . . . in dreams.

It can even be a form of enjoyment to change oneself into others in dreams or to acquire the waking habit of merging into the experience of others and viewing the world through their eyes. Thus fellowship with another cannot only help in self-discovery (as in the eros of Goethe's *Urworte Orphisch*); it can have the opposite effect of approximating the I to the other and thus blurring the frontiers of its own identity. Not to be oneself but to live in and through others can be lauded by André Gide in his *Faux-Monnayeurs* as an enjoyable transcending of one's own identity: "My heart beats only in sympathy; I live only through others, *per procura*, as it were, vicariously, by cerebral marriage. I never feel more intensively alive than when I escape from myself and become someone else."

What is meant may be illustrated by a very innocuous and everyday observation. When friends visit me, they want to tour the harbor. I go with them very cheerfully, though I know the area so well that it is no treat for me. For oddly enough I still see it as if for the first time, since I now see it through my friends' eyes. These landlubbers are fascinated by the strange world of ocean giants and tugs, and they obviously enjoy the stale jokes of the guide, which for them are new and fresh. I catch myself waiting for their exclamations of admiration. I am seeing and hearing it all with new eyes and ears, and so each tour opens up new perspectives for me. If I were alone in the sight-seeing boat, I should be bored, for I myself have long since absorbed every impression to the full. I can take in more only when I pass over the boundary of the self and take up a standpoint outside, where I see things as they appear to the eyes of my friends.

It may be the same with the ears. It is a Sunday morning and we have some visitors. I ask them if they would like to go to church to hear a pastor who has something to offer. Two go with me, one out of curiosity, the other out of politeness. Both admit that they seldom go to church. The preacher is good and I like to listen to him, but today things are different. I do not feel that I myself am being addressed; I listen with the ears of my friends. The mono becomes stereo. One of them had told me the evening before that he was put off by the moralistic scolding in his home pulpit when he did go to worship God. I now listen with this expectation in view and ask myself what the effect will be, and how surprised he might be, when he hears about gifts and graces here, and there is no moralizing. The other friend had believed that the pastor always said the same thing, and he was bored by the monotony of constant repetition. He knew in advance what was coming. I note how I put myself in his place and experience his surprise when, as he admitted later, things were suddenly said about himself that he had never heard before.

Astonishingly the breadth of my experience of reality, the vividness of my seeing, and the polyphony of what I heard seem to be immeasurably extended when I hear and see through others and thus take leave of my own identity. What is the attraction of the great tragedy that I see in the theater? Not least my solidarity with the hero as I enter into his destiny, which is not mine but the destiny of someone else, but which is played out in the same world of conflicts as that in which I also live and am exposed to similar possibilities. Fear and cleansing, which were for Aristotle the effect of tragedy, take place as phenomena in a tremendous extension of the ego as I discover in another my own place in the world and its menacing possibilities.

And what is the attraction—several stages lower—of the Western with its horses and guns? Is it not again identification with someone else who is battling for law and justice but who in this battle has far more potential at his command than I do and fights with a determination and ingenuity of which I can only dream?

Again, why do I look with fascination at acrobats and contortionists in the circus? These artists do vicariously things which I cannot do but which are potentially present in the humanity to which I also belong. Here, too, there is identification with the artist and thus a transcending of my own identity.[8] The other, whether my friend or the tragic hero, the champion of right or the artist, represents an aspect of the world that transcends my limited identity. They all of them supplement my finitude as they make it possible for me to move out of myself.

The diagnosis and longing are always the same. My identity makes me into one standpoint from which to view the world. It ties me to myself. Only a change of standpoints opens up to me a plenitude of new ways of viewing the world. As a moral being, Goethe said, he was a monotheist, as an artist a polytheist, and as a scientist a pantheist; he could not rest content with a single way of looking at things. Here we have nothing less than an overcoming of the limitation of perspective in virtue of which I can see the world with new and different eyes. Potentially I have all these ways of seeing things within myself. They are my own possibilities, and yet not mine. What embraces all of them as subject is what Schleiermacher and Kant call "humanity" and not the separate and limited individual. I get nearer to the full range of perspectives the more I learn to see myself and the world through others and thus identify myself at least fragmentarily with humanity. Behind the wish not to be oneself stands the painful experience of not being able to do justice to the riches of life in terms of one's own identity, so that one has to break out of oneself and change into others in order to get a view of the whole. Wilhelm Windelband had this in mind when he said that only the history of philosophy, which gathers up all views of the world, embraces the truth, not any particular philosophical system with its one-sided outlook.

Perhaps a similar thought lies behind the pseudonyms of Kierkegaard, namely, a concern to look at the world first from the standpoint of the aesthete, then from that of the moralist, then from that of the religious person who is addressed by God. The Portuguese author Fernando Pessoa even tries to snap the chains of his identity by using six pseudonyms and adopting different styles and expressions, each of which represents a clearly delineated literary personality (G. Kaltenbrunner).

The longing to transcend one's identity and change into someone else could well be the usual impulse in masked feasts such as the Roman Saturnalia and carnival.[9] A simple and honest housewife becomes a vamp she has seen in a movie, or a prosaic white-collar bookkeeper becomes a gypsy. Each is seeking a contrast to the self, a complementary extension of it.

The basic experience behind all this is as follows. If I am diligent, I can advance in my profession, but I can no longer choose my vocational possibilities freely. Certain junctions are behind me and I now have to go ahead on the chosen tracks. The older I get, the poorer I am in possibilities and the stronger the riveting to my identity appears. I am a professor and can no longer be a train engineer, even though there is still within me a desire to be this, and one side of my nature could only develop if I were. I am a slave to duty, strictly regulating my time, and can no longer fool around, but I envy the hippies because there lives in them something that has withered and died in me.

Society, too, has imposed a certain role on me. A professor does this and that and behaves in this and that way. It is from this enclosing of my identity that I want to break out.

This is what takes place during carnival when we play other roles. For Freud, masked feasts of this kind are legitimate excesses in which the limits imposed by the superego are set aside and for a time one may break certain sacrosanct laws. Johan Huizinga's *Herbst des Mittelalters* is full of juicy instances of the way in which Christian morality is suspended at carnival time and foolish jests and inversions invade the realm of the sacred, even involving a mocking of the liturgy so as to burst through every limit. It is as if the world before the birth of individuality were being celebrated. One can understand why Freud thought he had to interpret it all in the way he did. From a psychoanalytical standpoint, individuality and the role imposed by society seem to be forms of repression. I am not the other whom I bear potentially within myself but with whom I cannot identify myself but have to draw apart. I dwell in the fine house of my personality but hear the wolves howling in the basement. I know that I myself am this basement but I do not want to be a wolf but to celebrate humanity. I have limited my identity to the main part of the house. My name stands there to show this. It is not on the basement door.

Individual identity is a repression of what I am not and do not want to be, but of what is still potentially within me.

Nevertheless, all the gifts I do not use and all the burdens I do not bear press upon me, assert themselves, and come up from the dungeon of their repression. All this takes place at carnival time, when we can thrust off the usual controls. Impulses and instincts long held in check can be given free rein, and I can desperately (or in a repression of despair and transforming of it into pleasure) cease for a moment to be myself and change into someone else. The carnival is the time, as Wilhelm Busch says, when, as always and everywhere, we try with unusual cunning to seem to be what we are not.

ROBBING OF IDENTITY?

Torture, Biological Manipulation, and Ideological Alienation

Thus far we have noted, first, how the question of identity pursues and harasses us no less than does the fate of humanity itself. To be human is to be forced to ask about oneself, to be impelled by the image toward which one is thrust and which enforces a congruence of essence and existence. Basically our own existence brings to light here the tension between what is and what ought to be.

We have seen, second, how this question becomes more pressing in the stages of history and life in which the orientation of being is insecure, in which insecurity about ourselves threatens us, in which we become "question"-able in the full sense of the term.

We have gained some impression, third, of the extreme ways in which the question of our human identity can crop up: in the despairing attempt at self-discovery and the equally despairing attempt at self-renunciation in which we break out of the enclosure of identity.

If we want to complete this list of possibilities systematically, we come up against a final question. Thus far the problem of identity has arisen only with ourselves as the subject moving either toward or away from us. Either way the reality of identity (even if hidden) is self-evident. Only thus can it be sought or renounced.

But is it really an unquestionable and stable entity of this kind, a constitutive part of being with an indestructible character? Might there not be a *break* in identity—a break of such a kind that I seek in vain to resume it, that I not only seek or reject myself in vain but am taken out of myself and see myself robbed of my identity from outside? Might there not be violations of my selfhood that are "done" to me, so that I am not the subject as in repudiations of identity but the object and victim, being subject to them as negligently or unsuspectingly I enter on a slope at the end of which the self is lost (as in taking drugs into whose power to alter identity I have perhaps slipped).

This may sound abstract, but it takes on life at once when we consider an acutely urgent phenomenon. The crass depriving of identity that we see today has always been present in various forms. One might think of cultic rapture—getting out of oneself by psychagogic rites, especially dancing, rhythmic processes, and exercises in concentration. One might also think of such pathological forms of deprivation as schizophrenia or the extension of consciousness by taking drugs. One might think, too, of possession such as we find in the New Testament accounts of demons and more recent instances. Particularly macabre forms are also provided by modern methods of torture which aim at an artificial robbing of identity with the help of a perverted psychiatry.[10]

These methods use refined scientific techniques which ideological governments in particular impress into service with the enlistment of psychologists and psychiatrists. With their help they bring the I to a frontier where it can no longer decide for or against a truth, a mode of conduct, or a confession, but is trained to be the instrument of conditioned or desired reflexes, ceasing to be a center of decision when the pain becomes too intense. Torture of this kind does not force a decision out of the victim by promises, threats, or bribes, by the awakening of fear or hope, by an appeal, therefore, to the instinct of self-preservation. Instead, it bypasses the sphere of decision by rendering it inactive.

In the same way the center of the I can be harmed by such drugs as Pentothal or derivates of scopolamine. When the Hungarian archbishop Joseph Cardinal Mindzenty, under the influence of such methods, made very odd "admissions" at his trial, did he really have to say later that "I" said this or "I" denied that? Did he not instead read with astonishment the reports of his statements at the trial, being forced to say that these were merely a verbal expression of predetermined reactions of his neurological system, but he himself had not said anything of the kind?[11]

Biology undertakes to manipulate genes and thereby to alter or retouch the personality. Electric stimulation of parts of the brain can make people blindly aggressive or reduce them to peaceful indifference.

The surprised question after a return to normalcy, Was it really "I" who said or did this or that? can also be asked when the mass suggestion that propaganda knows how to induce loses its force after the fall of an ideological system. Related to this may be the puzzling fact that Nazi criminals who had human blood on their consciences, or had been guilty of wild speeches, were later able to live quite virtuously as anonymous citizens and deny what they had said or done when accused. It is much too easy to explain this by cynicism or mere self-protection. Probably they did not recognize themselves in what they had formerly done, and were thus inclined to assume that some other I had spoken or acted in that way. The spirit of the age had taken possession of them and robbed them of their identity. This is the kind of identity crisis that we find in those who are possessed.

Destiny and Responsibility:
Two Different Forms of the Loss of Identity
and "Possession"

At any rate, we must make a careful distinction. Loss of identity may be unconditioned or conditioned. It is unconditioned when it comes from outside—neurosurgically or by chemical or psychiatric manipulation—so that the self is removed. It is conditioned when I put myself at the disposal of an alien spirit, when I am ready to let myself be possessed by it, when possession and the associated loss of identity are in the first stage a responsibility of my identity.

Paul speaks about this second type in a famous anthropological passage in chapter 7 of his Epistle to the Romans. Here the Christian observes an identity crisis in himself. Encountering the law of God, he declares: "I do not do the good I want, but the evil I do not want is what I do" (7:19). What, then, is my identity? Is it defined by what I want or by what I do? Who am I if two opposing subjects contend within me and tear my identity apart?

If I understand the apostle aright, in the first part of his argument he seems to take it that the true self is the self that *wants*. His heart —the real center of the I—assents to the command of God. His inner being "delights" in it (7:22). Here is where the self is at home; here he is truly himself. But what, then, is this other factor that is at work in him? Does he not still have to say "I," even though it is just as absurd as saying that a thing both is and is not at the same time?

When the problem of identity is put in this way, a question arises that reminds us of the theme of possession (even though the term is not used). For Paul refuses at first to admit that the forces within him that resist God's law really belong to his I. He experiences them as alien powers that invade the house of the I and seek to occupy it. He even uses mythical terms to denounce these tendencies that are hostile to God's will as an alien factor in which his real I, the inner person, has no part. Twice (vv. 17 and 20) he refers to the "indwelling sin"—not himself—that strives against God and does not let him achieve unity with the will of God. He can also speak about a "law in his members" (7:23) which is at odds with the law of God and to which he finds himself subject. The mythical element in these statements is that in them he hypostatizes a power of the id that possesses him and will not let him be himself. Epigrammatically one might reformulate what Paul is saying as follows: Here is the "I" that is seeking union with the will of God, and there is the "it" that is stopping me. Thus my I is in constant conflict with this other that "I" am not.

Here, then, we have a kind of possession that brings an identity crisis inasmuch as there is an "it," a non-I, that occupies the territory of the I like an alien power. We thus have a confession that is familiar to us in criminology when offenders say that an "it" came over them and it was not "I" that did the deed.

In distinction to the robbing of the I that takes place from outside with the help of manipulations, we find here an initial stage in which I have to say Yes or No to the occupying power of the "it." If I say Yes, I am occupied and possessed. From then on I am directed by an alien will and lose my identity. If I say No, the battle does not cease; I am still in conflict with that which presses its claim to dominion on me. But I do not become subject to it. I grant it no authority over me. I am still watchfully and critically on guard against it.

Paul, then, does not simply solve the question of identity by saying that my I is that in me which knows it is subject to God and oriented to him in mind and conduct. This I is also characterized by its critical self-demarcation from that which triumphantly claims to be itself the I replacing the real I. But in so doing it takes this alien force into itself on its own responsibility. Even here, then, there is an ultimate identification. At the end of the chapter Paul stops speaking mythically about an "it" in himself. He stops making evil the hypostasis of a non-I. Instead he confesses, "Wretched man that I am! Who will deliver me from this body of death?" (7:24.) It is "I" who bear both factors within myself, who am both *for* God and *against* him. I am the one who needs forgiveness. This would not be so if the "it" in me were a fate or destiny to which I were subject as to an alien force and with which I did not have to identify myself. "Deliver me from evil" now means, "Deliver me from myself." And if I have to say what my true identity is from this angle, then I must confess that I am the one whom God has accepted in spite of everything; that I am the one whom he has affirmed for all my questionability and in all my conflicts.

In my view a great deal depends upon a clear differentiation between the two forms of deprivation of the I. Common to both is that they are both a form of possession. In both an alien government is enthroned on the territory of the self. But this enthronement may come upon me from outside like fate or destiny, or it may meet me as a question whether I will accept its rule or not.

In the latter case I have to face the question of preserving my identity in the initial stage. I cannot escape this question. To take another example apart from that of Paul, the responsibility of the Nazi criminal, or of criminals in other ideological systems, is of this type. The spirit of an ideology, a collective spirit of the age, undoubtedly achieves mastery over these people and carries them where they originally do not want to go. Yet initially they sell themselves to this spirit. The spirit then makes them fanatics. It makes them its instruments. It seems to act through them. They think they are speaking and acting on their own. Their values are reversed. They regard as good and bad, as right and wrong, what the spirit suggests. But they themselves have initially opened the door to this subjection. They have not been fatalistically depersonalized as when the I is chemically or psychologically changed. Hence they must identify themselves with what they do. They themselves are the I that has been possessed. When Faust makes his pact with Mephistopheles, he is led where he does not want to go. But he has signed the pact with his own blood. The drama triggered by the pact is thus the tragedy of his own identity. The masks and roles of Mephistopheles have only a triggering function. They simply bring to development what is potentially there in Faust's entelechy. Hence Faust has to stand by what he does. He has to confess: "It was 'I'; 'I' seduced Gretchen."

Having made the necessary distinctions, we may now return to the question how identity can be manipulated and made into non-identity. In two fields this question has become a very urgent one today, and for some time to come, namely, in the field of medicine, especially biology, and in that of criminal law.

C. THE NEW QUESTION OF HUMANITY IN INSECURITY

SURVEY OF THE PROBLEM

Within the framework of the biological possibilities of medicine the question is increasingly that of limits—less the limits of the possibilities themselves and more that of the exercise of them. The question that is now put on every hand is whether we should do all the things that we can do. Might not an unthinking use of all the biological and technical means at our disposal be criminal? Might not our "great learning" make us "mad" (Acts 26:24)? But against whom or what would we be committing crimes or acting madly? Before we bring in the theological category of *hybris* (pride)—which will be the ultimate answer to our question!—we ought to say what we mean by "criminal" in the anthropological sphere. Manipulations here are seen as a threat to human identity. They might be a crime against humanity. Here again, therefore, there are situations of insecurity that raise the question, What is this humanity that arises within the question of identity? It is no wonder that this basic question of anthropology is being put unmistakably in medical and biological conferences. What exactly does it involve?[1]

The expanding possibilities of modern medicine compel us first to be clear about the goals that are sought, e.g., in hormonal or neurosurgical manipulations or the influencing of heredity. As the London symposium of the Ciba Foundation in 1962 made vividly apparent, the questionable nature of these goals may be seen when we consider what the realization of all our possibilities might finally entail. For we then face shockingly utopian ideas of a humanly produced supercivilization for which we are not by nature adapted. "By nature" means that the biological and mental endowment of the race cannot handle what it is able to produce, so that it loses control over the changes it brings about. Its limited intelligence is outmatched by the superintelligence of its computers and other aids and thus redirected to goals that it neither desires nor governs. The powers it unleashes, as in the case of the sorcerer's apprentice, are too much for it.

Thus an American military school champions the thesis that in comparison with the technical possibilities and tasks of space exploration, humans are of faulty construction. They need to be reconstructed if they are to keep up with the instruments constructed by them. Thus the situation of astronauts would be greatly alleviated if they had the prehensile tails of Gibbon apes instead of superfluous bones.

Here the question unavoidably arises whether we should allow biological interferences of this kind, or interferences with heredity. The shock that accompanies the question is caused by the situation that gives rise to it. For it seems that here humans are no longer the measure of things, that they are not subduing the earth, as the command of creation enjoins, that the earth as thus subdued by them is organizing a kind of revolt of means that will rob them of their freedom and subject them to an ineluctable process. It is shocking indeed that in our place the structures that we have created, technology, progress, the apparatus of civilization, should direct the shaping of our human constitution, that superconstructions should mount an attack upon us with the aim of seizing power over us. Not just to cooperate but in the simple interest of self-preservation we seem to be put on the defensive and forced to manipulate ourselves or let ourselves be manipulated.

It is along these lines, partly with hope and partly with fear, that certain final utopian visions speak of a transformed humanity that transcends identity with its present state and embarks for new shores that we cannot as yet imagine. To the degree that we compete in the technical race and allow our acts to be determined by the extension of technological activity, we can say, with tongue in cheek, that this, too, is a kind of "possession." We come under a regime that contradicts our self-determination and as an alien spirit threatens our identity.

Apart from the basic problems raised by this process, which we shall not pursue here, there are on the empirical level certain eloquent signs indicating how dubious this path is. Thus doctors are put in a vicious circle with their increasing abilities, for the greatly increased power to heal the sick threatens to impair heredity. Lives that would have ended before reaching the age of procreation are now prolonged, so that their weaknesses are passed on and multiply.

Not only, then, is our endowment inferior to our accomplishment but our very accomplishment turns upon us, diminishing our original constitution and increasing its helplessness.

This sapping of heredity has produced macabre visions, not only from the wilder popular writers but even from respected scientists. The combination of the population explosion and pathological hereditary weakening threatens in a measurable period to turn the world into one big hospital full of cripples, neurotics, and the mentally ill and unstable—people who can live only if they have external support.[2]

The crisis to which humanity is thus condemned raises the question of identity in two ways.

I. THE FIRST CRISIS OF IDENTITY:
GUILT AND INNOCENCE
IN AUTONOMOUS PROCESSES

a. Autonomous Processes: *Example, The Way from the Theory of Relativity to the Atom Bomb*

Of the human "exemplars" whose selves are made the object of massive manipulations and are thus depersonalized, we are forced to say that they are robbed of their humanity, or at least that their identity is temporarily suspended. This robbing and suspending may be seen in their momentary or permanent loss of the decisive mark of humanity. They have ceased to be centers of action. They have lost the freedom to govern themselves. They have as little responsibility for the nature added to or thrust upon them as those who are psychologically tortured and robbed of their identity. They no longer have the "I" that must confess itself to be the subject of what they speak and do.

This dehumanizing and exculpating of the victims of manipulation, however, does not rule out but rather demands that those who initiate the process not be relieved of their responsibility. The ineluctable necessity of the processes unleashed when the devilish pact is made with Mephistophelian mechanisms certainly deprives people of freedom and subjects them to the irresistible movement. But they freely took the initiative in starting the process. In distinction from the victims, the initiators are forced to say even of what is now an ineluctable process that they are its authors. It was they who unleashed it; it was they who made the pact.

I hope I can put this instructively by using the example of Albert Einstein.

It was the pacifist Albert Einstein—no less!—who in a letter to President Roosevelt found himself forced to speak about the dreadful possibility that a madman like Hitler might achieve command of atomic explosions. With this warning he undoubtedly influenced the President's decision to go ahead vigorously with the building of the atom bomb. Later, when the disaster of Hiroshima had occurred and Einstein was shattered by this provisional result of the interplay of forces, a visitor, it is reported, said to him, "*You* pressed the button first." Einstein supposedly accepted the accusation in silence. He had not wanted the end of the process, but his theory of relativity was the formula that released the avalanche. At this moment he represented humanity and had to say: "I am homo sapiens, unwittingly taking the first step on a road that leads us where we do not want to go."

How if this road becomes one of revolt against divine creation, of reversal of this creation? Alluding to the underlying effect of Einstein's theory of relativity, Eduard Heimann once said that whereas God laid the foundation of the world by changing energy into matter, we are turning matter back again into energy.

What is humanity? one might ask in face of these entanglements. What does it mean to call dominion over self the mark of humanity if this freedom is blind to what it might do with its progress and discoveries and unleashing of possibilities, so that it is lost in the automatic nexus of these effects and makes those who initiate them into collaborators and unwilling components.

At this point we come up against an even deeper entwining of freedom and necessity than that envisaged by Kant. Arnold Gehlen described this loss of freedom very profoundly when he regarded even the activity of research—the idea of the theory of relativity and the signal it gave—as grounded in a necessary process rather than free decisions. For scientists neither put the problems nor decide upon the technical use of the knowledge they acquire. Problems arise out of prior knowledge. And by the logic of experiment pure science already includes control of the practical application. Thus no special decision is needed to make the application, whether in the form of biogenetic manipulation or the military use of atomic energy. The object takes the decision for us. It is thus taken away. Robert Oppenheimer, the father of the atom bomb and opponent of the hydrogen bomb, once described this inevitability as an irresistible mental slide when, with reference to his own work, he said that what was "technically sweet" proved to be irresistible even when it meant the evolving and constructing of the atom bomb.

The form of the autonomy of the processes of research and technology is thus a combination of question and answer, of theoretical knowledge and technological effect. Research scientists seem to be reduced to the status of means whereby the process advances. Their own intellectual contribution simply comes through their ability—brilliant sometimes—to recognize and trigger the "waiting" chain reaction of question and answer. But are they really responsible pilots? Does not the intellectual ship of scientific and technological progress sail with an empty bridge?

Gehlen thinks that a decisive change—a kind of ethical intervention or assertion of freedom—is conceivable only at the extremes, i.e., at the beginning, where I decide to know, and at the end, where I face the question whether I want to be consumed and destroyed. Once I want to explore radio electricity, an automatic process is initiated that cannot be interrupted ethically. There is no stopping advance in the technological production of television. Even if, for example, I believe that television culture works on the whole to degrade human and intellectual standards and is pedagogically dangerous, I cannot arrest the process. I can only refrain from using my set, or dismantle it, or refuse to buy one.

But here, quite apart from individual decisions at the beginning and end of the process, we come up against the fact that the process does not come upon us from outside like a natural event, but that someone has pressed the button. In this regard there seems to be profound significance in the way in which the Bible finds humanity represented in a single exemplary or collective person. This symbolizes the suprapersonal character of the nexus of guilt in which I, too, am implicated as a participant. I cannot exclude myself from the circle of those who bear the human countenance. I, too, am "Adam."

For all the ineluctability of unleashed processes that degrade people to the status of mere components, for all the deprivation of the human self that they suffer under the mechanisms of such processes, humans never lose their identity. They still see themselves accused of the evil that they and no one else have brought into the world. They cannot appeal to any power of fate or destiny, even though they themselves play the role of fate for those who are their victims and whom they rob of their identity.

b. Original Sin, Tragic Guilt, and Self-Justification

We thus come up against a fact—recollection of Adam was a first indication—that is expressed in the Christian doctrine of original sin. If this is construed as "hereditary" sin, it evokes misleading associations, giving rise to the misunderstanding that we are referring to something that is genealogically determined like a hereditary disease. But this is to miss the point. A hereditary disease comes upon me from outside and I have no responsibility for it. Similarly, if original sin is seen in this way, it becomes a matter of fate rather than guilt, and it is put in the extrapersonal sphere. This is not what is meant, and for this reason we should emphasize that the proper term is "original" sin (Latin: *peccatum originale*).* In this sense the term denotes a nexus of guilt in which I myself am always implicated. It describes processes in which I am both implicated and also have a part, so that I cannot hold aloof from them as though they were those of others. I have to recognize that I am a responsible subject. I have to say concerning them: "My fault."

What happens in the great structures of the world, e.g., the autonomy of the sacred egoism of states, is also at work in the microcosm of my own heart. I am forced to say that I am the world; it is a macrocosmic reflection of myself. Great Babylon is only a joke when it tries seriously to be as great and immoderate as our Babylonian heart (Francis Thompson). Just as the world is there ahead of me—we shall discuss this more fully later—so I am ahead of myself. I am already present in my nature, but not in such a way that I can cease to say "I" to myself.

Purely moral categories cannot encompass this reality. For in them it seems that I always face open decisions. This is undoubtedly an unrealistic as well as a banal view of things. In fact, experience itself teaches me that my room for decision is limited. Many factors narrow it: forms of autonomy that determine the course of politics and

---

* Thielicke stresses this because the usual German term is *Erbsünde*, not *Ursünde.*—Translator's Note

economics and even science and technology, conflicts and various forms of strife that are part of the nexus of our world. Thus the duties of my job are at odds with my duty to devote myself to my family and the upbringing of my children. My time is too limited to do all that I am required to do.

The morally perceived polarity of good and evil is indeed the most innocuous problem. Much more aggressive is the conflict between good and good, the constraint to leave one good undone in order to do another. I do not want this conflict. It is part of the nexus of the world. It comes upon me as something suprapersonal. Yet I find my failure painful. I cannot complain of the evil world instead of myself. I might, of course, speak like the blind harpist in Goethe's *Wilhelm Meister* and accuse the gods as the responsible representatives of this world structure, arguing that they bring us into the world, make us guilty, and then leave us to our suffering, since guilt always avenges itself on earth. But this kind of outburst can only be an interlude in self-reflection. Greek tragedy, which very profoundly illumines the awareness of original sin in this situation, does sometimes refer to a suprapersonal nexus of guilt, but it rejects this attempt at exculpation and demands that we confess our guilt as responsible agents. Thus in Aeschylus' *Oresteia*, when Clytemnestra passionately asserts that she is innocent of the murder of Agamemnon, since she is only the unwilling instrument of vengeance, her form having harbored the "old, fierce daemon of the house," the chorus imperiously requires her to accept her guilt. The boundary between guilt and fate, between personal and suprapersonal sin, is broken down here. Clytemnestra must say "I" to the deed that has been done. The chorus tells her, "Yours was the deed. No witness clears you of the murder. No, no. The sins of the fathers are merely accessories to the crime." Here, too, within a completely different outlook on life, guilt is found to have its basis at a point of decision. There is suprapersonal bracketing by both destiny and personal imputation. The act to which I see myself forced is still my own act. The forces that trigger it in me, the "sins of the fathers" and the "old, fierce daemon of the house," simply bring to light and release something that is present in me, changing it from potential to kinetic energy. They are accessories, midwives; the fruit they bring forth is my own. In this sense the term "original sin," resisting any attempt to render it innocuous along the line of morality or fate, expresses the fact that guilt is never just a future possibility but is something from which I already come. I have decisions behind me. Being already taken, they enter into my new decisions. But they are still mine. Hence they do not remove my identity; they chain me to it.

This burden of humanity, of "my" humanity, which I thus share and take with me, clashes with my innate impulse to justify myself. In self-justification I turn the tables, as it were, and use the suprapersonal background of guilt as an argument in my plea to be pronounced innocent (as in Goethe's *Wilhelm Meister*). I see myself as the victim of uncontrollable forces in the way Clytemnestra did. In so doing, I change guilt into fate. As Luther might have put it, I change necessity into coercion (*coactio*).

c. Interpretation of the Biblical Story of the Fall, the Great Example of Transferring Culpability

The classical example of this kind of self-justification may be found in the biblical story of the fall (Genesis 3). When God walks through the Garden of Eden in the cool of the evening, seeking to bring Adam to account for taking the forbidden fruit, Adam replies that the woman God had given him as a helpmeet had handed him the fruit, and he ate. Adam sees himself as merely the effect of a cause, namely, his temptation by Eve. And since God himself had given him this companion, God himself plays the role of a first cause and is thus ultimately the author of evil.

As if to show that this is a model of exculpation that will be copied again and again, we find the same procedure when God turns to Eve and asks what she has done. For Eve's answer is that she herself did not really do it, but "the serpent beguiled me, and I ate." Grammatically we have here a consecutive construction. If an act is done on false premises, because of a deception, "I" am no longer the responsible subject but simply an effect of the other that deceived me.

God abandons the trial at this point, for dialogue with the serpent, in which the latter could present its case, would imply a partnership between God and the demonic power, which does not exist. But if we might give free rein to our imagination for a moment, we might invent a rather bold discussion in which, when God asks the serpent why it has tempted Eve, it would reply with the rhetorical question: "Why did you put me in the garden? If you are the cause of everything and all things, then I, with my functions, am your creature too."

This would close the circle. Everyone would be caused by someone else and would thus claim to be a mere effect. And everyone would implicitly advance the thesis that God himself is the first cause and thus bears guilt for it all, having brought us into the world.

When in 1945, after the Second World War, the question of German guilt for Nazi atrocities became a dominant issue in Germany, the same game of transferring culpability was played: The desperate situation of 1933, with its six million unemployed, resulted in the cry for a strong leader; the unemployed were the result of the power politics that dictated the Versailles Treaty, so that the Allies were to blame. They, in turn, claimed that they were only reacting against the imperialism of the Kaiser. But the Kaiser imperialists argued that they, too, were simply reacting rather than acting responsibly. Was it not the envy of the English and the French at Germany's economic development that made it necessary for them to build up military and naval defenses and for the emperor to try to scare them off by bombastic speeches? And did not Bismarck stand behind the rise of the German Empire? And behind him Frederick the Great? And behind what was called the German spirit of subjection to authority —which allowed the great leaders to speak and act as freely as they did—did there not stand the old princely system, the force of tradition, and, of course, Luther's doctrine of the two kingdoms?

This transferring of culpability leads us farther and farther back in an infinite regress until finally we come to Adam and Eve, and in the background God. These are all to blame, not we ourselves. Arguing in this way is simply a variation on one and the same attempt to change guilt into fate. It is part of the plea for an acquittal. Psychologists and sociologists are called in to support the argument by interpreting criminal acts as the logical consequences of something else. The word "punishment" is increasingly proscribed. For how can one deal out punishment when no one knows where the guilt lies? Social defense is the final slogan in rejection of criminality. Assessors have the last word in court. Judges, it seems, have only the restricted role of putting into effect their findings. To put it somewhat epigrammatically, they merely have the function of saying such a case comes in a very restricted sense under the relevant criminal law.

Once we see that arguing back in this way, or transferring culpability, can lead only to exculpation and the elimination of the very

word "guilt," we understand why the question of the origin of evil—
how it came into the world—is wrongly put and therefore cannot be
answered. This statement is not a compromising admission that we
do not know any answer. Our answer consists of showing why there
can be no answer. It thus resembles Kant's proof why freedom cannot be demonstrated.

Why, then, cannot we say how evil came into the world? Because
every attempt to exhibit the origin of evil can only take the form of
an effort to derive it, to put it in a causal nexus, and thus to rob it of
the essential condition on which alone it can be evil, namely, freedom. Evil cannot be derived for exactly the same reason freedom
cannot be derived.

The biblical story of the fall puts all this in striking fashion,
though naturally not in the form of philosophical reflection. Two
points in particular demand our attention and perhaps will evoke our
astonishment. First, in spite of malicious attacks, the nonderivability
of evil is respected even so far as very definitely not making the serpent the cause or author of evil. It is a constantly repeated calumny
that Christianity attributes evil to the devil and posits a mythically
dualistic principle. Such a view blocks access to an understanding of
human autonomy, for it is in this that responsibility is grounded and
we are our own first cause and not victims of the devil. When Adam
and Eve try to transfer culpability, with the serpent at the end of the
line, the game is a total failure. Otherwise there would be no sense in
their expulsion from Paradise. The point of this is that Adam and
Eve are nailed to their offense, that they are identified with their
deed. It was they who took the forbidden fruit. The "old, fierce
daemon" of Paradise was simply an accessory. It released possibilities
—no more—that Adam and Eve grasped and in which their fallen
identity is manifest. This is confirmed by the second point.

Second, Adam does not believe his own arguments for shifting the
blame. His conduct refutes them, presenting his true face behind the
mask of his excuses. It is the face of an anxious person well aware of
his guilt.

Long before the dialogue with God begins and Adam advances his
defense, he has hidden from the face of God among the trees of the
garden. Behind and beneath the zone of his protective maneuvers he
knows his fault, for which there is no defense. He knows that God's
face is against him. When God calls him out of hiding, he argues
that he fled because he was naked and afraid. Is that just a pretext?

Yes and no: yes because he is trying to disguise in this way the real reason for his flight, his taking the forbidden fruit; and no because he unwittingly reveals and blabs out his real offense with the reference to his nakedness. For the next phase of the hearing shows that he is aware of his nakedness because the fall has opened his eyes. God's question: "Who told you that you were naked?" already contains the answer: Adam's taking the forbidden fruit has made him aware of his nakedness. The innocence of a nakedness of which he had no consciousness, the self-evident nature of the state in which God had made him, so that it raised no question, was now a subject of reflection and questioning. He was ashamed.

d. Taboos and Shame as Protection for Human Nakedness and Vulnerability

Shame is a sign that something vulnerable has to be protected. This is why what is vulnerable is ringed around with a wall of taboos. The covering of nakedness is due to the desire to reckon with this vulnerability. Taboos arise as a rule only in the field of sexuality. The story of the fall is often taken in this sense and viewed as a biblical covering up of sexuality, even to the point of forbidding naked baths. This interpretation narrows it considerably. It makes the symbol of a mystery into the mystery itself, the sign into the thing signified. But what is the thing signified?

It is the mystery of humanity itself. This is, as we have seen, the fact that human beings are not things like others. They realize that they are an open possibility that must be grasped—or missed. They can betray the identity they are given. They can misappropriate what is entrusted to them.

This mystery of humanity, which is also the mystery of human nakedness, finds twofold expression.

First, the mystery is open to me only when I am already fallen. To know the polarity of good and evil—and hence the basic state of all human existence—I have had to do evil. That I live in decision, that I may succeed or fail, is clear to me only when I have already decided and taken the forbidden fruit. Prior to this Adam lived in the unselfconscious and suspended state of an eternal liturgy that bound his thoughts solely to God. I am aware of a choice between good and evil only when I have taken a decision and taken it against God. The serpent knew this very well when it said to Eve: "When you eat of it, your eyes will be opened, and you will be like God, knowing good and evil." Schiller took the serpent's part when he extolled the fall as the most fortunate event in history because in it human beings learned to decide, opted boldly for freedom, and thus transcended animality. In this way Schiller makes a "necessity" of humanity—the knowledge of good and evil, of freedom and decision, which results from the fall—into a "virtue," and thus changes the thrust of the story. Nevertheless, he did grasp one decisive point, namely, that I know decision only in hindsight, when I have made a decision—a mistaken one. The dancer in Heinrich von Kleist's *Marionetten-theater* knows the secret of dancing, its weightlessness and unconscious grace only when he has had his special fall, contemplating himself in the mirror and beginning to reflect on his movements.

That the mystery of the knowledge of good and evil—the true human mystery—may be realized only in the state of lost innocence is very strikingly shown by the structure of the Ten Commandments. For these have a negative emphasis. They do not point positively to a goal that is to be reached, that will give identity to the idea and form of humanity. They do not say: "Be honest, respect property, preserve life," et cetera. They have in view the failure to do such things, not as a future possibility but as a present reality. Hence they carry a kind of backward reference to the fall, which is already behind those whom they address. One must always catch this backward reference, which is the concealed background of the Decalogue: "Thou shalt not kill, for thou art (already) a murderer"; "thou shalt not commit adultery, for thou art (already) an adulterer." Only by reason of this background, this decision that has already been made, do you really know what is at issue and perceive the relevance of the commandments.

It is because Adam has passed through the crossfire of the knowledge of good and evil, and as a guilty person has become unsure about himself, that he knows his nakedness, his vulnerability. From this standpoint, too, our thesis is confirmed that we ask about ourselves only when we are insecure, when our identity has ceased to be self-evident and unquestionable, when we see ourselves exposed. Adam sees himself exposed. This is the discovery of his nakedness.

e. The Breaking and Changing of Taboos: Sexuality and Death

That the reference is to the nakedness and vulnerability of humanity itself and not to the simple concealment of the sex organs is confirmed by a concrete observation. We can state that taboos and the breaking of taboos change. Hence the points at which the mystery, vulnerability, and insecurity of humanity manifest themselves are in constant flux. Nakedness "localizes" itself in different places. Hardened by the various sex-revolutions, many people hardly feel sexually vulnerable. Sex has been objectified and dehumanized by minute statistical examinations from Kinsey to Kolle. One can speak about it without emotion. Whether this will continue, whether human nature itself will not see to it that the lost ground is regained, that taboos, even if not of the Victorian or Puritan type, are reestablished, and that the indescribable impoverishment of sex is in this way prevented, is another question. Psychoanalytical approaches also strengthen the tendency to abolish taboos as intimate questions, such as complexes, including one's own, become the subject of daily conversation at parties.

A taboo can be removed, but not completely. It changes shape and reappears in some other place. People may feel less threatened in their sexuality today, so that they see no reason to hide in the bushes. No threat to their identity is seen at this point. Once sex is construed as an impersonal glandular affair, the taboo drops away. It does not touch the center of my person. In spite of its elemental nature, which no one denies, it is only marginal to my identity, having no influence upon it.

Perhaps the main site of the sense of taboos today has shifted from sex to death, i.e., our being in finitude. In the past, death was not subject to any taboo. It was a matter of public and open awareness. But today the inevitability of death has come under the seal of a taboo. Condemned to die, we do not talk about it. The natural processes of decay and corruption have become as shocking to us as those of copulation and birth were a century ago. Whereas our ancestors said that children were found among cabbage leaves or brought by storks, we shall perhaps be telling our children that the deceased change into flowers or sleep in lovely gardens, says Geoffrey

Gorer in an essay that bears the striking title *The Pornography of Death.*

The sign of vulnerability indicated by this taboo on death might perhaps be reduced to the formula that we are unable to cope with our finitude. Perishing is felt to be an attack on our identity, for we all desire eternity, "deep, deep eternity." We want fulfillments and triumphs. If we cannot fill our finitude with this deeper meaning, we cannot accept it. And if we cannot accept it, we have to repress it. Thus unmastered finitude compels us not to take time seriously. It leads to a protest against aging. It causes us to put the mask of youth and the deceitful symbol of an eternal present on wrinkled faces. Hence it can be regarded as no less than pornography to present an aging film star, whose role as a lover has become a cliché, without the aid of makeup. For the same reason limousines have replaced hearses in many cities. It is not the thing to remind people of their finitude, of that undomesticated factor that is the basis of our insecurity. Funeral directors are well aware of this.

f. Summary and First Result

The story of the fall and study of the phenomena of modern life point in the same direction.

Freedom is what identifies us with ourselves and constitutes the humanity of our existence. Freedom is the condition of responsibility for what we make of ourselves, how we fulfill or fail to fulfill the task we are set. But this freedom is threatened, especially by suprapersonal forces and pressures which seem as though they will achieve the power to control us. These apparently relieve us of the possibility of being guilty, which is an essential mark of freedom, for they threaten to change guilt into fate.

We have seen that what threatens identity as a suprapersonal force can also be regarded as a release, and that its imperious features can be a bush behind which we hide. The curse on the house of Argos, "the old, fierce daemon of the house," tragic entanglements, the autonomy of the historical process—all these things can take from us the guilt-liability of freedom and hand us over to suprapersonal chains of events. The story of the fall showed that this game of shifting responsibility is arrested. No "stony guest," but God himself interrupts it. Adam cannot attribute his fault to someone else and in that way minimize it. Unmasked, he has to leave his bush, step forth with his freedom, and identify himself as the first cause.

The story of the fall also showed us that nakedness is native to us. The hour of breaking through to freedom is not just the solemn moment of finding identity beyond animality (as Schiller said), but also the moment of vulnerability, of forfeiting true identity, of betraying the plan of creation. Freedom is thus bought at the price of guilt. Knowledge of good and evil comes only when Adam and Eve are pinned to evil. They have this knowledge only in painful nakedness, in shame. Their nakedness is covered; they come under taboos. What they conceal is the wound of their humanity.

Hence human identity, in the deepest dimension at which we can plumb it, is from the very first a threatened identity. It is this threat, this nakedness, that forces us to ask who we really are. It thus brings up the subject of identity. Only after the fall do Adam and Eve see why the Creator made them. Only in retrospect can they measure his intention for them.

II. THE SECOND CRISIS OF IDENTITY: MODELS FROM MEDICINE, BIOLOGY, AND LAW

After these principial discussions, it might be as well to return to the empirical realm where we started. We have achieved some new insights which we will want to demonstrate and confirm by empirical data. In view of the wealth of material offered by medicine, biology, and criminal law, we must be content with a few examples.

a. Coming Humanity as the Goal of Breeding

We have already considered some aspects of the significance of biology for an understanding of human identity, e.g., the possible influencing of genes and the bearing of manipulation upon identity. In this context, however, the question who we are arises much more drastically at another point.

The ability to manipulate life biologically has given rise to utopian

ideas. If human beings are plastic material that can be shaped by bi
ologists, it seems to be possible to set new goals for human evolution
Those who entertain such visions are not just dilettante dreamers. At
the London Conference of the Ciba Foundation, to which we have
already referred, prominent biologists accepted them.[3] Teilhard de
Chardin also dreamed of human self-transcendence in future devel
opment. To be sure, he based such dreams on theological presupposi
tions, but they still need biological manipulation for their actualiza
tion. The theological basis is that by creation there are from the very
first certain spiritual elements that direct the course of evolution
Once the human brain and human self-consciousness come into
being, we can take these elements, which previously worked on us
and gave us our present form, and make them the conscious content
and basis of action. We thus become collaborators in creation, God's
partners. We become junior heads in the firm of the cosmos. We
have the right of signature and can help to control evolution instead
of being its passive objects. We are empowered and commissioned
not merely to accept ourselves and see our identity as given and
complete, but to actualize our present being in new forms as yet unknown to us. This further course of human evolution can be
influenced by obvious biological means at the disposal of the human
brain.

Purely biological visionaries do not share this fully rounded and
comprehensive conception of coming humanity. Teilhard de Char
din had a picture of the human goal that he derived from universal
theology as well as biology. Biology interested him only insofar as it
seemed to provide the means to help achieve the goal. The experts
reverse things and thus fall victim to the besetting danger of all ex
perts. They posit anthropological goals on the limited territory of
their own discipline. Hence the picture is distorted. For the human
ity whose actualization is at issue transcends the isolated field of ex
pertise. If we project our picture of humanity on the basis of psycho
analysis, physics, or biology alone, we arrive at the caricature of a
truncated homunculus and finally come to the rather melancholy
conclusion that human beings are "nothing but . . ." (V. E.
Frankl).

The limitation of this approach is even worse if we look only at
the available means of influencing genes, consider the result of using
them, declare that the product of this consideration is the utopian

goal of humanity, and then dedicate ourselves to this goal as if it meant our exaltation to superhumanity.

The biological instrument at our command, which also delineates the humanity that may be achieved in the future, is the art of breeding. What its use involves for us may be seen from zoological experiments. For evolutionary progress has, in fact, been achieved by planned breeding in animals.

Yet the parallel breaks down. The reason why it does so is very characteristic. When we see what it is, we shall come up against the noninterchangeable human identity that animals do not have.

Why does the parallel break down? In the breeding of animals the goal is always limited and highly specialized. Thus in breeding pigs or horses those in charge have a specific end in view. They want pigs that will produce better ham or horses that will jump better or be better workhorses. But to what end will we breed humans? This is the decisive question.

A fatal error in thought may be seen at this point. Since the instrumental possibilities at our command are made the measure of the goal of breeding, the goal in view becomes a person who can be used instrumentally, who can work in gadgets like spaceships, with a prehensile tail bred in to replace superfluous bones. Or it might be a person with inbred aggressive instincts who could serve in assault troops, or a person with passive qualities who would make a good robot working stupidly but without boredom at an assembly line. Imagination knows no limits in this field.

But this is a mistaken conclusion. For in humans the drive toward specialization in breeding leads to the limitation of life to a narrow sector. And usefulness in one way or another is the criterion by which this sector is chosen. Humanity is thus betrayed not merely by an intolerable decimation of its fullness but even more so by the erasure of its dignity as an end in itself and its degradation as a mere means to some other end.

How far human identity is damaged in this way may be seen when we pursue the line of argument further. For we can say that everything that we regard as specifically human—conflicts, attachments, private self-fulfillment—is undoubtedly sand in the technical machinery and therefore in the putting of people to specific uses. What are we to seek then, what *must* we seek, if we are to achieve this end? Will we take from Faust his unrest so that we can use his dynamism productively, or from Hamlet his indecisiveness, or from King Lear his torments of conscience, or from Romeo and Juliet their conflicts, so that the energies thus released may be put in the service of concrete ends? Or do we want the hormonally directed stupidity of homunculi who in animal "innocence" live the nonhistorical life of vegetables beyond both fear and hope?

What is the world that comes to meet us here out of the twilight of the future? Even less finely tuned natures will surely regard it as apocalyptic and ghostly, as less than human. It is a world of robots and lemures, of humans that have become homunculi.

When we see where a nonhuman, purely biological approach is leading us, the question of the nature of human identity becomes an urgent one. As humans we have a broad range of possibilities. Control of our humanity is one of these. It is a task for us in every sphere of life: in our encounter with the destiny with which we have to wrestle; in the guilt that lays upon us the task of becoming human; in the anxiety that can release creative impulses in art and action; in the hope that launches us out and enables us to grasp the future; in the very conflicts that bring us to maturity. But the question what we *can* do threatens to cause us to forget what we *are* and what in the name of what we are we *can* do but *should* not. In this oath of renunciation we might well recall the skeptical saying of Albert Einstein that we live in an age of perfect means and confused ends.

Identity is not to be found in the limited sector of the individual faculties. These can display only one fragment of humanity. And woe to those who take this fragment for the total picture! The totality can be known only from other sources. And these are to be sought only in territory where the fullness of humanity is known, where humanity itself is investigated. Is there much territory of this kind?

One part of it is surely where humanity is viewed in its relation to God and in terms of God's purpose by creation. At any rate, we must explore this sphere. Only when certainty is achieved—in some way— about the nature of human identity can the faculties come and add their bits of mosaic to the picture. Biology does not produce a possible picture of humanity. But the biologist can have such a picture and then ask about the relevance of his science for it. When he has it, however, it derives from some other source than biology, perhaps from religion, perhaps from a philosophical view of the world, perhaps from an unreflecting knowledge of life resulting from love and hate and all kinds of conflicts. It can spring from many sources, but not from a specialized discipline.

b. Beginning and End of Human Life

1. BEGINNING

Investigation of the boundaries of human life also puts the question of identity. When and to what end are we human?[4] The legalizing of abortion and the growing cry for euthanasia give particular relevance to this problem.

In this context and within our present terms of reference we cannot seek solutions to these questions, but we might emphasize the crucial point of the problem of identity raised by them.

Among experts there is hardly any disagreement regarding the fact that the human fetus is not just a part of its mother but an independent organism. We may leave out of account certain popular ideologies with empty catchwords such as, "My stomach is my own." The embryo can die even though the mother still lives, and for a limited period, when the child can be kept alive, the reverse is also true. As both organisms have their own possibilities of living and dying, so both may become independently ill. The fetus has its own circulation and its own brain. There is agreement, therefore, concerning the independence of the developing life.

But when does this begin: at conception or later? Even if a consensus could be reached on this point, there would still be the question whether biological autonomy is the beginning of human life. Among supporters of a limited period for abortion without penalty—during the first three months after conception—this discussion is important. The unformed core does not come under the same taboo as the fetus with a human form. Although I reject this view—for reasons that need not concern us here, and in spite of my respect for the motives of many who hold it—our present interest is not in the answer to this problem but in the question itself. It is a justifiable one in its distinction between life in general and specifically human life. Whether or not what distinguishes human life (especially self-awareness, or the ability to communicate, or what have you) belongs as yet to the fetus, we have good reason to ask in what way the fetus enjoys more than purely biological life. This applies even though we find the distinction only in the developing organs that define its humanity, e.g., its brain, or its hands, which will later take shape and make use of tools. The reluctance to expel an embryo as though it were merely a fertilized egg is probably due in the main to an indefinite sense of this distinction between purely biological life and human life.

Once this difference is noted, we find that it has been sought across the centuries. Thus it is easy to discover it in the bold thought of endowment with a soul, which goes back to Aristotle and was handed down by Scholasticism. The fascination of this theory lies in its postulating of a break in the process of biological development when the embryo is endowed with a soul and thus acquires a share in the dignity of humanity. On this view an attack on the budding life is the slaughter of an innocent. But to establish the border between what is legitimate and what is illegitimate we have to say when the soul is acquired. In this respect an odd distinction is made between male and female embryos—the former acquiring a soul after forty days, the latter after eighty. But this should not be allowed to blind us to the seriousness of the question when "human" life begins. This is no less than the question when the developing life takes on its human identity and thus needs to be protected and has a right to be protected.

It is hardly possible to make any further advance with this kind of ontological question. Insuperable obstacles seem to stand in the way of the attempt to clarify the beginning of humanity, to fix objectively the boundary between mere bios and the rise of human life. The ongoing and inconclusive controversy about the break testifies to the difficulty. Even within the moral theology of Roman Catholicism there is disagreement on this point. On the theory that the soul is acquired the break comes fairly late, but today the beginning of humanity is located at conception and a corresponding taboo is imposed. The fact that no consensus can be reached, and that even the refined discoveries of modern medicine cannot help us to fix the essential break, is no indication of an ignorance that might be overcome in the future with further progress. Instead, we can state precisely why the break cannot be fixed. The reason is the same as that advanced already in our epistemological discussion. In principle, humanity cannot be objectified. The impossibility perceived in the question of human freedom may be seen again in this matter of the embryonic pre-stages of personhood. The transition from bios to humanity cannot be made the subject of scientific investigation. In this area we have to rely on an indefinite "feeling" (a very unscientific method!). And this feeling makes the humanity of the fetus more vivid and compelling when it has begun to take human shape or developed into an independently active and discernible being. The jolt experienced even by hard-boiled gynecologists when they see the limbs of a half-developed embryo twitching in an induced abortion bears testimony to this feeling.

Ontologically we can go no further. We shall be anticipating if we advance here a consideration that will be of decisive significance in our own anthropology, namely, that if we see in humanity the design of the Creator that is imparted to us and that it is our task to actualize, then we shall find in this relation to the Creator the decisive point of humanity. We are not just beings that enjoy certain special qualities such as reason, conscience, or an upright stance. Our dignity and inviolability is that we come from the hands of the Creator and that these hands are upon our lives and direct them until they go back to the one from whom they came. The mystery of human life is that the Lord of life summons it to a history with himself. Hence the nature of human life is not discovered by investigating its state and being ontologically. Nor does its worth consist in its attributes but in its relations, namely, in its reference to him who creates and addresses and calls us, setting us goals that we may reach or fail to reach.

For this reason we do not speak about a dignity of humanity that is based on qualities but about an "alien dignity" in Luther's sense. We humans are the apple of God's eye. Those who touch us, touch him. Our worth is based upon this imparted sharing in the divine life. The history with himself to which God has called us constitutes the basis, goal, and meaning of our existence. It is the secret of our identity.

Our investigation of the beginning of human life inevitably takes a new turn in the light of this alien dignity. It is no longer an ontological search for the marks or qualities by which the beginning of human life may be discerned. It now asks, When does that history with God begin, which is the basis of our humanity? That this history cannot be objectified, that it is the basis and object of trust is the key to our earlier phenomenological finding that humanity itself evades all attempts to objectify it. When we regard the history with God as the basis of human identity in this sense, then this identity is established by the creative fiat of God that summons us to life. We do not perceive human life in the unformed fetus—we have seen why this is not possible—but *God* perceives in it the identity of one who is created and called by him:

> . . . Thou didst knit me together in my mother's womb . . .
> My frame was not hidden from thee,
> when I was being made in secret . . .
> Thy eyes beheld my unformed substance;
> in thy book were written, every one of them,
> the days that were formed for me,
> when as yet there was none of them. (Psalm 139.)

When human identity is viewed from this standpoint, there is a stage of pre-existence even before conception. It lies in the thoughts of God, which conceive all that is to be and precede all being, calling it out of nonbeing with their fiat (cf. Romans 4:17). We shall later reduce this essence of human identity to the formula that our divine likeness—that which finally constitutes our humanity—may not be discerned in demonstrable states of being but has to do with the image that God has of us. We live in the thoughts of God even before we are.

2. END

The question of the distinction between purely biological and human life is raised by the other aspect of our finitude, by death. Here the remarkable skills of modern medicine have given a particular urgency to the question. With the help of certain techniques of reanimation, medicine can now keep the organism functioning even when the activity of the brain has been irreversibly halted, self-consciousness has gone, and the person—or former person?—is now no more than a vegetable.[5]

If medical ethics demands the preservation of life according to the Hippocratic oath, the question arises whether preservation of this remnant of the organism is included in the duty. The question might be put as follows: Does the postulate of preserving life extend only to human life or to life in general? If we give what seems to be the obvious answer, namely, that only human life is put in the care of doctors, then this initiates immediately a chain reaction of further questions. First, we have to ask where the boundary is between the two forms of life, namely, where human identity ends and organic vegetating begins. Second, the question arises whether doctors have to do all that they can do, namely, whether they should give free rein to their art, which may be a different thing altogether from healing. Finally, and quite apart from the extreme case of the organism that is deprived of its human identity, we have to ask whether medicine may validly keep on postponing death, and artificially prolonging life, with increasingly refined techniques. Is not finitude a part of human identity? Do not individuals have a right to the death that is ordained for them?

If we are to make headway in the question of the boundary, we must raise the question of the criteria of specifically human life in a new form. These criteria undoubtedly differ from those used in evaluating cardiograms or encephalograms. From early biblical times to our own day—we need only think of the ontology of Martin Heidegger—human life has been differentiated from purely animal life by the twofold capacity of self-consciousness and self-determination. At this point we need only mention the decisive factors, since we shall have to go into the matter more intensively at a later stage.

In the biblical creation story, plants, animals, and stars are passive products of the creative fiat with which God calls them into being. But humans are addressed in the second person. They are thus summoned to partnership with the Creator and they must make a responsible answer, either accepting the summons or rejecting it. In distinction from things or other living creatures, they are not just objects of the divine will but are posited as subjects by this will. As the story of the fall shows, they do not lose this identity as subjects who are summoned to responsibility even with the most refined cultural developments that seem to make them the abducted victims of suprapersonal forces and processes. The attempt to slough off identity by changing guilt into fate is nipped in the bud. We have discussed this already.

Heidegger makes a similar distinction when he says that we have an awareness of ourselves and must take hold of ourselves. He relates this self-consciousness particularly to awareness of the future, to anxiety and death. Animals live only for the present; humans anticipate the future in anxiety and hope.

Only on the basis of this distinction is it possible that we humans, unlike animals, can suffer "ethically." For we are given the task and possibility of reacting to suffering, whether by fighting it or accepting it, whether by surrendering to it or by opening ourselves to its purifying power, whether by protesting against it or by integrating it into our lives and making it part of our identity. In contrast, suffering is only a burden for animals. Hence it is right to put them out of meaningless misery, whereas active euthanasia is wrong in our own case, since it violates the self. Only what is obviously meaningless can be destroyed without question.

But when does a state of meaninglessness arise in the case of humans? The question is a delicate one, for it seems to demand objective criteria that cannot be given for reasons already stated. Is life meaningless when we can no longer achieve the happiness and self-fulfillment that all consciousness thinks to be demanded? Or is it meaningless when pain becomes too great and patients ask to be put out of their suffering? Or when pathological criminals are incarcerated and their situation is irreversible? If we once begin to tread this path, where will it lead us, and who can judge the inner history of the afflicted from outside and thus dare to assume the function of becoming lord of life and death?

Perhaps we may very cautiously say this. If human identity is characterized by self-consciousness and self-determination, then the complete and irreparable loss of self-consciousness might be a criterion for pronouncing the cessation of a truly human existence. Without the trace of this self-consciousness, we are only a biological preparation. Artificially to keep this preparation alive by modern medical means is certainly not covered by the Hippocratic oath. Instead of being part of the medical task, its preservation is to be commended only in order that it might function as a kind of bank for organ transplants.

But what seems to be clear in principle immediately gives rise to problems when we turn to specific instances. For we are attacked by the question whether we can speak about self-consciousness in this general sense. Does not the quantitative question arise whether there might not be a minimum of self-consciousness? How minimal does this have to be to enable us to speak about complete extinction?

Here again there can be no possibility of objective registration tested by machines. My reference is rather to the expression of self-consciousness by communication. So long as traces are present, they will manifest themselves in traces of communication. Where a subject is present, there will never fail to be human contact; it will never be unable to express itself.

This does not mean that such traces, or their absence, can be evaluated by rational standards. Pastor Fritz von Bodelschwingh, who had a great deal of experience in dealing with the mentally deranged, constantly advised caution at this point. He believed he could find reactions to love, perhaps through Holy Scripture, as it penetrated into otherwise closed areas, or through chorales. Even when the self-consciousness can no longer express itself verbally and, as in the case of schizophrenics, is controlled by dimensions of the ego that escape our hermeneutical grasp, I would not dare to contest the self-consciousness or deny human identity. Thus a dying person might be in a state where human communication has long since been left behind but a special form of self-consciousness remains. Hence only a complete and irreversible loss of every kind of self-consciousness is the lower border where humanity ceases and we have only a biological preparation.

But what do we mean when we say "biological preparation"? Are we saying that these people who have lost their identity and left only a shell behind have now become objects that we can dispose of in any way we like?

When we put the question thus, our previous concept of identity is no longer adequate; we come up against its theological dimension. The thesis remains intact that self-consciousness and self-determination are the sign of human identity. Their destruction by what we have called negative psychiatry shows plainly how identity can be mortally violated. Yet we have still to consider that self-consciousness and self-determination are not of our own making but something assigned to us by creation. In judging who enjoys them or is deprived of them we cannot overlook him who controls both the giving and the taking away. If our thesis is correct that human identity is finally grounded in the history that God has initiated with the human race, so that the essence of humanity is being addressed and called and chosen by God, then God's address continues to be our human identity both in giving and taking away. It is not tied to states that we can analyze or that permit the diagnosis that in this or that instance we have complete dereliction by God and these people have become mere objects that have lost their divine determination. The constancy of our identity is the constancy of God's faithfulness. Hence we can believe in the permanence of humanity only in the same sense as we believe in the God who promises his faithfulness.

Once again it is evident how important is the concept of "alien dignity" in fixing human identity. Since the basis of this dignity is to be found in God's promise, it does not lie in the sphere of what is ontically present. It is not a quality of us humans or our human state. It does not lie in the term "human," which we might forfeit to earthly eyes, so that people might say that the shell that remains no longer deserves to be called human. The basis of this dignity is to be found in him who has called me by "my" name. The one who calls, and the call, will remain even though no ear seems to hear them and no eye seems to see any reaction to the call. The one who calls, and the call, grant the alien dignity and make those to whom it is given inviolable. Even though, when confronted with the husk of a person, we might say that this *was* once a human being, the "was" is said only according to the manner of our human temporality. For him who was and is and will be, the past tense, too, is a present. We are, and always will be, the image that he has of us. Before him the dead are alive. The love that never fails (1 Corinthians 13:8) sustains what is past for us. Analogously something of the same may be seen in human love. To the partners or parents of those who only have the form of what they were but have no recognizable identity with the communicating I of their conscious life, even the shell may still be precious. Hence one cannot ask them (as is sometimes done) whether the machine should be shut off. Yet what we have here is only the pale reflection of a faithfulness that holds fast to the identity of loved ones, and continues to love them, even when they have left all recognizable existence behind.

Because of this alien dignity, the shell that remains is not under our control. Actively killing it off is a crime; it violates what is inviolable.

Incontestably, however, we do not have violation of this kind when we let people die, when we do not heroically keep the flickering torch of life alight by medical artifices. We should also allow people to die when they are suffering hopeless torment that cannot be eased, or have sunk into an irreversible coma. Pope Pius XII took this view when welcoming a conference of anesthetists. (November 24, 1957). In general, he said, the rights and duties of the family that must make the decision depend upon the supposed will of the one in the coma. As regards the family's own independent responsibility, it extends only to the use of conventional treatment. This obviously means that it does not entail the use of the extraordinary measures of advanced medicine that can keep some of the vital functions going when the totality is no longer present. Thus there are cases when the family may legitimately ask the doctors to desist and the doctors should comply.

It does not need any vivid imagination to appreciate what a burden this permitted decision imposes and how a kind of feeling of metaphysical guilt might arise even among doctors.[6]

The "alien dignity" enjoins this readiness to let people die because he from whom it comes has destined us for finitude. "It is appointed for men to die once" (Hebrews 9:27). The history with God to which we are summoned and which constitutes our identity makes of our earthly life a mere phase which after death yields to other forms of being. The continuity of existence is broken in death, as Paul declares in his great chapter on the resurrection in First Corinthians (15:42 ff.): "It is sown in weakness, it is raised in power. It is sown a physical body, it is raised a spiritual body." But our identity persists. To all eternity we are those who are called by name. "Those with whom God has begun to speak, whether in wrath or in grace, are immortal" (Luther). With reference to our present problem, this means that, since the history with God that is the basis of our identity does not cease, we are upheld in our identity even beyond death. What endures through death and dissolution is not our entelechy, not some immortal core of the soul in the platonic sense, but the faithfulness of him who will not let his work perish nor forget the name that he has written in the "book of life." To put it metaphorically, we are not like rivers that flow into the ocean of the all and one, merging into it and thus losing themselves, as eastern religions aver. We are tied to our names; we are upheld in our identity; we are always those who are called and known.

"Alien dignity," then, watches over both the living and the dead: the living inasmuch as it forms the final basis of their inviolability; the dead inasmuch as it makes death their transition within a history that can never end because God's promise guarantees it.

From the standpoint of our alien dignity, then, it is wrong to stop people by force from crossing a threshold that is appointed for them and that will lead them into new rooms. We hear the same call and the same name as that which led us into life. And as we feel that we are known by the naming of our name, so we for our part shall know (1 Corinthians 13:12). We know him who calls us as the one whose word we received in our bodily life. And in so doing we know ourselves. This is our identity.

c. Criminal Law and Identity

1. IDENTIFICATION WITH DEED

The concept of punishment implies a particular understanding of identity.[7] Punishment makes sense only if the crime for which it is imposed is imputed to its perpetrator as a guilty act. Imputation of this kind, however, is possible only on one condition, namely, that self-consciousness and self-government can be attributed to the perpetrator. Self-consciousness is necessary inasmuch as the perpetrator has to be clear about what has been done or not done, and about its purpose or lack of purpose. It is also necessary inasmuch as the criminal ought to have, by claim at least, an understanding of the basis of punishment and hence the possibility of seeing why the act is a guilty one, i.e., of self-identification with it. Self-government must also be assumed if responsibility for what is done or not done is to be charged to the doer. Penal codes usually have a clause excusing criminals if they obviously do not know what they are doing and hence are not identical with themselves or true subjects of their actions.

There is another reason why the problem of identity has a part in criminal law. The past and present are a unity for those guilty of criminal acts. Together, they are *their* time. Conceivably they have changed between them. There may be a break between their former state and their present state. Perhaps they have moved to a new environment that has given their life a new direction. They may have undergone a religious conversion that enables them to say that they have become new people. Yet a time, a past, remains when they committed the act that merited punishment. On the basis of their change in character, they may now regard this act of many years ago as that of another person. Yet, as in General Yepantchin, who says this about a base act in his cadet years in Dostoevski's *Idiot*, remorse and the impulse of self-identification remain. That other person that is, and always will be, himself, is the ghost of an "as if." The past of the Third Reich, when some people were guilty of sharing in the deporting of Jews, is still *their* time, even though they have now not only become blameless citizens (in what may be only a banal and superficial change) but are also making active amends in a startled recognition of their guilt. "I am the person I was" is the ontological presupposition that punishment is meaningful.

2. SOCIOLOGICAL ABOLITION OF PUNISHMENT

Connected with this understanding of identity is the fact that the concept of punishment becomes meaningless and superfluous as an extreme sociology, which is the fashion today, declares that society as a whole is guilty of crimes rather than individual criminals. If people are viewed essentially from the standpoint that they are under the pressure of social structures and are deformed to the point of unrecognizability, then as the victims of such relationships they are free of all guilt. Instead society itself is in the dock on the charge of having caused the slide into crime. To this view of things there corresponds a utopian vision, namely, that of a classless and justly structured world in which envy, aggression, and the impulse to commit criminal acts will be eliminated and paradise lost will come again to earth.

Since society is in the center of this view, it is presented not merely as the guilty subject that has to be changed but also as the object that has to be protected. One can hardly try to change something if one is at the same time exposing it to the possibility of destruction. But this will be done if the victims of perverted structures, who have now become criminals, are allowed free rein. So long as the state of social perversion persists and crime results, society has to be protected against its effects. Punishment is meaningless, of course, and therefore the slogan "Social defense" is used instead for this task of safeguarding society against criminals. Safeguarding, however, means not just locking criminals up but resocializing them. What was previously a part of the purpose of punishment, i.e., reeducating criminals, has now become its sole point.

This undoubtedly changes our understanding of human identity. Whereas in punishment the past is imputed to criminals as *their* time, in social defense the past is eliminated as a time of guilt, or, rather, it becomes the time of the guilt of society. The time and identity of criminals lie only in their *future*, i.e., in what they may achieve with the help of the society that now reeducates them.

The resultant truncation of identity may be strikingly seen in extreme cases. For example, how may one legitimately condemn those Nazi criminals who have long since attained the goal of resocialization and established themselves in society as worthy citizens? Against what will society be defending itself in such cases? Against their past? But what is that, for this past is no longer their identity. Their identity is restricted to what they are *now* and what they will be in the *future*. This partial identity, deprived of its backward extension, permits no punishment. If punishment is still imposed with the help of an earlier penal law on the ground that such monstrous acts cannot be left unexpiated, an inconsistency results to which, in spite of all rational argument, we are perhaps impelled by an instinct for justice that shows a deeper acquaintance with the mystery of identity.

3. CASTRATION AS A BORDERLINE CASE

Some other extreme cases connected with the capacities of modern medicine force criminal law and its administrators very emphatically to show their colors and to declare what anthropology,[8] what understanding of identity, is valid for them and validates their pronouncements. In order that we should not be lost in the ocean of very complicated problems and materials, we shall try to identify at least one of the most important issues. Here is an example.

Some time ago a sex offender called K., the press reported, had himself voluntarily castrated while in custody. He then married and stated that he was completely free from his fatal impulse. He was well, loved his wife, and was at peace. In court he defended himself with the argument that he was no longer the person he had been and so he ought to be acquitted. As the reporter put it, the fact that K. was now a completely different person from the one depicted in the accusation left the prosecutor and judge helpless, even though he was one of the most dangerous sex offenders who had ever appeared in the Hamburg courts.

The impression of almost complete helplessness made on the reporter derived from what might be called the isolation of the judge. For anthropological questions were under discussion here that had been given particular pertinence by medical progress, especially as hormonal injections might play a role as well as the surgically simple procedure of castration. The underlying questions raised by these needed to be tackled by law, and especially the philosophy of law, but the judge had to pass his sentence in the actual situation with no proper preparation.

Since the judge was an acquaintance of mine, and I knew he was interested in matters on the frontier between jurisprudence and theology, I wrote him a letter that might perhaps have helped him to reach his decision. I quote from its contents:

The subject of this trial interests me from the theological and philosophical standpoint. You are in fact forced to advance into new anthropological territory, for the problem of human identity is raised here in a new and baffling way. The not very intelligent accused instinctively thinks it is right to tell the court that he no longer feels he is the same person that he was at the time of his act. To put this claim in philosophical terms, he is saying that he is no longer identical with the former K. The judge thus faces the puzzling question whether, if he is no longer the same person in the dimension of the relevant impulse, he can be regarded as responsible and punished. We are now dealing with the present K., who is innocent and does not understand his earlier deed. The whole difficulty of the law in dealing with sex offenders is pinpointed here. The responsible subjectivity of such offenders is called in question by the fact that they seem to be victims or mere objects of impulsive mechanisms or of forces in the social situation. And now this subjectivity is made additionally questionable by the crisis in identity.

In my view the problem of identity is more than a legal one and cannot be reduced to law. This very circumstance will make it very difficult for the judge, who can neither ignore the problem nor solve it, and has no rulings or commentaries to which he can appeal.

Quite independently of what I might say as a theologian, it may be stated that there is certainly no total elimination of identity. Normative contours of character remain even after castration, though the emotional conditions are no longer the same and their forms of expression change. To someone like K., looking back on the past, it may seem puzzling, now that he is free of his impulses, that he did this or that. But he can hardly refuse to use the first person in referring to the one who did these things. If there is any justification at all for punishing offenders, then in face of his terrible acts he cannot be totally unwilling to make some expiation. Particularly in view of the fact that the problem of identity raises insoluble legal questions, can punishment be completely remitted? In my view, no.

This line of argument, of course, still leaves a very uneasy feeling. For in this case the offender voluntarily accepted an extraordinary assault on his personality by letting himself be castrated. This assault undoubtedly released and liberated him. Nevertheless . . . by accepting it he did at least see the culpability of

his acts and demonstrated his active remorse. He thus became
different in many ways and let his identity be modified. If the
point of punishment is simply resocialization, then there is no
problem and the man should go free. But if punishment has
more than this pragmatic purpose, some insoluble questions remain which we have to take up if we accept this purpose that
goes far beyond resocialization.

How are we to find our way out of this dilemma?

I believe that for the reasons mentioned—namely, that identity can be modified but not eliminated—an appropriately reduced sentence should be passed and the way of grace followed.
I have learned from the excellent book by E. T. Sehrt, *Verge-
bung und Gnade bei Shakespeare*,[9] to what extent Angol-Saxon
law as distinct from German law simplifies the problem of
identity by punishing the offense rather than the offender, so
that there are unequivocal objective factors by which to go.
Offenders are identified as those who commit the offense and
are thus responsible for its objectionable nature. Only when
these clear and geometrically calculable factors have been
established do such questions as the state of the offenders, miti-
gating circumstances, and the modification of identity arise.
Grace can then relieve the pressure of a cold and calculating law
of recompense for acts. An irrational element thus plays a role
in the criminal process, including the problem of identity which
cannot be reduced to a legal code. It is highly symbolical that
the ruler with his or her gracious pardon has to bear the burden of such problems, not the judge with his or her sentence.

Readers can easily see that the slogan "alien dignity" stands behind this discussion of identity. We have noted that according to
this concept an identity is ascribed to us that is grounded in God's
history with us. Hence this identity is independent of our condition
at any given time; it applies equally to the genius and the idiot. It is
thus the basis and safeguard of human inviolability. But it can also
become a law that judges us. For because my identity is based on
God's history with me, I am identified as the one I was yesterday, am
today, and will be tomorrow. The penitential psalms of the Bible can
thus sing about age and youth as both being times of the same person and both in need of the forgiveness of God (Psalm 25:7, cf. Job
13:26). Even as one who has become new in God's grace, even as a

"new creature," I still look back on what I was, on that other element in me (Romans 7:14 ff.), and I realize that in the mind of God I live in two ways, first, as the one whose old life, whose "old Adam," he knows well, and then as the one whom he embraces in his mercy, justifies, and accepts. Hence the mind of God binds my diffuse existence, my division into once and now, the schizophrenic cleavage of the individual spheres of the I, into the unity of my identity. In all the things that I myself cannot bring into congruence or perceive in their congruence, I am in God's mind the one I truly am. I am the image that God has of me. He alone knows my identity. I am "known" (1 Corinthians 13:12). Hence the identity that I learn in alien dignity is both terror and comfort at one and the same time. The accused K. faces both.

d. The Theological Dimension of Identity: The New Creature

Who, then, "is" a person like Cardinal Mindzenty in this ultimate sense? Is he the confessor he once was and became again in his place of refuge and his exile in Rome and Vienna? Or is he the one who renounced his faith under the pressure of torture and negative psychiatry? What is his image in the mind of God?

Again, who is the prodigal son (Luke 15:11 ff.)? Does his identity lie in what he was before he set off for the far country? Or in the potentialities of his entelechy that he developed there? Or is he totally himself when he leaves his mistakes and confusions, comes home, and finds his father's forgiveness? Is not his identity always hidden—regardless of the stages and circumstances of his life—in the image that his father has of him, in his alien dignity?

I know of no one who has been able to express this thought of our identity hidden and sheltered in the mind of God so pregnantly as Dietrich Bonhoeffer did when confined at Tegel, and hardly a year before his execution. When he asks, "Who am I?" he cannot go by what others say of him or what he knows about himself, nor can he conclude that he is at one time the former and at another time the latter, or both at the same time. All that he can finally say is this, "Whoever I am, thou knowest me, I am thine, O God" (*Letters and Papers from Prison* [1973], pp. 347 ff.).

In closing I should like to illustrate the identity that is expressed in the term "alien dignity," and is indicated in Bonhoeffer's poem, by a rather daring flight of imagination.

I see myself at the Last Judgment, and, as at an earthly trial, my identity has to be established before the proceedings begin. But there is an interruption. The Supreme Judge has hardly put to me the question, "Who are you?" before my satanic accuser breaks in and answers for me, "Who is he, you ask? I will tell you. He is the one who has done such and such, and failed to do such and such. He has ignored the plight of his neighbors because he himself was always the neighbor. He has been silent when he ought to have confessed. The gifts you have given him have not made him humble but proud." He goes on for a long time in this strain. But then the counsel for the defense interrupts; he is the exalted Son of God. "O Father and Judge," he says, "the prosecutor has spoken the truth. This man has all these things behind him. But the accusation is without substance. For he no longer *is* what he has behind him." And although he who sits on the bench knows very well what Christ is saying, for the sake of the audience he asks, "Who is he then if he is no longer what he has behind him?" To this Christ replies, "He has become my disciple and believed me that you have met him in me and want to be his father, as you are mine. Hence I have canceled his past and nailed the accusation to my cross [Colossians 2:14]. Who *is* he then, you ask? He is the one who has accepted me and thus gained the right of sonship that you have promised. Look upon him, then, as you look upon me; he is my brother and your son."

This is the story of our identity.

In that which Christianity calls forgiveness and justification, past, present, and future cease to me *my* time, the temporal description of my identity. The past really becomes the past; it is liquidated. The new creature is present, loosed and redeemed from its old status (2 Corinthians 5:17).

III. THE QUESTION OF IDENTITY IN PROCLAMATION. THE RELATION BETWEEN THEOLOGY AND ANTHROPOLOGY

The theological deliberations into which we have been plunged suggest that the problem of identity plays a role in Christian proclamation too. I think I can see, and will try to show, that the much decried crisis of preaching in the modern period, and especially today, has its root here.

First, and very simply, one might describe this crisis as follows: Average contemporaries can no longer identify themselves with the form and content of preaching.[10] They do not feel that what is said applies to them. They react to what they hear with statements like this: "I was not there in that sermon," or "Who was the preacher talking about anyway?"

Representatives of the church who are easily discouraged, or follow the line of least resistance, press such diagnoses to the dubious conclusion that preaching is out of date. People today, they say, do not want to be preached at. Unwittingly they thus adopt the mentality of poll-takers and make those they consult the standard of what they should do and say. They thus argue that, since preaching has become anachronistic, they should replace the impotent personal word by the suprapersonal word of the liturgy, or that they should set up political services in which they report on instances of torture or the repression of minorities, interpret the daily newspapers, and discuss problems of the day in dialogues rather than the monologues of sermons. Only in this way, they think, can their hearers identify with what is offered.

In attempting to clarify the background to this situation, we shall examine two of the most vital objections to preaching.

a. The Changed Pre-Understanding

People today, before the message reaches them, have certain pre-understandings related to the secular sphere: to experience, common sense, the social situation, the means of communication, and personal background, mostly things that are not shaped by Christianity. Naturally the resultant understanding of the self is not determined by belief in creation, awareness of guilt and alienation, and even less by a desire for salvation. Certainly all this may be present in the background, and indirectly, for it is an element of humanity itself and not just a matter of Christian reminiscences. In utopian longing, or flight into the imaginary world of drugs, or the trivialization of life in popular novels and movies, background forces of this kind might well be at work. But usually they are so latent and unconscious that it would almost need psychoanalytical investigation to bring them to light. In the pulpit, however, we act as though our hearers were openly confronting us with these forces and simply expecting us to provide answers that would give them release. But this is not so even in the conventional congregation, let alone among people who are secularized and dechristianized. Our contemporaries feel more enslaved by social pressures and manipulations than by guilt and alienation. They want freedom from boredom, futility, and the loss of identity more than from guilt and death.

For this reason the complaint is made today against the average sermon that the preacher posits presuppositions in his hearers that are not really present, that answers are given to questions that are not put, and that the pressing questions of the day are ignored. Hence people do not know what preachers are talking about. Sermons make no impact and sound anachronistic.

Under the ongoing influence of existentialism nothing is more popular in contemporary sermons than the statement that "this applies to you." And no promise is so seldom kept. Or existential application is overdone as an attempt is made to divine what is "relevant" for the age, and there is then an exclusive focus on this, and the theme of what is said is dictated by the audience. Out of a sincere desire to let modern hearers into the church and find places for them, so many doors are opened in the walls that finally the sanctuary disappears altogether and the contemporaries who are won over find themselves in an empty place. It is a kind of marketplace where they hear only familiar voices, especially those of politicians and social revolutionaries. How are they to get the idea that they are now in a church and not the marketplace?

This overkill in our encounter with contemporaries is an extreme and distorted reaction to pallid timeless preaching that lacks relevance and resides in the ivory tower of an esoteric tradition. This failure to deal with modern issues is just as bad as losing oneself in them. If we are to speak in a pointed and purposeful way in the pulpit, and not blindly, then we must indeed address the self-understanding of our own generation, relating our material to it so precisely that no one can fail to see the connection. Preaching must not be a monologue in which we "preach at" people; it must be a dialogue. Dialogue does not mean that there have to be conversations between two people in the chancel or pulpit. This is often tried, but is not a very good solution to the problem. What dialogue means is that our preaching should be within the context of a dialectic of question and answer. Preachers should see that questions are put to them. They must take notice of these. But they should not just answer them. They should also put counterquestions in order to draw attention to the true and authentic questions that only the gospel raises. We can see this process in the pastoral conversations of Jesus. In the form of feedback preachers should then collect the answers of their hearers to their message and put these in their sermons.

Obviously preachers can establish the pre-understanding and reactions of their congregations only if they engage in the kind of reflection in which these are to be found, as, e.g., in Karl Marx, Sigmund Freud, Teilhard de Chardin, Konrad Lorenz, or even Jürgen Habermas. Even though few of our hearers realize it, something is said by these thinkers that is present in a muffled and unreflected way in almost all of us. I have in mind, for example, the thesis of Marx that our thinking and destiny are determined by our social situation. It is obvious to any observant person that there is "something in this." All working students will sometimes have the experience at work (cf. Leo Tolstoi's *Diaries*) that although they are doing the same work they cannot understand their mates, for these are chained for life to the same occupation, whereas they themselves will spend only a short time in this dreary field and will then be free again to go their own way. What comes to expression here is the conviction that we are tied by our social situation. Again, all of us are aware that the thesis of Marx that in action, disposition, and thought we are dependent on the social infrastructure, has made headway in modern theories about the environment. We have noted already the impact of such theories on criminal law, e.g., in the belief that society and not the individual is responsible for crime and must repent, so that no punishment ought to be exacted, and prisons should be turned into social hospitals whose only duty is to give treatment in resocialization.

Who can deny that such matters, and the anthropological theses that lie behind them, are familiar to innumerable people or are seriously pondered by them, and that for this reason few of these people are affected by any direct confrontation with the message of guilt, judgment, and redemption? We have to take issue, therefore, with theses of this kind. That is, we have to show their representatives what the words "sin" and "guilt" mean in relation to them, and how far redemption is something other than a mere movement of political and social liberation.

This cannot be done by simply demonstrating negatively how very different the Christian message is. For sin and guilt are not confined to the individual sphere. They have structural, and, to that extent, a social and suprapersonal side. What we have to show then, in terms of this example, is that structural perversions do not exhaust the nature of sin and guilt, as Marxism thinks, but simply display one aspect of them. As the status of existence, human alienation precedes its structural expression. The prior history with God is the key to the significance of the structural expression. It brings to light the true priorities. We ourselves are the key to our world, including its structures. The story of the fall has taught us this.

Naturally the point of these observations is not that we should engage extensively in such debates in the pulpit. But preaching will have a different note, and its statements a different edge, if preachers have wrestled personally with these problems, if they have a background acquaintance with them. When we have to preach to university students who have a good grasp of literature, we do not have to introduce a single quotation from the poets. But those whose questions have their source in the poets can soon tell whether the preacher has any relation at all to literature or is personally involved in the dialogue between literature and the gospel.

To take another example, one of the theses of Konrad Lorenz is that much of what we call morally bad is grounded in the very "natural" instinct of aggression that runs through the whole of nature. Again, few of our hearers will have explicitly thought out questions of this kind or become acquainted with them. But all of us can see that the thesis that what is called bad is in reality only the expression of an antinatural attitude to nature is germinally present, in a muffled and unreflected form, in most people.

This applies especially in the realm of sex. For what has happened here is not just a throwing off of taboos or a movement of emancipation. What we really have is a naturalizing of sexuality, or, negatively, a depersonalizing. The representatives of the movement no longer direct us to an I-Thou relationship in sex. The goal they set is simply that of libidinous pleasure; the instruction they give is in the art of orgasm. Typically, then, they refer more to "enlightenment" in sex than to "education," as one may easily gather from the appropriate texts. All that we need to do is to understand the natural processes in a remote and objectifying way that is totally different from what is meant by sexual knowledge (*yadah*) in the Bible. Once we have learned to know and master the right positions, we qualify as experts in the art of love.

If preachers react to all this merely with moral rearmament, if they simply bring about an ill-thought-out confrontation with the divine commandments, they will fail to deal with this theme as with other problems of the day. For the victims of this naturalizing of sex will find in such exhortations to repentance only an incompetent and irrelevant assertion of moral standards. For them what is natural is amoral and cannot in principle be related to morality.

Instead of reacting "legalistically" in this theologically dubious way, preachers should point out that this whole approach carries with it a terrible distortion and denaturalization of sex itself. When personal fellowship is replaced by animal coupling, sex is impoverished and falls indescribably short of what it was meant to be by creation. For what is left for the pair when orgasm is achieved? Nor does liberation from earlier taboos really lead to new forms of freedom. It results instead in new pressures, such as the drive for sexual achievement, of which pastoral counselors and psychotherapists have a good deal to say in this period after the sexual revolution.

Many of our listeners will come with this distorted and "non-human" view of sex. The task of preaching is to meet them with their prefabricated attitudes. We can do this, however, only if we preachers ourselves have traversed the same problem areas and related them to the picture of total humanity that is presented in the biblical view of creation, the fall, and redemption.[11]

The first form of the crisis of preaching, then, is its failure to see the preliminary anthropological questions and to meet members of the congregation in the conscious or unconscious pre-understandings within whose sphere of influence they live.

b. Accommodation to Contemporaries

1. SOCIOLOGICAL, PSYCHOLOGICAL, AND OTHER CONTEMPORARY APPROACHES

The fact that the Bible tells us about *past* people and relations constitutes a temptation to bypass modern problems. The patriarchal structure of ancient Israel is miles apart from our modern mentality with its orientation to democracy and equality. That world is no longer ours—or it is so merely in a background sense that can be seen only as it is drawn into *our* world. Its view of things is different. It evaluates history by different standards from those of modern historicism. The nature psalms have an understanding of nature that has little in common with that of modern science, and certainly not the decisive aspect. If we simply quote these ancient texts, as many preachers do, without interpreting their message at the deepest level, in which it is an element in our own existence, then those who live in the modern world will see no relevance to themselves and will rightly be left with the impression that the whole thing is anachronistic.

In our own lives we are harassed by very different problems. We have referred already to some of these. For the rest, we need only read the question-and-answer columns in the press to find out what the recurrent problems are, e.g., bringing up children, marital difficulties, competition at work, boredom, lack of communication, loneliness, especially in old age, and such issues as abortion, euthanasia, and many others. Although these are mostly individual matters, the social background is plain to see. Obvious things like common sense no longer suffice in a pluralistic nexus. No well-honed style of life that is common to all allots us our place and at the same time relates these various places. At the personal level we are all of us left very much to ourselves, without orientation. Because the world of the Bible, at the first, superficial level, is a different world, because, for example, it is not pluralistically structured, we do not find our modern questions either posed or answered in it in such a way that we can consult it as we might consult a book of law or medicine to find the appropriate case described. The "cases" that the Bible offers, e.g., when Peter says to Jesus, "Depart from me, for I am a sinful man, O Lord," I cannot stand your presence! are such that we do not immediately recognize ourselves in them. We do not suffer from the guilt that Peter confesses, but from a guilt complex. The reality that the Bible has in view is so shifted by our psychological categories that we find such texts to be naive and unenlightened.

Hence the *immediate* subject of the message—with a stress on the word "immediate"—lies beyond the horizon of our present existence. The problems already mentioned (e.g., anxiety, boredom, pressures at work) stand at the center of life. To reach this center, we must address these problems. We must deal with anthropological themes in our preaching, or, more sharply, we must show that the theological themes of creation, the fall, and redemption stand in a basic relation to the anthropological questions that are put to us here and now.

But an objection arises here that we may not overlook. Does this not mean that preaching and theology must be enriched by alien materials if they are to be interesting and to provoke interest in hearers? Many—painful—instances can be given of attempts to attract people along these lines, e.g., the use of jazz or beat to breathe new life into dead worship services. Has not the church taken up all kinds of issues in daily life, such as nuclear weapons and the use of the pill, to try to give itself the attraction of relevance? (But is this the only motive?) Have not preachers adopted fashionable approaches and vocabulary from the lavish stock provided by, e.g., sociology? Thus the grotesque impression is sometimes given that since people will not look at our own wares in the window, with what is offered by grace and redemption, we must lure them in with attractive goods that are borrowed and imported from other areas of life. Or else an attempt is made to give the old stock a more attractive image by packaging it in new terms.

But will all this increase the readiness of Christian consumers to buy? Will not people soon spot the intention and be put off? Along these lines the American sociologist Peter L. Berger asks the ironical question why anyone should buy psychotherapy or a discussion of race relations in a Christian package when they can get them around the corner in a secular (the original) package, which is in any case more up-to-date. The Christian label will probably appeal only to those who are sentimental enough to cling to the old symbols. But the sun of secularized theology will quickly melt this group. Christian borrowing from the secular world recoils on those who do it. This kind of action is no less than a self-surrender of theology and of all the institutions in which the religious tradition has thus far found embodiment.

Where are we heading, then, if we take the center of modern life into account but threaten to destroy ourselves in the search for points of contact? In a very one-sided and violent attack, Karl Barth once thought he had caught out Emil Brunner in a fatal search of this kind. Barth threw out the baby with the bath water, completely ignoring the quality of the gospel as an "addressed" message. Nevertheless, he rightly diagnosed the danger that arises when we try to bring our contemporaries into focus and find points of contact in them. The danger is that this pointed address might finally become all that is heard in the pulpit. In other words, the anthropological deliberations that aim at our contemporaries might change, distort, or completely absorb the theological contents. In fact, theology from the time of the Enlightenment offers numerous examples of the way in which theologians who seek to be modern are so concerned to be up-to-date, and accommodate themselves to the spirit of the age in such a way, that their ideas have more to say about the intellectual situation of their age than about the gospel that they are trying to bring to this age.

At the same time, our horror at the more recent history of theology should not induce the blind reaction of dropping like a hot iron the whole question of contact, of aiming at people, of addressing them, of the anthropology of proclamation.

There can be a legitimate as well as an illegitimate form of anthropological address. This is the act itself. The illegitimate form is absorption into the act. In the first case, we fetch hearers in order to bring them into encounter with the substance of proclamation. In the second case, we leave them where they are, give them the impression of closeness and solidarity, but tell them nothing that they do not or could not know already. The question, then, is whether I discharge my theological task in constant correspondence with anthropological inquiry or whether I surrender this task to anthropology. In the latter case, the result is assimilation to the age, or bondage to it.

2. UP-TO-DATENESS ILLUSTRATED BY EDUCATION

We can best illustrate this problem by the example of education. The pedagogical task has always been classically related to anthropological inquiry. As we reflect on the role of the gospel in educational matters, we thus enter a field where we can test legitimate and illegitimate relations between theology and anthropology.

The task of education confronts us with the final questions of anthropology. Thus it puts human beings before us as "givens" that we cannot shape at will but have to accept. It makes us responsible for other persons who are entrusted to us, not just to enrich our own existence, but with their own ends. It also confronts us with the mystery of evil and hence with something that is especially linked to forgiveness and pardon. It also lays upon us a task of love to whose claim a natural love cannot do justice but which has also to wrestle with very dubious elements in others. Finally, it constantly leads us beyond the material problems of clothing and nourishment and care and brings the horizon of human existence into view—its meaning, destiny, and theme. Why do we educate people? What image are we trying to develop on this negative? These are indeed questions that take us to the very horizon of anthropology.

But they are also the precise questions that faith is concerned with, and with it the preaching and pastoral care that stand in the service of faith. They are coded forms of the questions of creation, justification, and human destiny. When as pastors or pastoral counselors we talk with parents about their children and discuss the problem of educational responsibility, even in detail, from problems of lying to choice of vocation, we cannot fail to bring these ultimate aspects into view.

We thus introduce the gospel, since it contains questions that the educational situation raises already, so that we do not have to bring them in artificially or ingeniously. We thus let the gospel come in as a co-reference in questions of life in which other people and entities are also references, e.g., the parents with their sound common sense, who also have their ideas on the topic, the teachers, philosophers, the writers of leading articles, aunts, and many others. The gospel is thus in competition with many other diagnosticians and therapists, just as the church in a plural society is one voice among many others. In this competition it is ready to be tested. Is it the normative voice? Can it set the right standards? Does it explore convincingly the depths of human existence? It offers a possible answer to some specific questions that are put to it. For this reason, there is no longer any need in this context to search for points of contact or artificially to open up relevant questions. These are already present.

Studying this situation leads to some very important conclusions about the relation between theology and anthropology. These may be clarified by some intellectual and historical observations. In a rather crudely abbreviated form, one might express the matter as follows:

Originally theological work was concerned with dogmas in the narrower sense. The first Christian centuries were fully occupied with the struggle to achieve a doctrinal understanding of Christ and the Trinity. But very early, more clearly after the Reformation, and expressly from the time of the Enlightenment, people began to investigate the life-setting of these dogmas. This question is the central one in Gotthold E. Lessing and Friedrich Schleiermacher. Both in different ways start out with the presupposition that I can appropriate and take up into my existence only that which is unconditionally relevant to me and has thematic rank for my own life. From their day on, it has increasingly become the self-evident task of theology to bring out the existential relevance of dogmas and church teachings. Theology is trying to show me that in statements of this kind I do not have something past and left behind, but something that concerns me and my here and now.

But I can believe in this sense only if the connection is clear to me. The necessity of the "one thing necessary" has to be demonstrated to me. Without evidence of this kind, access to the legacy of faith is blocked. I either give up, or I become an adherent who accepts the yoke of tradition in a purely passive way, with no personal commitment.

It is my conviction that today we have entered upon a new stage in this process. A great deal depends on our clearly recognizing the break.

Our question today—this is at least true of secularists insofar as they ask at all and are open—is no longer that of the life-setting of given dogmas. For the dogmas are no longer given; they have an air of complete unreality. We are beset by specific problems whose setting in life is quite clear and whose existential rank does not have to be demonstrated.

One of these problems is that of finitude. It seems that we live in permanent meditation on death, even though we may never speak about it (though existential philosophy babbles a good deal about it). We are well aware that youth passes quickly and we must try to enjoy everything because the past will not return. We hurriedly try to gather together all that we want from life, for the time-line is irreversible. We protest against old age and worship youth. Many people try to preserve youth artificially or even to restore it to their furrowed faces. Time and finitude are problems whose life-setting is plain and indisputable.

All the faculties have to deal with these problems.

Medicine, for example, faces the question of health and the inviolability of human life. Law seeks a normative court in answer to the threat of positivism, whether in natural law, the divine commandments, conscience, or common sense. Technology, or humanity in confrontation with it, has to consider whether we are not heading toward Einstein's world of perfect means and confused goals.

Education, too, faces questions of the same elemental and existential significance. As we bring the gospel into contact with these questions, discussion of its life-setting is superfluous. We start out from this. This is what leads to confrontation with the gospel. Here we already are; we realize that this is where we are.

Thus the process of inquiry now takes the opposite course from that taken previously. We no longer begin with the dogmas and investigate their setting. We begin with the setting and let the gospel be a question or an answer or a co-reference for answers already given.

Naturally, this account is very much simplified. The reversal does not mean that the questions that arise in life are prefabricated for us or that they are so finely cut that the cogs of the gospel fit into them exactly. That this is not so may be seen from the questions raised in the pedagogic situation. The fact that a child is "given" me does not automatically raise the question of creation. The fact that I find some bad in the child does not mean in itself that the subject of sin is raised. Having to pardon does not carry with it from the outset a reference to forgiveness and justification. Rather shallow apologists have made conclusions of this kind and thus engaged in the erroneous attempt to demonstrate faith in this way, even pointing out to people that they already have faith without realizing it. This is not so. Problems that have their setting in life itself are often like bells that we hear without knowing where they are. We certainly hear these basic questions. We are even harassed by them. But we do not know what, ultimately, they are asking. The what—not the question itself, but its true substance—has to be opened up.

3. THEOLOGY QUESTIONED AND COUNTERQUESTIONING

How this is done may be seen from the conversations of Jesus.

These usually begin with questions that people put to him, e.g., whether taxes should be paid to the Roman emperor, or who had given him his authority, or what one must do to win eternal life, the ultimate goal. But Jesus never simply answers these questions. He does not view them as prefabricated forms to which the answer of his message must be adjusted. Instead, he first corrects the questions. He does so by putting counterquestions. In so doing he opens up the background themes that lurked in the questions as they were put but had not been clear to the questioners. For usually the questioners did not really know what they were asking or what was finally troubling them. Hence they had to be shown that they themselves were the question within their questions. They became the question in this way when they learned that their own destiny was the hidden theme of the questions.

Thus questions that arise in relation to the education of our children are also questions that apply to us. They raise the issue who we are and what we want. In discussions of the education of our children, our own identity becomes the theme.

Since themes of this kind are also the subject of the gospel, its witness is a contribution to the matter. The relevance of what is said in its name does not have to be laboriously sought or demonstrated. It is obvious. The hearer or partner in the discussion does not have to be a believer. Faith is not a prerequisite of the necessary disposition to listen and understand. It is not demanded as a precondition. If it were, it would be a legal work, an act of repression, a suicidal act of the will. No, it has to be awakened as the partner in the discussion hears the liberating word of the gospel on the matter at issue, appreciates its relevance, and perceives its life-setting.

For this reason the gospel may be heard at first only as one voice among many others, one contribution to the discussion within the pluralism of opinions. It will prove itself in this competition. To learn who Christ is, and that after him we cannot look for another, I do not have to fulfill the prior condition of regarding him as the Son of God, or the Messiah. Even to think this is dreadful! I may regard him as the founder of one of the world's religions, or as a teacher of wisdom, or as a psychotherapist. If he really is who he is attested to be, he will transcend these prejudgments and categories of interpretation and display his incomparability. Then, as the result of the encounter, the hour of faith will strike, not before. By proceeding in this way, I ascribe to the message the power of self-attestation, the power to make itself known as the solo voice amid the chorus of voices, and to produce faith as *its* work, not *mine*.

We might sum up the relationship between theology and anthropology, as thus unfolded, in the statement that in the context of the basic questions of anthropology the gospel makes itself heard as one voice among others, as a co-reference along with other references, whose validity has to be shown. The question, then, is whether and how far it will pierce through the purely material questions in the foreground and in and through them raise the question of humanity itself, its whence and whither, its alienation and deliverance.

Always and everywhere theology has an anthropological reference. There are theological reasons for this. If God has revealed himself as our God, if he has created and accepts us as a Thou—which is the core of the biblical message—then we cannot speak about him without also speaking about his self-revelation to us. Conversely, we cannot speak about ourselves without constantly understanding ourselves as the work of God, as those who have been unfaithful to God's plan for them, but also as those whom he has accepted and saved.

This anthropological reference of theology needs, of course, to be supported and supplemented. For who are we as those to whom this message comes and who seek to understand ourselves as partners of God? If this partnership and our alien dignity constitute our identity, as we have said, this view of identity needs to be filled out concretely. Hence we have not only to seek the origin of this identity, which we have found in our alien dignity; we have also to examine its structure.

c. Humanity in Secularity.
Against a "Docetic" Anthropology

1. THE HISTORICAL SITUATION AS THE "BODY" OF HUMANITY

Formulated more precisely, the question is whether the individual alone is the issue in this question of identity. Is not this suggested by much of what we have hitherto adduced as anthropologically significant, e.g., our finitude and alienation, our boredom and meaninglessness, our projection into the future and consequent anxiety?

In fact, existentialism has thematically stressed the individual in this way. In Heidegger's ontology the world shrinks to the sphere of the useful and the world of naked and meaningless reality in all its resultant deficiency. No place is found for a reality that has its own meaning, for the organic life of plants and animals, or the sphere of human culture in any worthwhile sense. The external world is similarly oriented in Jaspers. In relation to the unconditional radiance of personal existence it becomes an insignificant background (O. F. Bollnow). For Sartre, the world is an outside thing that is limited, established, and fixed by human existence, and thus prevented from developing any identity of its own. In Rudolf Bultmann, too, the external world is from the very first hostile to us. It presents a threat to our existence, so that existential self-realization is possible only as we keep it at a distance in eschatological disengagement. But are these anthropological theses of existentialism right? Can we accept their implications for theology as Bultmann does? Does Kierkegaard's "individual," from whom they derive, really exist? Is there any such thing as an isolated person?

In what follows I want to show that this so-called individual is an unreal and shadowy phenomenon that does not really exist. I also want to show that an anthropology based on this individual falls victim to "docetism."

The term "docetism" needs some explanation. It is normally used for a heretical movement in Christology.[12] The heresy is that only an appearance of corporeality is ascribed to Christ (*dokein*, "to appear"), so that his full and concrete humanity is impugned. The divine predicates ascribed to him seem to make it impossible to call him human at the same time, and thus to see him subject to the same factors of finitude, suffering, and temptation as we are. The result is that he is depicted as a more or less unreal and shadowy heavenly being that is not truly human but hovers above us. In the present context I want to use the term "docetic" for a particular conception in anthropology, namely, the conception that is based on an unreal and abstract humanity, on the individual that has only a sham corporeality.

Why this individual does not exist I will try to illustrate with another example taken from the field of proclamation.

Let us suppose that we have to tell the people of our own age what is meant by neighborly love. We at once come up against a problem, for it seems obvious—or is it?—that we are dealing only with two individuals, myself, from whom love is demanded, and another to whom it is to be shown. But is this thesis of an encounter between two individuals correct?

It will serve us best to be more specific. Perhaps I can succeed in displaying neighborly love in a vital and convincing way on the individual level. Thus I might read to an old person in my locality, or put in a good word for a harassed colleague, or make a regular financial contribution to feed hungry children. Docetic anthropologists and preachers who go along with them can depict all this in many ways, and no one will be put to sleep in view of their sharp closeness to life. Nor can it be contested that what they say is illuminating and authentic.

Nevertheless, after a sermon in this individualistic strain, a young businessman might come to the preacher in the sacristy and say something like this, "All you have said is fine and good. But unfortunately it does not meet my own particular situation." (The old objection again!) "Why not?" the preacher asks. "Are you not one of those who owe love to others?" "But you did not need to tell me about reading to old people or putting in a good word for colleagues," is the reply. "I am fairly generous as an individual. I am so philanthropic by nature that I do such things in any case and do not need to be exhorted to do them. Good-hearted people cannot help doing them. Friends of mine who are not Christians do them. But if I am to live consciously as a Christian and thus discharge my social task of love, I am surrounded by very different questions. For instance, as a businessman I am in competition. And this, God knows, is hard. My main competitor is geographically very close. His business and house are in the same street. I know him and his family very well personally. They are good people and deserve every sympathy. Because he is my rival and I also see him almost every day, I am constantly faced by the question, What should be my attitude to him? How am I to love this competitor? Without wanting to boast, I am better at business than he is and more capable in every respect. I also have more capital and flexibility. I have a nose for development. My superiority is so great that as my business flourishes, his declines. . . ."

"What does it mean for me personally," is the young businessman's question, "that I should love? It does not mean having sentimental feelings or putting myself in his situation, although that is naturally demanded. What am I to *do*? That is the decisive issue. Does loving mean that I should raise my prices, sell poorer goods, and restrict my volume so as to give my rival a chance and halt his decline? Does it mean that I should no longer fight the battle of competition according to its own laws but philanthropically make it easier in a way that is inconsistent with the process? Do I have to go 'half-throttle' as a Christian? Must I be ready to let my business go on the skids financially—for the sake of love?"

The businessman also considers the consequences if the answer to this question is Yes. "If as a sacrifice to love I cease to be competitive and perhaps have to close down, what will this mean for my employees, to whom I also have an obligation as a neighbor? Look you, this is my problem. Love, according to your message, is being there for others. Well and good—when put in general terms, it sounds fine. But put it concretely and in detail, and difficulties arise at once. They always do. In what way can *I* be there for others in *my* situation? I am not just an individual with a hard or soft heart. I am businessman X in a specific economic and competitive situation. Is not all this part of my I too? Is it not included in my identity? Or are the laws of economics, and the situation, forces for which I am not responsible, which exert power over me from outside, which are in a special way not part of my I, which point to a *heteros nomos?*" (We will let him talk here as though he had had two semesters of theology or sociology!) "Am I, or am I not, all these things that put pressure on me and work through me?"

The problem delineated here is the problem raised by what we have called docetism. Do we not have a very unrealistic, a sham corporeality, if we isolate our individuality from the context of the situation in which we are? These considerations bring the businessman up against his final question vis-à-vis the New Testament.

"Perhaps I differ here from the man who asked the Lord, 'Who is my neighbor?' (Luke 10:29). I think I know this, for I have heard Jesus' parable of the Good Samaritan and understood something of it. But the question of my identity still remains. Who am I that am supposed to be a neighbor? Am I really an individual who can be isolated from my job and from the autonomous processes of economics? Or am I still a businessman or whatever in my quality as a neighbor? What is the neighborly love that God requires of me?"

We can formulate this question even more sharply as follows: "What makes me 'historical' and puts me 'in encounter,' in 'being for others'?" I am obviously these things only by way of the structures of history, the medium of transsubjective factors. I am always "in situation," as Jaspers puts it. But this means that I am in relation to others only as this relation is mediated by structures. The relation is vocational, economic, political, erotic, et cetera. This situational nexus in which we meet one another is, as it were, the body of the nexus in which my personhood resides. Any attempt to bypass it, to see my personhood apart, is a modern form of spiritualizing, an attempt to understand humanity as a free and disembodied spirit, and hence in its own way a repetition of the ancient heresy of docetism.

In resisting docetism, the early church rightly viewed the body as an inalienable, co-constitutive element of humanity. Without the body and its desires, the seizure of the forbidden fruit would be inconceivable. Without corporeal being, there would be no being in the world at all and no being for others. Without the body our finitude, our being for death, which is an essential mark of humanity, would make no sense. If the body, the *soma*, is thus an essential part of our identity and belongs to the I, this raises considerable questions regarding the modern situation as we have depicted it.

We have understood the nexus of the social and economic situation as a phenomenon of our corporeality. We have said that it is docetic to treat this historical body and its immanent pressures, e.g., the principle of competition, as though they were not part of the I, of our identity.

But this poses the question how these historical structures are to be understood theologically, and what it means to see them as part of my identity. But while keeping this question in view, let us consider for a moment the attempt to view these forces that pressure me from outside along the lines of what Luther called *coactio* (coercion).[18] On this view, I am, within them, what I am not really in myself but am plunged into. I regard the situation as something that is posited by creation, as instituted for the world in a way that is beyond our control. In Kantian terms one might say that in all this I am face to face with "dispositions." I can do nothing about these dispositions as such; I am responsible only for what I make of them.

One can also isolate oneself from the situation by saying that what we have here is the fallen world that has alienated itself from God's purpose in creation. In this case, too, the fate of the world is not my fault; I simply find myself involved in it; I see it suspended over me.

A third and very different possibility is to admit that the world which is structured in this way is my world, that it is a macrocosmic reflection of my heart, as we put it earlier. On this view, I have to identify myself with the structural law of sacred egoism that encounters me from outside because I recognize the strivings of the self in these suprapersonal trends. I have to confess: "That is I," when I meet this world of mine. The principle of oppression and the battle of competition that I encounter as suprapersonal forces are also an objectification in the world of what I myself am.

I can no longer say then, "Here 'I' am, a good person who wants to do the best, and there is the 'bad world' that forces me into modes of conduct that I do not want." Instead, I have to understand myself as the subject of the things to which these necessities seem to force me. At issue in my being in the world is an indivisible identity from which no intrinsic I can be docetically separated.

2. THE IDENTIFICATION OF I AND THE WORLD IN THE SERMON ON THE MOUNT

The Sermon on the Mount is obviously a model text for my identification with being in the world. Unlike Kant's ethics, it is not content to make demands upon me on the basis of given dispositions or within the framework of historically posited situations. Its requirements transcend all given factors, not regarding these as supposedly suprapersonal forces, and hence not taking them seriously as such. Thus I am made responsible not merely for the act of adultery but for the desire that lies behind it (Matthew 5:27–28). Desire is not regarded here as libido, as a disposition that is placed in me and that I cannot control. I cannot say, "There is a desire in me." I have to confess: "I myself desire." The Sermon on the Mount also refuses to recognize the compulsive nexus of "an eye for an eye and a tooth for a tooth" (Matthew 5:38). It demands that I should take a creative initiative in face of it. Because it does so, the nexus no longer has the appearance of a suprapersonal fate that makes me its victim. I myself am part of the nexus. I am not just an effect but one of the causes. Encountering the structured world, I encounter myself.

Thus the Sermon on the Mount places my world as well as me under its radical demands, i.e., demands that go to the very roots of my existence. It views my world and me as an indivisible unity. It identifies me with this present "aeon."

This is carried so far that the Sermon has been called hostile to the world in the sense that it sets itself above it. It does this. But rather than being hostile to the world, it wants to bear witness that this world of ours is hostile to the kingdom of God, that it cannot of itself achieve conformity to God, that it is structurally involved in the fall. The Sermon addresses us as if we were "still" in our original state, in Paradise, in the world as it left the hands of God. It addresses us "already" as if the kingdom of God were come. It thus runs up against both our subjectivity and the structure of our world.

This has the following implication:

If we accept the identity of the I with its world, then all acts, not just personal and private acts but those done within the autonomous nexus of the world, are shown to be in need of forgiveness. This need can extend only as far as I identify myself with my acts, have to accept responsibility for them, and cannot claim to be the excusable victim of other forces. Thus devout soldiers defending their country with the conviction that this is a divinely willed task may sometimes think (or be reminded) that the war in which they obey and seek to do God's will is the expression of a secular structure that God does not will. And when they pray the words of the Lord's Prayer: "Forgive our debts . . . ," they will not just think of their individual faults but also of what they are being compelled to do within this secular structure.

3. THE "WORLDLY" DIMENSION IN ORIGINAL SIN

If it is true that we have to see ourselves and our world together and cannot evade this identification, this has profound anthropological consequences. The doctrine of sin and the secular orders has to be thought out afresh. For our alienation does not just affect us at the individual level but also at the supraindividual level of our world. Once that is seen, the suprapersonal element that we note in original sin takes on a new dimension. It acquires a reference to the world inasmuch as the fallen world is now meant as something that is there before us. The understanding of the world's orders also takes on a new aspect. These are now seen to be structural forms of the present aeon, which can never as such be pure orders of creation but are also objectifications of human guilt, its expression in terms of the world as a whole. They thus lie in the half-light between creatureliness and alienation. Finally, this understanding of identity throws new light on eschatology. Structured in this way, the human world cannot fulfill the will of God unconditionally. Hence the kingdom of God can in no sense be a state that evolves in this present world or can be achieved by it. It is a force that comes to us from the other side of the world's frontier, from the *end* of the present world.

Hence its breaking in is at the same time the breaking up of this world. This is why we do not pray, "Thy kingdom evolve," but, "Thy kingdom come."

The businessman implicitly opened up these questions when he wanted to know whether the autonomy of competition, which is obviously at work as a structural form of this aeon, is in some sense a part of him. Is it to be added to his identity so that he has to accept co-responsibility for all that he does in its name? Or is it just a trans-subjective law to which he is innocently subject as to fate?

In our discussion of docetism in anthropology, of being in the world as our corporeality, we began with the situation of proclamation, and in conclusion we may state that if the reaction of hearers is that they cannot see themselves in the sermon, or identify with it, this does not have to be because what is said is too weak or too poorly illustrated or not vivid enough. The reason may be—and usually will be—that it rests on a docetic anthropology. Those who do not find themselves in the sermon are the people whose lives are particularly affected by the pressures and laws of the secular structure —who are at the heart of life. And those who are reached are the older people, possibly in a home for senior citizens, who are relatively more remote from the world. I say "relatively" because the home and even the monk's cell is a world in miniature and cannot be totally isolated. As an example we need only think of Luther's experiences in the cloister. Perhaps this is the real reason for the shifts in age and social status that investigators and statisticians have found among churchgoers.

Looking ahead to the tasks that are set us by these deliberations, we may sum up the results as follows.

The theme of anthropology is our being in the world. To define our nature in terms of our being in the world is to understand it as the point of intersection of many relations. If we mention some of these by way of example, we shall exclude the relation to God, since this is not one alongside the others but the one that sustains all the others.

At the head of the web of relations stands the relation to the Thou. But this is a multiple relation. As there is no I in itself, so there is no Thou in itself. Both are "in situation" and hence their meeting is tied to situations. They do not meet directly but through the mediation of the structure of historical situations. Thus they meet within the family as parents and children. Or they meet within the relation of eros, so that age, sex, and certain forms of attraction shape the meeting. Or they meet in the economic or social sphere, as employers and employees, as competitors or partners, as manufacturers, sellers, and consumers. All these relations—and one may easily extend them—come within the identity of I and Thou and their multiple relationships.

But the web of relations goes beyond that of I and Thou. It includes, for example, the relation between people and nature, not just in the sense that nature is something outside us that we urbanize or destroy industrially in our civilizations, but also in the sense that we are part of nature so far as concerns our bodies, our biological existence.

This web also includes our relation to time. By way of tradition we are on a path that leads out of the past. We do not begin our lives at a zero point but within a history that is shaped and that shapes us. We take over a legacy, and perhaps in so doing we take on too much. (We have referred already to Sartre's *Flies* in this regard.) We cannot be blank pages; there is already some writing on us. We also stand in constant relation to our future, which we anticipate in anxiety or hope, and in any case with expectation, whereas animals live only for the moment.

Our primary anthropological task, then, is to illumine this web of relations at whose point of intersection our human existence stands.

D. HUMANITY, HISTORY, AND EXPERIENCE

I. THE ENCOUNTER WITH HISTORY
AS AN EXTENSION OF THE SELF
(DILTHEY, NIETZSCHE)

In his work on various ways of viewing the world, Wilhelm Dilthey said somewhere that the riddle of historical life, the one, dark, terrifying subject of philosophy, is the sphinx with an animal body and a human face, i.e., humanity. In this statement Dilthey was perhaps pointing more to the content of anthropology than its theme. If I were to point to the heart of this content along the lines of the quotation, I might put it thus.

In viewing humanity in its historicity as the subject of philosophy, Dilthey has something similar in view to what we have called humanity's being in the world. The puzzling nature of humanity is characterized by its being not just the theme of philosophical knowledge but also the "subject" (or bearer) of it. To this extent anthropology is always a form of experience of the self. It results from obeying the command: "Know thyself."

We have said already that this self-experience does not come by way of introspection or contemplating one's navel, but by meeting other people, and especially by way of history. We recall Goethe's saying in *Tasso* that we know ourselves only in others; life teaches us who we are. Dilthey finds life summed up in history. This is why he finds in history the usual means of getting experience of the self. We find ourselves in history.

What does history teach us about ourselves and human nature? In Dilthey's sense it teaches us especially that human nature is always the same, that the basic elements in experience of life are common to all of us. Among the constants in the changes and chances of history are the transitoriness of human affairs, our capacity to enjoy the fleeting hour, and the impulse to overcome this transitoriness by surrounding life with a solid scaffolding. Experience varies, of course, with individuals. But the constants can always be seen. "The common foundation, that which is the same in everybody, is constituted by the power of chance, the corruptibility of all that we possess and love or hate and fear, the continual presence of death, which omnipotently determines for all of us the meaning and significance of life." As we reflect on the permanence of these elements and realize that we are subject to them, the horizon of our self-experience broadens. Experiencing the past, we are taught by the drama of life, and our nature expands.

But can history really perform this service if our relation to it is only that of spectators at a play? Since historians, who really do study it at a distance, do not seem in experience to be visited by any unusual access of self-knowledge, we have our doubts. But what is the basis of such doubts?

When, as historians, we consider a bit of history, it is part of a closed past. We see how things developed and what resulted from that to which people once looked ahead in fear and hope. But this knowledge of what resulted distorts our view of history. We *know too much*. We know *more* than the generation that actually lived through the history that we today are merely studying. This additional knowledge divides us from that generation and damages the solidarity that might make the study productive for our own self-experience. As those who know, who have hindsight, we cannot imagine that the people whose acts we are studying were moving toward a completely incalculable and hidden future, that they had to *venture* their diagnoses of the situation and their decisions, and that to that extent they were filled with fear and hope in face of the unknown. Even when I try to reconstruct situations in my own life, e.g., my experience of bombing in World War II, I come up against psychological barriers that prevent me from achieving full solidarity and identification with my own past. I can depict actual happenings in shelters during an attack. I can recount the sounds and cries and explosions. But as a survivor I can no longer revive the emotions—the elemental part of the experience—that I felt as I faced the possible extinction of myself and my family in the next few minutes. Undoubtedly these hours contributed decisively to my experience of myself, but does looking back at them historically perform the same service? Does not survival establish a distance that prevents me from integrating the actual situation and its anxieties and hopes with my present self, and thus causing the latter to grow?

The problem that faces us here can be felt with particular intensity by people who both acted at the time and now look back as historians. Winston Churchill is one such. In his *Memoirs* he repeatedly points out that he can hardly conceive of his anxieties in 1940. For much of what he feared, of what kept him and his staff in suspense night and day, e.g., the invasion of England or the capture of Malta, never came to pass. On the other hand, many of his hopes, e.g., the early entry of America into the war, were not fulfilled. But it was these fears and hopes that motivated his decisions and acts at the time. As they become fainter and fainter in later recollection, and can no longer be reproduced, the whole complex of motives behind the acts that made history becomes increasingly distant and alien. How much more does this process take place in later historians. Future readers, says Churchill, must remember how thick and deceptive the veil of the unknown can be. With the benefit of hindsight it is easy to see where there is a lack of perception, or too much worrying, or negligence and bungling. The same applies to those who were under the Nazi regime. How much that we see in retrospect is false because we project our knowledge as "burnt children" into the past and thus conceal the open future of the time with the haze of knowledge—for there is such a thing!

Observing our vanished past may rightly lead to some resignation in the face of history, to the conclusion that we never learn anything from it and never have. This is precisely the reason why there is no progress, why we do not become wiser through our previous experiences, and consequently why experience of the self profits little from history.

One thing, at least, is sure: historical understanding that helps us to discover and expand our identity can never consist of merely acquiring information about the past. To do this is to kill history. As one who comes later, I am confronted by fossilized realities. But those who lived then faced open possibilities, the fiery lava that had not yet hardened, so that no one could say what forms it would take as historical facts, as petrifacts, at a later date. According to Dilthey, then, I can understand history only if I make myself contemporary with the people of the past by empathizing with their decisions as though they were my own.

But how can I do this? Is there not a threat of falling victim to a kind of hermeneutical romanticism from which Dilthey himself is not wholly free?

History certainly cannot contribute to my experience of myself in such a way that even the most careful and sympathetic consideration of the past can teach me about myself. The reverse is true (though the dialectic of interaction should not be overlooked). I rise above the banal information available to a later age, and pierce through it, only if I make my existing knowledge of myself fruitful for the understanding of history, and only then, in a backward reaction, receive from history corrections and extensions of my self-experience.

Dilthey has some sense of this, though we only get glimpses of it. Thus he can say that the goal we posit as our future determines the significance of the past. A standard is set for the present shape of life by evaluation of the meaning of what is remembered. Thus our own understanding and planning of life are the starting point for historical understanding. But then what we discover in this understanding affects us and leads to an expansion of individual and collective experience. Starting in life, understanding constantly forces us down to new depths. Only in their feedback to life and society do the arts achieve their supreme significance. The objectivity of academic knowledge is not an end in itself but only a transitional stage.

Thus I may encounter myself by the way of history, of the microcosmic reflection of humanity and myself actualized and depicted in innumerable examples. But I do so only if I understand history in terms of myself, my own decisions, and my open present. This is the hermeneutical circle into which I must put myself. And we should be aware of the limitations of the process to which we have referred.

The attempt to link history and self-experience in this way may be found in Friedrich Nietzsche's classical early work on the value of history for life (*Vom Nutzen und Nachteil der Historie für das Leben*). Nietzsche, too, begins by stating that mere objective information about the past not only will be of no use to life, i.e., experience and self-fulfillment, but will be hostile and destructive. Too much historical knowledge disturbs the instincts of a people and prevents individuals as well as the whole body from maturing. It plants the idea that we are latecomers and epigones, so that our forces are damaged and finally destroyed. This is why, one might add, ancient Europe, which is so rich in history and tradition, is often so hampered in its dealing with the future as compared with America, which has relatively no history. A sterile encounter with history, which is concerned only about history as such, condemns the personality to an eternal loss of subjectivity or to an overblown objectivity. Thus historical knowledge can give rise to nonhistoricity and produce an omniscient homunculus whose own existence is stunted and taken out of history, a "cold demon of knowledge."

Nietzsche finds only three forms of encounter with history that can lead to fruitful application, transcend the spectator-perspective vis-à-vis the historical panorama, and help observers to achieve their own historical identity. He describes these as monumental, antiquarian, and critical history.

Monumental history focuses on the great moments of conflict that combine to form the mountain range of humanity across the centuries. Consideration of these high points strengthens our faith in humanity, for it assures us that the greatness that was present once is still possible and always will be. Thus, although the monumental approach is in a sense distorted and one-sided, it is a great encouragement in the historical present. It makes us weigh the possibilities of our identity and motivates us to realize them.

Antiquarian history also contributes to self-experience and self-confirmation. It deals with local history and hence with our own immediate background. As the history of my city, it is the history of myself. Again, it is one-sided, and I may be tempted to conserve that which molds me and put it in a limited parochial perspective. Nevertheless, the antiquarian aspect helps me to find my identity. Through it I see my collectively extended I. I see what forces of tradition, heredity, and environment influenced me and helped to make me what I am.

Finally, critical history in particular stands in the service of life, for it confronts us with the task of breaking up and dissolving the past so as to be able to live. We do not just understand ourselves as the product of our past and thus stay in the limited circle of the status quo, but are sometimes compelled to throw off the past, to bring it to judgment, to investigate it carefully, and finally to condemn it. In this process I may come to realize how unjust is the existence of a thing like privilege, caste, or dynasty, how much it deserves to perish. This critical attitude to the past means putting the knife to the roots, trampling on all that is sacred, breaking taboos. Although we cannot totally emancipate ourselves from this chain, being always the products of earlier generations, we can refuse to be the results of their aberrations, passions, mistakes, and even crimes. We can try to give ourselves a posteriori a past from which we should like to have come instead of the one from which we did come. This is how legendary and stylized pictures of the past, and retouched traditions, come into existence.

Critical history shows more clearly than monumental or antiquarian history what is the relation between identity and history. We have pointed out already that it is my own self-understanding that opens up history to me. The eye has to be attuned to the sun to receive its light. Only when history is seen and understood in this way can it have its effect on me and make my implicit identity explicit, helping me in this way to come to myself. I have to have some sense, however dull, of what possibilities there are in humanity to be receptive to the monumental features of history, even though the impression these make on me is what gives certainty to what I only sensed, and makes it a driving force in my life.

Critical history in particular is helpful in this regard because it helps me not to understand myself merely as the product of past generations but enables me to come before the past as a prosecutor too. To be able to do this I have to be certain about my own being. I am not just in process of becoming but already have an independent being. I can let the horizon of my identity be extended by history only if I can distinguish the historical horizon from my own (Eckardt Otto). To be able to do this I have to have a horizon. I must be able to oppose my own identity to history.

Only then can the interaction with history begin. Only then can history help me to become myself and find my own historical identity. Merely acquiring information about the panorama of history destroys this identity and produces the homunculus. Where there is no self that can oppose itself to history and be its partner in dialogue, there can no longer be any experience of the self.

II. HUMANITY AS SPHINX: THE UNION OF NATURE AND HISTORY

a. The Human Face

Who or what do we see when we look in the mirror of history and thus extend our self-experience?

Dilthey answers this question by pointing to the sphinx, which has a human face and an animal body.

As concerns the human face, we will not be wrong if we take it that what Dilthey has in mind is what we might call today, following Heidegger, human existence. Human existence, as we have seen, means that humanity is the only form of being that has to know and comprehend itself, that has thus to act in responsibility to its destiny. This is what distinguishes human being from animal being. Johann Gottfried von Herder made the same point in his *Ideen zur Philosophie der Geschichte der Menschheit* when he said that we are not infallible machines in the hands of nature but the ends and goals of our own handiwork. We are not puppets directed from outside but by creation are endowed with gifts that make us centers of action and thus expose us to the risk of winning our own identity, as the Creator intended, or failing to achieve it. God himself has taken this risk.

Friedrich von Schiller says similarly in his *Anmut und Würde* that in plants and animals nature has not merely set the goal but leads to it. In humans, however, nature simply prescribes the end and leaves it to people themselves to reach it. This means that the goal is given (*gegeben*). We do not govern ourselves in the sense of being able to fix our own destiny. But the way to it is given only as a task (*aufgegeben*). There is thus a possibility of failure. The experiment of existence may not succeed. We may fail to become truly human.

The reference to the human face means, then, that we are given our destiny and have to act as those who are intrinsically "in decision." This also means that we are pointed to the future and stand in a special relation to time. This relation is the existential factor. It is the reason why we are summoned to self-awareness and the discovery of our identity. We can thus find it in all the factors that constitute our humanity as their sustaining basis.

First, we are rational beings. This means that we are not taught by our instincts but teach our instincts (Goethe). We are not at the mercy of a deterministic evolution but with the help of reason can choose among the available possibilities and thus plan our future.

Second, we have a conscience. This means again that we cannot just "go along" but have to go toward an awaiting end. Our future becomes our task.

Third, we are tied to the body. We thus live with the awareness that we have only a limited span and have to make good use of it.

"For everything there is a season." The future of death is ahead of us. But not only that, for we also know that decisions must be made for whatever future we still have, that the future we choose cannot be revised at will, and that we are thus confronted by the irreversibility of the time-line (John 3:4).

b. The Animal Body

Dilthey also refers to the animal body of the sphinx. He means that the natural reaches deep into the human sphere, so that no sharp line of distinction can be drawn between nature and history. We shall discuss this overlapping later in connection with Teilhard de Chardin, but we may already make a few points concerning it.

Death is biologically ordained for us. The instincts of aggression and self-assertion are at work in human action, in history. This is incontestable and needs no special demonstration. The real problem does not lie in these facts but in their understanding and evaluation. For the question arises whether our biological destiny and instinctual activity have not to be regarded as ethically neutral and ascribed to "innocent" nature. But this is obviously impossible. The businessman to whom we referred illustrates in model fashion the question that faces us.

Those of us who are in competition and subject to external forces (whether in profession, business, or eros) know that they cannot fight blindly and absolutely in this battle to emerge as the stronger. They are suddenly brought up against values that lie outside the mechanism of competition. They see in their rival the face of a neighbor who will suffer in the struggle. The fate of others is at issue as well as their own. I recall a story from World War I that illustrates the situation with impressive urgency. In a bayonet attack a German soldier fell into a deep shell crater where he came across a wounded Englishman. In the heat of battle he spontaneously aimed his bayonet at the enemy, and the latter, though weak, responded in the same way. But when the German soldier noted that the man was severely wounded, he let his weapon fall. The Englishman gave him to understand that he was very thirsty, and so the soldier let him drink from his own flask. Then the Englishman pointed to his coat pocket, which he could not reach. The German reached in and drew out a wallet with a photograph of his wife and children, whom the dying man wanted to see once again. When the grateful glance of the Englishman fell on him, and the soldier looked at the photograph with him, a radical change took place in their relationship. They ceased to be the representatives of hostile fronts, and as such objects of the unleashed instinct of aggression, of the attempt to play the role of the stronger. They suddenly became neighbors.

We can find the root of this change only if we pierce through the sentimentality of the story and press on to its anthropological point. This is that at a certain moment they found themselves in a new and altered nexus of relations. At first they were representatives of opposing fronts in a life-and-death struggle. But now, with the quenching of deadly thirst and contemplation of the family portrait, they find that there is more to their lives than this representative role. They transcend it. They are no longer German and English. They are both married men and fathers. They are both human beings who are loved by other human beings and constitute their lives. The animal function of the released instinct of war and aggression is not all there is to them. Revealed to them is another dimension of their existence in which they meet, not indirectly through the mediation of a front, but directly, in which each sees the human face of the other and they enter into communication with one another. If at this moment both are overwhelmed by the terrible nonsense of war, by its alienating effect, as is humanly understandable, this is shown only by the fact that the natural force that has previously directed them as the collective emotion of assertion and the desire to destroy, is not "innocent" nature or an animal upsurge, but makes them face up to the question of their humanity. If human beings fight, this is a very different thing from what deer do in the rutting season.

Once the animal element enters the human sphere it undergoes a mutation that gives it a different quality. It is impossible to say, "C'est la guerre," or, "Natural laws are at work that we cannot control." We are compelled to take up this animal element into our identity and recognize that we are full subjects, not mere victims or objects.

Finding that they are neighbors in the shell crater, the two soldiers are oppressed by a sense of shame that they formerly had a distorted picture of one another. The equation of person and function brings about this kind of distortion. One form of the temptation that arises here is to see people only in the nature-inspired autonomy of action and reaction, in a "role."

We might think of other examples to illustrate the mutation that the animal element undergoes when it enters the human sphere.

The powerful corporation chief who can crush his smaller rivals suddenly comes up against the question whether the concentration of power in one hand does not overturn the structure of democracy from within, whether unrestricted competition is not destructive, whether it does not have to be the object of responsible decisions.

The same demand for decision arises in another area where the animal element enters the human sphere, namely, in relation to the sexual instinct. In animals this instinct is regulated and channeled by the rutting season. Among us, however, it may be invoked at any time. What is controlled by mechanisms among animals is something we ourselves have to control. (Thus we humans can also overeat.) All the impulses deriving from the animal body can be given free rein and become irrational and self-destructive. Once they enter the human sphere, as in the case of sex, they are changed, broken, and set in question. The question is how we humans will relate them to our destiny, for they do not propel us automatically toward our future. They assault us and threaten to denaturalize us.

c. The Transforming of the Natural in the Human Sphere (Eros)

This is not to be taken along the lines of Kant's view of personality, as though we humans, as the bearers of practical reason, as reflective and rational beings, were simply in opposition to natural factors, as though those were subhuman, the "sensible" world, the cellar in the house of the I, in which "the wild wolves howl" (Nietzsche). It would again result in a docetic picture if we were to locate what is truly human, the personality, solely in the sphere of reason and conscience, and find the true self—to use our earlier metaphor—only in the main rooms of the house of the I. No, the cellar, too, is part of us, and determines our identity along with all else. Natural factors are not simply that from which personality differentiates itself as truly human. They are the medium through which it actualizes itself, the stuff of which it is shaped. Eros is the illustration of the indissoluble interrelation or union (which we are not even to seek to dissolve) between the human face and the animal body.

I cannot demonstrate the worth of my humanity in this sphere by acting as though I saw only neighbors in others, as though our only communication were ethical. For there are laws of attraction and repulsion that are based also, if not exclusively, on biological factors such as sex, age, shape, temperament, et cetera. I cannot ignore these in the name of supposed higher motives; I cannot even wish to do so. Thus I cannot marry merely out of the very humanitarian motive of pity. If I did, I should not enter *into* marriage. The natural factors that are involved here would be either rejected or put on a lower level as inferior. I must accept the fact that I am a sexual being of flesh and blood and thus have very vital impulses and instincts. In so doing, I do not, like the animal, make the other the mere object of my impulses. Through the medium of my sexuality I make the other a Thou, a neighbor. This Thou has, then, a sexual and natural aspect. Toward the beloved I have a different I-Thou relation, or, better, a different form of this relation from that which a nurse in a home for senior citizens has for those under her care. But it is still the living Thou of the neighbor that is at issue within communication that is shaped, or partly shaped, by bios. Thus a human form of love does not arise *in spite of* the sexual or natural element. This love needs the sexual and natural factor as the material out of which it is formed. But this is possible only when this factor has the significance of a physical medium for the wholly human relation of love. Thus there will be in this medium just as much self-surrender, self-giving, and desire to make happy as there will be egoism, aggression, and disregard for the other.

This is supported by what happens when the bios or impulse aspect of sex is absolutized and *laissez-faire* characterizes erotic behavior. This is not just an attack on the finer side of humanity; it denaturalizes it, for eros ceases to be an expression of the encounter between two people and is reduced to a dreadful manipulating which is cut off from all that the human sphere contributes, is robbed of all nuances and deeper joys, and makes the participants bored and empty and indifferent once orgasm is achieved. As an American once told me, Hollywood is basically sexless, for all that its films are overloaded with eroticism. When I expressed surprise and asked what he meant, he said that in these films desire is directed only to a beautiful bosom, shapely shoulders, or attractive legs, and thus only to a part, not to the whole. He called this sexless, with some exaggeration, of course, in order to show not merely that there is blindness here to the higher personal spheres, and the acceptance of a kind of sexual materialism, but also that the sexual itself is corrupted and loses the riches that are dormant in it.

We see vividly here what it is our aim to show, namely, that once the bios factor comes into the human sphere, it comes under new and separate laws and either becomes a medium for love and hate, self-giving and egoism, and other human qualities, or it is isolated in a kind of game preserve, severed from the totality of the human, and thus turned in upon itself.

III. HUMANITY IN RELATION TO THE ANIMAL, GOD, AND THE GODS

a. The Question of the Basic Relation of Our Being

The present question is whether the human self can be defined in terms of this relation between the personal and the animal. Can one say that we are beings that transcend nature, not in emancipation from it, but by integration of nature into the human, and its transformation thereby?

Although such statements would not go beyond what we have said, it is not really possible to define the human with the help of this relation of personal-animal, or human face–animal body. We have introduced the concept of alien dignity precisely to take the mystery of humanity—on good grounds—out of the sphere of what can be fixed objectively and to find its basis in an ultimate relation, the relation to God, that is accessible only to faith.

The implication of this relation for the duality of human face and animal body may be fully seen only from something that Kierkegaard said in his *Sickness Unto Death*. In this work Kierkegaard stated that the human self can be understood only from its relations and not from itself as a self-contained entelechy. But the specifics of the relations to the animal and God then need to be discussed. The human self receives infinite reality from its awareness of existing for God, of being a human self for which God is the standard. A cowherd who is a self only in relation to his cows (if this were possible) would be a very lowly self, and so would a master who is a self only in relation to his servants; indeed, he would be no true self at all, for there is nothing by which he can measure himself. Children who have had only their parents as a standard become selves when as adults they have the state as a standard, but what an infinite emphasis it puts on the self to receive God as the standard!

For Kierkegaard the question, then, is not *whether* we are to be understood in terms of our relations, our "extra-political" relations, instead of our ontic state; it is the question *which* of these relations are truly basic. When we consider them, it is apparent that the relation to the animal, as of the cowherd to his cows, cannot be a basis for the human self. If we can say only, "I am more than these cows," or, "My human face is superior to my body," we have not really traversed the horizon of human identity but simply played the old game of dividing the self into a higher and a lower part. Things are a little better in relation to the state, for here we are relegated to the cellar and the standard is relatively higher. Yet no true conception of the self emerges, for the trouble is that, in this relation to the state, or to society, as we put it today, the self is only partly committed. I am relevant here only in my capacity as a citizen fulfilling certain obligations and being a useful member of society, as someone who is law-abiding, loyal, and honest, as a neighbor, a subordinate, the holder of a job—in many different capacities. But many dimensions of the I are not affected by this relation to the state or society: my personal relation to other people in love or hate, my solitariness, my despair at an incurable illness, my dereliction in death. Furthermore, my joys and celebrations and enthusiasms are irrelevant from the standpoint of the state. Thus I am only partly involved in this relation; my identity cannot be grasped in terms of it.

It can be fully seen only in the light of something that sustains the whole nexus of my relations, to which I owe both my human face and my animal body, which commits both to me as both gift and task. Kierkegaard calls this something God. He indicates thereby that the self can find itself only in him from whom it receives itself in the fullness of what it *is*, from whom it also receives the goal that it *ought* to reach, and from whom finally there is imparted to it the direction, power, faithfulness, and forgiveness that are needed on the way that leads to the promised salvation. Only in this light may the fullness of my identity be perceived, not by myself, for my identity can only be believed by me, but by him who knows me through and through (Psalm 139:23; 1 Corinthians 13:14). There thus opens up a new aspect of our thesis that human identity is enclosed in an alien dignity, that only here does the totality of the human appear.

b. The Crisis of Identity Under the Domination of Penultimate Relations (Example: East and West)

The attempt to define our humanity, not in terms of this ultimate nonobjective reference, but in terms of our objectifiable function as material beings, is a characteristic of modern empiricism. It is thus understandable that we find particularly marked examples of this kind of anthropology in the sphere of dialectical materialism. By way of illustration I might quote from a letter that Maxim Gorky wrote in 1926 to the celebrated Soviet pedagogue Anton Semyonovich Makarenko, who had entered a pedagogic collective. Gorky told him he was doing "a glorious work." "The earth," he said, "is *our* earth. *We* have made it fruitful, *we* have adorned it with cities, criss-crossed it with roads, done all kinds of wonderful things on it—we humans, once insignificant specks of dull and formless matter, then half-animals, but now the pioneers of a new life." Here one sees in a few sentences the process to which we referred. As we are reduced to our Promethean functions and thus to what may be seen objectively in our works, the feeling for personality is crushed. We take our rise from things ("dull and formless matter") and are ourselves things. That the omission of the nonobjective relation does, in fact, have this result is confirmed by Makarenko's answer, in which he says that he wanted to join a healthy human collective, since to submerge one's personality in this manner is the best way to put oneself to rights. With the extinguishing of the nonobjective relation, there also disappears the unconditional emphasis that is laid on human existence by its alien dignity and that makes submergence impossible.

Naturally this process of losing identity—for that is what it is!—does not occur only in the ideological sphere of dialectical materialism; many traces of it may be found in the West as well. Gottfried Benn points to this in his verses on the lost I. As a particularly impressive witness I might also quote Thomas E. Lawrence (Lawrence of Arabia) in his *Seven Pillars of Wisdom*, who gained world renown for his part in the Arab revolt, whom Winston Churchill called one of the greatest hopes of the British Empire, whose work George Bernard Shaw revised, but whose ideals were shattered by bitter experiences, so that as an act of despair of all meaning, of any possibility of doing anything significant, in spite of his high rank, he enlisted and served in a ground crew in the Royal Air Force under another name. When asked why he took this unusual step, he replied that he did it in order to serve a mechanical purpose, not as a leader who makes decisions, who has programs, who is his own center of action, but as the shadow of a machine simply going along automatically and vegetatively without making any decisions. In this way we learn that things do not depend on a single individual. On another occasion he spoke of extinguishing his free will, of overcoming his desire for life, of keeping at arm's length every act that still speaks the language of responsibility and pride.

The elimination of specifically human existence by erasure of the ultimate relation of faith and reduction to objective functions is, as we have said, typically modern.

The reverse, i.e., basing humanity on the nonobjective relation, is not just Christian but is one of the traditional axioms of Western anthropology even in its pre-Christian phase. A short glance at the anthropology of classical Greece will demonstrate this.

c. The Theonomous Relation of Existence Among the Greeks (Humans and Gods). Rationality and Autonomy in the Ancient and Modern Sense

The sixth Nemean ode of Pindar (c. 470 B.C.) begins by saying that while the human race differs from that of the gods, both have life from one mother. The distinction is in power, but there is a similarity in the power of thought and the disposition for immortality. In contrast to this way of putting it, our own reference to the nonobjective ground of human being sounds almost pathetically prosaic. But our theme compels us to cite Pindar as a confirmatory witness that this understanding of humanity rests on a relation to the immortals whom we resemble in thinking power and disposition and who surround our existence without being objects or forms within it, without our being able to objectify them. This is true even though we are told by classical philologists that our common mother is *physis*, or the totality of creative being. For this being is more than the sum of all existent things that can be documented. It is a mythical power, and as such has a share in the nonobjectivity of what is all-embracing. Hence there is no thought here of seeing the essence of the human merely in its function or technical capacity, or in its being more than one of the things which it subjects to itself. Pindar's cowherd, like Kierkegaard's, is not understood merely in terms of superiority to his cows.

In Plato, too, we find the same reference to the nonobjective world of the gods, as when he says in the *Theaetetus* that avoiding evil is becoming like God, which is being just and devout in conduct based on reason. To understand this, it may be helpful to realize that "reason" here is not just an epistemological organ by which to know the objective world, as in modern rationalism of various types. Instead, it is an ability to perceive and appropriate, which extends beyond the sensory world of experience. As Plato explains in the *Phaedo*, the reference is not just to the distinction between rational thought and deceptive sensory apprehension but to the higher stage of pure thought within the thinking self, whose objects include the good and the beautiful and the true, indeed, the ineffable. But the term "object" becomes a dubious one in this context, for what is thought relates in this instance to ideal entities that cannot be grasped objectively but form, in Kantian terms, the basis of the possibility of all experience. Among the nonobjective entities that underlie all human being is what Plato calls "God."

As the relation here is not to things or animals but to ideas and deities, another typical modern relation does not arise for the ancient Greeks. I mean the relation to the self that comes to expression in the concept of autonomy.[1] In many of its versions, though not all (cf. the Kantian), this modern term denotes humanity that is its own lord in self-resting finitude and does not see itself in its relationships but relates only to itself. At the end of this train of thought there does not stand an encounter with humanity in its real humanity but only an encounter with humanity as a thing. Max Stirner is the best representative of this sterile understanding when he says that "humanity" is a mere abstraction, a mystical nonobjectivity that does not really exist. Now, of course, it does not exist in the same way as houses and trees, or rocks and hills, as we have already seen. But modern empiricism with its object-related rationality can accept the reality only of things that exist in that way. And if we take away from humanity all that does not exist in that way—personality, conscience, relationships—all that is left is a thing, a purely natural object, a wingless biped.

The relationship of the ancient Greeks to the gods is worlds apart from this modern understanding of autonomy, and especially from its perversion. Although we must be cautious in applying and comparing terms that belong to different epochs, one may say that the ancients were theonomously and not autonomously oriented. Humans in Homer are "mortals" (*thnetoi*). Their determinative relation is not to the animals from which they have developed and from which they are distinguished by their human dignity, but to the gods, the immortals (*athanatoi*). As Pindar says, we are not to try to become Zeus. Only mortal things are appropriate for mortals.

Even Prometheus, who has become for us the symbol of revolt and the struggle for emancipation, has been misunderstood and stylized in secularist fashion, as Karl Reinhardt shows in his work on Aeschylus. In the writings of Karl Marx, for example, Prometheus is taken to be a hater of the gods, a symbol of revolution, and a personification of human autonomy and autarchy. Precisely by viewing him as a Titan, Aeschylus puts him in a context that is indispensable to his understanding. As regards the power it is given, humanity should remember its Titanic origin and find grace there. The figure of Prometheus the Titan symbolizes this polarity of force and grace.

In all these texts the idea of autonomy that has become the symbol of humanity is so far distant that with perhaps only one exception the concept of autonomous humanity never occurs at all, the term being reserved for sovereign states or free-ranging animals! The one exception understands the concept of autonomy in a way that is completely alien to modern usage and stands in total antithesis to it. It may be found in the *Antigone* of Sophocles. When King Creon, misusing the law, will not allow Antigone to bury her brother Polynices, she defies the royal edict. The king then has her walled up as a punishment, and so the chorus speaks of her as going to Hades for living according to her own law (*autonomos*) and referring only to herself. But in this context the term has almost exactly the opposite sense to that of "self-willed" or "being a law to oneself" that we would give it, for Antigone does not obey the voice of her individual conscience but defies Creon's arbitrary "positive" law in the name of eternal, unwritten, divine laws. For her, then, "autonomous" does not mean emancipated or under no obligation but expresses the inescapability of a final obligation. She stands in a reference to the self, but brings this self (*autos*) into play only on this ultimate basis. Theonomy and autonomy are not sundered here but have a basic identity. This again will occupy us more fully later.

The same referring of life to its divine basis explains Vergil's use of the term *pius* for Aeneas, the ancestor of Rome. The linking of the term "pious" with the "hero" sounds odd to us, because we are more accustomed to think of heroes as madmen racing through the world, as in Nikolaus Lenau's poem "Der Indifferentist," which Otto von Bismarck liked so much, or as those who defy every force and precisely in so doing evoke the arms of the gods, as in Goethe. But here it is different. "You rule because you yield to the gods, this is the beginning and the end," is the motto with which Horace refers to the greatness and fall of Rome in his sixth ode to the city.

Incontestably there were other anthropologies in the Greek world. Plato's thesis that God is the measure of all things was directed against the famous dictum of the Sophist Protagoras that humanity is the measure of all things. The attempt of the Sophists to refer us back to humanity when skepticism rules and all values are questioned is one color on the rich palette of the Greek spirit. But what one finds in the Sophists is more in the nature of counterpoint to the true theme of the theonomous relationship of this spirit.

Our existence in a binding relationship may be found unmistakably in Plato. The soul as the center of the person dwells originally in the realm of ideas and is a follower of deity. But it is then drawn away and deflected by emotional impulses. In the *Timaeus* only the rational (*noetikon*) is divine and immortal; it is the daemon that the godhead has given to each of us. The other parts of the soul that can break loose from their source are mortal. Existence on earth is thus given the task of reversing the alienation or emancipation from our origin. Step by step the soul must move back into the world of ideas, being helped in the process by recollection (*anamnesis*) of its earlier stay in this sphere which it has now left.

Those who break away from the relationship to deity and the ideas fall into futility and lose their humanity. Thus Plato has a premonition of what has become a collective phenomenon in later developments. I mean a humanity that has lost its original reference and been reduced to what may be apprehended objectively.

Even that which dialectical materialism would regard as the expression of pure rationality, i.e., understanding humanity only in material circumstances that may be improved scientifically, would have been viewed as nonrational by Plato, since the action is motivated "emotionally." He would have regarded the whole thing as a concept of the degraded soul and degenerate personality. On Plato's view there need be no contesting the existence of guilt in exposing humanity to this degradation by means of unjust social structures.

For the rest, Marxism does not want to *interpret* the world but to *change* it. For Plato this means that it is closed to the question of the nature of humanity and its world. Its acts of cognition are not directed, like Plato's, to the basis, goal, and meaning of the world, its "idea," but to its objectifiable functioning mechanism, which is to be manipulated and toward which one has, therefore, a purely pragmatic relation. Not truth as the self-disclosure of being (*aletheia*), but interest in action, and hence an "emotional" motive, forms the decisive impulse. Thus the basic relationship of Platonic anthropology is left out of account.

I hope readers will have perceived why we needed to get at least a cursory view of the Greek understanding of humanity at this juncture. In spite of all the differences between the Christian world and the Greek world (e.g., in the view of time, the connection between soul and body, cosmogony, and many other things), and in spite of the fatal intermingling of the two (e.g., in the disparagement of the body or the confusing of resurrection and immortality), it seems to me to be highly significant that the anthropologies that have done most to shape our culture have many formal resemblances in approach. For in both cases the picture of humanity is determined by the relationship to something unconditional, even though this something unconditional bears a totally different name and the nature of the relationship is thus qualified in very different ways.

Negatively, this means that in neither case is humanity construed along the lines of a closed entelechy that can be understood in terms of itself and is not therefore to be defined in relation to anything unconditional, to any basis, goal, or meaning of existence. Nor is it grounded in a relation to something conditional and objectifiable, as, for example, the biological or social conditions of existence.

We are thus given a clear view of the task that lies before us in our anthropological inquiry. We have to explore more thoroughly this relation to something unconditional. We shall do so by investigating it in the individual human spheres, the relations to the animal world, to society, to death, and to many other things that constitute our existence. At every point we shall have to establish the presence and relevance of the fundamental relation. We shall thus be asking with Kierkegaard how far we achieve our self-hood and identity by being "before God."

We shall keep this task in view as we now turn parenthetically to the question how our self-understanding has changed in the modern period, and in particular how far we have broken loose from that basic relation.

E. THE IMPACT OF THE MODERN UNDERSTANDING OF REALITY ON ANTHROPOLOGY

I. THE DIRECTION
OF THE UNDERSTANDING OF REALITY

a. The Relation of Time and Eternity
as the Key to the Secularized View of Humanity

A modern sociologist defines secularization as a process by which parts of society and culture are freed from the domination of religious institutions and symbols, or as the retreat of the Christian churches from spheres that were previously under their control or influence. Though these definitions agree with the usual understanding and are phenomenologically accurate, they are superficial and do not address the fundamental impulses behind the process.[1] They confine themselves to the institutional outworkings. We shall attempt instead to apply our earlier anthropological results to an understanding of secularization.

If we begin with the fact that both the Christian world and that of classical Greece, even if with different content, view humanity in relation to its goal and make it responsible for the choice of this goal, this understanding, as history shows, has always had one of two effects.

On the one hand, it may mean that projection to the goal becomes the normative category by which to understand "earthly" things. We see history in the light of it, including individual histories. It determines our approach to dealings with others in marriage, reproduction, and death—in short, everything that has to do with human existence. Naturally all such things, events, institutions, et cetera, take on a different appearance if (1) they are simply described as phenomena or (2) they are seen in the light of their meaning and given a final teleological reference.

On the other hand, the goal of humanity may determine the anthropological understanding so absolutely and exclusively that the individual items no longer receive their accent from it but completely lose their specific significance, becoming shadowy images that pale into unreality in the light of our true destiny. An example is the depriving of earthly things of all reality when there is very strong eschatological expectation. One may see this in 1 Corinthians 7, where the return of Christ, the goal of history, is presented as imminent. The power of the imminence of this goal makes existing things seem to be purely interim phenomena that have almost no reality of their own at all. Thus it is hardly worth it to marry or to change one's social situation, e.g., as a slave. Since the time of the present world is short, those who have wives should "live as though they had none, and those who mourn as though they were not mourning, and those who rejoice as though they were not rejoicing, and those who buy as though they had no goods, and those who deal with the world as though they had no dealings with it. For the form of this world is passing away." The nearness of eternity makes the temporal insignificant. In strong expectation of the goal, which carries with it the breakup of the present aeon, the coming kingdom of God takes on almost docetic features. It no longer penetrates this world and ceases to give it the meaning that causes us to see what is earthly in the light of eternity and to recognize in the many the one thing necessary that discloses the real priorities to us. The kingdom of God threatens here to be robbed of its embodiment and to lose all reference to the earthly sphere.

In contrast, when the kingdom of God as the goal sustains and illumines earthly things by setting them in its own light, one can see its relevance in every form of secularization. One thinks, for example, of a person like Dietrich Bonhoeffer, who decisively represents the type of theological thinking that takes account of secularization. Here, then, we find common ground where Christians, agnostics, atheists, and secularists of all kinds can meet for discussion. Social questions such as the problem of property or that of equal rights or that of structures may be put in different frameworks. But even with these different frameworks the theme is the same. And as it is addressed, the question of the ultimate relation can be introduced as well. We have seen already that proclamation can find a valid starting point in the theological interpretation of the world, in this material dialogue.

When the second position is taken, however, and the kingdom of God totally transcends history and loses all contact with earthly

hings, then secularization can become total too, and take the form
of secularism. As Peter Berger said somewhere, the only link between
a radically transcendent God and a radically immanent world is the
word. When the plausibility of this disappears, when it is no longer,
as today, the content of a universal and self-evident conviction, the
last narrow channel is broken that binds this world to the next. And
then indeed only the world remains as self-reposing finitude in which
"God is dead." Berger thinks this danger is a greater one in Protes-
antism than in Roman Catholicism. For the latter lives in a world
in which holy things are mediated through many channels—the sacra-
ments, the intercession of saints, the irruption of the supernatural in
the form of miracles, a fluid boundary between the visible world and
the invisible world. Time and eternity are related here by a whole system of analogies.

b. The Radical Diastasis of Time and Eternity in the Early Barth. The Secularizing Outworking of This in the Third Reich

The way one views the relation of time and eternity, of the world
and the kingdom of God, is thus highly significant for an understanding of secularization. I might illustrate this from the theology
of Karl Barth, and I come up here against a sizable contradiction.

Barth in his early years championed the absolute diastasis of time
and eternity and was thus guilty, as we see it, of a certain docetism.
God is for him the "Wholly Other." He pronounces his negation
and judgment on all the values and norms proclaimed by the world.
He exists in a transcendence beyond all analogies. The resultant
snapping of all relationship between time and eternity comes to expression in our helplessness in face of the ethical questions of life
and the world. If we are to be able to live responsibly as Christians
in the name of God's commandments, there has to be some connection between the will of God, our conscience, and the structure of
our world. God does not simply negate all this. But when there is absolute diastasis between time and eternity, there can be no form of
action or decision that may appeal to God's will. In principle, no
validly unambiguous position is possible. When I am asked how I
ought to decide in a given situation, I can only reply, "Perhaps in this
way, and perhaps not."

Everything, then, is left up in the air. Rather naughtily, and with some element of caricature, I might describe the position as follows: Whatever I do in this wicked world on which God pronounces negation will be corrupt. All that remains, then, is a certain indifference: "Perhaps, but perhaps not."[2]

The resultant crisis obviously makes us helpless when theologically valid decisions have to be made in the political and social sphere. One may see this in the blundering of the Confessing Church, which Barth virtually directed, during Hitler's Third Reich. This church had clarity of vision over against ideological tyranny only as it perceived this to be a threat to, and an assault upon, the word of God that was its only link between time and eternity. At this point it made a resolute stand. But this left an unpleasant taste for two reasons.

First, the church seemed to be defending only itself and to be speaking only on its own behalf. It was indeed the agent of the word, but in championing it, it was also presenting its own cause. This found expression in the slogan of the day: "The church must remain the church."

Second, in its protest against the ideological undermining of God's word by the German Christians and the Nazi party, it reached only those contemporaries who felt bound to the word and were thus Christians. It had no basis on which to join with others in a common protest. The things of this world, problems of culture and education and minorities, were theologically irrelevant. When as students we asked Karl Barth to give his opinion on specific issues in his courses, since these matters were of interest and concern to all of us, he refused to give an official theological answer, and told us to come to his discussion group, where he would willingly offer his private view.

Now it is incontestable that the ideological system of Nazism did not attack God's commands and the claim of eternity by directly doing battle against the Christian faith and the church as its institutional representative. One might say with relative confidence that the regime would never have made any objection to the Augsburg Confession or other confessional writings. It never once made any mention of them. It could allow itself this limited tolerance because it was not incorrectly convinced that a Christianity that had lost touch with the world and was vegetating in its institutional life would wither away of itself. On similar grounds Marxism-Leninism can tolerate the orthodox cultus behind the walls of the church.

When, however, the Nazis spoke about "de-confessionalizing public life" they were raising the true and suspicious challenge of Antichrist. New gods were to rule our secular life, replacing the old God of Christianity. Thus a new image of humanity was being proclaimed. Humanity with an eternal destiny would yield to a superhumanity pledged to the supposed voice of blood and given only a functional role at the behest of the party managers who officially represented that voice. Education—another secular affair—would be primarily antichristian, not because of any attack on the gospel, but because of its corruption of the young by making them no more than the personal elements of a national collective. Minorities—the Jews and the mentally unfit—would be eliminated, and this could be justified by an ideology that no longer viewed humanity in the light of its "alien dignity" and thus robbed it of its sacrosanct status.

One might pursue this theme at length. The battle was not fought within the church but in the world. An ideologically manipulated reality of existence replaced that of the Christian interpretation. For the most part, however, the summons to confess and stand fast and resist at this point was not heeded. Only a few individuals, e.g., Bishop Wurm and Father, later Cardinal, Galen, stepped forward. Dietrich Bonhoeffer, who was one of these and perhaps their leader, entered the political struggle in the name of this confessional obligation and put up secular resistance in the name of God. He sacrificed himself for this cause.

In the name of Barth's theology, however, the Confessing Church could not meet this claim. In relation to it, it was blind and helpless. It had lost sight of the way in which worldly things relate to the kingdom of God. The radical manner in which it made the total difference and transcendent sovereignty of God its magna carta led to an equally radical demission of theology from its secular commitment. Hence the church conflict was almost exclusively about the question of dogmatic confession and not about the obedience that Christians owe God's commands in their secular tasks. It was a great misfortune that on very different grounds, namely, a misunderstanding of the doctrine of the two kingdoms, the Lutherans, too, shuffled off their responsibility to the world. They, too, thought they could restrict their resistance to the regime to the confessional sphere. The persecution of the Jews was a secular matter and seemed to have no theological relevance. The radical diastasis of time and eternity in the younger Barth (and the Confessing Church that was normatively influenced by him) worked in with the Nazi slogan "the de-confessionalizing of public life" (which in fact meant its de-christianizing) in a basic manner that was quite macabre.

Barth himself, of course, very quickly noted what dead end he had run into and what the problem was with his system. He was politically too alert and involved not to see the total devastation caused by Nazism on the secular level. He thus exerted himself to modify his theological thinking so as to make secular issues a legitimate theme and to establish a basis for action. It was clear where the modification would need to take place, namely, in the relation between time and eternity, between the world and the kingdom of God. The complete absence of any analogies between them, which he had declared in the name of God's total otherness, had led to a complete ethical blockade. Hence unwittingly and, of course, unwillingly, he had exposed a flank to the Nazi attack. Barth undertook the necessary correction by finding his way to a new concept of analogy.[3]

From all that we have seen, it is certainly understandable that the emancipation of world that understands itself solely in terms of immanence, and hence the repudiation of a goal that lies beyond this world, is more natural, and will take place more radically, the more theological anthropology itself ignores the relation between time and eternity. Hardly anything has done more to provoke and produce secularization, and in the upshot full-blown secularism, than the docetic, de-secularized, and disembodied concept of the kingdom of God in the sphere of the Protestant churches.

c. Secularization as a Legitimate Child of Christianity (Gogarten)

Yet that is not the only impulse in this direction. Friedrich Gogarten in particular has rightly pointed out[4] that the secular understanding of the world derives from Christianity itself. Christ de-divinized and de-sacralized the world and thus made an objective understanding of it possible. A Hindu, one might say, is unable to study the anatomy of a cow because it is sacral and full of mana. An objective relation, which requires distance, is possible only when this numinous element vanishes from the world and things are seen as "mere" things. Only the demythologization of the world effected by

Christ produced the objectivity that has made modern developments in natural science and technology possible.

Christianity's relation to the technological revolution is like that of a father to a son who comes of age. Now that the son is an adult he can do one of two things. He can either administer his father's house as an adult or leave home, part from his father, and emancipate himself. Secularization as a form of adulthood is a legitimate consequence of Christianity. Secularism as a form of radical emancipation is the use of the freedom that has been achieved for revolt. It resembles the misuse of human freedom in the story of the fall.

This perverted relation to the true goal has an indelible character. For the emancipated world sets itself new goals and invents new meanings. Immanent parts of the world are blown up into the whole; the relative is absolutized. We see this in the new philosophies and ideologies in which individual areas of being are made a cosmic theme, whether spirit, or matter, or bios. Linguistically one may perceive absolutizings of this kind in words that end in "ism," e.g., idealism, materialism, biologism, structuralism, et cetera. What we have here are efforts to find surrogates for the lost basic relation. Recollection (*anamnesis*) that being is more than phenomenology and demands a point of reference is still present and active even in its perversion.

d. The Historical Beginning of Emancipation

Historically the process of emancipation begins with the Renaissance, when this world increasingly becomes an end in itself, not just an interim zone of decision, and humanity is accorded intrinsic worth. On this view humanity is seen to be divine, not absolutely so, for it is still human, but humanly divine. On this basis one can readily understand why the Renaissance has a regard for the individual person. Things were different for Gothic and Byzantine artists, who set their human figures against a golden background, thus relating them to heaven, to the glory of God. A radiance thus lay upon them and constituted their true being. Their being did not reside in their individuality but in this relation. External individuality was secondary to this. On icons the faces and drapings are stylized. Individual features and peculiarities would simply tempt us to look for the true essence in the wrong place. In Donatello or Mantegna or Van Eyck, however, the human figures are individuals with their own beauty or ugliness. A realistic approach is adopted in which humanity is shown in its relation to the present world and has meaning in itself, not with reference to something else.

Along these lines a Donatello can de-sacralize even his prophetic figures and present them as geniuses of flesh and blood. They are no longer subject to a transcendent calling in relation to which their bodily form is simply an indifferent vessel that is consumed and used by the calling. What fills them is the immanent passion of genius. They are transported from the sphere of the pneuma (*spirit*) to that of the psyche. It is worth noting in this regard that the masters flourishing at the height of the Renaissance, beginning with Leonardo da Vinci, cease to use the halo. It loses its significance in face of the new, this-worldly realism, for it is a sign of the transcendent reference.

The attitude to death changes as a result. Fear of death remains, of course, but it undergoes a decisive mutation. Previously, with a direct transcendent reference, it was fear of the Last Judgment. Now, however, it is fear of the ending of life, of corruptibility, and of an old age in which the ability to do things, to find pleasure in decision, and to enjoy life, is coming to a close.

II. THE FORMS OF THE UNDERSTANDING OF REALITY. FROM THEOLOGICAL TO PHILOSOPHICAL ANTHROPOLOGY

a. Ancient and Medieval Ontology.
Correspondence of the Divine and Human Logos

The trend toward this-worldliness or emancipation that we have noted manifests its deepest bases and impulses in the radical changes that we observe in philosophical cosmology and anthropology from the beginning of the modern era.

For antiquity, as for the medieval epoch, truth has a different meaning from that which it has for modern thinking under the influence of empiricism. For us saying that a thing is true always means a judgment on the quality of an insight and its appropriate expression. As a modern lexicon might put it, if a statement accurately reproduces actual relations or the actual state of affairs, then it may be regarded as true. Truth is viewed as the agreement between what is said and what is. Thus to say that something is true always involves evaluation of an act of cognition. The criterion of truth is the controllability of what is stated. Behind this understanding there stands, of course, the confidence inspired by empiricism that reality will assert itself over against our statements and falsify them if need be. The sun will bring it to light if what is said to be true is really false. Reality will add its confirmation if the claim to truth is justified.

In antiquity and the Middle Ages, however, people dug deeper. They would have found the modern criterion of truth rather superficial, pointing out that it refers only to the external symptoms of truth and not to its essence.

When we investigate its essence, we come up against the fundamental philosophical problem why there can be truth at all. The answer, as we see already in Stoicism, is that there has to be built into the world an analogy between our thinking and the being encircled by it. Only because being is thinkable can it be thought at all and become the theme of true knowledge.

The correspondence thus presupposed between thinking and being can be assumed only on one condition, namely, that there rules in being the logos that is active in reason too and makes it receptive to itself. There has to be agreement, then, between the noetic logos (that of knowledge) and the ontic logos (that of being). An insight is then natural that is found in medieval Scholasticism, e.g., in Anselm, namely, that God has granted his own Logos to both being and the organs of knowledge. God is the prototype of the thinker. He creates being in thinking it. Thinking and making are one and the same in him. Hence created being is thought being that everywhere bears traces of the divine intellect.

When we look at things in this way, there open up new perspectives on truth that are really very old and have simply been forgotten by us. In this light a thing is true when it agrees with this thought being, with the Logos imparted to the world. This is what Anselm means, for instance, when he can call a thing true, a part of being, and not just a judgment on it. A thing is true when it is what it ought to be, when it corresponds to the way it was thought, to the way God conceived it in his own thinking. Fire, as Anselm might say, is true and right when it burns and warms, for this is what it was meant to do.

This has several implications, of which two are of particular interest to us because they come almost as a shock to our mentality and have a direct relation to anthropology.

For one thing, the word "truth" has here a bearing on ethical action. We naturally draw back at this point because today the alternatives of correct and incorrect or good and bad are alone made matters of evaluation. How can an action be called true? In Anselm the matter is perfectly clear. An action is "true" when there is agreement between goal and deed, between what ought to be and what is willed. This agreement is present when the act fits into the order of being. This order is in some sense an institutional expression of the Logos of being that is itself a reflection of God as absolute Spirit. Only thus can we understand Anselm's thesis that the good and the true are one and the same: "Everything that is, is one, true, and good." Truth, then, is not a trait that is restricted to certain judgments and confirmed by their incontestability or their conformity to reality. It can also be predicated of things or acts to the degree that they correspond to being and order and consequently are what they ought to be.

This leads to the second implication, which at a first glance seems even stranger to us.

Today the term "truth" seems to be the opposite only of "untruth." The word "half-truth" is an ironical one that simply indicates the possibility of being misled by an appearance of truth. In reality there are no intermediate stages between true and untrue, no gradations of truth.

For the same reason there is no comparative for "true" that might enable us to say that statement "a" is more true than statement "b." Like the words "married" and "pregnant," "true" is not capable of any enhancement. Affirmation and denial are the only possibilities.

But things are different in Anselm.[5] In him there are different grades of truth. These are related to the position of a thing or person or act in the order of being. They are more true or less true to the extent that they are closer or less close to their goal. In mineralogy, for example, crystal is more true than quartz and quartz more true than flint, for crystal can create forms, break up light, et cetera, to a higher degree, thus coinciding with its purpose, whereas the purpose is still unrecognizable in flint. Similarly acts and decisions are true when they actualize their meaning and value and subject themselves to the supreme value.

In this *higher* context, as we may quietly put it, the modern, formally cognitive concept of truth occurs only as a partial instance. For according to Anselm a statement is true when it does justice to its purpose and reality just as they are. A modern mathematician can certainly understand that formulas might be simpler or more complex, more elegant or more intricate, more pregnant or more prolix. But he could hardly copy Anselm and equate these comparatives with more or less true. For Anselm, however, statements, too, may be in the form of flint or crystal.

We can sum up as follows the older view of truth of which Anselm is an example.

At the head stands the primal creative Spirit, the Logos, who as truth in being produces all other truths. Then follows the truth of things that is called into being by this creative Spirit and localized in the order of being. The truth of things produces the truths of thought and action. But these truths are not the cause of any other truth. Thought is human in the sense of our prior anthropology inasmuch as it refers itself and the thinker to their final purpose and meaning and to him who gives them meaning. Only when thought does this, and thus orients itself to its final purpose, is it truth itself, and thus able to recognize the truth of things and their place in the order of being.

Clearly thought that understands itself in terms of its function in the order of being can give a proof of God and anchor faith in the intellect (faith seeking understanding). But strictly this is not a "proof." For proofs involve a movement from uncertainty to certainty. For Anselm, however, there is never any uncertainty about God, as the introductory prayer to his *Proslogion* shows. Anselm already knows God in faith and simply wants to make the certainty of faith a certainty of understanding so that his reason, too, may have a part in worship. Prior faith in the creative Spirit or absolute Spirit implies faith in the being thought and created by him. This faith in the being posited by God also carries with it faith in the order of being which is oriented to God and which establishes the basis, goal, and meaning of our thought and action. When thought is understood thus, so long as it functions within its own principle of correctness, it cannot fail to come up against the divine basis of being. Human beings can thus follow the thought of the Logos, the meaning of being, and will finally come up against themselves, because their own logos, their reason, is a thought of the primal thought. They are, as it were, chips off the cosmic or spermatic Logos. Thus the cosmic Logos recognizes itself in the mirror of human reason. We know how Hegel adopted this idea and made it the center of his philosophy of spirit.

Anselm's thinking—and the same applies to other examples of ancient ontology—rests on a presupposition that is believed and not objectifiable, i.e., on the axiomatic correspondence of thought and being. He is not just wanting to play theoretical games or to indulge in speculative fantasy in trying to comprehend the incomprehensible. He is driven by a basic question that we have largely forgotten, namely, why and with what right we can speak about truth at all and give an answer of this fundamental type. Only those who are superficial enough to take the mere symptoms of truth for its essence, e.g., the agreement of statement and reality, or the absence of contradiction, will fail to understand this venture of thought and faith, this essay in metaphysics, as we might call it.

b. The Modern Breakthrough in Descartes and Vico: Centrality of Humanity

1. CONDITIONAL MODERNITY OF DESCARTES.
HIS RESERVATIONS ABOUT HISTORICISM;
THE BURDEN OF THE GREEK LEGACY

The radical departure from this grand conception that binds together thought and being, humanity and the cosmos, as the embodied thoughts of God, takes place with Giambattista Vico (1668–1744). Even though the theological reference is retained, especially in his idea of providence, it is on humanity that his searchlight is focused. His *New Science* (*Scienza Nuova*, 1st edition 1725) initiates an anthropology that increasingly replaces the older theology and carries clear traces of an emancipated view of humanity.

Three quarters of a century earlier, Descartes (1596–1650) had taken a first step toward an anthropocentric view of being.[6] To find ultimate certainty, Descartes questions everything that had been regarded as self-evident. Are we really sure that the external world in which we move, the trees and houses which we see, do actually exist and are not just dreams? Might not the values that we take for granted be just suggestions of common sense and tradition instead of having properly established validity?

The purpose of this methodical doubt is to find something that cannot be shaken, a basis of absolute certainty, behind everything that falls victim to it and proves to be vulnerable. But the only part of being that cannot be doubted is the identity of the self. With my critical thinking I may doubt all else, but it is evident and indisputable that I am the one who thus thinks and doubts, that I am posited as a subject in the act of thought.

From this certainty about the I, this anthropological fact, Descartes then achieves certainty about the existence of the outside world and the existence of God. He does so by a process of deduction that uses the ontological schema already observed in Anselm. Both presuppose a relation between the I and God. But the priorities in the relation differ. In Anselm certainty about God comes first. Deductions from this follow because the intellect is to share in faith as well as the heart. Certainty about God is the first stage. Understanding of one's own identity is achieved from it. I can see *that* I am, and *who* I am, only in the light of God who sustains all relations and gives rise to the nexus of being. In Descartes, however, the converse is true. The I achieves certainty about itself as the subject of thought. It is thus the axiomatic starting point for all other certainties. These are achieved out of uncertainty. Even certainty about God is secondary in this sense. It is not grounded in itself but is given by certainty about the I.

Descartes, then, took a decisive step toward the anthropocentric thinking of the modern age. He shattered the theological architecture of the Anselmic world-structure, even though he used the same materials, to build instead a temple to humanity.

Yet we still find in Descartes' thought some obstacles preventing a complete breakthrough to the modern understanding of life and the world. This understanding is characterized by empirical realism insofar as history plays a dominant part in it and is normative for our being in the world. Today we do not regard institutions and values as metaphysically sanctioned facts that have fallen from heaven and that we have to accept. We see that they have developed historically. Hence we do not grant them absolute validity. Ernst Troeltsch was undoubtedly right when he equated historicism and relativism. We are very much interested in the question of the forces at work in history. Do human beings themselves make history? Is a world-spirit really actualizing some rational conception in what seem on the surface to be the contingencies of history? Do material and economic relationships constitute the basis of the historical process? What lies behind the attempt to solve this question is not metaphysical curiosity but a pragmatic concern to shape the world, to achieve mastery over the earth, to subjugate the driving forces of history, to make possible their manipulation.

But there is no sign of this type of historical thinking in Descartes. For all the modernity and anthropocentricity of his philosophy, he shared the ancient prejudice against history that may be found among the Greeks—the prejudice that history is not a proper subject of science, that it represents a dimension of being in which the question of truth has neither purpose nor answer. In the search for absolute certainty there is no place, then, for knowledge based on sensory experience and historical tradition. Tradition and the senses are sources of permanent deception. We cannot possibly find truth in them. The final basis of certainty that Descartes discovered, the thinking I (*cogito, ergo sum*), does not lead back to history and its contingency and delusions. From the I and its ideas one can get back to the physical world only with the help of the mathematical ideas that determine it. Only in this way can the true language of nature be heard and truth found. In nature, then, and not in history!

In this nonmodern caveat against history one may see that Descartes was trapped in a long tradition that derived from the Greek world and lived on under the cover of the Christian West. The Greek world could not produce any real philosophy of history because the contingency of historical events did not seem to yield any truth and could not, then, be the content of genuine philosophical reflection. Truth could be sought only in the calculability or rationality of nature—at any rate when it was being sought in the empirical world.

The drive to see truth in what is uniform and not in what is contingent and changing—this is well symbolized by Plato's world of timeless ideas—led the great Greek historians to look for laws and continuities in history and to treat them in analogy to the uniformities of nature. Thus Herodotus finds in history the "law" that human pride brings down divine punishment. Thucydides is much more radical in this pursuit of uniformity when he finds the historical process to be dominated not only by objective factors in politics and economics but also by impulses and passions, i.e., by subjective, psychological emotions.

The movement of history is thus the movement of cosmic occurrence in which we can discern the same driving forces through every change. Plato's remark in his *Georgias* is relevant here when he says that a mathematical relation (resting on timeless laws) rules between gods and humans. Thucydides thinks that regard for the timeless laws of historical movement gives a better view of what happens, and not only that, but also of what will happen, since it will always be in accord with human nature. To see the timeless in time makes prognosis possible and thus enables us to plan for the future.

In broad outline this is still the view of history that influences the reservations of Descartes. It may mean on the one side that history is simply contingent and hence is no part of the orderly course of the cosmos and is declared to be irrelevant to the question of truth. Or it may mean on the other hand that history is integrated into the cosmos but has to be seen in analogy to processes that are controlled by natural laws. Either way history is robbed of its force and discredited scientifically.

2. VICO'S INITIATION OF THE NEW VIEW
OF HISTORY AND HUMANITY

It was the great philosopher of law and history, Giambattista Vico, who made the real breakthrough to modern historicism and a decisive break with the earlier tradition. As Karl Löwith rightly says, he was too far in advance of his age to have any direct influence. The bell that from the standpoint of intellectual history tolled the beginning of the modern epoch in his *Scienza Nuova* can be heard far better by us who hear it in retrospect than it could by his contemporaries.

For him history—and with it anthropology—is a possible and privileged object of science, whereas the natural sciences are, from the noetic standpoint, burdened by a lack of truth. This is a truly revolutionary and shocking reversal of the usual movement in the search for truth. But as in almost all academic revolutions, so here there is no radical or total rejection of what precedes. On the contrary, Vico accepts much that is normative in tradition, tries to borrow legitimately from what is universally acknowledged, and then goes on to make new and unexpected inferences from it.

Thus he begins with an idea for which, formally at least, he can appeal to Aristotle. This made it philosophically credit-worthy in his age. The idea is that real knowledge of something is present when it is understood to be caused and its cause or basis is known. The revolutionary conclusion that Vico draws from this is as follows.

If knowledge is a knowledge of causes and we can speak of truth only as we can establish these, then properly and basically we know only what we ourselves have done. We do justice to the Aristotelian equation of truth and the knowledge of causes only when we ourselves are the cause of something. Since history is the sphere of human achievement and it is here that we function as causes, we can attain to true knowledge in the sphere of history as in no other sphere. There can be no greater certainty than where we ourselves do things and narrate them, as Vico says in his *New Science*.

Over against the certainty that can be attained in history as the extended autobiography of the human race, the certainty granted in the natural sciences is suddenly seen to be defective. Have we ourselves brought the physical cosmos into being? Not at all! Since we are not its cause, then, it is largely hidden from us. At any rate, it is more hidden than our own history, which is revealed to us hermeneutically as "spirit of our spirit."

From this standpoint, even mythically veiled prehistory is accessible to us. Remotest antiquity may be wrapped in a night of complete shadow, yet still the eternal light of truth shines there as well, leaving us in no doubt that this historical and civilized world was caused by human beings. Hence its principles can and must be found in modifications of our own human spirit, as he says again in the *New Science*.

Precisely in this concern of Vico to show that even the shadows of the most distant past may prove to have more truth than the exact sciences, one may see the far-reaching implications that begin to open up. I shall describe the most important of these as follows:

First, the facticity that the Greek world despised is now worth knowing, can be known, and is decked out with the privilege of truth. In Anselm the cosmos that God conceived and made was the object of truth. This truth consisted of knowing the Logos content of the world; facts were not its content, but the reference of facts to the Logos. In Descartes the ontic givenness of the thinking I was truth of the first rank; deduced truths were thus secondary to it. In both Anselm and Descartes one form of being was the truth; whether being as a conceived and made totality, or being focused on the existing subject of thought. One might say, then, that something is true because it has a share in being. In Vico, however, historical facticity is privileged to be the content of possible truth. We know it and its cause because we ourselves are causes. Hence the thesis now obtains that something is true as and because it is made or done by us.

Second, if Vico lights up mythical prehistory with the light of truth even though an objective knowledge of facts is largely debarred in this sphere, he has the courage to do this because he has found a new and modern form of knowledge that is familiar to us from hermeneutics, which knows not only a truth that is disclosed in the grasping of causes but also knows, as we have seen already, a truth of understanding. Understanding is present when something reveals itself to us that is related to us, e.g., when we encounter another personal life that affects our own personality. This is precisely what Vico means when he says that we may find the principles of the prehistorical world in modifications of our own human spirit. There is thus an analogy between prehistory and us that makes it intelligible. This approach of Vico is in fact followed up in Bultmann's attempt at de-mythologization and Carl G. Jung's interpretation of myths. Even though Vico does not use the term "understanding,"[7] it is evident that he is entering the field of hermeneutics and is thus breaking through to new and modern aspects of world-experience in this respect too. Humanity comprehends history because history derives from it. One has a sense of the many implications of this thesis. It proclaims a historicizing of the understanding of reality which at the same time triggers historical relativism and all its incalculable philosophical consequences. The modern age is the story of these implications.

Vico himself does not go so far. Even though anthropology becomes for him the key science—humanity being the cause of what is authentically true as historical fact—his anthropology is still theologically based.

This may be seen, for example, in his restriction of the human knowledge of truth to the knowledge of history. The world of nature is accessible only to divine insight. For God is the one who has made nature and therefore he alone can see it as his work. Even when Vico allows that we humans can know history as "spirit of our spirit," this does not mean for him that history is regarded as our creation. No, when we treat the historical past as a kind of objectification and echo of our own spirit, this is possible only because our spirit is privileged to have a part in the divine Spirit and is thus put in a position to see in history the providence of God, the thoughts of this divine Spirit. The meaning of history is manifest to our spirit to the degree that we look to providence.

Connected with this is the fact that Vico rejects a conclusion that might possibly be drawn from this anthropological outlook, namely, that philosophy can replace theology as the representative of the human spirit. He expressly opposes the thesis of the rationalistic philosopher of history Polybius (second century B.C.) that religion is unnecessary when philosophers undertake to explain the world, and Tyche is manifest as the organizing force in world events. In opposition Vico argued that philosophers did not fall from heaven but emerged from groups that were there before them—groups that could not have arisen without religion. Belief in providence alone can relate us to the orders of family, tribe, and state. Only when these institutions are transparent and let the divine planning that is operative in them shine through, can they bind us together.

Although Vico seems to make the decisive breakthrough to an apparently anthropocentric view of history, or at least to one that works in this direction, we cannot speak of real emancipation or secularization in his case. In spite of his principle that things are true and perceptible only for those who caused them, humanity is not for him the lord of the history made by it. His concept of providence gives things a very different aspect. Humanity meets itself in history only because it is built into it as the agent of providence. Only for this reason can it perceive the earlier self-manifestations of providence.

That the path of intellectual history is not yet at its end may easily be guessed from the way in which Vico's understanding points. The breakthrough to the emancipated secularism of the modern age will spread and deepen—as did in fact happen. In Vico himself the idea of providence is still a barrier, though a weak one. Inasmuch as this idea is dubious, and humanity begins to see that it can master historical facts even when they are understood in self-reposing finitude, the establishment of an emancipated secularity results. The religious link in Vico is a very thin thread that will soon be broken, and is actually broken. Then humanity encounters only itself; outside it, there is no Thou.

c. Consequences: Humanity's Control of the World in Karl Marx; The Eighth Day of Creation

1. THE TRUTH OF WHAT CAN BE DONE

The path has led from the Logos of being to fact, to the human world, to humanity encountering itself in its this-worldliness. But this path to emancipation and secularity is not yet at an end. The name of Karl Marx denotes a new turn. If Vico said that truth relates only to what is done by us, that binding statements can be made only about that of which we ourselves are the cause, the Marxist position might be stated in the thesis that a thing is true to the degree that it can and should be done, that what can be done is true.[8] We have in view here the well-known saying that philosophers only interpret the world in different ways, but the real need is to change it (11th Thesis against Feuerbach). If we wanted to alter this saying a little to incorporate what we have seen thus far, we might put it thus: Up to now philosophers in their contemplation of the world have started with an immanent logos,[9] but we must now start by bringing the logos into the world by our acts. We must rescue the world from the non-logos of its alienation and make it into what it means to be as our logos.

By truth, then, we are no longer to understand the truth of being (the logos-content) or the documented truth of the facts that make up our history, but the truth that is to be brought into the world. Truth is thus related to the possibility of changing the world, to what can be made or done. Its characteristics are thus pragmatic. It is the truth of interests, ideological truth, even though this carries with it an inner contradiction and means that we have to put the word "truth" in quotes.

The result is that not only does the ancient idea of a cosmic logos necessarily seem to be a metaphysical ghost to the ideological pragmatist, but doubt is also cast on the facts of history. This happens in two ways. First, turning to the past kills off openness to what can be done and is being done. Fixation on facts (*facta*) means missing the future (*facienda*). Second, the truth of historical facts is fragile. Concern for accuracy, ruthless investigation of what really took place (Ranke), cannot alter the impression that we cannot really recapture the past, that as we look at it we see ourselves, that we are never without presuppositions and never will be. We allow specific interests to help in the formation of our view of history. We cannot determine the facts of history in the absolute sense that the norm of truth contains within itself as a claim.

To the degree that the view of what can be done is distorted, we are thus compelled to abandon the field of history and turn to spheres in which the postulate of truth as what can be done finds satisfaction. If what can be done becomes the criterion of truth, there seems to be a possibility of exact truth only where something can be repeated in a controlled experiment. The method of natural science thus acquires the prestige of truth, along with its application in technology. Both of these make what can be done the foreseeable possibility of shaping and actualizing the future. Homo faber now becomes the creative God who takes over the government of the world and initiates the eighth day of creation.

Finally, then, humanity itself confronts a world of its own creation which is its alter ego. And we know—it should be inserted—how increasingly sinister this world is becoming. To the degree that humanity seeks to be the creator and hopes to shape a new form of itself and thus become a self-creator, it alienates itself. Its world, within the boundaries of the belief in what can be done, gives rise increasingly to anxiety. One need only think of the possible results of thermonuclear energy, or the possibility of manipulating genes, or the threat to the environment, to arrive at the urgent question whether this world that is in the hands of Homo faber is not on the way to ruin and can perish like a veil of dust in the cosmos. Are we not confronted by the questionability of this world that we have synthetically constructed? Do we not find in its secondary systems a macrocosmic objectification of our own questionability? Is not the microcosm of our own heart magnified here?

If we get this impression that humanity is seeking its own truth in radical self-actualization with the help of a world under its own control, then the vision is distressingly close that Werner Heisenberg once expressed when he said that with the apparently unlimited extension of its material power humanity is like a captain whose ship is so strongly built of steel and iron that the magnetic compass will point only to the ship itself and not to the north. With such a ship one can no longer reach the desired port but can only journey on at the mercy of currents and the wind.

Why is this world so sinister? Why are we self-alienated? Perhaps because we are sinister to ourselves, because the fall is behind us and we have betrayed our origin. This origin lies in our relation to God as the ground of our being. This ground of our being put us in the position of being able to entrust ourselves to being, because higher thoughts were thought about us, and in the design of the world we were the product of one whose gracious purpose was known to us.

But I am anticipating a little. As the result of our discussion the following points may be asserted.

If truth is seen in the logos that I, a human being, have to import into the world and actualize by changing the world, then I reject any hope of finding this logos as something given on the ground of being. I must make of the unensouled material of this world whatever it is to be according to my own hopes and wishes and ideas—or interests! Hence I can meet this world only as one who acts. I have to assert myself in it and manipulate it.

Here again we find a weakening of the transcendent relationship. Perhaps *homo christianus* prior to the Renaissance, when asked how to achieve life and meet the world, would simply have replied, "By doing God's will. If I seek first God's kingdom, other things will be added to me, including what step to take next, the imagination that sets aims to be achieved, where to live and what companions to have." Within the transcendent reference my relation to the world is primarily only an automatic by-product of my real activity. What is essential is my relationship to the one (Matthew 6:33). The New Testament imperatives that set goals for me are all grounded, then, in preceding indicatives, in the statement that I *am* established on a new basis of life and that everything else will result from this existing backward connection.

2. THE LOGOS IMPARTED TO THE WORLD, NOT SOUGHT IN IT

When this sustaining relationship is weakened, the whole inquiry changes. I no longer have to ask how I can entrust the world's problem to God and thus receive my own tasks and find the truth of my destiny in the course of this entrusting. I now have to ask what I must do to shape the unformed and meaningless world on my own initiative and impart meaning to it.

To know how to act and change the world along these lines, I have first to know how the world acts on me, i.e., what are the laws of its course and how it moves in them. Is it dominated, as Niccolò

Machiavelli thought, by the morally neutral forces of *virtú* and *fortuna?* If so, I must assert myself in it as pure and amoral energy. Or is it the material, economic substructure that determines the course of history? If so, to act historically, I must examine this substructure and bring it under my control. I can change the world only if I first diagnose its substructure and thus create a presupposition for influencing it strategically and tactically.

This was the question of Karl Marx. I can have freedom to affect the world only if I exploit the trend of history and swim with its current. But to do this I have to know the current and the real forces behind it. A mere proclamation of freedom without a knowledge of the possibilities of having an impact, and without insight into the material that has to be influenced, will necessarily be an illusion. For Marx, then, middle-class postulates of freedom are naive and are not to be taken seriously. Those who do not know the waves on which they are swimming, or the currents that carry them, may have a desire for freedom, but they are driven along helplessly, mere playthings of the elements, which they do not understand.

Thus Marx takes over from Hegel the definition of freedom as "insight into necessity." Only those who know the ineluctability of historical processes can enter into them, influence them, and exploit them without being delivered up to the unknown and tilting futilely at windmills.

The goal of freedom as thus defined is to bring the logos into the world in the name of the dogma of what can be done, and thus to impart to the world the ideologically desired meaning. What is proclaimed thus with the assurance of a supposed scientifically supported insight, and hence claimed to be a realism far removed from the logos-dreams of the ancient metaphysics of being, ends in blind faith. For the meaning that is to be brought into history and actualized in it is not at all subject to the insight that might be claimed for the disclosure of historical processes. The fulfillment of the goal of history is still a matter of promise. The eschatological state when the conflict between existence and essence, between freedom and necessity, between individual and species, is at an end, when humanity is naturalized and nature humanized with the formation of social organs in us—this state can never be achieved. The logos of a final historical state—a logos that is oriented to the future and that is to be fashioned by us—stands outside all experience, and is thus an object of faith, in exactly the same way as the Logos that was previously embedded in being. Thus the establishment of a closed world for which we are responsible and to which our truth is entrusted seems to lead to a dead end and an insoluble self-contradiction. On this view we constantly cross the boundaries that we ourselves have drawn and unwittingly and unwillingly allow a place for transcendence.

3. THE THEOLOGICAL ENCOUNTER WITH THIS VIEW OF THE WORLD

Far-reaching theological questions arise here. In abbreviated form one might formulate them thus. The extreme this-worldly reference and the related dominion of humanity over logos give the impression of a complete loss of transcendence and the presence of naked secularism (though our concluding sentences disturb this impression). With this impression, short-sighted thinking might feel driven to the postulate that we must go back and correct this false routing. That would be reactionary. It is an impossible attempt to reverse the wheel of history. It would entail an absurd effort to liquidate the empirical interest of the modern world, its curiosity about material things, with all the knowledge and technical mastery that this has brought. As though we could put out the light that has been shed on being! No, we have to live with this light, and even those who repress it cannot break free from it but are related to it in a negative mode.

Theology, which is particularly affected here, finds in its own field a striking example of the irreversibility of intellectual and spiritual processes. The historico-critical investigations of the nineteenth century shattered a naive and simple relation to the Bible. For those who are open to these investigations and do not repress them, it has forever become impossible to be passive and uncritical consumers of what is imparted and demanded in this book. Here, too, the objection was and is quickly raised that a threat is posed to faith, that we have to avoid this threat, and that we can do this only by treating the critical breakthrough as though it had never happened, repressing it by a retreat into what were thought to be happier times. Even in saying this we put our finger already on the dubious element in this attitude. But there is a further point that what is regarded as a critically destructive invasion which seems to destroy the relation to the Bible is not in reality a negative thing at all. On the contrary, the fact that I must now cease to be a passive recipient, putting the question of truth in a critically feeble manner and simply being preached at instead of entering into dialogue with the biblical message, means that I attain to a deeper dimension of faith. I no longer take things on trust. I have to inquire into the binding content of truth that must be separated from its time-bound husk. (Luther himself did this.) Furthermore this critical research, while it may seem to be merely destructive, opens up previously unknown riches of the biblical message. It brings out the contours of the individual witnesses and their relations to one another. It forces us to seek the unity of their witness for all their individual variations and multiple wealth. New dimensions come to light and an incomparably greater fullness (*pleroma*) of content is revealed.

The situation is the same with the breakthrough to modern empiricism and the consequent orientation to this present world. This is irreversible and even in the name of what seems to be a betrayal of the transcendent relation it must not be regarded as mere apostasy and negation. What is true of the historico-critical investigation of Scripture is true here as well. New theological tasks arise out of this new turn in the understanding of humanity and reality. Theology must now begin by interpreting reality as thus discovered and experienced in terms of its eternal aspect. In so doing it will enter into competition with other interpretations, including the thesis that truth is what can be done. It must accept this competition, trusting that the evidence in favor of its own understanding of truth will prevail. In the modern situation of pluralism it cannot compete merely by marking off its own position from that of others, e.g., by saying that what it stands for is the truth that is divinely set in being, whereas what they stand for is the truth that is imparted to it. Delimitations are not dialogue. Dialogue demands that theology demonstrate the reality of the claim to truth that it makes by offering an open interpretation and cogent evidence.

Bonhoeffer was right when, following what Hugo Grotius (1583–1645) said about natural law, he defined our modern adulthood as knowing reality "as though there were no God." Those who do research in physics, biology, and chemistry act on the heuristic principle that the world is a closed natural system, self-reposing immanence. They investigate the laws that rule this system and do not count on transcendent interventions. In the sense of the French physicist Pierre de Laplace (1749–1827) they thus abandon the hy-

pothesis of God, at least as it might influence the methods and results of research.

Christian scholars follow the same course. Like their secular colleagues, they cannot use the hypothesis "God" to explain what they
cannot as yet understand and thus make God the warden of an asy-
lum for ignoramuses. Where that has happened—and it has—it has
led to the fatal embarrassment of continual retreat. As the gaps in
knowledge are closed, the place for the hypothesis has narrowed.
Hence it has had to be smuggled out of spheres in which an attempt
was made to retain it.

Our new question, then, is not how we can continue to think
naively as though nothing had happened but how we can learn to see
"before God" the newly perceived world that we cannot escape even
if we wanted to, and whose empirical reality we have to view in exactly the same way as everyone else. How can we learn to understand
God as the "ground of being," to use a phrase of Paul Tillich? How
can we find the transcendent reference of reality as we look at it in
this new way?

When Grotius used the words "as though there were no God," he
did not mean that the rational evidence of natural law and its independence of divine commands enables us to ignore the question of
God and treat it as outmoded. What he meant was that God has so
bound himself to his own order in natural law that this order would
be in force even if we were to assume—which we cannot do without
committing a serious offense—that there is no God. Grotius, then, is
not postulating an atheistic belief in immanence but extolling the
world as God's creation. What God has established is so good that it
would maintain its order without him and it is so inalterable that
God himself cannot alter it.

Here already we are on the frontier of the new age toward which
the new impulse in theological thinking is pressing. The undoubted
commitment to transcendence in Grotius does not prevent him from
ascribing to rational insight the competence to recognize truth, i.e.,
in this instance the validity of the norms of natural law. Grotius
even adopts a position in which he does not consider God but directs
his gaze on pure rationality with no religious commitment.

This position, however, is heuristically provisional. As regards the
reality at issue, i.e., that of natural law, a retreat to transcendence is
open. To extol the order of being that may be seen in it is to extol
the one who manifests himself in the establishment of this order.

We have a model here for the future putting of theological questions. They arise out of the encounter with reality and are attested and call for attestation in face of other encounters. We have already pointed out earlier what new tasks and goals are set for proclamation when this is the starting point.

III. MODELS OF THE NEW UNDERSTANDING OF REALITY FROM MEDICINE AND ITS ANTHROPOLOGY

a. Speculative and Mythological Medicine (*Aristotle, Hippocrates*)

I will now illustrate the theological and anthropological issues by a historical example taken from medicine. Medicine—and especially its history—can offer eloquent models for anthropology and its development. For the constant medical problem of the interrelation of body, soul, and spirit raises the general question of the unity and nature of human beings.[10] My task, then, is to show by this example of medical anthropology how the concern of the Renaissance for this world, interest in the biological phenomena, develops in such a way that there is not only a flight from the commitment to transcendence but also the emergence of totally *new theological* aspects.

In the Middle Ages prior to the empirical orientation of modern natural science, including medicine, the anthropology shaped by Aristotle held sway. This was not based on exact empirical observation, e.g., in anatomy and physiology, but concerned itself with metaphysical deductions. For us today, living in the age of exact natural science and empiricism, it is hard to grasp to what extent the doctors of this earlier period either did not observe nature at all or pressed their observations into the framework of empirically nonverifiable speculations.

When we nowadays define bodily "health," we answer along these lines: Health consists of the intactness and proper functioning of all our physical organs. Naturally this is not meant to be an exhaustive definition of a complex matter; my concern is only with the direction and approach, which differ from those taken in speculative medicine. Thus to be able to say that someone is "healthy," we have to know the function of organs such as the heart. Only when we know that all parts of the system are working together properly can we say that the person is healthy. We have to study life from an anatomical, physiological, and biochemical standpoint. The concept of "health" is the result of this kind of study.

But not so in Aristotle. To see the difference one need only consult his definitions of health in the Nichomachean Ethics. I will give a few examples without more detailed interpretation, for my purpose is merely to give an impression of the speculative style of his thinking and thus to bring out the difference from the empirically influenced science of today.

He calls health the logos in the soul and in the recognition of knowledge. Medical skill is described as the logos or form (*eidos*) of health. Logos and *eidos* are both metaphysical terms with an ontological reference.

The metaphysical background is even clearer when the normative concept of ethics, that of the "mean" (*mesothes*), is adduced to describe health. The role of this concept of the "true mean" in ethics is that it defines the essence of virtue. Virtue can be determined only as one avoids both too much and too little. It thus resides in the mean. Thus courage lies between foolhardiness, which is too much, and cowardice, which is too little. The mean, expressing balance, is thus a synonym for righteousness (*dikaiosyne*), which is above parties and thus stands once again in the middle.

Both terms occur in medicine for moderation. What we might describe today as the medicine of sport offers pregnant examples of the golden mean in Greek antiquity. The Greeks abhor bulging biceps just as much as they do underdeveloped muscles. In modern terms, they would dislike specimens from a body-building school just as much as they would bespectacled intellectuals. All such polarizations of humanity miss the true mean and are thus unhealthy. For the Greeks gymnastics is the training designed to prevent unhealthy one-sidedness and to achieve moderation, the harmony of body and soul. Moderation is the aim of the gymnasium. Its work is not restricted to the bodily sphere but extends to the intellectual as well. The postulate of the golden mean always relates to the whole person. In this sense health is indivisible.

Only when this is clear to us can we turn to the true secret of speculative medicine and see how it differs in orientation from modern empiricism.

The form of health, the golden mean, cannot be known therapeutically in the practice of medicine if it is not known already prior to all empirical observation, if there is not already a concept of the mean in the mind of the physician. In Kantian terms one might put this as follows.

The concept of the mean is not won a posteriori from experience but is part of the a priori structure of my consciousness which makes experience possible and precedes it. Aristotle thinks in this way because of his ontology. Form (*eidos*) and matter (*hyle*) are originally separate for him. Pure form, not yet embodied in matter, exists in shadowy unreality. Naked matter, not yet formed, is without essence. The two look for one another and are driven toward self-fulfillment by a kind of eros. Pure form yearns for material fulfillment and matter for fulfillment in form. Only when the two meet do they become "something" and give rise to things in the world of experience. Because we ourselves are formed matter, we can know things that have the same structure of being. Like can be known and understood by like.

At this point we can see what it means that the transcendental presupposition of all experience lies in our consciousness and its structure.

I could know nothing—neither table nor street nor tree—if the formed character of things did not give them their identity, and our own formed character did not enable our consciousness to identify and know them, thus showing itself to be the given condition of all knowledge. A hare might settle on a freeway and give birth to young there because it cannot identify the freeway as such and can form no concept of it. It sees only a clear space, a kind of forest glade, instead of a traffic artery.

Because human beings, or doctors, have an innate concept of righteousness and the mean, and because their form, their picture of what they ought to be, is already formed in their consciousness prior to all experience, they can know a priori what health is. They thus bring prior knowledge with them when they begin to deal with objects in the world of experience such as human bodies and their ailments. In other words, they do not know the harmonious balance of the whole organism from anatomical and physiological studies. They already have the concept of the formed, functioning totality in their consciousness. They know the form of the whole prior to all experience. The logos (or reason) in nature that they find outside is recognizable only because the same logos already has a bridgehead in their consciousness. This is what Aristotle means when he says that health is the logos in the soul and in the recognition of knowledge.

No wonder that here the theses in a medical textbook are not based on experience (like those in the textbooks of modern, empirically grounded medicine) but are deduced from concepts and put together from analogies. Doctors in this sense are speculative philosophers rather than natural scientists, just as earlier they were mythologizers who found in sickness and health the working of the disharmony or harmony of cosmic forces.

This is plain even in so significant a physician as Hippocrates, who did study nature. I will just give a few sentences in illustration, namely, those in which he speaks about the sacred illness of epilepsy. The distinction from modern descriptions of the illness, which always track down the biological or psychological cause, is striking. This so-called sacred illness, he says, derives from the same influences as others. (He thus seems to want to de-mythologize it and fence it off from superstitious interpretations, but he himself also uses mythical and cosmic imagery.) It originates in coming and going, in cold and heat, in the winds in their restless and ever-changing movement. (This is meant to explain the spasms.) These are all divine, and hence this sickness is no more divine than others. For all illnesses are both divine and human.

Now we should not get the idea that this mythological and speculative medicine, which represents all science and anthropology at that time, is so primitive that physicians looked only at themselves, consulted only their own reason, and went through the world completely blind to its phenomenology. To a large degree they were also observers and recognized many empirical and statistical relations. But the decisive point is that they did not gain their knowledge empirically but regarded what they observed empirically only as a confirmation of what they already knew a priori, of what came to them from the link with the cosmos. Naturally high temperatures are a symptom of sickness. But why? Not because they are a symptom of some somatic disturbance, e.g., an infection, but because the mean or balance of normal bodily warmth is upset. Being too cold and too hot are forms of disturbance parallel to foolhardiness and cowardice in ethics.

Thus the speculative approach does not prevent the observing of phenomena and the collecting of experiences. But these can have only secondary rank. They can only be confirmatory. I know the logos of health from other sources than the empirical world.

b. The Shock of the Empiricist Revolution

1. THE POSTULATE OF THE ABSENCE OF PRESUPPOSITIONS AND THE PRIMACY OF FACT OVER INTERPRETATION

I do not think we wasted our time reflecting a little about the shape of ancient thought. We have to feel our way into it and not just summarize it if we are to realize what an indescribably shattering break was involved when people turned to the present world of experience at the time of the Renaissance. In the preceding speculative and mythological periods there could be an unbroken unity of the consciousness and all the faculties. Theologians, philosophers, physicians, and natural scientists, when developing their concepts, could all use the same metaphysically oriented methods and draw on the same sources. But today it is different. We observe and probe and discover the laws of the immanent nexus of being. And suddenly the phenomena that we observe block our path. They will not fit into the prefabricated order, into the patterns suggested by metaphysics.

So long as people observed life in the name of speculative prejudgments, they could continue in accordance with the principle of Christian Morgenstern that nothing can be that ought not to be. They knew in advance what ought to be and what ought not to be. They were thus forced to contest or ignore anything that did not fit into this framework. But we can no longer do this. The spell of speculative prejudgments has been broken. We begin to wonder.

Thus we no longer accept the prejudgment—partly based on theology—that the sun has to go around the earth because Christ is the center of the universe and he did his work on this earth. Nicolaus Copernicus and Galileo studied the heavens, made some exact calculations, and revolutionized astronomy. This had to be an unparalleled shock. If we today laugh in superior fashion at the trial of Galileo by the Inquisition, which was the result of this shock, we simply show not only that we are blind to the problem of the nonsynchronization of discovery and the philosophical handling of discovery, but also that we are gravely lacking in imagination.

We shall now try to formulate more strictly what took place and how it profoundly affects our modern theological and anthropological inquiry. In so doing, we shall also consider some of the theological implications.

Since observation of the phenomena of this world has begun, and the question has become what *is* rather than what ought to be (for speculative reasons), two fundamental tasks have developed that determine the modern concept of science, including theology, and involve a radical break with all that preceded, thus ushering in the "modern" world.

First, the postulate has arisen that we must conduct all our studies and calculations with a complete absence of presuppositions. This involves a readiness not to want to know in advance what ought to be and may be, but to examine being realistically with no conditions and without regard for metaphysical losses. This readiness carries with it an openness to possible surprises. It also involves a readiness to question traditions, to put the knife to one's own roots (Nietzsche).

Absence of presuppositions thus becomes the axiom of all modern science, or, if it cannot be attained, as in anthropology, then reflection on presuppositions. Marxism will not allow any questioning of its axiomatic presuppositions or any reflection on them. It thus discredits its own claim to be scientific. Theology reflects on its presuppositions (of faith). It thus has a scientific side.

In our consideration of the understanding of history we have already stated that hermeneutical presuppositions are unavoidable in a human science such as history. The self-understanding that we bring with us has an essential bearing on our radius of action, on our approach, and on the selection and arrangement of phenomena. Thus the threatening swamp of subjectivism can be avoided only if we direct conscious criticism not only on the objects of our study but also on ourselves and our presuppositions. This applies in every area that has anthropological relevance. We are too close to the objects of this discipline not to be burdened with secret premises. If actual examples are desired, one need only think of the debates about homosexuality, in which social, moral, religious, and instinctive prejudgments stage a macabre meeting.[11]

Second, we have the task of interpreting what is discovered, of asking what it means. Thus when humans are found to lack instincts, what does this imply? We might say with Herder, and more recently Gehlen, that only through this lack is freedom possible, and with it civilization. Thus Goethe argues that animals are taught by instinct, whereas humans teach their instincts. Here we are not assuming (as people did earlier) that we know in advance what the cosmos means, what its final purpose is, and can thus postulate how it has to be structured. We are taking the opposite course, first examining the world and establishing what it is, and only then putting the question of its meaning. Interpretation—at any rate in terms of the postulate and the intention—comes only when the facts have been established. It is no longer a premise.

2. NO METAPHYSICAL PRESUPPOSITIONS BUT OPENNESS TO METAPHYSICAL DEDUCTIONS.

THE RELATION BETWEEN EXPERIENCE AND MEANING

A very challenging fact emerges here, namely, that in the anthropological sphere not merely the view of things but their interpretation in particular can vary widely, so that the universality of exact sciences such as mathematics cannot be attained. Many illustrations might be given (we have already alluded to some). I will choose only one which fits very well into our present project.

From the standpoint of interpretation the result of the empiricist revolution does not have to be that we must all be "secularists" and that we are confronted only by a world stripped of all transcendence. Metaphysical inferences do not have to fall away with the loss of metaphysical and theological presuppositions. So as not to be abstract, I will give an illustration.

In the records of the Austrian Academy of Sciences, S. Meyer states that early in the twentieth century the Patriarch of Jerusalem visited the old Institute of Physics in Vienna. He had heard about radium and wanted to see its marvels. They showed him X rays, and for a while he was silent. He then said, "I now begin to understand the Bible. We read there: 'God said, Let there be light; and there was light.' Only later do we read: 'Let there be lights in the firmament of the heaven to divide the day and the night. . . . And God made two great lights; the greater light to rule the day, and the lesser light to rule the night; he made the stars also'" (Genesis 1:3, 14, 16). "But how could we understand it," asked the patriarch, "that God first divided light from darkness and only later made the sun and moon and stars? It seemed to be an insoluble riddle." But now that he had seen radium and its luminescence, he began to see how this was possible.

I might add in explanation that in the fact that light was created prior to the astral bodies Old Testament scholars find an important assertion, and even polemic, against Babylonian and Egyptian astrology, which attributed luminous power to the constellations. The biblical creation story emphatically wants to de-mythologize the sources of light in the universe and to deny them a monopoly of light. There is even a touch of irony in the original when it states that God put "lamps" in the sky. Lamps! The light that derives from God's creative power is distinguished from the created objects that dispense it. These objects are relativized; the undertone of irony serves to do this.

The worthy patriarch did not know this. Apart from it, the biblical text was for him an unsettling absurdity. Whether radium, another created entity that might be put in place of the Creator, like sun, moon, and stars, can really explain the biblical statement, I will not go into here. But that is not the essential point. The patriarch realized that the Creator's act is sovereign and independent vis-à-vis the functions that he assigns to his creatures. He obviously did not see himself forced to interpret the luminescence of radium as though the nature of light were grounded in the potency of something that belongs to the nexus of immanent causalities, as though it amounted to no more than that. But he also did not say, as the ontology of antiquity and the Middle Ages suggested, that light is subject to God alone, so that no object can be its bearer, and we have thus to postulate the existence of some radiant matter alongside such conventional dispensers of light as the sun, moon, and stars. No, the patriarch's train of thought was simpler and more modern. He used neither deduction from considerations of metaphysics nor induction from the facts of physics to arrive at a kind of proof of the Creator or God. On the one side his faith was sustained by certainty about the Creator even though he was disturbed by puzzles like the creation of light before the stars. On the other side, obviously out of scientific curiosity, he took note of an empirical fact, the luminescence of radium. The two together led him to use empirical observation to interpret his belief. He did not derive this belief from observation but had it in advance. He saw, however, that observation shed a new light on the belief and thus gave it, too, a new luminosity.

This is important for our thinking on the empiricist shock. It shows us that the bridges between research into this world and commitment to a theological interpretation of being are not down. Theology and metaphysics (the latter in the sense described) now hold a different place. They no longer offer axiomatic presuppositions from which I deduce the nexus of being without needing empirical studies. They do not do this even though my faith precedes my research, even though I am a Christian before I become a scientist. What they do offer are decisive signposts when I later interpret the insights that I have gained by empirical or mathematical methods.

In elucidation I might recall some of our earlier anthropological theses. Thus I might explain the genesis of humanity along the lines of the evolutionary theory or investigate the sociological or ecological conditions of human life. I should then be writing chapters in empirical anthropology that would not be found in biblical or any other religious teaching and could not be deduced from this kind of teaching. But would I grasp the essence of humanity by means of these empirical data? Not at all! I can arrive at the essence only when I interpret the data. I am then confronted by the difficulty that the genesis of humanity tells me nothing about the basis, goal, and meaning of human life, that I am in a dead end when I try to wrest such a statement from it (as has been done). I thus maintain that information about the essence of humanity must be taken from some other source. For this I might turn to belief in God or some other philosophical interpretation.

No matter where I gain this information, it has to be confronted by empirical study in the field of biological, sociological, and ecological anthropology. By way of example, I might turn to the empirically demonstrated lack of instinct in humans. If as a Christian or Kantian or Heideggerian or whatever, I understand that humans are beings that must grasp themselves in freedom, so that they can win or lose, the light of meaning is cast on the biological fact of the lack of instinct. Then, as in the case of the patriarch and radium, a hint is given that the biological structure of our existence is not unrelated to its final purpose, its metaphysical meaning. Both spheres of reality, that of experience and that of meaning, stand in a relation of interdependence on one another that must not be broken if faith is not to be blind to reality and experience is not to be devoid of meaning. Illustrations of this are innumerable. A very typical instance will occupy us when we discuss the anthropology of Teilhard de Chardin.

The change of position of theology (or metaphysics) in relation to the empirical sciences is something we have to understand if we are to measure what modern theology is, i.e., a theology which is in dialogue with the changing world, which takes it seriously and does not simply continue threshing the old corn in a sterile attempt at restoration without noting that all the barns and scenery around it have changed.

I should like to give another illustration showing how one can still be a Christian and a theologian, in a new way, in face of the modern orientation to the present world, to realistic experience. The this-worldly theology that I shall be presenting is, to be sure, a little outmoded for present-day ideas. It sounds naive. We undoubtedly need to revise it. But that can wait a moment. It is only one of many forms in which empiricism is referred back to transcendence, the sphere of experience to the sphere of meaning. It is taken again from the story of medicine. But this time I am turning to an incredibly interesting person who is not generally known today either as a physician or as a theologian but whom it is fascinating to study. I refer to Niels Stensen.[12]

c. Empiricism United with the Return to Transcendence, Illustrated by Niels Stensen

Niels Stensen was born in Copenhagen in the middle of the seventeenth century. He was one of the great natural scientists and theologians of the baroque period. His unusually extensive travels, not only in Germany but in France, Italy, and Hungary, gave him cosmopolitan breadth. He was in correspondence with many prominent contemporaries, including Gottfried Wilhelm von Leibniz and Baruch Spinoza. He was a leading member of the famous Accademia del Cimento in Florence. Pope Innocent XI appointed him bishop and apostolic vicar of Hannover. His scientific studies were especially in the fields of anatomy, geology, and paleontology. Even as a bishop he gave anatomical demonstrations to doctors. As a theologian he engaged particularly in the practical theology of preaching and pastoral care. He was concerned to give a personal example of Christian life.

Stensen's life was lived at the very time of the break that I have described. He became a Roman Catholic by conviction and made a sensational change of calling when, as one of the leading anatomists of his day, he became a bishop in northern Germany. He showed thereby that there is still a path from the orientation to this world which marks presuppositionless science to transcendent connections.

I will give a few indications of the way in which he made the transition to empiricism in anatomy and survived the shock.

In the name of empiricism he constantly inveighed against the metaphysical principle of analogy which, adopted from Aristotle, was openly abstract and used deductions from what ought to be instead of tracking down what is. He stated with almost the passion of a confessor that we must stop the error of those who try to explain the phenomena of nature only by like phenomena, e.g., by saying that the fetus is connected with the womb by the umbilical cord in the same way as a plant is connected with the earth by its roots, or the veins are nourished from the intestines as roots from the earth, or a magnet attracts iron as the mind attracts the object of its striving.

His medieval and contemporary opponents were using the logos of being, the axiom of true being, to hunt out analogies in every dimension of being, whether biology, physics, or the arts. One might perhaps define their position as follows: The logos, or truth, is indivisible, and so examples of it must occur everywhere in the form of analogies, permeating the totality of being.

In the same way Stensen attacked Descartes for not observing the processes of life but deducing them from principles. One of these principles was that of heat. It is highly characteristic that Descartes made a principle out of a sensory experience, or, in physics, a special form of mechanical energy. Heat was a principle of life for him and he believed that the fire in the heart causes the blood to circulate. Becoming hot, the blood expands, and when it joins the air sucked into the lungs, bubbles up in such a way that it is driven into the arteries and expands them.

Stensen showed how fantastic all this was by studying the heart of an ox and the foot of a rabbit. He realized what this implied for his theological as well as his scientific understanding of reality. If these people, as he wrote in a much later letter to Leibniz, were so wrong in material things that are accessible to the senses (i.e., which are within the competence of empirical observation), what assurance could they give us that they are not wrong when they speak about God and the soul? (Cf. John 3:12.) The very thing that was meant to establish the idea of God by a comprehensive interpretation of being and the demonstration of higher analogies was now compromising this idea. How can we trust this system which is constructed with such theological perspicacity when it fails so blatantly in the sphere of what is empirically controllable and can be refuted by simple investigation? When Descartes talks so absurdly about the circulation of the blood, we can no longer adopt his underlying metaphysical presuppositions. What seemed to be an apologetic for the faith is now an assault upon it.

We have thus to make a 180-degree turn. We must begin, Stensen thinks, with what we can know and prove. Only then can we make theological statements in the form of an interpretation of our findings. Truth is indeed indivisible—this thought is still in the background. What we believe as truth cannot be in contradiction with what we know as truth. We must let our belief in the Creator be confirmed by what we can know in the sphere of creation—or else we must modify it for the sake of the indivisibility of truth.

What this new approach involves may be seen, e.g., from his *Disputation on the Glands of the Mouth* (1661). Again in polemic with the "scholastics," who have ignored all this and disregarded observation, he describes the various glands, the origin of spittle, and the meaning and purpose of the system. Only on the basis of exact observation does he allow himself a theological interpretation, believing that sound reason must admit that the human and animal body is the work of a wise Master who loves living creatures. A treatise on *The Vessels of the Nose* concludes with the statement that all these things make it clear how carefully the all-wise Creator sees to it that nothing impure sullies the head, that royal throne. The cavities of the ear and eyes and nose are to be kept moist, the mouth and tongue are to be coated with moisture. Nevertheless, we find no discharges from nose or eyes or mouth if we live in accordance with the order of nature. To modern ears, of course, this sounds very much like "natural theology," and those who know the Enlightenment will be reminded here and there of some of the naivetés of deism. Yet this need not disturb us. My point in adducing this example is to give some impression of the extent to which theological approaches have to be set aside when the relation between logos and reality is abandoned. This took place irrevocably with modern empiricism.

No doubt we cannot be as naive as Stensen in deducing a proof of God from the teleology of the human organism. We cannot be theologians who base our certainty about God upon the grass of the Alps (Barthold Heinrich Brockes), or the rocks (Friedrich Christian Lesser), or the wonders of shellfish. Yet these nature lovers of the eighteenth century did in their own childike way try to make a step toward empiricism and give it a theological interpretation. We today may have to do things differently. We have been burned too often to be led astray by the impressive analogy of time and eternity. Yet one fact remains. There can no longer be any theology, or theologically oriented anthropology, that does not permanently relate its statements about the basis, meaning, and goal of human life to the empirical insights that we owe to the so-called human sciences. We cannot derive theological insights from these in the sense that they provide us with premises from which we may infer eternal certainties, if possible in the form of a proof of God. Nevertheless, what we say about humanity as an object of faith will always have to be confirmed, and granted reality, by what we know about humanity empirically.

IV. MODEL OF THE CHANGE IN ANTHROPOLOGY: THE RISE OF INDIVIDUAL EROS[13]

We have indicated the great gulf that separates the modern understanding of the world from the ancient and medieval view, locating it particularly in the way attempts were made to understand being from the philosophical and scientific standpoint. On the one hand stood a metaphysical conception of the cosmos from which individual being was deduced. On the other hand was a concern to reach an objective and empirical conception of being from which possible, though not necessary, metaphysical deductions might be made. In this context we have also tried to say something about the changed place of theology.

We shall now evaluate our findings from the standpoint of anthropology. There can be no doubt that the split between the Middle Ages and the modern age had to have an impact on humanity's self-understanding. One may assume—and it will soon be confirmed—that humanity can no longer unquestioningly see itself as part of a divinely integrated cosmos oriented to a self-evident basis, meaning, and goal of life in virtue of this integration. Everything is changed.

Humanity, too, becomes an object of empirical investigation. It begins to grasp the connection between the phenomena of body and mind, as, for example, in biological and neurological research. It recognizes its animal determination in sexuality and the instinct of aggression. It is influenced by the social and economic rootage of its existence, and by many other relations that can be explored scientifically. This new situation can have some extreme results, such as those formulated by Sartre, i.e., that humanity finds itself in pure existence, and that this alone is the basis of the question how it is to understand itself, or, better, what meaning, or essence, it is to give itself, and how it is to write on the empty page of existence.

The distance from the Aristotelian and medieval view is particularly obvious here. The traditional interpretation of being is seen not to be based on encounter with concrete reality. It is totally wrong. Humanity is naked—not clothed with meaning. It has to see to it itself what essence or meaning it wishes to give itself.

Methodologically we shall proceed as previously by studying the changed self-understanding of humanity in a particularly eloquent case. In this instance we choose the fundamental change in the view of eros. In connection with this we shall ask whether and how far the changed relation of the sexes allows or even forces us to transcend our empirical findings, to inquire into the meaning of eros, and on this basis to achieve a new link to the Christian tradition and its understanding of sexuality.

a. The Understanding of the Sexes in the Bible and the Reformation

The ancient view of the sexes represented by the Old and New Testaments may be found primarily in what is said about marriage and its understanding. This makes it plain that the personally and individually colored encounter of the sexes that is so important for us today, namely, the experience of eros, has little or no part in fixing the significance of sexuality, or at any rate in the arrangement of a marriage (as in the case of Jacob and Rachel). The point is rather— and this reminds us of what was said earlier—that we have here a given order of creation to which all experience, as in the selection of a partner, is subsequent and secondary. Hebrews would never have dreamed of saying that they were choosing a partner because such and such a person was pleasing to them and completed them, or of adding that this was what marriage was all about.

One may rightly ask whether in Old Testament thought most orders, e.g., law and the state, are not emergency institutions to protect us against the fall, so that they must be related to the constitution of the world after the flood, to the Noachic covenant, but not to the intact creatureliness of the original state. In this sense Luther in his exposition of the beginnings of the biblical story said that in Paradise Adam and Eve constantly directed their gaze on God, so that he could guide them with a flick of the finger. But when they turned aside from him in the fall, they no longer paid any attention to these flicks of the finger. Hence God had to bring them to a better mind with palpable power. The institutional expression of this new direction by force that the fall had made necessary is the state.

But this does not apply at all to marriage and the relation of the sexes. This is a divine dispensation from the very first. According to the relatively late creation story, it applies already in the world of innocence. The partnership of man and woman is part of the original order (Genesis 2:18). They are created for one another (2:21 f.). They recognize themselves in one another (2:23). The original identity, which is depicted in the story of the rib, but which later splits up into male-female polarity, in many ways resembles the idea of completion and the search for original unity in Plato's understanding of eros. But the polarity bears no individual features. It does not point to a special person in whom I will find my complement. Adam and Eve represent the race. The thought of completion applies to our nature, to humanity in general. The modern concept of the person, which is related to the thought of the individual entelechy, does not arise. The same obviously applies to the familiar idea of partnership.

Only along these lines can we understand the status of woman in ancient Israel. The man is the master (*ba'al*) and the woman his property. This is why seducing an unbetrothed girl is listed among offenses that have to do with property (Exodus 21:15 f.; Deuteronomy 22:28 f.). As compensation (to the father!) the seducer has to pay the amount that might have been exacted in a regular engagement.

Once we see the nonpersonal side of this understanding of the man-woman relation, we can appreciate the basic change that has come with the discovery of individuality, of individual eros, and the modern experience of sexual love.

Let us take some further examples.

Whereas the rule of individual eros not only enables us to choose our own partners but also, if we wish, to remain unmarried, virtually everyone was married in Israel. The Old Testament has no word for "bachelor," in contrast to the Arabs, who have the ironic term *azab*, or "loser." We do not know whether there might not have been some unmarried people in Israel—marriage was such a general institution and binding ordinance. It was not a matter for individual decision.

Ludwig Köhler is undoubtedly right when he says that in a society in which all marry and are married, there are fewer tensions. In fact the Old Testament never speaks about the tragedy of unhappy lovers. Even the painful tests to which Jacob was exposed in his winning of Rachel can hardly be taken in this sense. Nor does the Old Testament talk about unhappy marriages whose partners suffer from unconquerable antipathies. The suprapersonal order built into the world dispenses with individual decision and confers stability. This is the way things are, and so people do not take themselves and their feelings too seriously. Marriage, even at the individual level, is integrated into a plausible structure which gives it unquestioned validity. This tendency is strengthened by the fact that two clans are united in marriage rather than two individuals. In this way the shifting emotions of eros are given a suprapersonal counterbalance that confers permanence.

We might sum up as follows the features in the Old Testament which stand in striking contrast to the individually accented relation of the sexes from the time of the Renaissance.

First, an order of creation precedes all individual experience, including that of sex. This suprapersonal reference comes to expression in the regulation of marriage by law and custom.

Second, marriage is oriented to the procreation of children, the continuation of the promised blessing, and mutual assistance and completion. The true basis of its meaning is not to be found in the earthly actualization but in an institution that orients the creature to the Creator and is thus transcendentally grounded. Only for this reason can marriage serve as an analogy for the relation of God to his people and later for that of Christ to his community (cf. Isaiah 50:1; Jeremiah 2:1 f.; 3:1 ff.; Ezekiel 16:23; especially Hosea 1–3, and in the New Testament, 1 Corinthians 11:3; Ephesians 5:22 ff.).

So far as concerns the core of our inquiry, namely, the question of the theological implication of the change in the modern understanding of the self and the world, we can be satisfied with just a few hints when we turn to the New Testament. We can look at the witness that it gives to marriage only from the standpoint already indicated.

In the New Testament, too, marriage is an order of creation. This may be seen in what Jesus says to the Pharisees about divorce (Matthew 19:1 ff.). Jesus appeals to the original order that precedes human history. In the beginning God created man as male and female (Matthew 19:4) and made them one flesh. "What therefore God has joined together, let no man put asunder" (v. 6). The Creator has made this link even stronger than that to father and mother (v. 5, cf. Genesis 2:24). If, then, the possibility of divorce, the Mosaic certificate, is conceded, this cannot be the original and proper will of God (v. 8). God allows it because of their fallen state, their hardness of heart. Express reference is made here to the beginning when creation was as yet unsullied, to the normative order. This is the standard of marriage and the criterion by which to judge the law of divorce. Negatively this means that the law of marriage and divorce is not based on concrete experiences in the encounter of the sexes—the experience of fulfillment or its opposite in hatred or unconquerable antipathy. Instead, this law is based exclusively on a declaration of God's will. The true purpose of God may be seen in marriage. In divorce one sees God's "improper" will relative to our actual state. Thus, even though God permits divorce as an emergency measure in the fallen world, it does not correspond to his will in the same sense as marriage. This is interesting because law is here characterized as belonging to the present aeon, the world after the fall. This is emphatically *not* an order of creation. It is a kind of emergency order along the lines of the Noachic covenant (cf. Genesis 9).

In Paul, too, though in a modified form, marriage is a suprapersonal order, which does not in any sense have the accent of individual fulfillment and experience. Nor are we doing the worthy apostle an injustice if we say that he leaves us with the impression that a certain "erotic unmusicality" helps him formulate the corresponding theological theses. What are these theses?

In 1 Corinthians 7 it is plain that marriage as an order of creation occurs only in shadowy form in the background. Preparation for the last days and their troubles (vv. 26–28) makes it advisable to remain unmarried (vv. 1, 8, 26, 38). The orientation now is not to the beginning of the world but to its imminent end. How can one seek fulfillment in a world that will soon break up? Even the institutions that serve as forces of stability and order in this world are now given a provisional rank and no longer have any specific significance of their own.

By modern feelings and the modern view of eros there is thus a twofold relativizing. The search for personal fulfillment in sexual encounter is not even considered—here relativizing is too mild a word. The individuality of the encounter and the encounter of individuals are swallowed up in the emphasis on the suprapersonal character of the institution of marriage. The second form of relativizing is that the order of marriage loses some of its significance in the light of tense eschatological expectation of the end of the world. Love, Paul thinks, binds us to people instead of the returning Lord (vv. 32–34). The unmarried will get through the troubles of the approaching end-time more easily, and will be spared many of the problems that we cannot avoid when we are closely related to others (v. 28). If we are married, we should not try to get out of it (v. 27) but should keep a kind of inner distance, having as though we had not: "The . . . time has grown very short; from now on, let those who have wives live as though they had none, and those who mourn as though they were not mourning, and those who rejoice as though they were not rejoicing . . . and those who deal with the world as though they had no dealings with it. For the form of this world is passing away" (vv. 29–31). Those who belong to the Lord, Paul thinks, are no longer involved in the final phase of this world. They no longer participate in a way that should excite them. Their concern should be to withdraw from the world in anticipation of its end. Many cannot achieve this. It is thus better for them to marry than to burn with passion (v. 2). The relativizing of marriage goes so far here that in contrast to the creation story this passage treats it as an emergency institution to deal with the ardor and canalize the passion that might lead to stronger relations and worse aberrations than the institution of marriage that tames it. Here the point is reached that is furthest from modern feeling and experience.

It is well known, and has often enough been pointed out in historical confirmation, theological criticism, or antichristian polemic, that one may see here one of the two strands in Christian aversion to the body and this present world. The other consists of the Hellenistic legacy that Christianity took over to its hurt.

Even Luther, who in his doctrine of the two kingdoms and his emphasis on the body manifests a theologically considered orientation to this world, presses on only sporadically and not fundamentally to what we have called the modern experience of individual eros. For him, too, the original purpose of suprapersonal order overshadows all that later generations can say and sing about the riches of eros. Sometimes, like Paul in 1 Corinthians, he can view marriage as an institutional canalizing of what would otherwise be rampant libido, as a refuge for the weak. From God's standpoint Luther thinks that marriage stands related to the procreation of children and the satisfaction of the sexual libido. The Creator uses sexual desire to achieve this purpose even though lovers may have no awareness of it (Weimar Edition 34 I, 40.59). With tongue in cheek one might see something similar here to Hegel's "cunning of reason." As in world history individuals pursue their own goals and satisfy, e.g., their lust for power, without suspecting that they are also realizing the purposes of the World Spirit, so they satisfy their sexuality without ever seeing, or at least without having to see, that in this way they are serving the purpose of the Creator.

In our present context the theologically interesting thing here is that the place of the psychological experience of eros is indeterminate in Luther. This experience is simply accepted as given. God knows why he has made us thus. One can formulate God's purpose theologically, as Luther sometimes does. But it is outside the horizon of his thought to make the experience itself the theme of theological interpretation and to evaluate it, e.g., as a gift of fulfillment or a chance to form bonds with others.

In this sense Luther seems to belong to antiquity or the Middle Ages. We find in him no reflection of our own experience of eros. At the very most we trace only some slight movements in this direction —movements that are of little theological account. Thus Luther can sometimes ignore the aim of procreation and describe sexual love as the inalienable bond of marriage. He can even say that God smiles and rejoices when two people have a good marriage in which they love one another (34 I, 61).[14]

b. The Discovery of Individual Eros:
The New Secularity and Sexual Love

1. THE NEW BEGINNING IN ROMANTICISM

It might be as well to delineate at once the problem on which we are focusing. When we consider the tremendous gulf that yawns between, on the one side, the suprapersonal view of the order of the sexes and marriage that we have just depicted, and, on the other, the modern idea of self-fulfillment in the sphere of eros, we cannot avoid the question whether the biblical statements on this theme are not antiquated and outmoded. In this situation what possibilities are there of still taking them seriously and advancing their claim as a normative authority? Possibilities of this kind are present when we are able, and if possible compelled, to integrate the new, this-worldly experience of eros into the coordinate system of the biblical interpretation of being, if we thus find in this interpretation a place that is open to our understanding of life and "provides" for its integration. But how can we count on this, and what form will it take? This is the main question, in answer to which we are collecting material and studying models. To this end we must scrutinize the change in the understanding of eros more closely and develop our previous indications of the shift from the earlier view to the modern one.

Prior to romanticism, and especially the Renaissance, the order of sex and marriage was determined, as we have seen, by the fact that marriage was not an individual matter but a matter for the family and clan. These were the main subjects in the action (or transaction!), and to a large extent they controlled the candidates for marriage. This does not have to mean that only rational, economic, and similar considerations were taken into account. One may assume that parental instinct played a part, and the suitability of the children for each other was not disregarded. Nevertheless, it is incontestable that in more recent history, only the period after the Renaissance and romanticism has made individual eros a normative criterion in the question whether two people are "made for one another" and ought to marry.

Certainly individual eros was not totally left out earlier. From the very earliest times and in all places we hear about it in stories and poems and philosophical reflections, whether we think of the myths of Plato or the songs of the medieval troubadours (to limit ourselves to our own cultural milieu). What is new in the strict sense is only that individual eros is now publicly felt to be the presupposition, indeed the only basis, of a possible life union. To put it rather bluntly, one might venture the statement regarding our own time and culture that prior to romanticism people married, or were married, with a view toward individual love within the union thus effected, whereas since romanticism they marry on the basis of a love they already experience.

Personal love as a consequence or a presupposition. In the simplified form of a slogan this embraces the estimation of individual eros in marriage. Public consciousness today recognizes that the mutual personal attraction of two individuals is the legitimate condition of a life partnership. Presupposed here is that this kind of attraction, called "love," is an indication of mutual suitability and completion. Now of course we cannot go back beyond the historical break any more than we can go back beyond modern empiricism in history and natural science. We cannot secure the direct adequacy of the biblical message by repressing or bypassing the new factor. The historical path that has been entered is irreversible. With the awakening of individuality and the sense of identity, with the related striving for maturity and self-actualization, eros awakens too. Eros is the decisive means of self-actualization. In his commentary on the verses on eros in his *Urworte. Orphisch*, Goethe remarks that lovers are inwardly aware that they cannot determine themselves alone (as though they were alone and could find their identity solipsistically); they cannot just violently seize but have also to appropriate what fate has sent them; what is more, they can embrace the other, like themselves, with an eternal and indestructible attraction.[15]

2. THE UNDERSTANDING OF THE HUMAN THOU
IN SEX PARTNERSHIP

In biblical thinking, as we have seen, the meeting and union of the sexes were regulated by the transcendentally based, suprapersonal order of creation and were certainly not based on the individual experience of the partners. In contrast one might say of individual eros —or it seems one might say—that it is purely this-worldly—just as much so as modern empiricism. In the last resort the choice of partners that is made in its name is based on experience, and obviously this experience is not related in any way to philosophical or religious factors, even though these might play a role in the matter of individual suitability. Fundamentally the only question is whether and how the one experiences the other in nature and relationship. The choice thus made calls for freedom of selection and freedom in dealings with the other. It thus demands several decisions.

One of the basic decisions thus demanded consists of the question what I am looking for in my encounter with eros, and who the other is for me. The alternative that confronts me is as follows.

In the one hand, I can regard the other as a means for my own gratification and self-development because at root I am seeking only myself. In this case I am an egoist. We need not think that egoism is simply brutal. It can be sublime and find expression in veiled form. Thus in the neo-humanism of Wilhelm von Humboldt the egoistic focus on an ultimately Thou-less self-actualization appears in the garb of a highly refined culture. Perhaps one might view Goethe's Faust as a variation on this type of sublime egoism. Faust wants to develop his own entelechy. He strives for supreme self-actualization. He tries to do justice to this search by being active, by turning to the outside world, by finding his identity in encounter (in Goethe's sense). He strides through the faculties without stilling the urge within him. Even his love for Gretchen is a means of self-discovery. This is where he incurs guilt. A living Thou cannot be used as a mere instrument in this way even though the incident might seem to serve the "ethical" goal of personal self-development, the imperative of one's own higher ego.

The alternative to this sublime egoism is the desire to bring happiness to the other, to release the other for extreme, ecstatic possibilities of the self. As a rule this ministry to the other in sexual partnership is called agape rather than eros. For agape, the Christian variant of love, is determined by this motive of unselfish, serving, and helping self-giving.

What might seem theoretically an alternative expresses in reality a complementary relationship between two forms of love. It would be stupid to think that Christian ethics wants selfless, ministering love of neighbor to replace eros. The one who marries with no erotic feeling but simply out of neighborly love and because of the other's need will bring unhappiness to them both, as we have noted in another context. On the other hand, sexual happiness is not to be had where there is only an egoistic eroticism, a desire to possess. To make happiness possible there has to be cooperation, initiative, the possibility of self-giving, and readiness for it, on both sides. The art of love might achieve these things in the form of bodily reactions, but not as the surrender of the total person. This total self-giving can be achieved only when the dominant motive is not personal self-gratification but bringing happiness to the other. In this case self-fulfillment will come almost as a by-product.

The important question here is how I understand the other, who the other is for me, whether I use the other instrumentally or view him or her as a separate end. This question does not arise out of the attempt, remote from eros, to apply the concept of agape in every sphere, including this one. It arises out of the understanding of the other within the zone of eros itself. It thus arises as an immanent problem in the partnership of the sexes. It is not brought into this partnership from outside, thus pointing to a heteronomous authority. Those who are asked for pastoral counsel in the problems of love and marriage will thus act very foolishly if they tell those who come for advice simply to apply to their partner what they have learned in the catechism: "Love thy neighbor as thyself." In the circumstances this is a hollow and even ridiculous phrase. What might be said is that you are destroying your partnership, and not even achieving personal satisfaction, if you consider only yourself and not your spouse. Hence you are losing out not merely as an ethical person or a Christian but primarily as a sexual being.

The statement that the question of the Thou, of the understanding of this Thou, is a problem that arises within the sphere of the erotic, of sex itself, as may be learned from experience, seems to me to be highly significant. For with it the experience of sex presses beyond itself and proclaims here, too, that humans are beings that transcend themselves. I see myself required to ask about the nature of human fellowship, including that of sex. But this question can be answered only if I first face the different problem who or what is the human Thou with whom I have to do. Only then can I fix the role that I myself may and should play. I am thus face to face with the question of humanity itself. And it is easy to see that this involves the ultimate problems of anthropology, e.g., the problems that we have discussed under the headings of infinite worth and alien dignity on the one side, and utilizability or instrumental significance on the other. As we have also shown, the question of God arises when we choose between the alternatives.

We thus get another hint of the way in which theological questions arise afresh, and in another place, in the changed situation of the modern age as well as within its this-worldly empiricism. The tradition in which the final and enduring questions of the basis, meaning, and goal of humanity confront us is not broken. The new thing in the new age is not just new. It is not really different. The old play is still being acted. Only the scenery and the perspective have changed.

The same question of the human Thou encounters us from another angle.

Egoistic eros, which treats itself as absolute, constantly plunges us into new crises. If we adopt the pure aim of self-fulfillment in its name, then in the choice of a partner we subject ourselves exclusively to the criterion whether the other will be complementary and thus complete us and fit in with us in every way. Only thus can the other serve the development of our own entelechy and bring sexual satisfaction in the process. But if we focus on this criterion alone—as is often the case when eros is aroused—we are forced into permanent checking and are thus delivered up to a permanent state of crisis. The counterquestion that is forced on us is whether the other is really and always "right" for us. Does this other really bring maximum fulfillment? There are three reasons why this question is forced upon us.

First, the initial assumption that this other is our best complement demands constant scrutiny and possibly revision. Both my partner and I are historical beings who change with the march of time. What might have worked well when the union was made can change as the two partners develop in different ways. There are many examples of this. The immanent interest of eros in my own individuality constantly forces this question on me.

Second, isolated eros is interested not only in the being and nature but also in the functions of the other. It asks whether the other satisfies me in erotic and sexual functions. Is the other a complement in this sphere? Here again sexuality is at issue. We know that time and age are not without a bearing on sexual ability. The changes they bring may not synchronize in the two partners. The result will be disruption and disharmony. The functions of individuals are historically more variable than their being.

Third, the rhythms of the two sexes differ. Moments of ecstasy are followed by phases of indifference or even aversion. At such times the question whether complementarity still exists or has been shattered can become a tormenting one and even take on neurotic features. Thus a crisis often follows the honeymoon in what is a purely erotic or romantic attachment. The increasing instability of marriage manifested since eros achieved domination is historically evident. The earlier principle that love would come with marriage has proved not to be so wrong, as far as the solidity of marriage is concerned, when compared with the post-romantic principle that eros-love must be the basis and prior criterion of marriage.

This does not mean, of course, that we can use the "good old days" as a model. It certainly cannot be taken as a proof of the absurd idea that one can reverse the course of things and can or should go back before romanticism. It can only mean that we are shown that certain questionable elements lurk behind a sex partnership or life partnership that is based on eros alone.

At any rate, it is important that we should see that both eros and agape point toward the uniqueness of the sex partnership. This uniqueness is a theme in both. Eros postulates it by pointing to specific complementarity. Agape aims at it by keeping in view the unconditional and unique nature of the other. Here again the basic anthropological question who the other is, who he or she is as a representative of humanity, is an acute one. As indicated, this question crops up here in the immanent context of experience. But it is not answered in this context. In regard to their essential nature, human beings are still an object of faith and transcend experience. This is not just a Christian thesis, for it holds in philosophically grounded anthropologies as well. But it embraces the Christian view of humanity too.

3. THE HUMAN QUALITY OF FREEDOM IN SEX PARTNERSHIP

The modern world of experience, then, does not forget the question of the human but puts it in a new way. The question only arises subsequent to experience. We have no answer, prior to experience, on the basis of some religiously grounded ontological system. But as we put the question of the human in this way, the question of what transcends the human also arises. What is there in us that is not covered by the empirical or phenomenological model?

When we embark on this discussion, it is as well to take some more illustrations. Anthropology has many paradigms at its disposal here. I will choose only two that have a high degree of symbolical pregnancy. It is also of value that they come from the sphere of physiology and thus seem to be emphatically this-worldly and remote from transcendence. Both are taken once again from the area of human sexuality. I refer to the incongruence of male and female curves of stimulation and the absence of rutting seasons.

The Incongruence of the Curves of Stimulation in Men and Women

The structure of human impulse, although like that of animals, has human factors that transcend it. It is common knowledge that the curve of stimulation rises and falls steeply in men, but rises and falls more gradually, and stays up longer, in women, covering longer stages of pre- and post-play, of erotic atmosphere. If the two partners were to think only of themselves, they would inevitably leave the other solitary and unsatisfied. The incongruence would recoil on themselves. They would lose their rhythm in the process and fail to achieve the necessary cooperation.

If we had only physiological categories by which to evaluate this incongruence, we would probably conclude that there is here an unfortunate mistake on nature's part. For through this disharmony one partner (usually the female) would miss out, the orgasms not merely failing to synchronize but not even being achieved by both. Frustration would thus ensue, with fire on the one side and ashes on the other, stimulation on the one side and exhaustion on the other.

If we consider the implication of this for human sexuality, we reach a point where we have to go beyond physiological laws and consider once again the transcendent element. For the difference in curves of stimulation does not seem to permit us blindly to follow impulse in animal fashion. The reason is to be sought in the physiology itself. The impulse that looks only for its own satisfaction, as a kind of end in itself, fails to achieve it. This special element in human sexuality sets us the task of transcending nature. Creatureliness means that we are constantly summoned to move toward a goal, the specifically human element, that goes beyond natural factors. This applies even to the corporeal side. The body with its libido represents us. Being human, we are made for communication. We live for and by others. We are meant to serve and be served. This is true even in the sphere in which the body represents us.

Thus the difference in sexual nature rules out laissez-faire not just because of higher duties but even for its own sake. As Arnold Toynbee might have said, it forces us to meet a "challenge" with an appropriate "response." It provokes us not to be ruled by natural laws. It makes us face up to success and failure. It is thus the theme of human communication and not just animal copulation.

We think it important that all this is proclaimed on the level of impulse itself and not merely on that of lofty reflection or conscience, which has to do with conscious decision. Ethical decision does not come down from above into the lower sphere of impulse to ennoble it, to impart to it something new and inaccessible. This would be an idealistic falsification of humanity, dividing up its unity into a higher and a lower part, into soul and sense. The fact is that the potential for moral decisions is already present in the structure of human impulse. These decisions are evoked, kindled, and put into practice here. In this sense we are, if one wills, a closed system. What transcends us, and constantly calls for self-transcendence, is not something additional to what may be seen in our natural phenomenology, to what is accessible to empirical observation. Indications of it may be found in this area too.

I should like to interpret this in terms of the integration of the libido. This is "human," not because it is directed by reason and conscience, but already in its own self-direction (if we might put it rather forcefully). Wanting itself, the human libido cannot want itself alone but has to want the other too. It has to affirm and not just desire the other. It must carry with it a "diaconal" element if it is not to be abandoned and hurt. The incongruence of male and female curves may be an imperfection of nature from a natural standpoint, but it offers us a chance to be human even in the physical sphere. The automatic operation of animal impulses is thus transcended.

What may be found at this point in the physical sphere has the character of a *sign* of humanity. What is signified may thus be found in other human spheres as well. What is largely instinctive (but humanly so) in the sex relationship becomes a motif in the total sphere of communication, and as such, in the form of feedback, it flows back again into the physical sphere. For we achieve true partnership in sex only as we give to one another, only as we give one another sexual pleasure and "serve" one another in this way. When we help the other to fulfillment, fulfillment comes to us. Satisfaction in this optimal sense can never be had directly as an end in itself. It is a by-product.

Here, then, we see how agape manifests itself in the sex relation, how it is present, and how it is used. Its character is that it does not "seek its own" (1 Corinthians 13:5), and yet incidentally it receives all things. It takes up what is present as a sign in our sexual nature and makes of this challenge a motif. It gives meaning to what instinct does unwittingly and relates it to the destiny that creation has given to our human existence and fellowship. As thus governed by agape, the partnership achieved in sex works back upon the physical elements as well.

The Absence of Rutting Seasons

A no less striking model of the way that physiological phenomena take on a new quality when they enter the human sphere, so that they can no longer be understood in purely physiological and empirical terms, is presented to us by another feature in the structure of human impulse.

In animals sexual impulses have a fully automatic character. Males and females come together by constraint and not by decision. The rhythm of rutting seasons is regulated automatically. If something from outside interferes with this, it is broken. We never find any replacement for it in which the nonoperative impulsive energy is sublimated or transferred to some other field.

This automatic element is lacking in us. If "normal," we are not under the constraint of impulse. An essential reason for this in the sexual area is that there is no rutting season, or at the most only a seasonal increase in hormones that finds expression in an intensification of impulse and makes May the special month for the joys or sorrows of eros. Because of the absence of any rutting season in the strict sense, we are not subject to cycles in the sphere of sexual impulse.

This observation carries with it an interesting allusion to mythical anthropology and its underlying view of time. This concept is based on the alternation of days and seasons and has a cyclical character. The humanity of myths sees itself embedded in nature and its seasonal rhythm. Post-mythical humanity, however, no longer sees itself as subject to natural processes. Being "historical," it transcends nature, asserting itself over against it and molding it.

Like the incongruence in male and female curves of stimulation, this liberation from the rhythm of nature might at first seem to be a negative thing, a loss. Can one really speak about transcending nature? Do we not fall short of it? This question takes on greater urgency when one sees what instability and disorder result from it. Animals are spared these negative consequences. Unlike humans, they can hardly fail or go wrong, except for young animals that lack experience and are not yet adequately adapted to their environment. If we do find failures in animals, they are not due to any organic lack of success, perhaps as a result of experimentation, but because they are deceived for a moment by their environment, as when a bird flies into a glass window.

Yet our human emancipation from the constraint of instinct is not just a defect. It is also a possibility, and as such a sign of our greatness. The proverb that "to err is human" has much to tell us in this regard. It is undoubtedly equivocal. On the one hand, it says that our humanity is a mitigation, an excuse. We are "only" human. We have neither the sure direction of instinct nor the wisdom of the gods. But the proverb also denotes our distinction in being exposed to risk, to the possibility of failure. The prodigal son in Luke 15 is human precisely in the fact that in his aberration he manifests the possibility of decision and a readiness to take it. He is thus a "historical" figure. The older brother who stays at home, for all his virtues, is of lesser human rank. He is thus farther from the father's heart. He is ruled by environment and custom and thus stands in some analogy to beings that are governed by nature. We cannot see him breaking away from his background or risking a riotous way of life in some far country. Hence we do not find much pleasure in the steadiness of his moral curve. The father, who stands for God, loves the son who takes a risk, who is himself an experiment, who might fail as such, but who in his very failure learns what is meant by the possibility of returning home and the certainty of grace.

The diminution of our powers as natural creatures offers us the chance of finding our true destiny. Not being given up to the order of life or regulated by instinct, but set at risk, we have the task of seeking the meaning of what we do and become, of seeking virtues and norms by which to orient ourselves. The possibility of error is thus the presupposition of being set between possibilities of being, of ourselves "being" our own possibility. This is the basic condition for the development of civilization, for the existence of a sphere of history (or humanity), and for the possibility of making nature arable and subordinate instead of being subject to its laws. We have already made it plain enough that we do not see here a simple antithesis between the animal sphere and the biological conditions of the human sphere. We shall back up this point in our dialogue with Teilhard de Chardin.

Herder in his anthropology, to which we have already made brief reference, understands our "defect" along much the same lines as our great opportunity, as the basic condition of all humanity. The sociologists Arnold Gehlen and Helmut Schelsky find here the "plasticity" of human existence. It is something that can be molded, and molded by ourselves. A sign of this plasticity is that the role of the sexes is not fixed for good and all or sharply differentiated. Thus in primitive tribes the woman may be in charge of agriculture, whereas the reverse is true among European and Asiatic peoples. Hunting and war are mostly male pursuits, while cooking and housekeeping are female, but here again, as Margaret Mead and others tell us, there are notable and dramatic exceptions, e.g., the dangerous and venturesome hunting of the seal by Tasmanian women, or their hunting of the opossum, in which they have to climb tall trees. We today make plentiful use of this plasticity in liberation movements, even if the most zealous proponents of women's rights do not perhaps go so far as their Tasmanian sisters.

At all events we can say that paradoxically the nondetermination of human sexuality and the sex relation by natural compulsion carries with it the impulse toward humanization. To take up a phrase of Sartre's, and to modify its original thrust, we might say, with tongue in cheek, that we are "condemned to freedom." The transition from natural constraint to conscious and accountable actions is both a possibility and a necessity. This transition, which we have called human self-transcendence, is potentially present already in the structure of human impulse. Consequently this structure calls for anthropological interpretation.

V. THE NEW SITUATION IN CHRISTIAN ANTHROPOLOGY.
SUMMARY AND CONCLUSION:
THEOLOGY AND THE HUMANITIES FACED BY MODIFIED THEMES IN ANTHROPOLOGY

Using the model of individual eros, we have seen how modern anthropology increasingly begins with empirical phenomena but in this very field comes up constantly against the problem of transcendence. The more individual eros becomes a criterion for the development of the sex relation, the more clearly and sharply the new situation comes into view. It will thus be worth our while to discuss the meaning of individual eros in its ultimate implications. There is still something more to learn from this fruitful model.

First, it is plain that the area of decision that is posited with the plasticity of the human sex relation not only extends further with individual eros but is also full of complications. The more developed and distinct individualities are, the more the law of attraction and repulsion tends irresistibly toward instability. We have already had an example of this. The erotic meeting of two individuals is directed by the question how they can fulfill one another. How well are they suited to one another? But implied in this question is the need for constant checking: How well do they still suit one another, or have they outgrown one another?

The more developed individualities are and become, the sharper this question is, and the greater become the vulnerable areas and the possibilities of giving and taking offense. But this opens the door to the whole scale of sublime and intimate tensions and an unheard-of increase in the potentiality for guilt. Greater individuality means greater vulnerability. When sensitivity is heightened, a glance, a gesture, a tone of voice can mean an attack, a withdrawal, a closing or opening of the self. Alertness to movements in the background of the I develops and becomes more refined. All psychologists and pastoral counselors know to what extent crises in a sex relationship are not occasioned by big things but have their basis in trivialities such as the habit of ignoring the other, of reading the newspaper when he or she wants to talk, of complaining when the other wants peace or encouragement, of being late at meals or when going out, of failing to take account of differences in rhythm and thus being too slow or too fast. Such things all take on greater significance when they are connected with the development of individuality and the resultant problem of complementarity, especially because they are regarded as symbolical, as an indication of the whole personality. Thus previously unknown forms of guiltiness appear, but also forms of nonalignment that seem to be outside any ethical categories.

With the awakening of individual eros the danger increases that one's own individuality or entelechy will become the measure of all things and therefore that the motive of self-fulfillment, which means self-love, will determine all life's major decisions. In this way individuality can unmistakably become an object of idolatry. The question, "What's in it for me?" can in a very suspicious way crowd out the other question, "Where and how can I serve?" The switch is all the more dangerous if the question, "What's in it for me?" is not put in a material or economic sense. It, too, can be sublimated and have the higher self in view, which seeks fulfillment and can thus make an ethical appeal. Faust did not sin against Gretchen for the crude reason of his libido but in the name of his metaphysically transfigured Faustian nature, his entelechy, and with the motive of self-realization (as we would say today). Thus the question can have an ethical and even a religious nuance when it takes on the form, "What do I owe myself?"

When individual eros and individuality, awakened in this way, carry with them enhanced possibilities of hurting others, of aggression and even cruelty, forms of disorder follow that force us to modify the traditional Christian principle of the indissolubility of marriage and to put the question whether it is really God who has joined together and whether one may rightly appeal to him for a radical and uncompromising practice of the principle.[16]

It seems to me to be fatal that the crisis in the sex relation, and especially marriage, which individual eros has caused, has passed almost unnoticed in the Christian churches and has occasioned very little theological reflection. Where it is even mentioned, this has usually been with a negative emphasis and with the criticism that people today take their individuality too seriously, worrying too much about what they owe their self-fulfillment and thus thinking they are obliged to dissolve their marriages. Now I will not try to contest the fact that this charge, and the call for correction, are often apposite, that they must even be included in the opposition that a Christian pastor has to put up against the idolatry of individuality. But the abuse of individuality does not invalidate its legitimate claim—the claim that has reached people today, and through the awakening of individual eros become an inalienable and irrevocable part of their humanity. In the last resort this claim forces us once again to grasp ourselves, to master and transcend ourselves, to become a task to ourselves. To that extent it repeats on another level, but with no final change, the original task of becoming human.

It is just because this is so, and the situation created by individual eros is not just a break or an emancipation, but raises and discloses the basic questions of humanity, that it seems to me to be fatal that the change, and the continuity in the change, have passed unnoticed by the churches. This may be one reason why people who suffer from crises in their sex relations and marriages often avoid the clergy and turn to psychotherapists or newspaper columnists. The churches ought not to be content to argue that people make this switch because they want greater freedom and the ethical neutrality of the mere expert. This is partially true. But there is a greater fear, it seems to me, that the churches do not take the problem of individuality seriously, that they have no theological place for it, that they still operate in the sphere of general dogmatic rules. That is why our present concern is to find a place for individuality. That is why we are not content with critical complaint against the changing times.

Taking newly developed individuality seriously means recognizing within it the latent chance of becoming human. This chance comes to light when we realize how intensely we are asked here how we understand ourselves and where we are going, whether we think that we are summoned merely to self-development, to sublime egoism, or to self-giving, self-outpouring, and service. Either way we are a task to ourselves and we will be actualizing the self (so long as this is not understood as a deified entelechy). We can certainly fail in this task. At issue is a chance, not an automatic mechanism. We will fail if we seek and grasp only the self. But even then we will be discharging a specifically human task, though only in a negative mode. The positive equivalent is self-actualization in a being for the other. This includes regarding the other as a self that is also charged with self-development and that summons me to have a responsible share in this self-development. I am thus compelled to decide how I regard the other, whether as only instrumentally important (as a means to my own self-development, as Gretchen was for Faust), or unconditionally as an independent end, as is plain in the concept of alien dignity.

When we put it thus, it is not difficult to see what form a theological interpretation of this anthropological situation will take. In terms of the polarity of law and gospel, or judgment and grace, one might state it as follows.

Grace is at issue inasmuch as the awakening of individuality stands under the promise that the destiny of being human, of being a free subject and partner of God, will no more cease than will "seedtime and harvest, cold and heat, summer and winter, day and night" (Genesis 8:22). From this standpoint the awakening of individuality and individual eros is a development of the fullness of creation, and especially of the Creator's intention to make everything "according to its kind" (Genesis 1:11). What the promise means for awakened individuality is that it is not a breaking free from the task of creation but its broader fulfillment and richer orchestration. On the other hand, judgment means that there is in the gift an increased risk, that new forms of guilt can be incurred against others, that there is the temptation to make the development of one's own entelechy an end in itself and hence idolatry, that there is the possibility of betraying agape and the honoring of others in their alien dignity.

It ought to be clear how far all these statements testify to the revolution in modern theological thought. Anthropology in the form of individual eros and the resultant understanding of the sex relation puts a very fruitful model at our disposal.

We may sum up our decisive results as follows.

The anthropological statements are no longer deduced from specific dogmatic principles and therefore limited by them.[17] The new approach means that empirical phenomena—the structure of male and female impulses and the difference between them—are now interpreted in the light of our human origin and destiny. In this light some references and relations are brought out that would perhaps be hidden if we did not set things in an eternal perspective. Theological knowledge, if I might call it that, takes here the form of a subsequent interpretation of phenomena with which we first become acquainted in the empirical human sciences. All that is presupposed is a certain approach to these phenomena, i.e., viewing them from an eternal angle. As regards the structure of the sexual impulse, we thus ask about its orientation. We look for indications of something transcending mere bios, namely, of humanity. This kind of inquiry and this perspective are not restricted to the confines of Christian theology. They can occur also in the human sciences with their philosophical orientation. These too, whether materialistic or idealistic, put certain questions to the phenomena. In some cases these questions might lead to more than a mere interpretation of the phenomena, to more than illumining them in this or that light. They might lead to the discovery of new phenomena that were previously hidden and thus to advance even in the empirical field. For example, the materialistic anthropology and historical understanding advanced by Karl Marx did not merely give a fresh interpretation of historical facts but brought to light many new facts, for, while history had previously been regarded mainly as the story of war and civilization, the reality of social and economic conditions was now given prominence by the materialistic view. Thus Greek antiquity was no longer presented, as in Johann Joachim Winckelmann or Jakob Burckhardt, merely as the world of the Acropolis and Doric pillars and perfect sculpture, but also as the world of slaves and workers whose proletarian destiny made all this possible.

This is what we had and have in mind when we want theology to take part in the new approach and to set itself the task of interpreting the this-worldliness of empiricism from its own standpoint. When it does this, it will keep in view the coincidence between what directs its earlier work and what emerges as an answer when it investigates the phenomena of the world of experience.

The new situation in thought is nowhere so plain, and nowhere offers such evident models, as in the sphere of anthropology. Only a radically positivist and empiricist anthropology or a consistent behaviorism (John B. Watson)[18] can ignore the problems of coincidence. But a terribly high price must be paid if one refuses to put the phenomena in the light of that which transcends them. For in so doing one refuses to put the question of the nature of humanity itself.

F. HUMANITY AND NORMS

THE PROBLEM:
HUMANITY IN THE WEB OF ORDERS
AND RELATIONS

If humans are beings who have to orient themselves to something and cannot just be the objects of processes, like animals, this means that they are beings in relation, that they are spiders connected to the outside world by numerous threads. What does this imply?

Our basic state, namely, that we have still to become what we are, that we do not come from nature potentially complete, compels us to ask about our whence and whither. Questions of basis, meaning, and goal thus come under discussion. In every case we have to give some answer to these questions, even though we do not do so in a conscious or reflective way but only de facto by our acts. We have to give some answer even though we repress the questions or escape into indifference. Simply letting things be, evading decisions, is itself a decision.

The fundamental question of humanity, who I am and what I ought to be, cannot be answered merely by introspection, by contemplating one's navel. We have already quoted Goethe and Dilthey in this regard. Both tell us that we can know ourselves only by moving out of ourselves and doing things in the outside world, finding out what is in us by mastering circumstances and doing creative work (Goethe).

This is so even when the theme is self-development. In *Urworte. Orphisch* Goethe uses the term "daemon" for our necessary individuality, which is directly stamped and restricted at birth, thus constituting what is specific and unique in us. Yet this daemon does not develop alone. It cannot know its whence and whither merely by looking at itself and observing its evolutionary powers. No, it fulfills itself, and can thus know itself, only by coming into contact with what is outside itself, by disclosing itself in encounter, and thus entering into a web of relations, exposing itself to the contingent (*tyche*), to love and therefore to the other (*eros*), and finally to necessity (*ananke*). Only as the daemon persists in these fields, and thus stands in relation, does the I come to itself.

This is so because my I is the point of intersection of many relations and these relations are a decisive part of my identity. They are not just outside things apart from which my human self has its own existence. If I do not take them into account, I cannot grasp the self. It becomes a shadowy thing with no reality, as in Steiner's daring vision of the isolated individual and his (or her) possessions. We need to have a look at some of these basic relations to confirm this impression.

I am the child of specific parents. Here is my first basic relation. Education and sociology both refer to the personal relationship in which the small child has its life and being. As a parent I stand in relation to my children. I have neighbors, enemies and friends, colleagues and rivals, to whom I stand in mutual relationship. I am a sexual being seeking fulfillment through a husband or wife. I find myself integrated into orders, social structures, and historical processes and traditions. I have to take up some attitude toward these, either complying with them or asserting myself against them.

I can never understand myself in isolation—for my identity involves more than isolation. What we understand by individuality, or Goethe by his daemon or entelechy, is something that is enmeshed in a system of relations and influenced by this system. I live and move and have my being in a being for others and the world with its infinitely differentiated nexus. Even the "final" orientation that I describe as the basis, meaning, and goal of life is something that I can achieve only as I define the "final" relations that surround and sustain my being. We have discussed this already in another connection when dealing with the way Kierkegaard looked at these basic relations: We can define our being by our relation to an animal and understand ourselves as something higher. Or we can orient ourselves to God who is above us and constitutes the ground of our being. Or we might simply orient ourselves (Kierkegaard thinks) to the state, which does at least transcend us and integrate us into a higher, meaningful order.

Precisely at this point it is evident that different understandings yield different views of humanity.

If I choose the downward relation to animals, I choose one that is external, but of such a nature that it does not make possible any self-transcending of my existence but makes me only a higher animal or even reduces me below the animal level because of my loss of instinct.

A most impressive example may be found in Nietzsche's understanding of conscience. Conscience is usually regarded as a human quality, a true sign of humanity, for in it I appeal to the imperative, the requirement that I should make decisions and grasp my destiny. This suggests the theological interpretation, namely, that in it I receive God's summons, that it is God's bridgehead in my consciousness to which he comes with the power of his word and with which he unites himself. Here conscience is understood in terms of my upward relation. But Nietzsche views it in its relation to animality—from below. So long as we live freely as animals, we turn our instincts for war and the chase to outside things. The instincts help us to assert ourselves. But once the break comes to what is called higher human development, and we find ourselves enveloped in society and peace, those predatory instincts become inoperative and superfluous. We are chained and lose our strength. This is what has happened to us half-animals who are happily suited to the wild, to war, to roving, to adventure. All the direct and spontaneous impulses mediated by instinct and the elementary will for self-assertion have to be reined in because they have no target or function in the sheltering edifice of civilization. Reflection takes their place.

What Nietzsche has in mind can be elucidated by concepts taken from Freud's psychoanalysis. The fighting instincts of the wild beasts of the steppes, or even of half-animals, cannot simply be negated when they are not put to use. At most they can only be repressed. Their strength can only be transformed into a different kind of energy (as in the process of sublimation). In this case the instincts of war and the chase, which were previously directed outward, now turn inward. They become forces in an inner struggle between will and impulse, flesh and spirit, (supposed) good and evil. Conscience, especially a bad conscience, is for Nietzsche the battleground in this conflict. It is the self-laceration of decayed and divided humanity.

No wonder that Nietzsche finds here a degeneration from the animal state, so that in his *Genealogy of Morals* he speaks of a profound sickness. Lacking external foes and opponents, we are driven into the oppressive restriction and regularity of custom. We impatiently tear and harass and gnaw and disrupt and mistreat ourselves, dashing ourselves like animals against the bars of our cage, consumed with longing for the wilderness. It is as such desperate prisoners that we have discovered conscience.

It seems to me that by this example Nietzsche very impressively makes it clear what I am trying to say. First, even in Nietzsche's rather daringly one-sided genealogy, human existence can be disclosed only with the disclosure of a basic relation underlying it, in this instance the relation to its earlier animal stages. Second, it is evident that the picture of humanity changes according to the relation that is selected.

This applies even to immanent, i.e., nonultimate, relations. Two different pictures of humanity can arise here. The one may be based, for example, on our relation to society in pure dependence on its structure and pressures. We might be understood as beings who are shut up in this relation and do not transcend it, so that we are no more than social beings. This is certainly how it is in popular Marxism among some left-wing extremists, but also among some ideological champions of totalitarianism on the right. All such movements think they are compelled to relate humanity to something outside, but they select a relation of total functional dependence that blocks human self-determination, the responsible grasping of the self, from the very outset.

On the other hand, while the relation to society and the state might be regarded as a constitutive element in human existence, it might not be viewed as exhaustive, but another side of humanity might be found outside it. This position can be seen, for example, in the phrase used by Luther when in the name of conscience he is said to have told the representatives of state and church at the Diet of Worms: "Here I stand, I can do no other." Luther, whose approach here has symbolical significance for us, accepts his relation to the emperor and the empire, to the institutions of state, church, and society. He finds in them a divinely established nexus. But he does not let himself be defined by this relation. He himself defines the limit of the competence of these authorities. He does not let them embrace and negate a decision of conscience.

But is it possible for Luther's self, his conscience, to escape and transcend his relation to the orders of this world in that way? Such a relativizing of the worldly nexus, such a refusal to be taken captive by it is possible only if a point is found outside the world that sets the world out of joint. The penultimate courts of emperor and empire can be relativized only by an ultimate court. (Philosophically one might say that I can set limits to *normae normatae* only in the name of the *norma normans*.) Luther grants full power over the self only to the ultimate relation, his commitment to God and his word. This is why he can stand above the penultimate relations. This is why they cannot take him captive. This is why he can confront and transcend them.

This helps us to clarify the significance of relations, both ultimate and penultimate, for our picture of humanity. Our finding is that an anthropology can be achieved only as we set humanity within a system of references. Looking back on our earlier discussions, we find that we have always proceeded along these lines. Whether we were considering the theme of identity, the human ability to understand, or the change in the view of truth, explicitly or implicitly we were always talking about humanity in relation. What was mainly incidental, although, to be frank, not purely accidental, must now be treated expressly and made a theme of its own. We must examine the web of relations more closely.

If the reader surveys the relations that follow, he might perhaps find it odd that the decisive fundamental relation, the relation to God, is missing from our sketch. This omission is deliberate. The relation to God cannot be one thread among others. It is not part of the web. The whole net depends upon it. It is present in the depiction of all the rest.

Readers familiar with philosophy might feel that our concept of the nexus of relations by which alone humanity is to be understood reminds them of the movement of structuralism founded by Ferdinand de Saussure and developed by the Prague school of linguistics. In spite of many similarities, however, the author does not agree that this would properly describe his position. A brief comparison, then, might help to clarify the present view.

Structuralism is originally a philosophy of language. Its starting point is that speech is not to be understood in terms of physically describable elements of sound or word units but is a connected system of relations, a structure. De Saussure finds an example in chess. The king, knights, and pawns are characterized, not by their shape or material, but by their function in the game. They are thus to be understood in terms of the nexus or structure of chess. Similarly, in words and things the relational nexus is the thing that counts. In contrast, their substance (or matter) is what is not yet formed and hence cannot be known. The basic thesis of structuralism, as stated by

Günther Patzig, is thus the supremacy of the relation over the elements that compose it, whereas for Aristotle the reverse is the case.

Once this structural thesis is applied to humanity, it may be seen that it is formally inadequate. We may see this from Aristotle, to whom, in spite of the difference between them, De Saussure likes to appeal. Aristotle views humanity in terms of substance, not relation. For him we are ontological beings. Only individuals are to be viewed relationally, e.g., slaves to masters.

A decisive and critical question arises here: Are we structurally enmeshed and conditioned only in our functions while remaining entelechies in ourselves? Are relations only added secondarily as a kind of appendix, without defining us intrinsically? If so, can this situation continue? Or will our inner nature (Aristotle's substance) finally be swallowed up in our functions and thus be integrated into the nexus of relational conditions? Does not this actually happen when Marx views us only as elements in a social system? Does not structuralism press necessarily toward this integrating of humanity into a system of immanent relations? Does it not have to become a philosophy, as the suffix "ism" denotes?

If so, it involves a negation of our own basic anthropological thesis that we are beings who transcend ourselves and hence have to inquire into the basis and meaning of existence. The system of coordinates within which we have to place ourselves and to which we are related can never be a nexus within which the question of meaning can be validly put, let alone answered. Here at best we can achieve only immanent teleologies. That we transcend ourselves cannot simply imply our relation to an embracing system of functions similar to that of the game of chess. It has to inquire into the meaning of this system or structure. This question does not involve crossing the frontier into metaphysics, for it is bound up with the need to grasp the self and clarify the thematic meaning of existence. Our approach to this basic question plunges us deeply into immanent relations. We will either be lost in these, e.g., in our quality as functioning social beings, or we will stand in an ultimate relation, outside the function, which constitutes our true essence, or alien dignity.

The question, then, that we have to put to structuralism and its anthropological implications is whether formally defined relations can determine the nature of human existence, or whether the decisive thing is not to fill out the empty forms and thus ask *what* penultimate and ultimate relations are finally at issue.

I. AUTONOMY, HETERONOMY, THEONOMY

a. The Commands of God and the Postulate of Autonomy.
In Debate with Kant

We recall that there are certain defects in humanity, especially the lack of instinct which offers the chance to become human. In his *Treatise on the Origin of Speech* (1772), Herder says somewhere that if our human senses are less acute than those of animals, they acquire thereby the advantage of freedom.

Now freedom, as we have seen, is undoubtedly more and other than caprice, than doing what we like. As a good in human existence, it does not mean that I can do what I like, but in its full sense it means that I may become what I should be. It confers on me the ability to be myself, to achieve my identity. The sphere of freedom opened up by the loss of instinct does not remain empty, then, but has to be filled by a program on which, and with the help of which, freedom can work. This means, however, that freedom asks for norms by which to orient itself. Freedom and norm are related terms. Freedom without norm is caprice, or libertinism, and leads to self-destruction. Norm without freedom is dictatorship and autocracy, a mere training or brainwashing, which can only manipulate and therefore destroy the human self.

Humanity has to have norms. But this opens up a fundamental question. Where is it to get these norms? This is a decisive issue. In thinking it through, we shall again come upon the difference between the medieval and the modern epochs. In this instance Kant stands on the frontier.

1. THE GULF BETWEEN GOD AND AUTONOMY

In the biblical period, and in the West prior to secularization, the question of norms seems to find a very simple solution. Humanity receives its norms in God's commands, or in systems of thought built upon them. These provide decisive directions for our acts and for the way that we have to traverse to reach our goal. To the degree that in the modern age we have broken away from these commitments, freed ourselves, and tried to become adults, these ostensibly or actu- ally promulgated commands have seemed to us to be a forcing or blockading of free self-determination. The magic word that Kant has made into the Magna Carta of modern ethics is autonomy. Briefly, what this word implies is that we cannot be told from outside, by God, who we are and what our end ought to be. The practical logos that comes to expression in our own conscience tells us all that mat- ters in this regard. Only as we obey this and not an external author- ity do we cease to be the functionaries of an alien will and to let our- selves be led heteronomously. Only in this way do we find the freedom of self-determination and thus find ourselves, our human destiny. The categorical imperative that alone ought to direct us is our own imperative. The commands of God can still apply, and thus live on, only if they can validate themselves before autonomous con- science as the final court. They must prove to this board of censors that they contain maxims which simply express what the imperative of our own conscience requires of us.

With this thesis the problem of norms becomes a delicate one. Does not the "Copernican revolution" effected by Kant mean that the commands of God, and with them the solution to the problem of norms proclaimed by Christianity, are set aside once and for all? That for us today the concept of autonomy is the only guiding star by which to direct our course? That every anthropology must be oriented to this maxim of autonomy?

Pushing these critical and self-critical questions even further, we ask whether Christian ethics is not, on this view, a self-contradiction. Is it not heteronomous, and therefore anti-ethical, inasmuch as it makes us the objects of a law instead of giving us the freedom to fix our own law and thus be moral subjects? Is not theonomy the same thing as heteronomy?

If we agree that it is, then theology—and Christianity as a whole— is in no position to establish an ethical discipline on its territory or even to allow one to be developed. If it still claims that it may do this, it is pushing back the wheel of time and feverishly trying to re- tain a medieval, pre-Kantian view, thus acting in a grotesquely an- achronistic and reactionary way.

One thing must be allowed in this objection.

Once we have taken up the idea of autonomy, we can no more reverse this advance than we can the other advances to which we have referred, e.g., the awakening of individual eros and the develop-

ment of the historico-critical sense which is not frightened off even
by the authority of the Bible. God as the author of binding commands can no longer be a kind of "given" that our conscience has to
accept, that we simply have to believe. To try to remain faithful to
him in this naive and unruffled sense is to be untrue to ourselves and
to betray the dignity of self-determination.

What conflicts does this involve us in? Bonhoeffer is simply expressing a common view when he says that the movement toward
human autonomy has become fairly complete in our age. We have
learned to handle all important questions ourselves without resorting
to the working hypothesis of God. Everything works very well without God, just as well as before.

Experience teaches that I have within me a conscience, or, let us
say, a functioning moral criterion, which operates, and continues to
operate, even when this world is granted supreme emancipation and
autarchy. Thus Kant's claim remains in force, and is irrevocable, that
I owe *responsible* obedience to commands. I cannot passively and
indifferently expose it to heteronomizing by commands. I have to ask
whether these commands will stand before the sovereign and supreme court of conscience. In certain circumstances I may have to
reject them.

But do I really need them at all? What relevance can they have
for me, things being as they are? They can tell me nothing that I do
not know already from my practical logos. If they tell me something
more and different, then inevitably they are regarded as a heteronomous authority. They slip by the censorship of my conscience.

Unmistakably the modern age, represented here by Kant, has shattered the previous nexus of norms in this area, and in so doing has
staged a revolution in anthropology as a whole.

Will things turn out at this new center of anthropology as they
did in the sphere of empiricism? Will the new orientation to this
world, to the autarchy of the moral I, be open to a transcendent reference and thus be amenable to a theological interpretation? Let us
consider how crucially important this issue necessarily is within the
framework of the Christian tradition.

If we cannot go back behind the newly awakened autonomous self-
consciousness, and if Christian anthropology cannot surrender its
principle of theonomy, then it seems that we have to try to synthe-
size two totally incompatible things. We have to try to achieve

wooden iron or square the circle. Is the idea of theonomous autonomy any less paradoxical?

To put this elementary objection to a serious test, we would be well advised to scrutinize the term "autonomy" more closely. We need to pay more attention to the meaning of *autos* than to that of *nomos*. We shall first consider the anthropological core of this concept.

What is meant by the self?

For Kant the self is the solitary person. This person is defined by a relation. It participates in the intelligible world. It hears the voice of its practical logos in itself, in its own conscience. I am thus related to myself, though it is to my higher and true I that I am related. I am related to myself as a representative of humanity. Only because humanity is sacred to us in our own person, only because it "is" in our own person, are we moral beings. To look outside, to seek grounds of action outside the self, is to disrupt the closed structure of the self (*autos*). We do this when that which evokes fear and hope in us becomes the motive for our acts. Thus fear of punishment, of what avenges itself, and hope for the fulfillment of desires, are not moral impulses. Again, looking to the orders of some authority does not do justice to moral impulses, for it means surrendering the power of decision to an alien entity and thus canceling or suspending moral subjectivity.

Why should we do this? Perhaps because we fear freedom and responsibility. Or because we want to woo that authority, hoping for its favor or fearing its displeasure. No matter what the motive, the impulse is not a moral one. In some way it is eudaemonistic and hence the very antithesis of a moral disposition. The moral self is the solitary I that listens only to itself and does not look outside.

Naturally this cannot mean that contact with the outside world is broken. That would be absurd, for we obviously move out of ourselves to act in the world. Moral action involves encounters, e.g., conduct toward others in love and friendship and all forms of dealings.

For Kant, however, this relation to the external world comes only in the second phase of the moral process, i.e., when the I seeks objects in the external world on which to bring to bear the disposition that is formed in the inner I.

What may sound very abstract in this form can be illustrated by considering what love of neighbor might mean on this view.

For Kant it is not the case that the impression made by neighbors and their need of help awakens feelings of sympathy, then loving concern, and finally altruistic self-giving. To give in to emotions stimulated from outside can only be a sublime form of seeking egotistic self-gratification and is thus a form of eudaemonism. Kant, then, takes the opposite path in his description of the development of a moral motive. First, I form in myself, irrespective of external impressions, a noneudaemonistic disposition to offer help. The ethical quality of this disposition may be tested by the criterion whether it can be advanced as a principle of universal legislation and has, therefore, more than an individual character. Only then, in a second act, will I seek neighbors in relation to whom to practice the disposition already formed.

For this reason we may rightly say that for Kant the self (*autos*) is the solitary I that is related only to itself and hence autarchous. An anthropological decision precedes and underlies the resultant concept of autonomy.

We thus arrive at an important principle. In the relation between autonomy and theonomy the crucial thing is not what is meant by *nomos*, or where it comes from (though this is still important for Kant). The real emphasis lies on the question of the prior anthropological decision, namely, how the self (*autos*) is to be understood. This, and no other, is the decisive issue. This alone is normative for the discussion whether the modern concept of autonomy leaves the door open for some kind of transcendent reference and therefore for a theonomous basis of human existence.

Only in the light of this question can one see the real difference. For in Christian anthropology the self (*autos*) is given a different interpretation. This difference forms the specific object of the decision that has to be made.

In Christian thought the self is to be understood only in terms of the relation to God. It is created by God, alienated from him, visited by him, and called to redemption. No theological statement about God or humanity can fail to reckon with this relation.

If we still attempt a "theo"-logical statement apart from this relation, we enter the unfathomable and inaccessible territory of a "God in himself," and hence a hidden God. The object of a true knowledge of God can only be Immanuel, the God who enters into a history with us. To know God is to know his history with us, to know him in his "for me," if we might thus adapt a famous saying of Philipp Melanchthon.

The reverse is also true.

No theological statement can be made about humanity that does not include its relation to God. If we attempt such a statement apart from this relation, we either find no more than purely psychological or physiological functions and their bearers, and thus remain on the purely phenomenological plane, or we have to resort to metaphysical theories and interpretations. Either way we miss the point of human existence if we detach humanity from the relation to its ultimate basis.

In keeping with this I can only *believe* in humanity, since God as he who determines and sustains its nature is an object of faith for me. Our infinite worth and hence our inviolability—what has been called our alien dignity—cannot be established empirically. Empiricism has at its disposal only the standpoint of our utilizability in sublime or brutal form. Function replaces person (Hans Freyer). I may thus reach the view (Nietzsche) that the human race is a parasite on the earth. Naturally I may also make more sympathetic diagnoses. But the true essence of humanity—human personhood—would still be out of reach.

If we take seriously the ultimate definability of humanity by God alone, the self that is at issue in human autonomy acquires a particular quality. I can come to myself only as I come to God. Apart from that I miss the self, or at most attain to it only in fragmentary hints.

The parable of the prodigal son may be taken as an illustration (Luke 15:11–24).

When this son asks his father to give him his inheritance so that he may go into a far country, he does not intend to play the role of a playboy or wanderer but has an ethical motive. At root he is in search of his self. He is afraid that he will not find this in his father's house. At home he stands under authority and has a system of values that is fixed by tradition and determines what he should do or not do. All these things seem to be heteronomous influences that make the son the object of forced growth, deprive him of the freedom of decision, and thus prevent him from being an autonomous subject. Only abroad can he be his own man. In this way he is in search of himself.

But he does *not* find himself. For in casting off the higher authority of his father he comes under the rule of a lower authority. He comes under the influence of impulse, ambition, anxiety, and homesickness. When he finally ends up in the very depths among the pigs, he finds out that the freedom he wanted is not the opposite of commitment but a special form of commitment. Only in an ultimate commitment am I penultimately free. Only the conscience that is bound in this sense can enable me to say, "Here I stand; I can do no other." Commitment is this inability to do anything other. But because it is an ultimate authority that binds me, so that I can do no other, I am free to throw off my commitment to penultimate powers, to emperor and empire. The converse is also true. Commitment to these penultimate powers makes me the slave of an alien will and does not free my I for itself but robs me of my identity. This comes out in the parable as follows.

With the father, or, better, in commitment to him (or to God), the son is free. He is a child at home with all the rights of a child. Apart from this commitment (or relation), he is a servant of inferiors. With the father, then, he finds his self, while outside he loses it. His self is not, as he thought, a self-grounded entelechy. It is his existence as a son.

This existence is *not* free because he is just a child and never leaves the childhood state of dependence (like his elder brother). It is free because he visits the far country and now accepts commitment to his father as an adult, finding his way to a commitment of a higher rank.

Again, his existence is *not* free because he breaks away from childhood, for the opposite of childhood is servanthood. He is free because he finds his way to adult sonship (cf. Galatians 4:1–7). The *autos* of the Christian view of autonomy cannot be the one who in emancipation focuses on the self but the one who is an adult son or daughter. Hence the assurance of freedom that is given with the saying, "All things are yours," is coupled with the other statement, "And you are Christ's" (1 Corinthians 3:31–32).[1]

It is evident, then, that on this level theonomy and autonomy are not antithetical, for God is not an alien law (*heteros nomos*) for us. It is as we are with God that we find the self, while without him we miss it.

But we need to put this more carefully.

There is a possibility that God might be an alien law for us. John's Gospel holds out this possibility when it says that I might reject being "in the truth" and try to ground my life in the self. In doing this I would still be related to God, but in a negative mode. He would be for me a trigger of resistance, hostility, and doubt.

Paul's teaching on the law draws attention to this situation. Luther's comment here is that I can react against the God of the law only with aversion, servile obedience, and hatred. I am not on the side of the divine law, nor is my own will in conformity with it. Instead, I am its opponent (at least on one level of the I, Romans 7:22 f.). Hence if the law of God is the only thing that characterizes my relation to God, it presents itself to me as an autocracy, an alien law. What corresponds to it on my side is servanthood in every conceivable form, from unwilling obedience out of fear, by way of constant sabotage, to clever evasion that represses the image of the dangerous master and substitutes an image of mythical or intellectual desire.

One may thus say that from the very outset—if we start, that is, with humanity in its natural state—God is in fact heteronomous. Hence the objection with which we began is right in another sense. Redemption, however, consists not merely of learning to *understand* the self afresh but above all of *receiving* a new self, so that the "old man" ceases to be and I become a "new creature" (2 Corinthians 5:17; Galatians 6:15).

2. THE BRIDGING OF THE GULF.
LOVE AS THE FULFILLMENT OF AUTONOMY

Along these lines it is the work of the Holy Spirit to make me conformable to God so that I will what God wills. As my self is oriented to God, he ceases to be alien and encounter is no longer antithesis. We receive a new heart that impels us to walk in his statutes and keep his ordinances (Ezekiel 11:19 f.). For now God's law is no longer outside and alien but is put within me and written on my heart (Jeremiah 31:33), so that I incline spontaneously to it and it has become my own law. No longer, then, is it a demand. Indeed, it makes itself superfluous, for I bear it within me (31:34). It can thus be an expression of my autonomy, for my *autos*, my self, has been changed. The word of God is now near me, in my mouth and in my heart (Deuteronomy 30:14), so that I "do it." The doing does not originate with me, just as strictly the clause "and do it" is a grammatical consecutive. The impulse, then, is not an alien law that comes to me from outside. It arises out of the spontaneity of the self as in Kant's concept of autonomy. Formally, then, there are surprising analogies, but the understanding of the self, the *autos*, has changed fundamentally. To the new self there necessarily corresponds a new form of autonomy that is oriented to it. As I am called to "being in the truth," and as I respond to this call, I also want this truth. I want what I now am.

God ceases, then, to be one against whom I have to defend my autonomy. The very opposite is true. It is God who calls me as Father. It is with him that I find my true self as an adult son or daughter, and thus come to my autonomy. What previously seemed to me to be autonomy I now see to be a very sublime form of self-alienation: an intellectual instrument with whose help I evaded the final issue.[2]

Only in this light can one appreciate Paul's statement that "love is the fulfilling of the law" (Romans 13:10). One has to have the new conception of anthropology in view to be able to understand the background of this saying.

What does it mean to love God?

To love God is to want what God wants, to be at one with his will, to be conformable to him. For God's will has come to me as the declaration of one who loves me and enfolds me in the relation of father to adult son or daughter. The demand that I should love God with all my heart and mind and soul and strength does not reach me now as the claim of an alien law that goes against the grain and forces me to assert my own identity. It no longer has the characteristic mark of an alien law, i.e., the provoking of opposition. For those to whom God has revealed himself as one who loves, it simply releases a new spontaneity of the total I. The I is totally involved in the response of love. Since love is a reciprocal movement, even in our love for others, our will no longer chooses love as one among several possibilities. It no longer has to force itself to decide for this one possibility and to repress the other possibilities that crowd in upon it.

Real love involves no conflict (even in the case of eros). It needs no resolve or decision. I do not have to win it from the opposition in my inner parliament. That it may lead to new and different conflicts is another question.

The trouble, by the way, with a sick and purely physical sexuality is that in it the whole person is not involved. The bodily libido is temporarily satisfied, but the heart and mind do not participate and therefore they are not quieted by the encounter. Sexuality without love never achieves fulfillment, for when sexuality breaks free from love, it can never be total. This is probably the reason why there have seldom been so many sexual problems as under the sign of our modern emancipation. This is why there are endless courses in the arts of love. But they hardly meet the real need; they merely provide healing for conflicts that to a large extent they themselves produce.

Love—and even, as we have said, erotic love—engages the whole person. It arises whole and undivided, not through the conflict of decision. In love, then, the will does not seek to assert itself against opposing forces (as in Kant's teaching on duty). It wills that which love impels it to love. It is an element in love, or better, an agent of it.

This is why Jesus can say so strikingly that the command to love our neighbors is "like" the command to love God (Matthew 22:39). What is meant is that in relation to love, God and neighbor can no longer have the significance of different realities. God gives my neighbors the meaning they have for me by buying them with a price, by investing them with alien dignity, by taking them up into the same history as that into which he has taken me up.

For this reason the act of love is indivisible. It cannot be divided as regards its objects, i.e., between God and neighbors (James 2:14 ff.; 1 John 4:19–21). Nor can it be divided as regards its fulfillment, one half of me being invested in it and the other standing outside and perhaps protesting against it. This twofold indivisibility is conceivable only if God wins love from me and makes me a new self, a new creature, by summoning me to fellowship with himself.

When this happens, I cannot say in the strict sense that I have become "another" person. I must confess instead that I have only now come to my true self, found my real identity, and become congruent with the plan God had for me. When I let myself be determined theonomously (not resisting under the law but being made conformable to God under the gospel), I achieve autonomy in the true sense. My present self is my true identity. Thus the contradiction that was originally perceived between theonomy and autonomy disappears.

What we said at the beginning of this section still stands. We cannot go back on the discovery of the autonomy of the moral sense. No form of authoritarianism, however pious, can claim ethical quality for itself. It is impossible for us to call a servile obedience to the divine commands moral. We may indeed go further and say with Kant that the claim of supposed commands, even though they maintain an honorable origin on Sinai, can be accepted, because of the dignity of the moral person, only if they pass through the censorship of the ethical consciousness, receive its approval, and thus present themselves to the ethical consciousness as simply an objectification of the imperative that sounds forth within itself. The only difference from Kant, though this is a basic one, is that for Christians the ethical consciousness is that of a new I, the I of adult sonship.

On this changed level all the formal structural marks of autonomy are the same. The discovery of these marks by Kant, and their varied fixing since Kant, e.g., in existential philosophy, can be helpful to the Christian ethicist. For they help to establish the difference between servile obedience and childlike love as it finds reflection in the philosophical postulate of self-determination, so that new dimensions of its meaning come to light. Just because a secular ethics is inclined to understand (or misunderstand) theonomy as heteronomy, it forces self-criticism and self-reassurance on theonomous ethics: self-criticism to the extent that the possibility and even the inevitability of heteronomy is always present when theonomy means the dominion of the law and God is regarded as the author of the law; and self-reassurance to the extent that by way of this philosophical misunderstanding the postulate of autonomy illumines and discloses what might otherwise remain a hidden dimension of the gospel, since in it being in love is shown to be the new self that makes the will of God its own will and experiences its authenticity in the relation to God.

Theonomy and autonomy thus point to one another as law and gospel stand in polar antithesis. This polarity is the core and guiding star of the fundamental dialogue between theological and philosophical anthropology.

b. Humanity in Relation to Authority and Tradition

1. THE QUESTIONING OF AUTHORITY IN THE NAME OF ANTI-AUTHORITARIAN SELF-FULFILLMENT

When we grasp our humanity, and have to become what we are, self-determination, or the freedom to discharge this task, is part of this humanity. We have seen that the postulate of autonomy is bound up with this. In that connection we have examined some real or apparent threats to this autonomy in the religious field. We have put the question whether theonomy, i.e., the authoritarian "God has commanded . . . ," does violence to autonomy.

But such challenges to freedom occur primarily on the plane of society. Here one may find in authority and tradition forces that resist human self-determination and thus have the significance of heteronomous pressures. Enlightenment, according to a celebrated saying of Kant, is human self-discovery through emancipation from authority in the sense of an ethical task oriented to human destiny: "Enlightenment is the emergence of humanity from self-incurred immaturity." By immaturity Kant means surrender to an authority to which the role of subject is delegated. It is an inability to use one's own understanding without guidance from someone else. In this way we fail to reach our true humanity. We do not discharge the task of autonomy that makes us human. Surrender of this task obviously has ethical relevance. This is why Kant says that immaturity is self-incurred. His verdict is just if the cause of immaturity is not a lack of understanding but a lack of the resolve and courage to use it without external guidance.

This is why the slogan, "Have the courage to use your own understanding" is, as it were, the motto of the Englightenment. The heart of this emancipated rational activity is, for Hegel, philosophy. This has arrived at the concept of free thinking and made it a principle, so that it is free from authority. Hegel can even say very pointedly that philosophizing is putting another basis in the place of authority. As the mobilizing of one's own understanding, it is diametrically opposed to authority.

The demand for an anti-authoritarian life-style is undoubtedly a continuation (albeit extreme) of this line of thinking. This postulate goes far beyond the purpose of simply wanting the independence of one's own powers of understanding in contrast to immature dependence upon authority. Its goal is the liberation of all existence in every area. Positively this intention is perhaps best expressed by saying that it seeks the smooth development of one's own entelechy unhampered by any form of "repression."

If this is not to lead to a chaotic confrontation of different individualities and thus to block all social dealings, this type of self-development can be meaningful and acceptable only on one condition, namely, that the self that is to be developed in this way is equipped with the social organs to which Marx refers in his early writings. Only when individuality is absorbed into the species can the leap into freedom occur that harmonizes unlimited self-development with the interests of society and thus makes it seem desirable.

The way to this final anti-authoritarian possibility is paved, of course, with all kinds of restraints and remodelings and even perhaps brainwashings, so that it seems to be the very opposite of anti-authoritarian (just as a strict authoritarianism has been set up in all the areas where Marxism has taken root). The slogan of the anti-authoritarians is thus the premature proclamation of a state which—if it is to be realizable at all—will need a lengthy learning process with many preliminary stages. It is anticipating the eschaton.

No wonder, then, that the project has misfired both in America and West Germany. Yet the experiment is heuristically fruitful even in its failure. For when we ask *why* this wave has necessarily receded in every observable area, we reach the assured finding that commitment to authority and the related tradition is one of the constants of humanity. Hence no anthropology can overlook this theme.

It is a by no means irrelevant approach, then, to seek the meaning of authority by inquiring into the reasons for the failure of anti-authoritarian ideology. What are these reasons?

First, it is noteworthy that this ideology does not distinguish between the noun "authority" and the adjective "authoritarian." The adjective, in our penetrating usage, normally denotes the characteristics of social and institutional structures. This critical labeling is meant to show that we have to do here with governmental relations that lead to division into a superior exploiting class on the one side and a subordinate exploited class on the other. If we belong to the former, we have an authoritarian position that confers privilege without the need to earn it personally. If we belong to the latter, we are exposed to the dictatorship, the "heteros nomos," of the ruling class. No matter what may be our individual merits, we are unable to achieve maturity and use our own understanding without guidance by someone else.

There is no doubt that the protest against an authoritarian nexus that hampers the attainment of maturity is justified. But the passion of the protest leads only too easily and frequently to a blind and deluded anathema against any superiority and hence against all hierarchical ranking. It causes those who make it to overlook the difference between authoritarian structures that automatically confer superiority and the individually merited authority that attests and manifests itself in superiority.

It is easy to level down this distinction. For superior natures necessarily seek to create relations in which their superiority can express itself. There is a connection between personal authority and authoritarian structures, and this can easily lead to the corresponding confusion.

Nevertheless, one must keep in view the difference in the two understandings of authority. Only when this is done can one see why the relation has been disturbed. This kind of disturbance takes place when solidly established structures give positions of leadership to nonqualified people and thus rob the system as such of all credibility and evoke justifiable protests. Inability to differentiate between person and system, authority and authoritarian structures leads necessarily to a radical rejection in advance even of legitimate authority. Shakespeare bewails this rejection in *Antony and Cleopatra:*

> O! wither'd is the garland of the war,
> The soldier's pole is fall'n: young boys and girls
> Are level now with men; the odds is gone,
> And there is nothing left remarkable
> Beneath the visiting moon
>
> (Act IV, Scene 15).[3]

2. THE FORMS OF QUESTIONING

The Postulate of Equality

The rejection of authority on this basis has a generalizing and ideological character. Both aspects find an echo in the misuse of the postulate of equality. We shall demonstrate this briefly in what follows.

The generalizing tendency in the rejection of authority may be seen in the fact that the principle of equality is radicalized and generalized far beyond its originally restricted meaning. To show in more detail how this mutation came about, we should have to discuss the history of the understanding of the term. But we must be content with some mere hints in the present context.

Generalizing of the Postulate

Originally, before the modern mutation, equality had a specific sense. It had its validity in a particular sphere or limited relation. Thus there is equality before God. Here is neither slave nor free, man nor woman (in spite of the order of supremacy and subordination in the world of antiquity), but all are one in Jesus Christ (Galatians 3:28). Even where hierarchical rankings are assumed, as between men and women, the path to equality is pioneered by this appeal to the relationship with God. Thus Paul says that the head of the woman is the man, yet he adds at once that husbands are to love (*agapan*) their wives as Christ loved the church and gave himself for it (Ephesians 5:22, 25). This command of love, which is an isolated one in antiquity, has the implication, strengthened by the appeal to Christ, that the one who loves is summoned to serve and thus to take the lowest path. Hence the external order that gives men a privileged role is relativized and transcended by the dimension of being "before God." In this dimension hierarchical rankings fall away; each is for the other without distinction.

Luther, too, referred to this equality before God. We see this characteristically in his relating of equality to freedom and brotherliness. Whereas the French Revolution adopted the threefold slogan of freedom, equality, and fraternity, Luther, as Johannes Heckel has pointed out, had the very different order of fraternity, equality, and freedom. Brotherly love, which is put first, is grounded, like the command of love, in our being God's sons and daughters. It is on this basis that we accept our neighbors. Hence equality is set within a specific relation. In spite of all the outward distinctions that will always develop in different societies, we are all equal before God in our commission, in our failure to fulfill it, and in our need of redemption. That this equality before God is a permanent challenge to unjust inequality before our fellows, and contradicts their irreligious trimming of it, may at least be noted in passing. The story of Christianity manifests, of course, a dreadful series of offenses against this principle.

A modern variant in the understanding of equality may be found in Kant. Here, too, equality is set in a specific relation and thus given a particular meaning. In Kant the relation is that to the law. We are all equal before the law and no one can claim privilege. Thus Kant says in his work *On Perpetual Peace* . . . that external or legal equality in a state is the relationship of citizens by which no one can bind someone else to the law without being subject to the law and thus open to the possibility of being bound in the same way.

The modern generalizing of the principle of equality to which we referred may be seen in the fact that it is no longer limited to a specific relation, e.g., to God or the law, and thus oriented to a fixed point of reference, but is extended instead into an equality of all people in principle. The justifiable protest against authoritarian structures or the crassness of the distinction between rich and poor, privileged and nonprivileged, develops into the opposite extreme of a demand that all social distinctions should be eliminated and that we should move toward a collective leveling.

Naturally in ideologically less deluded spheres there is still some realization that the difference between equality and inequality persists and that it is identical with the difference between various dimensions of our humanity. We are thus forced to ask today from what standpoint people are equal and from what standpoint they are not.

Along these lines, equality is understood qualitatively. It is defined by human dignity and finds expression in human rights (i.e., in relation to the law, as in Kant). Distinction, however, is measured by the quantitatively different contribution to society, i.e., by difference in function. Since the second aspect tends to catch our attention first, it threatens to become the dominant one and in inhuman fashion to push aside poor achievers or the handicapped. Justifiable protest against this strengthens the tendency to demand not merely an equality of opportunity (which does too little for constitutionally poor achievers) but to postulate the generalized equality of which we are speaking. This postulate is usually linked to a corresponding criticism of society, using the argument that the inequalities and the ensuing privileges, or lack of them, are due exclusively to the social structure and can be corrected only by a change in the system.

The ideological character of this hypothesis, its remoteness from reality, may be seen at once from the fact that it ignores the question, which has become a very acute one in America due to the researches of the psychologist Arthur Jensen, whether intelligence (at least as measured by IQ tests) is not determined less by society than by heredity and hence biologically. Probably there is a very complex interaction between bios and society which makes it impossible to absolutize either factor or to make it an ideological basis of humanity. No one has more felicitously satirized this generalized view of equality and leveling down than George Orwell in his *Animal Farm*, in which he points out that all animals are equal, but some are more equal than others.

Ideologizing of the Postulate

As I have already noted, ideologizing of the postulate accompanies its generalizing. The term "ideology" has several shades of meaning. But it undoubtedly has a basic sense that recurs in every variant. Ideology—perhaps among other things—is always the attempt to furnish an interest with arguments and to integrate it into higher relations so that the pragmatic root is concealed and the eye is directed to something else, to the supposedly higher relations.

When we speak about the ideologizing of the idea of equality in this sense, we might say that behind the higher relations of its postulate of humanity the motive of a particular interest, i.e., a pragmatic concern, is at work. What might this motive be?

In the period subsequent to Helmut Schoeck's important theory of society, which bears the title *Envy*,[4] the conjecture has gained in strength that the motive of envy might be normative in the trend toward leveling down and equalization. Nietzsche argued already that this was the basis of egalitarian and emancipatory ideologies when he thought he discerned masked forms of the will for power in the demand for freedom and equality. His suspicion of ideology is so strong that even in Christianity, revolution, equal rights, love of peace, and truth he found no more than "big words" which have the value of standards in battle, not as realities, but as imposing fronts for something very different which may be in complete antithesis to what is ardently placarded as the motive.

What Nietzsche here describes as the front of imposing words corresponds exactly to what I called "higher relations" which are designed to conceal. In what Nietzsche finds behind the facade may be seen unmistakably the motive of envy, at least if one discerns in envy an impulse that dislikes every form of superiority and wants either to attain to it or to pull it down (naturally without saying so openly, but rather erecting a facade of words in front of the real purpose).

Thus Nietzsche in the metamorphosis of the will for power finds four stages among those who lack power. Each of the four is marked by envy of rulers and superiors disguised by the fervor of apparent moral motivation. The first stage sees a demand for justice from those who have power. The second talks about the freedom that those in power should confer. The third is the stage of equal rights that are wanted so long as we cannot stop rivals from increasing their power. The fourth stage is that of the simple demand for power itself, for a share in the privileges that are not conceded to others and whose justice is contested.

François Babeuf (1760–1797), who originated the idea of the socializing of the means of production and coined the slogan "the dictatorship of the proletariat," provides an impressive example of the underlying motive of the demand for equality. In his paper *Le tribun du peuple* he espouses egalitarianism with a revolutionary passion, especially with a view to a fair distribution of property, but also in respect to civil rights. But what he champions as a theoretician is decisively modified when he has access to power. He wants to secure himself against any use against his own privileges of the arguments that he deploys against the ruling classes. So, once the ideal of equality is actualized and has been established at the state level, human rights are again to be restricted for an indefinite period. (Naturally he has to save face and find higher reasons for this.) The masses are allowed only to learn to read and write and count. This will strengthen them in a certain inferior sense of equality but prevent the education of an elite that might be dangerous to the privileges of the new ruling class which derive from the new equality. It could hardly be demonstrated more plainly that the postulate of equality is here a mere slogan to conceal the envy that those who want power feel for those who monopolize it and the concern of those who achieve power to keep it. The motive of the will for power that Nietzsche unmasked may be seen again here.

Marx argues in much the same way in his work *National Economy and Philosophy* (1844). But he is more aware of the splinter in his brother's eye—the eye of "crude communism"—than the problematic nature of his own motives. He admits that in crude communism universal envy, constituting itself as power, is simply a hidden form in which greed satisfies itself in its own way. The concept of private property, as such, is at least directed against greater private wealth as envy and the desire for leveling down, so that these constitute the heart of competition. Raw communism is simply a final development of this envy and leveling down on the basis of a preconceived minimum.

Ernst Troeltsch rightly pointed out that with this motive the idea of equality is now concealed behind the slogan "democratization." We attack the elite with a view to toppling those who resist our own claims to total power. We inveigh against privileges in order to secure great and unjustifiable privileges for ourselves. We demand equality of opportunity but are really aiming at equality of success for unequal performance. In a cynical reversal of the purported goal, this leads to the exploitation and finally the interdiction of achievers and those who are rich in ideas.

As a first finding we might state that if the radical rejection of authority—and not just authoritarian structures—takes the postulate of equality as its basis, this basis may itself be based on a very different motive hidden behind ideology. Although, as Troeltsch says, we like to think of ourselves as rational animals, our race is controlled to a large extent by irrational motives.

If this irrational element consists of underlying motives of envy, the will for power, and self-aggrandizement at the cost of others, then not only is a psychological diagnosis required but we are forced to ask whether the self-alienation that is the point of the biblical story of the fall does not again come to expression here. In this story the desire "to be like God" (Genesis 3:5), to level down God's totally different being, is ideologically concealed behind the taking of the forbidden fruit. In the foreground is a fine show of discussion, a rational inquiry in religious philosophy. The serpent begins the dialogue with Eve by raising a problem. Has God really said that you may not eat of all the trees of the garden? How can he have said that? This question evokes a chain of unuttered but natural associations. With what right, one of these questions might be, has God conferred special privileges on that one tree in the middle of the garden? Are not all his works, including all the trees in Paradise, of equal rank? Does there not stand behind the prohibition an awareness that with its transgression you will enter into the polar tension of good and evil, that your eyes will be opened, that you will thus achieve true maturity? Is it God's purpose, then, to keep you immature, so that you will not come into the dangerous zones of decision and open rebellion? Does he not really want adult partnership? But how can he want this, and how can you achieve it, unless you venture to take the forbidden fruit and at the risk of guilt experience good and evil, exposing yourself to this knowledge?

These are all, if you will, intellectual questions. The serpent engages in no less than a theological discussion with Eve, raising the question of God's nature and will, and also the question of human destiny. But what we have here are only concealing words behind which stands an irrational motive, namely, the desire "to be like God," to cross the gulf between the divine and the human, the higher and the lower, to empty heaven—as later at the building of the Tower of Babel (Genesis 11)—and to seize the throne of God. Behind the drive for superhumanity there lurks an envy of God that makes it intolerable that we should be merely "human" and live in what is finally an absolute dependence. Here again we find the equality postulate defending itself against ultimate authority and hence rejecting all penultimate authorities.

The story of the fall has much to teach us about the problem of ideology.

3. FORMS IN WHICH THE REJECTION OF AUTHORITY BREAKS DOWN

We shall be content here to make the decisive points in thesis form.

(1) The slogan of self-fulfillment, when turned against authority, is a misleading principle whose destructiveness increases with its popularity as a fad. It is used against authority inasmuch as the latter is seen to be a tyranny that subjects the self to an alien power and thus leads to self-alienation. But the resistance to external forces proper to this ideology of self-fulfillment is too one-sided. It is directed against all external claims. A mother is afraid that she cannot find her true self if she devotes herself to her children and their education. A spouse is afraid that the self will be smothered in marriage and family and thus seeks liberation. Adolescents are afraid that being tied to their mothers or embedded in the family, in an authoritarian commitment, will nip their self-development in the bud.

In all these pedagogical ventures it is overlooked that self-discovery can never occur as an end in itself. (We recall what Goethe said about introspection and self-absorption.) It is paradoxical, but true, that the self is found only in self-forgetfulness or self-giving. People who have been found to be truly original, to be elemental and unaffected forms of a self, have always been those who have fully given themselves to some task or service or vocation. Only in self-giving are we given ourselves. Only in a readiness for claims, and in wrestling with them, do we find ourselves. Self-discovery does not come when concern for the self and its nature is the criterion of conduct. On the contrary, the real question whether a thing is right, whether we can do it responsibly, arises only when we forget ourselves. Hence it is absurd to want to be original. Attempts in this direction bring down upon us the curse of being ridiculous. Even the self-judgment that we are original, that we have brought it off, is nonsensical. Only others can make this kind of judgment. It lies outside our own knowledge and purpose.

(2) Child psychologists have long since established that an anti-

authoritarian pedagogy that is supposed to serve self-discovery achieves the opposite, fruitful though it may be as a temporary corrective to a patriarchal style of education. The child that is handed over to this kind of treatment, or nontreatment, does not honor the nerve-shattering freedom it is granted. As Christa Meves has convincingly shown, it feels neglected and starved of love when left to its own devices. It detects no concern but simply thinks it is left on its own. What is supposed to contribute to early independence is asking too much. It demands of the child decisions which it is not yet ready to make and which rob it of the blessing of protection. The question raised by a Hamburg child is highly significant: "Auntie, do we really have to play again today any game we want?" The wisdom of immaturity may be seen in this question.

Corresponding attempts to apply this style of education in higher grades have long since broken down in America. Thus Dennis Gabor can say that the permissive education that has done so much harm there is fundamentally wrong. In the very early years, according to the great Maria Montessori, there is a place for some self-development in play. But later, at least from the age of ten, students have to accustom themselves to the lifelong self-discipline without which a free, "permissive" society is impossible. This demands some severity if we are to do more than bring up unhappy and profoundly bored hedonists.

In particular the appeal to the principle of pleasure and sexual self-development makes people susceptible to consumer pressure and thus brings about the opposite of what anti-authoritarian methods are trying to accomplish. Unwillingly and unwittingly a strategy is followed that produces weak people and makes them defenseless against ideological indoctrination.

(3) We have already indicated, then, the consequences of the rejection of authority. No less a person than Alexis de Tocqueville pointed out that when the principle of equality is directed against authority and tradition, it simply exposes the helplessness of those who are left on their own, and thus produces a sophistical concept of freedom which confers on the state that rules the masses the freedom to do as it likes, without distinguishing between good and bad or truth and falsehood. When we are left to ourselves in a supposed freedom for self-development, we have no home in the past, we feel isolated in the crowd, and we have no specific function. The result is

a splintering of the will in respect to truly important matters. In reaction, mass movements of the will arise that force individuals to take part in affairs of state on demand. Thus we get back to despotism. The supposed emancipation from authority and tradition does not lead to the freedom that is sought but causes us to experience it as an impossibly severe pressure for permanent self-development, so that we finally delegate it to the strongest voice of command. Thus the movement against authority conjures up the pseudo-authority of despotism. Ideological tyrannies and total states need only rootless individuals who have no binding commitments but are left on their own. Ideological systems of government create this kind of vacuum so that they can exploit nature's abhorrence of a vacuum.

(4) Loss of authority in this way does not usually derive from an initiative on the part of the young or subordinate in the rejection of authority and the enunciation of a program of liberation. Such a loss normally results from a self-surrender of authority itself. Only when authority abdicates does it bring down on itself protests against its claim. Revolts, then, are not initiatives. They are reactions to what is already a loss of authority. They result from the emotional diagnosis: "There is no longer any authority here. No claim is made. Why, then, should we submit?" The subordinate self can no longer identify with this kind of abdicated authority. It rightly finds itself exposed to a self-alienation against which it rebels. Thus crises of authority among rebellious young people are always accompanied by crises of identity.

The change from the loss of authority to the pseudo-authority of tyranny takes place through the granting of too much uncommitted freedom. We have pointed out already that when too much is asked of freedom, it cries out for new direction and is thus vulnerable to the strongest voice of command. As Karl Marx showed, the reversal may come about when possession of the means of production, and hence the ability to impose one's own will, confers privileges on a certain class to a degree that leads to impoverishment of the masses on the one side and the constant accumulation of the property of the privileged class on the other. This leads, in turn, to a violent redistribution through the dictatorship of the proletariat that is sought.

Plato describes another form of the reversal in Book 8 of his *Politicus*. A democracy that grants too much freedom has to end up in tyranny. Authority itself surrenders here by giving in to an insatiable hunger for the good of freedom and producing anarchy by giving freedom to everybody. This surrender begins at home and then moves on to the school. The father no longer accepts his superior role and thus excuses himself, as it were, for his existence. He lives out the role of a boy and finally begins to be frightened of his sons. No wonder the sons usurp the role of their father and in their desire to be free have neither shame nor fear of their parents. When age ceases to be itself and coddles the young so as not to be rejected as inflexible, but to appear progressive and flexible and open to the future, it has already surrendered the credibility of its authority. Teachers fear their students and flatter them. Students have no respect for their teachers. The young make themselves equal to the old and seek to wear down their rank in words and deeds, while the old deal in over-familiar fashion with the young, in the spirit of youth constantly engaging in witticisms and jokes so as not to seem morose and overpowering. Finally all respect for laws in any form, written or unwritten, disappears, and no command is recognized. The anarchical element that lurks in this relaxation, or supposed freedom, then moves on to revision of the untenable situation and becomes in this way the fine and glorious starting point for tyranny. For too much advance usually turns into the opposite . . . to a return to too much bondage both for the individual and the state. Tyranny, then, has its basis in no other state than democracy when democracy cultivates freedom as an end in itself and understands it as liberation from all authority. The law of dialectical inversion that we note in plants, animals, and human society finds demonstration here.

4. THE DEVELOPMENT OF LEGITIMATE AUTHORITY

It would be mistaken, then, to regard the questioning of authority as an original act of protest. The protest is the result of a particular kind of freedom that eliminates existing authority. It eliminates it because this authority no longer trusts itself and therefore abdicates. It puts itself on an equality with what is subordinate, or subjects itself to it. All that we are left with, then, are empty and impersonal authoritarian structures which might originally have served as a social basis but which now, lacking authority, can no longer do justice to this function. Originally, therefore, the revolt against authority is not a denial of authority itself but the rejection of a lapsed authority and its residual structural shell. Thus a great deal depends on distinguishing between personal "authority" (the noun) and the "authoritarian" shell or structures (the adjective).

Regarding the development of rebellion, especially among the young, Cyril N. Parkinson in his book *Die pelzgefütterte Mausefalle* shows impressively that people never revolt against tyranny but against an authority that is becoming or beginning to become weaker. We do not hurl ourselves against barred and bolted doors but against rickety doors with broken locks. The story of all revolutions begins, not with the conspiracies of the rebels, but with the doubts and differences of opinion among those in office. The collapse of government, or authority, creates the vacuum into which rebellion is sucked.

Why is there this loss of authority? Parkinson replies that it is due to the ruling classes' not knowing how to give young people a goal because they have none themselves. It is not offering a goal to say to young people, as in the United States, "Look what we have to give you. You have schools, universities, culture, sport, television, travel, and counsel. What more do you want?" The more that they want is a goal that makes life worth living, and that rulers for their part have to represent credibly. When this is lacking, commitment to authority falls away. To win back the loyalty of a wandering youth, we must offer them a goal outside the society in which they have to live, a goal with which they can identify, so that they can then identify with those who represent the goal and who go before them, as authorities, on the path that leads to it. What are we trying to do in this regard, in nonmaterial categories? Parkinson thinks the Marxists have an answer to this question, and so they have something analogous, at least, to what we call authority, and perhaps even an outdated answer like theirs is better than none. So long as we cannot answer this decisive question, our society, and those who represent it as authorities, will have no magnetic attraction for young people.

Only when we see clearly along these lines that the rebellious protest is not against authority itself, but against lost authority and its residual but anachronistic structural bases, can we understand that the rejection of so-called authoritarian structures goes hand in hand with longing for the legitimate authority embodied in persons. The question arises, then, what we mean by this legitimate authority.

We have already set forth one decisive precondition for this legitimacy. It has to refute the thesis that it confronts the human self as a dictator and by alien direction thwarts its identity. One might make the same point in the form of a question. Does authority have to be hostile to autonomy from the very outset, or can it serve identity and open up possibilities of self-actualization?

Relation Between Authority and Autonomy

This question may be studied with the help of a very interesting and pregnant model, Lessing's work on *The Education of the Human Race*. Though one might have many objections to Lessing's Enlightenment view of God, by means of this possibly distorted picture he still makes it very clear what authority is by nature, simplifying it as on a blackboard.[5] For Lessing understands God in the strict sense as an authority that is set over us. The way that God exercises this authority offers some decisive insights into its nature and functioning.

It is with an absolute authority whose legitimacy cannot be questioned that God deals first with the race in its youth and immaturity. At this early stage he issues commands and performs miracles so as to demonstrate his superiority and authority. But he does not act blindly or capriciously. In line with the Enlightenment view, he proceeds in the name of a reason that is not yet accessible to the race in its childhood, but into which it is to ripen. Hence God uses his authority to make rational disclosures to the race that are unattainable at this stage and have to be told to it. Precisely by means of these anticipatory disclosures he hastens our evolution toward a goal at which we can handle the pure and everlasting gospel for ourselves. God's authority facilitates the development of human autonomy.

If we analyze this view of authority, we find two decisive features.

First, authority does not use power arbitrarily but to establish its legitimacy. The superior court that confers legitimacy is the logos, which has definitive and normative rank not only in the human world but also in the kingdom of God.

Second, God's authority is marked by the fact that it leads to autonomy and thus seeks to make itself redundant. In good rationalistic fashion it is understood as the authority of a teacher who pursues the same goal toward which the pupil's development also presses. A pupil gives poor thanks to a teacher by remaining a perpetual pupil. The teacher's goal is the pupil's independence.

We thus arrive at a reciprocal relation between authority and autonomy that we might not originally have suspected. As a rule we link the concept of authority with the impression that subjects must surrender some control of themselves, delegating it to the authority. The present relation (which replaces the assumed confrontation) may be stated in two theses on which commentaries will be appended.

The first thesis is that authority can never be conceded except by what is at least a potentially present autonomy.

The second thesis is that authority constitutes itself only in relation to an autonomous partner and must pursue the goal of allowing potentially present autonomy to become the normative factor of self-consciousness. Authority, in distinction from blind power, is present only when those who bear it are ultimately on the same level of norms as those over whom it is exercised. Only then do subjects have criteria that make the legitimation of authority possible. Only then can authority carry with it a readiness to let itself be legitimated by subjects. The two sides use the same measure.

We may again use an illustration, this time that of the authority of a judge in a trial. Authority has to be granted to the judge. It is he who finally conducts the trial. He also acts as a representative of the law. He and not the accused decides what is right. But this superior position of the judge does not put the accused in a position of pure dependence. It makes the accused a partner in the legal procedure. For both are under the same binding law, the one upholding it, the other its (actual or alleged) transgressor.

This partnership of judge and accused in the name of a higher third thing that covers them both has always been the subject of discussions of legal principle. Such discussion arises, for instance, when it is asked whether things like lie detectors and drugs and psychological examinations should be used to arrive at the truth. Legal writers (e.g., Eberhard Schmidt) have brought a decisive argument against their use, namely, that they rob the accused of partnership in the process and reduce him or her to a mere object. It is part of the partnership, of the rank of subject, that the accused should make the decision whether to tell the truth or not.[6]

That the judge has to give reasons for a verdict is also connected with the nature of his or her authority. The point of this is not just to explain the verdict technically or to validate its agreement with the law to the legal community. Its true target is the accused, who is to be shown that the verdict is just. The accused is thus granted the same privilege of demanding an accounting as is granted to the legal community, not being excluded, therefore, from this community, but included in it. The question whether the accused is in fact convinced of the justice of the verdict is unimportant compared to the basic position that is taken here, namely, that an appeal is made for his or her consent, so that the accused is also made a potential judge of the act that he or she has committed. The law respects the autonomy of the accused in this way and puts both judge and accused under the same final authority. The correspondence between authority and autonomy is thus illustrated here with all the clarity one might desire.

The same is true of other figures or institutions that represent authority. Thus Luther is a kind of church father for the Evangelical Church. In this sense he is an authority. But this is not because of his "blue eyes and beautiful blond hair," to use his own words. It is only because he speaks in the name of Holy Scripture as the court that authorizes him. Because this authorization is taken seriously, this means that his authority can be checked and that the church has criteria by which to check it. This is true because the church, too, recognizes the normative court of Holy Scripture and can thus test the authorization of Luther's authority. There is a plain analogy here to the judge whose verdict may be tested and, if necessary, revised in accordance with the law.

If it is true that authority always needs to be checked—because it has to do with the autonomy of those who are subject to it—then there can be no permanent authority that is established once and for all. Every authority is for the time being, until further order is taken, for so long as it checks out positively with the court that is above it. Only so long as we find that some binding norm is represented by an authority can we identify with that authority and let our autonomous will be taken up into it. Regulations that presuppose and claim both freedom and obedience must proceed from an authority that is not felt to be alien and hostile but is loved as their own by those whom it directs. Such regulations must be firm enough, and universal, and few enough, to be accepted by the spirit without fresh offense whenever a decision has to be made (Simone Weil).

The observation that authority has to be recognized in the name of our own autonomy, so that it is dependent on its autonomous subjects, leads on at once to a new problem: Is this not to maintain an ultimate equality of rank between those who have authority and those over whom they have it? But is it not of the very essence of authority that there should be some form of superiority? How are we to reconcile these two principles?

Equality and Hierarchy:
Fundamental and Empirical Aspects

The apparent contradiction is resolved once one recognizes that fundamental and empirical aspects overlap here. The fundamental side is that human autonomy and personhood are inviolable, so that only autonomous partnership can constitute authority, and one has to assume that there is in fact an equality of rank between those who bear authority and those who recognize it and identify with it.

The empirical side, however, is that experience shows that those who bear authority are in the right. They are there prior to my own insights and possibilities of decision. They see farther than I do. They seem to be in a position of greater immediacy and intimacy than I am vis-à-vis the court that binds us both. At first, then, I have good reason to trust the validity of whatever proclaims or orders authority. If Luther's understanding of Holy Scripture has proved to be true at decisive points, and has opened up perspectives that were closed to me, I am inclined initially, and until proof to the contrary, to trust his demonstrated perspicacity even where his theses seem at first to be strange to me.

Jawaharlal Nehru offered a good example of this empirical relation to authority when he said of Mahatma Gandhi, as a man of supreme authority, that at first many disagreed with him, but they soon recognized that he had done the only right thing. They thus came to rely more and more on his judgment, as they had already learned to rely on his principles.

The prestige of authority results from experience, from the finding that it has demonstrated itself. Experience is always limited to its own span of time. It is a temporal phenomenon. This is why we have to use such words as "thus far" and "at first" to describe the rank of authority. These terms tell us that authority is only for a time. Because it has demonstrated itself before, I trust it, but only until my critical alertness shows me that it has forfeited its rank and my own perception forces me to contradict it, to liberate myself from it.

The supremacy of authority, then, does not rest on the tutelage of those who are under it, on depriving them of their autonomy. It rests on the credit that adults are prepared to extend to authority because it has demonstrated itself in the circle of their experience.

It is less than accurate, therefore, to talk about the *authority* of parents or masters in relation to very small children or animals. In such cases there is no experience on the basis of which to extend credit. Nor is there the maturity to recognize authority. There is only the supremacy of influence, the radiant power of love, parental power, and the ability to train.

The credit that is granted on the basis of experience is extended in similar fashion to tradition. Authority and tradition have much in common.

Tradition hands down the experience of generations. Hence the credit that one's own limited experience initially extends to collective experience (expressed, e.g., in proverbs) will be granted until the legacy of tradition finds an adequate replacement in one's own experience or is limited or refuted by one's own encounter with life. This is true even when certain enduring elements are found in tradition, as in the Christian churches. For even here there has to be differentiation and distinction between that which is permanently valid and the ballast of what is merely time-bound. This distinction between the authoritatively valid and the outdated can be made only with the help of criteria which are at the disposal of adults alone and which thus presuppose autonomy (in the sense developed by us).

The limitation of authority of which we have been speaking is not just one of time, as though authority were merely provisional. It may take other forms. Thus the weakness of human nature gives rise to the possibility that there may be too much authority and that this excess will lead to the tutelage of subordinates. We can also grow used to overbearing authority, so that the will to be critically alert is injured and by the law of inertia authority degenerates into authoritarian structures. Finally, institutions that bear authority have a tendency to seek stability in structures and to expand in accordance with the autonomy of power of which Jakob Burckhardt has spoken in such an illuminating way. We have examples of this degeneration of authority in dictatorships, and especially in ideological tyrannies. These are usually connected with a personality cult that is willing to say that the "leader" or some outstanding ruler is always right. Here the provisional credit becomes permanent. It is frozen institutionally and it leads to the tutelage of subordinates and upsets the basic correspondence between authority and autonomy.

The democratic principle of the division of power is a structural means whereby to resist this degeneration of authority. The refusal to give complete independence to either the legislative, the executive, or the legal branch creates a system of mutual checks and balances which forces the authorities constantly to legitimate themselves and guarantees institutionally the correlation of authority and autonomy. The recognition of the weakness of human nature that makes such arrangements necessary may be based on distant recollections of what the biblical story of the fall has contributed to our picture of humanity.

5. THE ANTHROPOLOGICAL SIGNIFICANCE OF TRADITION

Tradition and Freedom

We have already had occasion to note that authority and tradition have much in common. Tradition has authoritative significance inasmuch as collective experiences and the collective sense of norms accumulate in it, and these precede individual experience and are—initially at least—superior to it. We may thus suspect that tradition, like authority, will prove to be specifically human in character.

Tradition does in fact occur only among humans. Animals do not hand things down. They simply pass things on. What they give their young is not handed down in the human sense. They merely activate instinctual conduct that is inborn or ground in. There is no discussion—no opportunity for acceptance or refusal—such as is demanded of us with our summons to adulthood. There is only a turning of the mechanism of instinct, with none of the problems that we humans face. In animals, therefore, we find typical behavior without the individual nuances that mark modes of conduct which involve decision and reaction to demands. In our case tradition does not have the compelling force that instinct has in the case of animals. We are able to move out of the influence of one tradition into that of another, and either to assimilate it or to free ourselves from it. Alexander Rüstow in his attempt to set forth the human character of tradition is even prepared to hazard the statement that our humanity consists in our ability, not to invent, but to hand down. Konrad Lorenz has characterized this side of humanity in the brilliant statement that humans are beings who have invented the passing on of inherited qualities (i.e., tradition).

By way of tradition we inherit certain values and modes of conduct that we may appropriate or critically vanquish. Either way, what is handed down is presented as a matter for our own decision. We never begin with zero or empty slates. Even in a revolutionary age, when people leap across past determination and live in the name of a future that they themselves have planned, they still follow courses that are set by such great figures as Nikolai Lenin or Mao Tse-tung.

It is also a mark of the constitutively human character of tradition that even revolutionary movements that shatter earlier traditions begin at almost the same moment to form new traditions, sometimes by way of legends. Without tradition we are without history. We are exposed, naked, as strangers cast into time. We freeze in isolation. One may illustrate this by Jacques Monod's description of human beings as a pure accident, as gypsies on the margin of the universe. Humanity totally devoid of tradition would be an extreme abstraction and would suffer a degree of alienation, which points negatively to the indispensability and indestructibility (or indelible character) of tradition.

What is human in the original sense can, of course, be plunged into inhumanity. The possibility of inhumanity, of complete self-alienation, is a dubious monopoly of the race that animals are spared. Freedom can conjure up total unfreedom by way of unrestricted misuse. The free resolve to take the forbidden fruit whirls us into the history of perdition which carries with it fratricide (Cain) and idolatry and makes us the slave of the processes initiated by us. The free resolve of the prodigal son takes him into the far country and delivers him up to bondage there.

In the same sense, tradition as a human institution can plunge us into inhumanity. It confronts us with specific values and modes of conduct. More accurately, it does not confront us but hems us in on all sides. We breathe it; it is the atmosphere in which we live and move. And as breathing in and breathing out are not done consciously but are an elemental act of life that is more done to us than done by us, so we are to a large extent unaware of the things that determine us. Over large sections of life we do not put the reflective question: Which part is the self and which part is tradition? In the naive sections of life we do not make this distinction but identify with tradition. It is almost like a new birth when in face of tradition we begin to ask about our own identity in distinction from it. Since this birth is painful—and the more painful, the stronger the motherly organism of tradition—tradition carries with it a temptation to cling to it, to be involuntarily carried along by it. It can thus lead to a self-deprivation of freedom and hence a dehumanizing. Here, too, what is most human is always the greatest temptation.

It is of the very nature of human personhood and freedom that there can be no gift (*Gabe*) which is not also a task (*Aufgabe*), and only thus a gift. When a gift is merely taken passively and consumed, it becomes a ferment of disintegration. In exactly the same way we have to win and possess what is handed down to us by our predecessors. Instead of passive reception there has to be personal appropriation. Sociologists speak here of an internalizing, a conscious or unconscious taking into one's inner self.

Tradition is appropriated in this sense when I can will freely what it gives and demands, when it thus passes through an act of critical reflection and receives the approval of my autonomous conscience. Only then does the struggle end between tradition and autonomy, between the despotism of what comes down from the past and my own freedom. But even if I reject a tradition in the name of my own freedom—perhaps a feudal, patriarchal, or middle-class tradition—I still need it in order to release my own freedom from it, and with it the free air in which alone this freedom can breathe. It then serves the function of creative provocation, of a challenge in Toynbee's sense.

This immanent conflict of human nature, which is caused by the creative tension between the poles of tradition and freedom, finds historical expression in the permanent conflict between parents and children, or, in psychological terms, between gratitude and repudiation. Here again self-knowledge and the discovery of identity do not come through pure introspection but are made possible only by encounter with others outside the self. This grows more intense (and correspondingly more fruitful) to the degree that the other comes to me with the claim to be my own. What encounters me with this claim is tradition. Wrestling with this claim enables me to know what is my own and thus to find my identity.

This has particular significance for what is called upbringing. This is also and primarily the bringing out of the self, self-formation. The mere devouring of knowledge never accomplishes it, even though the unlimited riches of tradition might be tapped. Such devouring can produce only pedantic dwarfs, learned eunuchs, and the homunculi that Nietzsche could describe so satirically in his work *Nutzen und Nachteil der Historie*. Real education can never come through the purely passive acceptance of what is offered but only, as Thomas Mann once said, when there corresponds to this some "educable material" that can be provoked to free development and therefore formed. In Goethe's sense what is entailed is the "reproduction" of what is received.

The antithesis between a tradition that takes us by the hand, functions as a despotic authority, and is passively received, and a tradition that is active and provokes us to self-discovery, may be expressed in a figure of speech. Truly exalting tradition, as someone once said, does not mean preserving the ashes of the past but guarding the flame. When we receive a fire we have to know what is burning, and why it is important to keep it burning. When we are truly concerned about the flame that we find in tradition, we cannot just warm ourselves at it. We have to work to keep it blazing. If this is a form of "conservatism," it certainly cannot be called a reactionary orientation to the past.

The Antitraditionalist Thrust of Emancipation:
Revolt in the Name of Human Rights

Talking about the emancipatory task of those who are progressively minded demands liberation from many things, and not least a repudiation of every form of tradition. This is denounced as an alienating force that makes us the involuntary functionaries of an inherited collective will. In this way we assist and preserve and forward the interests that are at work behind the collective will. In a fateful way, therefore, tradition hampers the discovery of the self. This thesis is necessarily alarming to us, for it radically challenges all that we have said and established concerning the human role of tradition.

For if our principle is correct that tradition is a constitutive part of humanity, then the antitraditional thrust of the ideology of emancipation moves inevitably toward a new form of inhumanity. It will thus accomplish the very opposite of what it is seeking. Pursuing the goal of overcoming human alienation, it will necessarily result in a new and perhaps more radical form of alienation. This issue applies in a very elemental way to the present generation. For this reason we must test it out.

In definition of the term "emancipation," we note that it derives from Roman law. Here it denoted the legally demanded releasing of an adult son from his father's authority, or the remission of a slave. Today the term has moved increasingly out of the sphere of individuals to that of groups who are trying to break free from legal, social, or political tutelage. Typical groups of this kind are peasants, workers, Jews, and women. Among the slogans ancillary to the postulate of emancipation are demands for equal rights, democratization, and self-determination. A curious fact that might be mentioned, since it has some symbolical significance, is that for some time in France the world's "oldest profession" has been demanding emancipation and a corresponding democratization of the center of eros. The theoretical basis on which demands for emancipation have been achieved—whether they be humanitarian, liberal, or socialist in nature—is formed by human and civil rights, which have come increasingly into the picture, though they have their basis in the ancient idea of natural law,[7] and which were finally codified by the United Nations in 1948, so that they have become the so-called fundamental rights in the constitutions of member states.[8]

Since movements of emancipation have their basis of action in human rights which an earlier social structure withheld, thus condemning whole groups of people to subjection, the decisive question arises: What is the model of authentic humanity which is to crystallize in a finally achieved adulthood and in whose name protest is to be made against the forces of alienation?

Karl Marx as an Example of a Negative Anthropological Analysis

When we put this question, we stumble upon the remarkable fact that the ideologists of emancipation seem to ask only from what we are to be freed—i.e., from what structural forces of oppression and disintegration—if we are to be ourselves. What the self is that throws off its chains remains an unknown or perhaps inexpressible quantity.

The anonymity of the self that presses for liberation certainly does not have to mean that there is not at least some vague idea of it or that the question is without interest. Nevertheless, one has to state that this being is nowhere defined, nor is any portrait of it given. Complicated interpretations and inferences are required to discover what the champions of this ideology, e.g., Karl Marx, mean positively by the human self. They can tell us very well what this self is not, and ought not to be. It is not, and ought not to be, the product of social structures such as we find in developed capitalism. But can one really speak about this kind of alienation without measuring it by the norm of what the human self authentically is? Can one say what is inauthentic without having some standard of authenticity?

It is a strange phenomenon that this piece of illogic constantly recurs. We, too, can say fairly easily what is *not* human. But when we have to say what *is* human in a positive sense, we quickly run into difficulties. To know what is bad is not by a long way to know what is good. To know what is human and good we have to indicate the source of this knowledge, e.g., whether we are made in God's image or simply serve economic processes. We need not do this if we restrict ourselves to negation, to a mere assertion of what is not human. For a massive mistreatment of people, their cynical exploitation, contradicts both views.

In Marx the anonymity of true humanity is the more glaring because he had opportunity in his system to say something about it, e.g., when he depicted the eschatological process by which we may throw off our former fetters and come to ourselves. He calls this process a leap into freedom. This leap consists of the seizing of the means of production by society and the consequent ending of the dominion of products over those who produce them. This will bring the battle for individuality to an end and lead us out of the animal kingdom and animal conditions of life into those that are truly human. Previously nature and history have forced social systems upon us. Today this can be our own act. This is the leap of humanity out of the kingdom of necessity into the kingdom of freedom.

We are authentically human, then, when we are no longer the objects of relations but acquire social organs and can thus shape society freely for ourselves. But is not this still a negative statement, a negation of the negation? Does it involve more than saying that we were previously alienated? Does it tell us, and can it tell us with its ideological approach, what we are positively; how, for example, we live and suffer and love and are merry and die? How will the history of this enigmatic and ghostly figure proceed? Will it proceed at all? Obviously there are no longer any hostile forces, whether externally in society (class warfare has ceased) or internally in the soul. There are no longer any conflicts. Are these people of the last days good, perfect, without evil? All this is obscure, and has to remain so. The writer Robert Havemann has given some thought to it in his book *Dialektik ohne Dogma?* But the very fact that he has raised the theme seems to confirm the instinct of the chief ideologist that it is a foreign body in the system.

Marx himself apparently gives us only one hint (in his *Deutsche Ideologie*) as to our true nature. For Marx, too, the monstrous power of evil as it is at work to proletarianize and dehumanize us in the economic disorder of capitalism is not self-constituted but derives from human beings themselves, who are thus ultimately to blame. Our own act develops into an alien power that confronts us and subjugates us instead of being controlled by us.

Is it by chance that this concept of evil as a statement about human nature is not expounded further and never occurs again, so far as I know, except under the symbol of alienation? The idea of radical evil is totally eliminated from Marxist eschatology. This presents only the utopian vision of a humanity that no longer has any history—a strangely unreal, docetic picture in which we cannot discern any essential features. At this point Marx simply gives up trying to portray us. He thus stops when we are most eager to find out what he means by unalienated and authentic humanity.

Where, now, is the evil whose traces Marx can find in historical or empirical humanity? Assuming that Marx is right and the social forms of dehumanizing, i.e., exploitation and the class structuring of society, are the product of evil in humanity, how may we hope that humanity will ever be essentially different if it merely eliminates the phenomenal forms of evil? Should we not assume instead that the potential energy of evil that slumbers in us will break out in new and different forms even in a classless society, e.g., in individual conflicts, in envy, hate, the need for prestige, and all the complications entailed by the biologically innate drive toward a pecking order? Will not the impulse of aggression remain?

Herbert Marcuse lets his imagination roam further than Marx did but still gets no closer to a positive statement. We recall some of the decisive aspects of Marcuse's eschatology that occupied us earlier (pp. 39 ff). In a free society the elements that provoke the aggressive drive when there is class conflict and the stress of competition will drop away. The happiness of inner balance will thus be achieved as well as external peace. The surplus energy that remains can be put into such positive tasks as construction and sport. This state of redemption will extend to the animal kingdom as well. Predatory fish will no longer need to feed on others because they will have other sources of nourishment. Marcuse cannot deny, of course, that a final ineradicable element of aggression will remain. Thus even in the last and golden age of history we have to reckon with the fact that two young men might fight for a girl.[9]

Do we not have here again a very unreal and shadowy picture? Does not this harmonious utopian society consist of stupidly happy lemures, of homunculi who can never be Romeo or Juliet and among whom no Shakespeare could ever find any dramatic stimulation? In all this, do we ever find even a single word about the ontological status of this new humanity, about its nature or essence? In both Marx and Marcuse humanity is exclusively presented as a mere function of future social conditions. It is simply the shadow of what will take place on the social level. It is no more than stuffing for the areas of freedom that are opened up by the automation of the means of production.

The picture of this eschatologically authentic humanity is made even harder to grasp by the fact it has no individual features and is simply the substratum of a collective consciousness. Only when the true individual reabsorbs the abstract citizen and becomes genuinely social in empirical life and individual work, only when he or she sees and organizes his or her personal resources as social forces, so that social force is no longer divided off in the form of political power— only then, Marx thinks, will human emancipation be achieved.

We thus find our human fulfillment only as we cease to be individual and become social. Only here does society accomplish a complete union between humanity and nature. Only here, through the completed naturalism of humanity and humanism of nature. In other words, humanity has returned here to union with nature and the world. It wants what nature wants, what society wants. All antitheses are at an end, for the emancipation of everything particular and individual is complete, and this emancipation of emancipation brings us to our true selves. Since history is inconceivable without conflicts, one might say that we cease to be historical beings here and become mythical beings who have lost our individuality and simply represent a collective will.

But is not this humanity with its collective instincts and consciousness an unreal sham? Has it not ceased to "be"? Is it not a mere synonym for the "humanity" which in the eighteenth and nineteenth centuries, including Ludwig Feuerbach, is no more than the sum of all our positive and complementary qualities?

With this unreality of the human X, Marxist eschatology confirms our previous insight that we cannot get at human nature along purely empirical lines or by adding up human characteristics. But this is what Marx did when he tried to show from the empirical course of history that we are simply economic beings. Authentic humanity, however, cannot be achieved by merely looking at the eco-

nomic aspects of life. That this is impossible is shown by the fact
that many phenomena of life, e.g., living, loving, suffering, and
dying, resist this attempt to explain it in terms of economic interests.
And can we really explain by this interplay of interests such figures
from world history as, e.g., Luther, Francis of Assisi, or even Adolf
Hitler? When we try to do so—and Luther has been the victim of
such attempts—we get distorted pictures and terribly amputated homunculi. The caricature of Luther presented by Dieter Forte is a
dreadful example. We achieve an authentic view of people only
when the transcendent element is also present. We have spoken
about this in connection with "alien dignity."

We recall the discussion that led to this brief analysis of Marxist
anthropology. When the ideologists of emancipation, we said, break
free from such a constitutive factor as tradition, this negation leads
inevitably to a new form of inhumanity. Marx is a test case. For him
history is a process of class conflict, and so traditions can form only
the functional superstructure of this conflict and we can only seek to
liberate ourselves from existing tradition. Social humanity, the goal of
history, casts off the tradition defined by class conflict, and with it
the alienating impact of this tradition. The obvious result is the
shadowy and docetic phenomenon of a lemur, a figure that we have
described as new inhumanity.

Permanent Change as an End in Itself

The ideologists of emancipation want a total detachment from all
that has gone before and therefore from tradition. By means of this
they hope to deprogram us completely. In intention, this depro-
gramming has a material goal. Even if this goal can be described only
in negative terms, and necessarily remains a hazy one, it is that of
humanity liberated from alienation.

The climax of this trend toward emancipation seems to be reached
when the act of change that is sought becomes an end in itself. This
occurs when no definite goal motivates the alteration but the act of
alteration is enough. This act is no longer oriented to a future that is
to be achieved but consists only of repudiation of the past. Change
then means no more than not remaining as we were. In this sense
the new left is polemically fixed on the past and is thus in a paradoxical way reactionary. Tradition is simply something that has to be
discarded because it hampers change and seems to enforce conservation. Those who are bound by tradition simply repeat what is past

instead of being able to achieve a present of their own. "Can we describe it as will," asks Peter Handke, "when people only want to do again what has been done before? Is an idle will to repeat things a real will at all? Is it not true that only the impulse to do something different can be described as will?" But to want to do something different, and to refuse to do a thing only because it has been willed before, is to reject in advance the question why it was willed and whether the reasons for it might not be reasons for us to will it too. In this way every kind of tradition is decisively repudiated.

This repudiation has some extreme implications. Thus it cannot desire a free order which will allow generous room for all kinds of emancipations of this kind. For once a program of emancipation is given institutional form, it becomes an element of tradition. Free institutions, as Robert Spaemann has rightly observed, are in direct contradiction with the emancipatory view of freedom. The activism of a desire for change which is an end in itself works in grotesque fashion against its own institutional results or fruits because achievement of the goal of change would bring activism to a halt. The goal of change, if attained, would invalidate the proclaimed thesis that change is an end in itself. It would thus involve the whole conception in self-contradictions.

It is perhaps for this reason that notorious changers such as we find on the New Left are very uncomfortable with the granting of freedom, suspecting that there is here a more dangerous opposition than in hard conservative countermovements. They seem to detect that an opposing readiness for emancipation will entangle their own desire for change in damaging self-contradictions. Thus they can hardly be *against* something that says it is *for* them. But they themselves cannot be *for* it because their fanaticism for change cannot be in favor of anything that is already present, even an order of freedom and toleration. They thus engage in their usual guttersnipe vituperation against liberals. Herbert Marcuse, who comes from an academic tradition, does this in Latin and speaks about repressive toleration.

But what is really "idle" here (to use Peter Handke's term)? Certainly a tradition can become idle when we are just passive consumers and do not try to win and possess it, nor to criticize it, nor to make it our own. Idling is simply the possibility of misuse. But is it not made into a principle when change is declared to be an end in itself and thus perpetuated (as the New Left puts it)? A car runs idly when the engine turns over without moving the car or taking it to any destination. Change for its own sake is really an idling of this kind. It does not try to move to any point or achieve any goal because carrying out a program of change would simply bring about a new contradiction.

Here again, and more decisively than in Marx, the repudiation of tradition ends in unreality and inhumanity. As we have seen, humans are beings who have to aim at a goal, who are furnished with a destiny, even though they may define this in arbitrary ways that are very remote from the biblical concept of creation. But when change becomes an end in itself, there is neither Whence (except perhaps as self-positing) nor Whither (except as the object of fear of the establishment). There is only the ghostly Now of the moment, an abstract present with neither past nor future. The movement that presses for this kind of change is a circular movement. It is that of a carousel. It simply goes around and around, without getting anywhere. The chosen task of those who break free from tradition and focus on the moment gives truth to the statement of Mephistopheles—though one may doubt whether it applies to the dying Faust—when he says that all is over, that all the striving has led nowhere, that it is as good as if it had never been, that it has all moved in a circle, and that he himself would prefer eternal emptiness. "As if it had never been" is a good description of the idling of which we spoke. Emancipation as a fundamental repudiation of tradition is inhuman. It is so in *every* case. Tradition, on the other hand, can only become inhuman, or, better, we can let it be inhuman. Whether it is human or not, whether it is used in one way or the other depends on whether we have the freedom to move toward a Whither. But this possibility is present only when we are seen in our Whence and responsibly confronted with this. Inasmuch as tradition represents this Whence, it is inalienable.

II. HUMANITY AND SOCIETY

In our chapter on human secularity and in many other places we have had occasion to note that we are enmeshed in a social existence. We do not just exist for ourselves as individuals. Our social life is not a mere extension of our individuality. Robinson Crusoe is not a paradigm of our original state but an extreme instance of the self-alienation into which the accident of a shipwreck might plunge us. In truth society is not an appendix of selfhood, an addition from outside. We live and move from the very first in our being for others and therefore in orders, in a system of relations, in the relationship of I and Thou. The order of man and wife is part of this. So is the relation of generations to one another. The great orders of state and society, with their many subsidiary groupings ranging from social clubs at work to indigenous choral unions, are impulses or outworkings of the implications of our social constitution.

Our intertwining in our social being is the point at which what we have called our relation to the world crystallizes.

a. Godless World and Worldless God

At this point a self-critical question arises for Christianity, especially since the Reformation. Has not this relation to the world been missed by faith? Can our modern knowledge and mastery of the world, our feeling for it be brought into harmony with faith, or do there have to be wrestings and violent convulsions here?

I remember a conversation with a teaching assistant in biology and religion. I had given a lecture on the relation between belief in creation and the theory of evolution, and afterward she surprised me with the remark that she had never previously realized that the two aspects of the world, that of biology and that of religion, stood in a relevant relation to one another. When I asked with some astonishment how she had been able to relate the lectures on biology and religion which she delivered to the same class, whether she had not had some interest in bringing them into harmony, whether she had not even experienced this harmony at least in the form of a question, she astounded me with her naive answer, "In the interval between the classes I simply switch over and have the sense of entering a totally different world." In its childish innocuousness, this may be rather exceptional, especially among educated people. But it brings to light the misguided possibility of suppressing the relation to the world and its understanding, of isolating the believing I in docetic fashion, of snapping its relation to the world. This can be carried even to the point of a cleavage in consciousness that undermines the personal union between the believing I and the I that exists in the world.

The question that arises here is shown to be an urgent one by the fact that since Luther's day decisive changes have taken place in our relation to the world. A sober empiricism prevails in history and natural science. The question of God seems to be excluded here. A methodological atheism is the rule. It is adopted even by Christian historians and natural scientists, whether with epistemological awareness or with the uncritical naiveté of the teaching assistant. Technology and organization seem to put the world under human control and hence to free us from absolute dependence in the religious sense. "We plow the fields and scatter—by machines, of course!—the good seed on the land." But for its growth we now have greater confidence in fertilizers than in "heaven's almighty hand." We now seem to have taken over the government and God is banished to a hereafter whose heaven is so small that he has to share his emergency quarters with the sparrows. No wonder that rumors of the death of God were spread abroad and he was faced with the choice of either demonstrating himself in this world or being written off altogether.

At any rate the Reformation, especially in its Lutheran form, finds itself suspected of not being able to handle the world. The thesis that we are justified by faith alone may have brought with it a new relation, a new immediacy, to God. But what good is that if this God has lost contact with the world and therefore with our being in the world? We cannot have a relation to him outside the world any more than we can have such a relation to ourselves. We work at our jobs, our desks; we compete for markets and positions; we have bodies with urges; we study their biological origins; we feel responsible for social justice and progressive forms of life. If God is not present in this implication of ours in the world, then he is unreal. We do not talk for long about those who have emigrated, whether into the hereafter or into their own inwardness.

Is this, then, to be the mark of the reality to which we have come either in spite of the Reformation or in consequence of it—that a godless world and a worldless God stand in confrontation? This is the decisive question.

That Lutheranism cannot handle the world, and has thus neglected the modern age, has in fact been alleged against it by serious people. We shall appreciate this if we underline some of the objections.

First, is there not in Luther's Small Catechism—and hence in a normative doctrinal statement of the Lutheran tradition—an antiquated and patriarchal view of the world, which is dominated by the figure of the father? And may not the influence of this be seen today in some detectable afterpains of the authoritarian state? For the sake of this tradition, have we not had difficulty in coming to terms theologically with free democracy? Is not the cult of authority that is championed here contrary to every adult relation to the world? Is not the thesis that each state of life is assigned by God, and must not be changed, a harmful restriction of modern mobility and every idea of progress?

Again, in sexual ethics and questions of marriage and divorce the reformation church does not seem to have found the right word for the hour. This critical conjecture does not have to doubt that marriage is a divine order. But it leaves the question open whether God's will does not present very different claims within the framework of a partnership of the sexes, equal rights for women, and the altered position of the father.

In the name of a reformation understanding of the faith, are we not committed too much to inherited customs instead of being reached by a relevant word for the age and thus being open to the future? Can we and dare we, in the name of faith, be reactionaries? Even proven traditions, when they no longer fit the present, can become dead laws. We need to remember how post-exilic Judaism passed on the ashes of the tradition of the law from urn to urn and ended with the rabbinic cult of the letter, thus providing us with a good example of the withering of traditions. Are we not going the same way when we let Lutheranism define our relation to the world?

Fundamentally it is an astonishing question whether the reformation has perhaps neglected modernity and hampered a theologically informed relation to the world. It is astonishing because the general view—and it is not totally wrong—is that Luther freed us from clericalism and theocratic tutelage and sanctified secular activity. Was it not he who tore down the barrier between the sacred and the profane and said that the mother who brought up children and the maid who wielded a broom were offering service to God in a secular estate? And did he not provide a theoretical basis for this emancipation of the world in his doctrine of the two kingdoms?

In asking whether Luther's theology might not have opened up faith to the world, and then for some reason run into new obstacles, we come up against the key construction that regulated his theological understanding of the world, namely, the doctrine of the two kingdoms.

b. The Kingdom of the World and the Kingdom of God— Humans as Pilgrims Between the Two Worlds. Orders of Creation and Emergency Orders

Although this doctrine marks a decisive breakthrough and incorporates the understanding of the world into faith, we can adopt it today only in a modified form. We have burned our fingers and note that a secularized, conformist Christianity can use this doctrine as an ideological excuse. This misuse has taken, and takes, the following form. Only the spiritual sphere (preaching, pastoral care, and the like) is regarded as within the competence of the divine claim and command. The secular sphere is viewed as a zone in which only economic, political, and social laws apply. Hence the laws of God have no place or competence here. They are irrelevant, disruptive, and ineffective interruptions. For us, then, who have become cautious, if not wise, through experience, this much mistreated doctrine needs some safeguards whose necessity Luther could not perceive at the moment of the breakthrough.[10]

In this context all that counts is the decisive *intention* of the doctrine and not the problems involved in its theoretical development. Our concern is with the situation at the time of the breakthrough, when it opened up the world as a sphere of divinely willed tasks instead of a zone to be rejected and neglected (as in Augustine and later forms of Pietism).

If we ask concerning the decisive impulse that triggered the doctrine of the two kingdoms, we come up against a dramatic conflict of faith, namely, the clash between the radical demands of the Sermon on the Mount and a world structure that seems to make these demands impracticable. The world obviously stands in essential contradiction with what the Sermon on the Mount requires.

Thus the Sermon tells us that even he who looks on a woman to desire her has committed adultery with her in his heart (Matthew 5:29). Or it says that if our eye offends, we are to pluck it out and throw it away. Or we are told not to resist evil, but if someone hits us on the right cheek, we are to turn the other also. The list of radical demands goes on.

Now a mere glance at real life shows me that I cannot do justice to these demands in any literal sense. This impossibility is not due to my lack of subjective readiness—which may well be present—but to objective relationships that form an insuperable barrier. (We have already had occasion to speak about this problem of the barrier when we had a look at the young businessman who wanted to love his neighbor but was trapped in the principle of competition, pp. 113 ff.) I can rightly see myself ordered to curb my desires, but I do not control the kindling of elemental desires within me. This is a vital process outside the grasp of my will. How, then, can it be the subject of an accusation? How can it be understood as adultery in the heart?

What is a drive within the individual meets us in objectified and suprapersonal form in the structural laws of the world. What will happen—we have already asked this—if I do not resist evil but offer the other cheek? Will not the result be chaos and the unrestricted dominion of the strong? Do we not see that the nexus of our world is shot through with orders that do resist evil and make life possible? Did God not want this life? Did he revoke his purpose in creation? Is there not a Christian ethics of calling which binds us to these orders, obviously regarded as divinely intended? In the name of love of enemies, judges cannot just "love" enemies of the legal establishment and let them go free. They *have* to oppose them and put them behind bars. And how about parents? Even if they want to be extremely anti-authoritarian, they cannot let every lie or egoism pass in the name of love. They may investigate as radically as they can how their children have come to offend as they do, but there will still be situations when they have to stand up to them, when they have to resist evil. If they let everything go, their children will become intolerable brats. And if they are ill-prepared for life, they will probably accuse their parents later of not having treated them with love, i.e., of following the law of convenience and least resistance.

Why is it that relationships obviously do not let me fulfill Jesus' command of love literally and uncompromisingly? The reason seems to be as follows.

The earthly orders and structures within which we have to act have a certain autonomy that we cannot ignore, as the enthusiasts attempted, and proclaimed to be possible. Within the legal order judges have to resist the evil of crime and cannot condone it. Politicians cannot passively and patiently watch hostile powers attack their country, turning the other cheek to their forces, but have to take action to repel those who are acting contrary to the interests of their state. The autonomy of politics demands self-assertion and the consolidation of power. Taking a humbler course is forbidden. In business, too, we have to accept the law of competition and cannot lag behind in the name of love of neighbor. We have already seen that in so doing we should damage the interests of our employees, so that we should fail to meet the law of love from this standpoint.

We cannot say this without recalling two points that avert possible misunderstanding.

First, if the structure of the world seems to make fulfillment of the radical demands of the Sermon on the Mount impossible, one may not conclude that these demands stand in a correspondingly radical contradiction with God. For he in whose name the unconditional command of love was issued is the same as he who established the orders of the world. These orders were set up after the flood to give structure again to a world that sin had disordered and thus to make human life possible (Genesis 9). If we were simply left to our own individual or collective egoism, we would destroy ourselves. We could not then fulfill our destiny. To reach this goal, we have to exist physically. The orders, then, have always been regarded as measures of providential care and love. But what was established in love limits the possibility of radical love. Is love itself in conflict here? A prospect of ultimate ontological contradictions opens up at this point. What is the reason for these? What we have already said about the fall, and will say later, leads us to suspect that the brokenness of human existence, the gulf between God and humankind, is responsible for the rise of these tensions. This is also one of the reasons why God's coming kingdom is not a future event of this world's history which the present aeon itself can bring about.

Second, the fact that we and our world cannot fulfill the radical demands of the Sermon on the Mount carries with it an accusation. It is a judgment. Nor can we set aside this judgment by pleading a tragic situation along the lines of Bert Brecht, who argues that I myself might live in conformity with God's will but the relations will not. As we have seen (pp. 116 f), I cannot detach myself from the relations of the world, saying that I am here, and they are there, and because of them, from outside myself, I am prevented from being the person I might be. For the sacred egoism and self-assertiveness of the political world are simply an extended form of that which lives and moves in my own heart. As I look outside, I have to say, "This is my world; this is what I am." I have to identify with my world. Hence it is not the wicked world that puts me in tension with the Sermon on the Mount but I myself. As I am the representative of this world of mine, I myself am the initiator of the tension and the reason for it.

In admittedly dubious fashion, but without evading the question that is put, the doctrine of the two kingdoms tries to express and make intelligible, in a theoretical model, the contradiction between God's radical demand and the conditions of the earthly order that oppose it.

What is meant may be illustrated by the so-called Noachic covenant that God made with the world which arose newborn, as it were, from the receding waters of the flood (Genesis 9). We have here a new beginning almost like that of the morning of creation. The promises and commands of creation are promulgated as at the time of origin when the world was summoned into life. Humanity is again charged to have dominion over the earth. God's world is entrusted to it afresh. It is called upon again to be fruitful, to increase, and to fill the earth.

But in all this there is now an alien note which the perfect world of creation never heard. Regarding human dominion we are now told: "The fear of you and the dread of you shall be upon every beast of the earth, and upon every bird of the air, upon everything that creeps on the ground and all the fish of the sea; into your hand they are delivered" (Genesis 9:2). This is no longer the eternal liturgy of the world of creation which rests hierarchically in itself because it is related to the Creator. This new beginning bears within itself from the very first the stigma of the breaking of the covenant. Dominion is no longer simply conferred and unquestioningly respected as such; it has to be asserted. It is bound up with fear and terror. The break with God, which is a liability of the world after the flood, is also a break with our fellows. If this break is not to lead to self-destruction, it has to be limited by force. This is why we read: "Whoever sheds the blood of man, by man shall his blood be shed; for God made man in his own image" (9:6).

The world after the flood, the fallen world, needs a legal order. If the death penalty is understood as an extreme instance of this,[11] what is its relation to God's will? It is undoubtedly ordered, but can this mean that it is in keeping with God's true and original will? Undoubtedly not! It would be absurd to try to find such threats in the creation story. What we have here is a new and modified will of God, a will that relates to the broken order of the fallen world, coming to it in a way that it can bear.

Luther in his commentary on Genesis distinguishes between these two expressions of God's will with a metaphor that we have quoted already. In the perfect world of the original creation God could direct the world with a flick of the finger. He could do this because our human gaze was fixed on him and could note every slightest movement, just as an orchestra looks at the conductor and obediently follows his gestures.

But everything changed with the fall. Turning aside from God, we humans no longer see his movements. God has to grasp us with his fist to make us do his will. The institutional form of this ruling fist is for Luther the state. Thus the orders of history (e.g., the state, law, economy, et cetera) are not original orders of creation. They are emergency orders to meet the new situation of fallen humanity. One might say that they are orders of the patience of God in virtue of which he keeps the fallen world alive and uses the means that are available within it for its preservation.

Jesus himself presupposed this distinction in expressions of the divine will. When he spoke to the Pharisees about the indissolubility of marriage ("What God has joined together let no man put asunder," Matthew 19:3 ff.), they replied by asking why Moses—in the name of God—had allowed certificates of divorce. Jesus answered, "For your hardness of heart Moses allowed you to divorce your wives, but from the beginning it was not so." A plain distinction is made here between the original and authentic will of God as this was promulgated at the beginning of creation and the expression of his patience which tolerated the hardheartedness of fallen humanity. If there is crisis or divorce, the original order of creation is disrupted. To try to uphold it, things being as they are, would be fatal and terrible. In a fallen world God uses its possibilities and upholds it by the orders of his patience.

Thus the Creator constructs laws of the fallen aeon, e.g., that fear and terror should rule in it, and that it should no longer be able to continue without force. In virtue of the miracle of his preservation and blessing these will not serve to destroy the world but to uphold it. As Gerhard von Rad says in his exposition of the Noachic covenant, these are orders which obtain in the violently distorted interrelations of creatures. They are emergency orders in which power and force are assigned a legitimate function.

The theoretical model of Luther's doctrine of the two kingdoms tells us along these lines that to the direct will of God as this is symbolized in the order of creation there corresponds another form of his will as this is expressed in the orders of the world, in divinely willed institutions by which God deals with the situation of the fallen world, upholds it with its own dubious means, and bears with it in patience. These, too, are signs of the loving providence which wills to preserve and to make room for redemption. The kingdom on the right hand is an expression of the direct will of creation, whereas that on the left hand is the kingdom of the world in which the will of God that is broken by hardheartedness is institutionalized in the form of orders.

If we do not distinguish between these two kingdoms and thus differentiate between God's proper and improper will, we will produce distorted pictures of humanity and its world. The two possibilities of failing to distinguish are easy to recognize.

The first is when we proclaim the radical demands of the Sermon on the Mount—the proper or authentic will of God—without considering the state of this aeon as the law of the world's constitution. In this case we treat the world as though it were still in the original state of the first day of creation, or as though the last day had already dawned. To think that the world must be ruled by the Sermon on the Mount, to make it a law, was and is the fatal error of all enthusiasts and utopians.

The second possibility of overlooking the distinction between God's proper and improper will is when the orders of this aeon are upgraded as orders of creation and existing conditions are thus given the sanctity of theological validation. In this case war, for example, is regarded as a divine institution and hallowed as such. God himself is seen as the God of iron. Statecraft becomes an expression of God's will and there is thus no theological barrier to its intensification in the form of totalitarianism and ideological tyranny. Historical examples on both the right and the left—the "German Christians" of the Third Reich and Christians who conform to the system in the Communist bloc—crowd in upon us in sinister numbers.

Humanity in this aeon after the fall and the flood becomes a distorted picture once it forgets that the two dimensions symbolized by the kingdoms on the right hand and the left overlap in it. For it will then place itself one-sidedly in either the one kingdom or the other, and either fanatically bypass this world, and therefore God's relation to it, or absolutize this world and equate its jungle laws with God's commands.

Without some consideration of the two kingdoms, no theological anthropology is possible. No bowdlerizing that the doctrine suffered, especially in the nineteenth century, should blind us to this fact.

c. Improvised and Planned Shaping of the World— the New Dimension of Love

1. NOT JUST BINDING UP WOUNDS, BUT PREVENTING THEM

The decisive point that is set before us is that obviously God's will does not always reach us in the same form. It is not a statically fixed thing but is flexible, dynamic, and many-sided, as may be seen in our dealing with history. For this reason the way in which we ask about it, and seek to do justice to it, will change in accordance with the media in which we exist.

Thus it may expect from us the improvisation of love when our neighbor lies unforeseeably at our feet (as in the story of the Good Samaritan in Luke 10:30–37). Then what is demanded cuts right across all planning. The priest and Levite pass by the man who had fallen among thieves. We do not know exactly why they prescribed this arc around him. It might have been due to fear, or the desire not to be involved. It is also conceivable that the priest's calendar had fixed the day's program and stopping to help would have thrown everything out of gear. Perhaps he had to give an evening lecture on neighborly love in the city of Jericho, and practicing this love would have disrupted his plan to give instruction on it. At any rate, the parable of Jesus is designed to demonstrate that a readiness to let oneself be disrupted is what God might want. God's will can require of us an improvisation of love that sets all plans aside, even those that we have made in the name of God or humanity. (In the last resort the lecture on neighborly love in the city of Jericho would also have been part of a plan that was pleasing to God and indicative of love of others.)

On the other hand, God's will might be quite different. It is possible that it does not demand improvisation—or only improvisation—but the planning of love. One may say indeed that love makes us inventive. But in the first instance it makes us investigative. It makes us ask what is the cause of the problem to which it brings its aid. For it might be that true aid is possible only when an evil is fought at its root. But in this case we have to know the root. Thus painful abuses might have social causes that are themselves grounded in the organized or political system. In this case love might be commanded to deal with the system which produces the intolerable social and human conditions. If so, love cannot stop at improvisation. It has to be a planning, organizing, prophylactically effective, and far-sighted love. Only thus can it properly discharge the task of change. Only thus can it not merely bind up wounds but help to prevent them.

2. POLITICAL IMPLICATIONS OF THIS FORM OF LOVE.
THE APPEAL TO RATIONALITY AND
READINESS FOR COMPROMISE

If this task of planning, this systematic form of activity is viewed as an aspect of the love that God's will might demand from me, a whole series of implications follows.

If we want to influence, and if possible change, the shape of the world—which is what planning love has to want—then we naturally have to act in accordance with the laws of the world. We cannot desire what is impossible and utopian; we have to act "politically," i.e., to pursue the "art of the possible" and to conduct ourselves accordingly. This means quite simply that we have to keep real relations and specific conditions in view if we are to fulfill God's commands here and now and be present for our neighbors in such a way as to help them in a planned, programmatic, foreseeing, and comprehensive way.

I will try to give an illustration of what I mean.

If God's will directs us to act, it does not give us a detailed description of our route. If it did, at every crossroads—where a decision has to be made—there would be an arrow telling us in what direction to go. I could read off in precise casuistic fashion which turn I should make in questions of abortion or tariffs or conflicts in personal or professional life. I should thus be subject to legalistic casuistry and guidance in which God's will would meet me as heteronomous compulsion. In this way it would not really meet me.

We have already seen how the gospel is in striking antithesis to this view of the will of God.

Instead of a detailed map I am given a compass reading with the requirement to let the pointer tell me in what direction I shall be doing God's will. The pointer directs me to love of neighbor, to what we have called planned and politically active love of neighbor. How am I to proceed in this direction? It is impossible to move forward undeviatingly and therefore without aberration. How can I do that when I am not marching on an abstract desert plain but in varied country with houses and fences and rivers and mountains that I cannot just traverse unseen? My only option is to go around these. The one thing that really matters is that I should keep the compass direction in view and come back to it after every crossing and turning.

This necessary regard for the terrain symbolizes the need to take into account the given circumstances in which I have to act. I cannot run my head against the wall but have to consider what is possible or practicable, things being as they are. I must use existing relationships and study constellations of interests, political antitheses and agreements, and many other matters. Otherwise I shall simply be acting in a fanatical, unrealistic, and ineffective way.

If the metaphor of the compass illustrates the manner in which the will of God claims me, an unheard-of appeal is made to my freedom. The will of God claims my rationality, my adult self-government.

I am compelled to consider how I can fulfill the command of love in existing relationships and with the use of existing possibilities, how I can do the best that can be done, things being as they are. The issue is how situations of conflict can be handled, if not resolved; how we are to decide in the battle of values as various demands confront us; how we can at least fulfill the command of love in the form of a compromise. Compromise between an unconditional demand and the concrete circumstances that hamper it by imposing conditions—that is the true task which is laid upon the rationality that God's will claims of us here. A refusal to compromise in principle is a form of radical utopianism which is shattered by reality and in the supposed name of the will of God will simply sabotage this will.

As the will of God, especially if not exclusively in this form of planning, causes us to ask about the possibilities of fulfillment, it claims our mind as well as our readiness of will. Paradoxical though it might seem at first, it is still true that openness to compromise, considering the terrain in our use of the compass, imposes a total commitment, claiming conscience, volition, and rationality: conscience with its assent to God's will; volition with its translation of this assent into the movement of obedience; and rationality with its interpretation of the claim into what it entails in a given situation.

Reason, then, has to interpret the circumstances and situation, and this involves evaluation. But obviously different people can come to different evaluations, for we are not following detailed directions with their arrows. Thus even among Christians for whom the will of God is a common norm of action, there may be different assessments of the situation. This finds outward expression in the fact that Christians belong to very different parties and groups. Another indication of the difference in evaluation is that synods can hardly ever reach agreement on issues of this kind, e.g., whether one should support revolutionary liberation movements, or pass resolutions against racial division. They may be at one in principle, i.e., in the set of the compass. The difference arises in their interpretation of the terrain or specific situations, and therefore in their assessment of the way in which the principle can be put into practice.

Just because we are so totally claimed in such questions—claimed in conscience, will, and mind—the disagreements which result lead in experience to particularly passionate exchanges. The intensity of the conflict reaches the same heat as that found in the battles against heresy in the early centuries. Sometimes offense is taken at this in church circles. A sign of the decadence of faith is perceived in the fact that in our synods we no longer fight primarily about the Incarnation and the Resurrection and the Last Judgment, but about questions of political ethics. It seems to me that this offense is unjustified and that there is no basis for the idea that we have here a retreat of dogmatic interest. Once it is seen what significance the reality, the situation, the terrain has for a fulfillment of the command of love—and this insight is our modern destiny—it is understandable that theological passions should be aroused precisely at this point today. We no longer look at people abstractly, "in themselves"; we see them in the web of real structures which are part of them and from which they cannot be detached.

If it is people viewed like this who are summoned to love, then at once the nexus of reality comes into play. For the neighbors that they are to love are also part of this nexus. They are competitors, or partners, or members of the same party, or of an opposing party. They have similar or alien political views. They have specific social positions and economic interests that may be compatible with mine or opposed to them. This nexus of reality to which each of us belongs erects a whole series of barriers which I have to leap across or circumvent in order to reach others. It raises the question how I can serve others in these circumstances and what conditions of realizability, of the possible, I will come up against in so doing.

The unconditionality of the claim—if we may use one of Kierkegaard's phrases—triggers an "infinite passion of inwardness," a commitment, to the exact extent that the realizability of the command of love is uncertain. (For what is certain, e.g., that two and two make four, leaves me cold and does not trigger any passion.) The realizability of the command is uncertain precisely because I confront the barriers of the structures of reality—autonomies, pressures, and suprapersonal fronts that do not allow me to follow the exact course indicated by the compass needle. It is this very uncertainty that leads to my total commitment. I am not just partially involved in the sense that I merely *want* to do good. My mind, or reason, is involved too. I am "condemned" to the freedom of responsibly interpreting the reality, the terrain; of making compromises with it; of finding the necessary ways by which I can serve my neighbors.

In this burden of freedom and responsibility which is laid on the mind there may be seen again the fact that we are not slaves or functionaries or immature people who have to be led step by step. We are called as the "children of God" (Galatians 4:1–7) who are summoned to serve in responsible personal decision and the venture of freedom.

Here, then, we have some indication of the way in which we can fit in our modern understanding of reality. Planned love—the form of love which deals with the barriers of reality, which is at work systematically, critically, prophylactically, and politically—this planned love has its place here in the free responsibility of the children of God.

d. Love of Neighbor in Today's Wider Horizon

1. IMPACT OF MARX

Discovery of this new dimension of love represents an unheard-of historical break. It does not throw overboard all older traditions in the understanding of love, but along the lines of these traditions it opens up new perspectives.

For centuries Christians were the deacons and Samaritans of the world. They bound up wounds, cared for the sick, visited people in prison, and gave alms to the poor. One should not document this display of love without respect. Yet the question immediately arises whether this alone can be the solution to the problems of the modern world. Does the command of love simply demand that we should set up a gigantic hospital—admitting that to do so is indeed a fulfillment of the command? If so, the Soviet author was right who wrote in a Moscow newspaper that the church has long since ceased to be a pillar of fire going before humanity and leading it to its supreme goal. It has become more of a sanitary service that follows the march of life and gathers up the wounded and broken.

As the church was dealing with the unfortunate victims of the trek of humanity, Karl Marx came along and analyzed the causes of social misery. He found these causes in the structure of capitalist society. Logically, then, he proposed a vast restructuring. Whether or not his proposals were right is not relevant here. The decisive thing is the new view that he gave us of humanity and serving humanity. Marx attempted to influence the social atmosphere, whereas the church— to exaggerate a little, and hence not to be quite fair—was simply offering umbrellas to those who had lost the shelter of their homes.

Medicine, hygiene, and technology have operated in a way that is formally similar to the experiment of Marx with society. They have changed the conditions of our communal life. They have not just devoted themselves to caring for those who suffer from contagious diseases but pressed on to find the causes of the diseases. They have fought bacteria.

We face here the question whether the children of the world with their scientific curiosity or political concern have not had to take up a task which the command of love ought really to have laid on Christians in the kingdom on the left hand, in the dimension of planning love. Did not this love itself require that Christians should render more than Samaritan service, i.e., that, faced with threatened individuals and groups, they should organize and do things and render institutional service that would prevent the human needs from arising?

This task of planned prevention also imposes material tasks of world control. These include research into the conditions which will allow the tasks to be performed. Hence we come up once more against the problem of the terrain which we have to traverse in our compass march.

2. THE PARABLE OF THE GOOD SAMARITAN
FROM A NEW STANDPOINT.
AGAINST "ONE-EYED" HUMANITY

At this point I will not hesitate to illustrate this very abstract problem by a little story, and I do not think the illustration will really mean any simplification.

Perhaps I may be a little overimaginative in wanting to consider how the stories told in the New Testament might have continued. Thus I am tempted to speculate what became of the woman of Canaan whose first meeting with Jesus was so momentous (Matthew 15:21 ff.), or of the rich young ruler whose dialogue with Jesus ended on such a sad note (19:16 ff.). More interesting, however, is the question what might have become of a figure like the Good Samaritan (Luke 10:25). We have seen that he was a man of improvising love. When he suddenly came upon the man who had fallen among thieves and was severely wounded, he spontaneously altered his day's schedule, cared for the man, and paid his expenses when he left him to be treated in a nearby inn.

My question is whether the Samaritan was content with this spontaneous aid or whether he considered some further steps. He was not a Samaritan by calling or the head of a Samaritan union. (To suppose this would be as foolish as saying that Goethe was a classicist by profession.) Allowing fancy free rein, I may thus suppose that he was the mayor of his native city. I might then imagine that when he was back in his office the same love of neighbor that led him to render spontaneous aid stimulated him to ask what he might do to prevent such a need from arising again. How could he see to it that in the future wounds would be prevented instead of having to be bound up when already inflicted, as at his own intervention?

As the mayor, which we have made him, he might then have seen it as his job to send two posses of police to comb the neighboring forests for robbers. This preventive measure would result one day in his scouts' arresting two dangerous-looking characters in a very suspicious situation. But when these two wretches come before him, caught red-handed, this Samaritan mayor suddenly realizes that the command of love bids him do something for these unfortunate fellows too.

He thus does some investigating to find out how they came to be on this slippery slope. Not to prolong the story, I will use some abbreviated technical terms which cause me no difficulty though the characters in the parable could not possibly have used them. One of the prisoners tells the mayor that he comes from an asocial background; his mother sent him out to steal when he was only a child. The other, who if he had lived today might well have used such terminology when undergoing psychological testing, tells him that he suffered from a youthful trauma through being bathed as a child in water that was too hot.

The command of love now forces the Samaritan to consider how to extend his defensive measures in the light of these disclosures. He tells himself that the slums that produce the asocial milieu must be completely cleaned up and that the man with the youthful trauma must be brought to a psychotherapist's couch. To make this possible, a host of ancillary measures is required which poses enormous tasks of organization and planning. But we will assume that the kind-hearted Samaritan indefatigably undertakes these.

It is certainly daring to continue one of the parables of Jesus in this way, and the fear might arise that an element of the grotesque is being introduced. But is the continuation really so off the mark? Does it do anything other than spotlight the many implications of the command of love? This command is like a rocket with many driving principles.

It is driven first by the direct need of neighbors that calls out for assistance. Then there is the impulse to take preventive measures and prevent the infliction of wounds. The final impulse is to engage in far-reaching actions that will tackle the social root of the lapse into crime. This undoubtedly leads far beyond the act of spontaneously expressed neighborly love and brings us into the sphere of basic reflection, advance planning, and organization.

With these final stages it may easily happen that the initial Christian starting point—the command of love—is lost to view in management and activity. Perhaps today a certain radical, left-wing, ideologized theology is a macabre model of this process of forgetting. It changes the community into a political club for social change without keeping in sight, and actualizing cultically, the commission that had this practical implication. Apart from this aberration, however, one has to say that insight into the many facets of the command of love shows us to what extent it claims us totally, for in face of the

needs of others it commandeers our mind as well as our conscience
and goodwill, demanding that we give ourselves to the tasks of reflection. One of these tasks is that of meditation on the final motive of
the command of love as we recall that we are accepted by God and
can thus accept others, being forced to pass on the experience that
has become ours. Then there is the task of rational reflection which
makes us engage in planning and confronts us with political, economic, and social tasks.

This total claim, which defines our humanity, can be betrayed in
two ways, the result either way being that our total engagement is reduced to a partial one.

A first restriction is when we do not go beyond improvising love
but simply bind up wounds from case to case. With all due respect
for the sacrifices that are made—we think of the many unselfish
helpers in everyday life and in charity organizations—one has to say
that a deliberate limitation to spontaneity and a resistance to planning love which claims the reason have the result of making love
one-sided.

A second restriction is when meditation on the relation between
love of God and love of neighbor is shriveled up by activism and absorption in rational projection. Everything depends upon keeping the
totality of the command of love in view lest we fall into the "one-
eyed humanity"—as Ernst Jünger puts it somewhere—which will
allow us to see people only in part. People are more than neighbors
lying directly at our feet. But they are also more than molecules in
larger orders that I am trying to shape or alter.

e. Unsolved Problems of the Reformation in Anthropology

1. FROM CHANGING THE HUMAN HEART TO CHANGING THE WORLD. DELAY AND NEED TO CATCH UP

There can hardly be any doubt but that this totality of the command of love has continually been neglected in the history of Christianity. Even if there was no desire to think nonhistorically, it is perhaps a disgrace that it had to be Karl Marx who made us aware of
the planning or sociopolitical dimension of love, although naturally
he did not appeal to love as Christianity understands it. In spite of
the doctrine of the two kingdoms, which forms a system of coordi-

nates that is well adapted for the purpose and can find a place for love in the sense of secular planning, this aspect was not considered and had not even been discovered, as it were. How are we to explain the delay at this point? Or, more positively, how are we to achieve a relation to the world and our existence in it that corresponds to the totality of the command of love?

We must begin with a historical statement. The Reformation focused on a question concerning the human heart. In biblical usage and the Christian tradition, the word "heart" designates symbolically the center of the person, that which makes us human. The concern at the time of the Reformation was that this heart should be freed from the unrest which was necessarily caused by the principle that we have to achieve righteousness by legalistic obedience. When the relation to God is thought of along these lines—the doing of good works and the earning of merit—there is necessarily a centering on the I that inevitably causes disquiet. I am then compelled constantly to look at myself and my standard of achievement and will either trust in this in a false security or I will despairingly note its inadequacy.

It naturally meant a tremendous liberation from this twofold "curving in on the self" (Luther), this narcissistic and self-tormenting egocentricity, when the Reformation started to speak about justification by faith alone. For this thesis means that God for Christ's sake accepts us as we are. We need not make ourselves acceptable to him by some fixed standard of achievement. He accepts us unconditionally. Because we can now live in this confidence, in a grace that receives us even in our lostness, we no longer need to be concerned about ourselves. Our identity is taken up and hidden in God. We no longer need to be bothered about merit. We are delivered from the urge to control our own destiny and hence from both false security and inappropriate despair. The heart is renewed. It has a new relation to God from which the burden of achievement has been lifted. The drive toward curving in on the self weakens.

Extraordinary though this liberation might be, one question arises and must not be overlooked (as later happened). This is the question as to the effect of the renewed heart on the blood circulation. Does this heart pump blood into the members, into the extremities? Are there numb and bloodless members? In plain terms, is it clear enough that the new relation of the heart has implications for all the spheres of life in which we are engaged, that of sex, that of business, our relation to possessions and to social structures? The question,

then, is that of the relevance of justification by faith to our relation
to the world, to our social and political conduct, to improvising and
planning love.

It is here that we find the true omissions whose symptoms and
theological explanation we have noted already. Reformation theology
did indeed put the question of the heart but neglected that of the
circulation. There is at this point an immense need to catch up. A
theological anthropology cannot fail to deal with this issue.

It has all the more reason to deal with it because the relation between the heart and the circulation is not a theme that Marx had
first to bring to our awareness. It occurs already in the middle of the
Sermon on the Mount under the slogan "hypocrisy."

Hypocrisy here is not a simple form of deception. It is understood
more radically and denotes an objective self-contradiction in us that
we may not be aware of, so that it has to be pointed out to us. Thus
we have hypocrisy when people offer a gift on the altar (Matthew
5:23) but perhaps do not realize that this sacrifice is in contradiction
with some quarrel they have with their neighbor. Or we have hypocrisy when people accept God's forgiveness but will not forgive their
neighbors (Matthew 18:21–35). Hypocrisy in this sense is the contradiction between a heart that appeals to a new access to God and rejection of the implications that this has for our relation to the world
and to worldly matters. The circulation is clogged. Some members
are numb. There is complete self-contradiction.

In face of this criticism we certainly must not fail to see what a
tremendous and far-reaching new start it was when the reformers
made the heart the strategic point where redemption begins. (Precisely in this regard, in relation to justification, Protestantism and
Roman Catholicism have come much closer since the days of the
Reformation.) From the heart as the center of the person one can
easily move on to the members or extremities. One can ask what is
the implication of the command of love or the new relation to God
(even though it may be non-Christians like Marx who have to remove our blinkers in such matters). The opposite course is hardly
possible. It simply tries to heal the members. Co-humanity is in-
scribed as a slogan on its banners and the goal is the transformation
of an unjust social structure. Important though this may be, it
reckons without the host. From this point it is hardly possible to
work back to the place where the decisive loss of the center has taken

place and where liberation has to begin, i.e., where the human heart lies in all its questionability and its need of redemption.

A decisive mark of failure here is that those who are trying to bring about revolutionary change are for the most part utopians. They assume that human existence is more or less dependent on structures, since it is primarily or exclusively located in the social dimension. Thus a thesis emerges like that which is so impressively championed by Robert Havemann or Herbert Marcuse, namely, that human perfection will come through the perfecting of social structures. True humanity, free of all defects, will appear at the end of history.

Theologically this is a new form of the doctrine of righteousness by works and therefore of the dominion of the law. The perfecting by us of the orders of history is the good work that we ourselves do. (It would be tempting to try to detect the individual symptoms of work-righteousness in this context.) Theologically again, this conception thrives because it ignores or denies the fall. Human existence is not thought to be alienated in the sense that it has betrayed its destiny (as the story of the fall believes) but only in the sense that it is self-alienated and has become the passive victim of unjust structures. Once we shake off the fate of distortion, or, rather, of being distorted, our essence, which is now under pressure, will get back to its starting point, so that there has to be a restitution of humanity and a leap into the freedom that has been lost.[12]

Here there emphatically arises the question of the origin of our plight. Has it come upon us or are we ourselves its root and therefore responsible for it? This is no less than the question how we understand humanity itself. Is it viewed, along Marxist lines, as embedded in principle in orders and structures, so that our concern is exclusively with structural problems? On this view, to use our illustration of the heart and members, we never get to the question of the human heart and there is no consideration of a basic alienation of humanity through the fall. Inevitably, therefore, there is a restriction of vision, a blind spot in the eye. In contrast, the opposite way of which we spoke, that which leads from an understanding of the heart to an understanding of the circulation and the flow of blood to the members, remains an open one.

The heart has been discussed in some essays, though obviously not with the thematic concentration of the Sermon on the Mount. Thus A. Mitscherlich (*Thesen zur Stadt der Zukunft*, 1971) has pointed out that planning should not entertain the ambition of creating new people through new houses and city buildings. Only those who see their situation can find the courage to break the taboos that stand in the way of the construction of new and gigantic cities. But where are these people to come from? What situation is in mind? What dimension of depth does Mitscherlich have in view? Is there really here something analogous to what the Bible calls the heart?

Working on the extremities, focusing on the mere shaping of the world does not arrive at the real secret of humanity. It deals only with the symptoms and does not touch the true sickness at the heart, at the center of the person.

2. THE NEW FREEDOM OF "CHILDREN" IN MASTERING THE WORLD

We argue, then, that there can be no creating new people through changing the world. To think otherwise is to engage in a utopian transfiguring of the world and ignoring of human questionability (the fall). When we do not make the essence of humanity our theme, we fail to see the goal and we are unsettled in our movement toward it. Concentrating on the means by which to master the world leaves open the questions of end (especially final end) and meaning. This being so, we are referred again to the starting point in the human heart. Only here can renewal and change begin. This in turn carries with it the question—we have come at it from every angle—how the step can be made from the changing of the heart to the changing of the world, i.e., to planning love. To stay with our metaphor, how will the blood that is pumped by the heart flow into the members?

Here again our metaphor of the compass, as distinct from a set of instructions with arrows, shows that independent decisions are needed on how we are to move over the terrain so as to avoid obstacles and yet still keep the goal in view. I have thus to decide in freedom, in the responsible freedom of the children of God (Galatians 4:1–7; Romans 6:15–18), on how to orient myself and which way to take.

This is in accord with the original meaning of the New Testament. In the gospels, not to speak of Paul's Epistles, there are striking indications that freedom is granted to God's children, and that this is what distinguishes them from servants who have to follow directions. Children can move around as they wish in their inheritance.

Three examples will clarify this.

The first is the story of the tax money (Matthew 22:15–22). Trying to trap Jesus, the Pharisees ask him whether taxes should be paid to Caesar or not. No matter how he might twist or turn, any conceivable answer might seem to embarrass him. If he said they should, he would seem to be championing the Roman party and would anger his own people. If he said they should not, he would be going against the occupying power. When he avoids the dilemma by replying that we should give Caesar what is Caesar's, and God what is God's (v. 22), this is undoubtedly a very clever answer, but we should not see in it merely a tactical maneuver. The answer has a programmatic rank that gives it significance beyond the immediate situation, and this is the real reason for the extreme astonishment which it causes. Jesus does not offer any clear or detailed guidance on how to split up the spheres of God and Caesar, the demands of church and state. We are not led casuistically by the hand but have to find out for ourselves the border between the two authorities case by case.

This border is not one that can be charted and fixed once and for all. It is historically fluid. In a democratic constitutional state it will be different from what it is in an ideological tyranny. The terrain will vary in the two cases and will thus demand different decisions as to the right direction to take. Leaving the border open, Jesus makes considerable demands on our own thinking. The mind with whose help we must interpret the situation is also put under the claim of obedience.

Because this makes the claim all the greater, we are inclined to evade it. Legalistic religions seem to be more pitiless and radical in their claims, but they are so only in appearance. In reality they burden us less because they make the decisions for us. This is why we like them. They seem to offer a place of sure retreat where we are protected from the fatigue of freedom and individual responsibility.

To measure how much we really want to be led casuistically, we need only recall the ethical conflicts imposed on us by a dictatorship like national socialism (but not, of course, by this alone). The strategy of this kind of rule is to sap those whom it governs of their resolution and to damage them by means of artificially provoked situations of conflict. These are the real torment of life under ideological governments. For they block the clear path of conscience. In paying taxes, we pay tribute to tyranny. Living constantly in the zone where the authority of God overlaps that of Caesar, and not being able to come down radically on the side of either the one or the other, we are under the pressure that whatever we do or not do is what we do not really will, and should not will, so that we are threatened with a loss of self-respect. This loss is the goal of the government, since it produces pliant subjects. People who have been through such situations know how much they would have liked to have had clear instructions and definite information on what is Caesar's and what is God's, and whether compromise between the two is permitted or not.

But this decision is not taken from us. We have the rights of children in our inheritance. We thus have the duties of children. The mind or reason is involved. It is asked whether it will let itself be drawn into obedience to the command, whether it will be the mind of "children," or whether it will simply serve to conceal with arguments our flight from obligation.

Reason is not a neutral intellectual organ. It is directed by the basic decisions that we make. Hence it, too, has to decide whether it will assess a situation of conflict in the name of God, as the reason of "children," or whether it wants to offer rational justification for dodging the situation. There is thus no dimension of the I, not even the rational, which lies outside decision, outside the claim of freedom. This is why our thinking and evaluations always stand in need of forgiveness.

The second example is that of the apostles when they say that we must obey God rather than man (Acts 5:29). This statement is a variation on that of Jesus regarding decision between God and Caesar. The "rather" can be decided only in a responsible assessment of a conflict of values.

The third example is the saying of Jesus that we are to be as wise as serpents and as innocent as doves (Matthew 10:16). Jesus makes this statement when he is sending out the disciples on their mission. They are sent out as sheep among wolves. If they do not survey the terrain carefully in this dangerous situation and use the tactical cleverness of serpents, they will soon be lost. They must see to it that they survive. For if they are dead, they can no longer preach. On the other hand, they are not just to act tactically or to put self-preservation above their task. If they did, they would obscure their message by accommodating and corrupting it. They would then survive in the midst of wolves, but they would betray their mission and lose their authority. They have thus to be as innocent as doves, delivering their message without hidden motives.

When either the one or the other will be right—either the wisdom of serpents or the innocence of doves—cannot be fixed casuistically; it is left for us to decide. With what is supposed to be the innocence of doves I may seek a martyr's crown or blindly and recklessly rush on to destruction. But with tactical cleverness I may become a traitor. Scylla and Charybdis lie on the two sides of my decision. My rationality has to be involved in it. I have to be able to reflect on the question how far the situation permits me to consider myself and how far my mission makes an irrevocable demand. I have to find the knife-edge between the two claims. I must survey the terrain but also keep my compass reading in view.

f. The Church and Politics. Faith and Objectivity

1. POLITICS AS AN ACT OF REASON,
BUT A PLEA FOR SKEPTICISM ABOUT REASON

Just because the claim of God is directed to people who are gifted with freedom and "condemned" to it, it gives them the chance to know themselves in their totality, i.e., as those who are claimed in conscience, will, and mind, and who also receive the offer of forgiveness in all these dimensions.

Under this claim and with this offer they move in the world and seek to shape it in the name of our given task. More accurately, this does not apply to all people but to specific people who have received the task and the promise, and are conscious of it. We thus refer to Christians.

If Christians try to shape the world, to follow their calling, to act politically, to improve the structures of society, and in all this to obey God rather than man, they can hardly be at one with their fellow-Christians here as they are in their common confession of the common faith. This faith is for all of them the binding goal toward which the compass points. What separates them on the way to this goal is their different assessment of the terrain, i.e., of the existing historical situation.

We have already come up against this fact of disagreement. It is based on the claiming of the rationality of adult children which leads to evaluation of the concrete situation. In this evaluation Christians will not agree. In another connection we have already pointed out that synods cannot reach agreement when they have to deal with issues that extend to political ethics, e.g., racial questions, or the right of revolution, of using force, or of terminating pregnancies at this or that period. For this reason there can be no common Christian program for society, politics, or culture. No conception of shaping and changing the world can legitimately claim to be "the" Christian one. There is no binding church approach to secular questions except in extreme cases.

It may sound a little contradictory if we also say that such an approach is still in some ways required. We must support this, and say more precisely what we have in mind when we use the phrase "in some ways."[13]

It is impossible for us to think that in all secular questions, e.g., the issues of politics and economics, Christians can decide and think and act only on the basis of factual arguments or only in the name of rationality. Even in the leading article of a newspaper, which may seem to argue very cleverly, soberly, and rationally, we cannot evade the question (especially if we do not know the newspaper but simply buy it on the street) what interest lies behind the article. What does the editor not merely think but "want"? By what emotions or prejudices is he or she moved? Everything that seems to be objective is not objective. The argument may be a garment wrapped around an interest to persuade and win over our skeptical reason. Did not Hitler use arguments in his speeches, never omitting to list his first, second, and third reasons?

Thoughts, even our own, are rightly suspect, for we know that the wish can be father to the thought. Fear and hope usually play a normative or motivating role in thinking. When we wish something, we easily believe it or think it. Our arguments are simply an intellectual excuse or cover which fear and hope know how to provide. Reasons are easy to find when one looks for them. They are all the easier the more talented the intellect and the more facile its gift of association.

The greater the talent, then, the greater the danger of providing intellectual justification for our wishes or intellectual criticism of what we fear. I remember a well-known cancer surgeon who did not diagnose his own growth. His assistants tried carefully to acquaint him with the painful truth and put the results before him. But precisely his highly developed medical rationality enabled him to make associations that interpreted the findings differently. He did not "want" to accept the dreaded truth, and he thus took rational measures to suppress it. Paul mentions this rational process of suppression when he talks about "men who by their wickedness suppress the truth" (Romans 1:18). We do this by means of arguments. This consideration probably led Luther to make his bold statement that reason is a "harlot," a prostitute whose services we can use to assert or confirm our impulses. It is a stupid if common misunderstanding to see antirationalism in this thesis. The complaint here is not against reason but against the way it can be used, or misused, as an instrument. The issue is the existential area of motivation behind the arguments.

It is at this point that we may discern the significance of faith for an objective relation to the world. The fear of God is the beginning of wisdom (Psalm 111:10) inasmuch as it frees us from fear of things and hope of things, from false fear and false hope, and thus grants us the victory over anxiety. Only as Christ the Pantocrator dedivinizes the world, "making a public example of the powers and triumphing over them" (Colossians 2:15), only as he de-mythologizes our world, does he seal up the sources of anxiety and thus make an objective relation to the world possible. Redemption in the sphere of reason is a redemption for objectivity. Even in intellectual history it forms the break beyond which objectivity can develop. Liberation from bondage means also liberation from prejudice.

It may be connected with this that natural science and technology have been able to develop in the Christian West even though they have forgotten their origins and lived only by the results òf a liberated relation to the world and a redemption for objectivity.

Karl F. von Weizsäcker has finely depicted this Christian root of the secularized world and its science in the metaphor of a secularized monastery. The buildings are the same, and the rooms still have the structure of cells, a refectory, and a chapel, even though they are now put to different uses. Thus the modern world still has the structure of a Christian world even if the colors on the plan are different, black having been changed into white and white into black, as on the print of a negative. Thus the Christian origin remains even in our secularized rationality. Self-reposing finitude still has transcendent features. The possibility of objectivity has to do with redemption.[14]

2. POLITICAL ACTIVITY OF THE LIBERATED REASON

Its Contribution to Criticism of Ideology

If the statement is true that reason is "redeemed" for objectivity, and if political decisions have reason as a criterion, it follows that the church is given a political task, no matter how we may define it. Yet one cannot say this without at once having to inquire into the limits of this task.

The thesis of liberation for objectivity ascribes especially a *critical* function to the watchman office in the political sphere. This function is set in motion when it seems that political thinking is not objective but is controlled by ideological idolatries or bedevilments. For this entails prejudice, or bondage, from the fetters of which there has to be liberation. Of the many illustrations at our disposal, we can give only a few fleeting glimpses. A couple of typical instances must suffice.

Thus this critical function may come acutely into play in Germany when political views are governed by an ideological overemphasis on the concept of the homeland. In America or Africa it may be triggered when the race problem is exaggerated or suppressed by an undifferentiated ideology of humanity. The politics of aiding development may also mobilize a critical function, especially when commercial or imperial interests are really at work behind the ardor of philanthropy and neighborly love. Thus one may be filled with either a hatred or a blinding love which dulls the objectivity of reason. Either way, ideological forces hold sway which need to be restrained.

The possibility that the egoism of a group or class or party may be triumphing in social or racial politics—and here particularly—is at least strikingly evident. Reason is hostile to the human race when it is not freed for objectivity. It evaluates people as mere instruments. For this reason a critical function combines against an ideologized function with what is almost a call for repentance directed to those who scorn humanity, an unmasking of the hypocrisy that talks in humanitarian terms but in reality treats people as though they were pawns on an ideological chessboard. This is where the Christian commission comes into play with its championing of the safeguard of what we have called our "alien dignity," namely, that people are more than the sabbath, than institutions, than ends and things (Mark 2:27).

Another brief section must now be devoted to demonstation of the church's humanistic task in the criticism of ideology.

Total Democratization

The fashionable postulate of "total democratization" can call for this task of criticizing ideology in many respects. For the postulate arouses the suspicion of being ideological, since it makes democratization a dogmatic principle and then extends it to every sphere of life, e.g., the university, the church, and even the Jesuit order. What is undoubtedly meaningful and valid in the state, when applied principially and uncritically in other areas, becomes a corrosive acid. The valid principle that all are equal before the law, i.e., in a specific and limited relation, becomes the ideology of egalitarianism (about which we spoke in connection with the phenomenon of envy). Quite apart from any question of competence, the same right of speaking, evaluating, and deciding is given to all. In the first instance I do not have participation in economic decisions in view. The problem here is too complex to allow of a simplistic Yes or No. I have in mind the troubled relations in the universities, which through the democratizing mania have become conglomerates of competing (in part incompetent) and mutually damaging interest groups. Friedrich Engels in his work on authority in 1872 specifically mocked this form of democratization and the destruction of authority that it pursues. "What would happen," he asks, "to the first departing train if we did away with the authority of those who run the railroad over those who travel on it? But the need for authority, for an authority with the right of command, is most evident on a ship on the high seas."

The loss of objectivity, the ideological bondage of the egalitarian trend, may be seen from another angle. I have in mind the threat to the fundamental legacy of freedom that is implied in this trend. Democratization, as Helmut Schelsky once said, means a greater participation of the masses in political decisions. It thus means more politicking. But more politicking in this general sense is not possible unless questions that are often complex are put in the form of a dramatic either/or, and consequently simplified. Ineluctably, then, polarization follows total democratization. Conflicts are sharpened, and by means of intensive propaganda and irrationalization people are whipped up by slogans and emotions are unleashed. Since it is no longer possible to see the full context in which one must come to a right decision, one resorts to the clichés of primitive friend-foe notions, and there is finally a call for leaders to personify the friend-program. Thus institutions lose their objectivity and fronts are an inevitable result. Those who speak about redemption, and who have to have in mind redemption for objectivity too, find themselves summoned at this point to discharge the watchman office of criticizing ideology.

Trust and Mistrust Within Pluralism

What is destructively at work in this form of democratization is connected with basic questions to which the biblical picture of humanity directs our attention. The crisis in the hierarchical principle —from parents who are asked to give anti-authoritarian education to courts that are denounced as the expression of a repressive system— this crisis in inexorable rankings rests on a programmatic mistrust. Mistrust, as previously mentioned, is often dictated by envy. We often underestimate its social and political significance. The pessimistic anthropology that lies behind it stands in strange contrast to the utopian dreams of ultimate human perfectibility. This pessimism found classical expression in Lenin's dictum that control is better than trust.

How does this kind of collective crisis in trust arise?

Wilhelm Herrmann, the great teacher of Karl Barth and Rudolf Bultmann, offers an illuminating analysis of this in his *Ethics*. Trust, he thinks, is possible only on one definite condition, namely, that I stand under the same norms as the person in whom I trust. When this is so, I can be confident that this person will act in a certain way. There will be nothing hidden or incalculable about what is done. Only thus can trust arise.

The biblical story of the tower of Babel (Genesis 11) provides us with a sketch of the meaning and development of trust. If it ends with dispersal and the confusion of languages, this is not because God—at a metaphysical stroke—brings down his fist on the table of the world and upsets everything as a penalty. The scattering takes place because the pride of those who are building the tower is trying to dethrone God and thus to repudiate the relation to a comprehensive and normative transcendence which is alone the basis of trust and which thus makes fellowship possible. The centrifugal force of dispersal develops out of a theologically based lack of trust.

Trust as that which holds things together on the basis of common norms is naturally hard to come by in our societies with their pluralism of values. For these societies, apart from those that are Marxist-Leninist or still theocratic, have long since split up, either openly or secretly, into different classes that hardly recognize any overarching values but are fundamentally controlled by group interests (by "interests," then, not "values"). Societies of this kind have no common values on the basis of which a final consensus is possible. Even secular humanism with its very general and faded scale of values is hardly in a position to provide a common denominator at this point. The minimizing of all norms, whether in taste or morality, is a mark of our age.

The truly explosive centrifugal force that is present and at work in this pluralism comes to expression in the fact that almost all of us try to discover with watchful mistrust what hidden aims and interests lie behind what are often the eloquent declarations of principle made by others. If we are convinced that ideologizing is everywhere present—as most newspapers, not without reason, now are—then we are compelled to suppose that these secret aims and interests are the true and authentic motives. When entrepreneurs, for example, speak about their concern for good social products, and stress the need for investment, and thus argue against unreasonable increases in wages, which from their standpoint carry the potential for economic disruption, their employees see in this only a concealed economic egoism which is really concerned only to see to it that higher profits flow into their own capitalist pockets. Conversely, when workers advance the thesis that capital and labor ought to be equal and thus share in profits as well as decisions, employers think they can discern an ideologically concealed purpose on their opponents' side to pander to the immoderation of the hunt for profits.

The watchman's task in criticism of ideology cannot mean that the church takes sides in individual conflicts of this kind. If it were to do so, it would come under the accusation of partisanship and would lose credibility. Above all, it would rightly be accused of exceeding its competence. Moral appeals for restraint are also out of place, for these would simply mean that the church joins the chorus of such appeals and cannot make people hear what is inalienably distinctive in its own voice.

The church will accomplish something when it speaks its own unique message. In this case, this means that it has to unmask the final reason for these destructive processes, namely, the mistrust which is a shadow on our "hearts." It has to show in its proclamation and pronouncements what is the basis of this mistrust. If in so doing it mentions pluralism and the chaos of values, this will certainly not be with the intention of simply proscribing this pluralism. This would be absurd, for we have attracted pluralism to us like a virus, and it is not in our power to expel it.

Part of the task of ideological criticism is to pour some water into the wine of stupid pride in pluralistic diversity. This will not be with the intention of legalistic carping, but with the goal of drawing attention to the "loss of a center" which stands behind it. The church has to put to humanity this question of the center, of the lost basis of its existence.

For a society that has lost its center but would like to overcome pluralism by a new homogeneity—for a society never wants to fly apart explosively, but always wants to maintain the possibility of historical existence—the only final option is to seek ideological equalizing and to become homogeneous at least in this dubious and fragmentary way.

What else can it do? We can observe the process today in ideological systems. When the center has been lost, only a dismal choice remains—either centrifugal pluralism and self-destruction, or the forced unity of ideological conformity. Ideological systems are characterized by the fact that they not only govern with the help of outward force and physical terror but also insert their ideas inwardly and thus seek to achieve total control. It is an essential task of theological anthropology and its criticism of ideology to point out the roots of this perversion and to set it in contrast to the true destiny of humanity, to the freedom of an objective orientation to the world.

The Anti-Authoritarian Principle

We have already referred to anti-authoritarian tendencies in our chapter on authority. In this context we shall pick out only one theme and put it under the microscope.

The thesis of those who champion the anti-authoritarian principle is that faults in children or young people (aggressiveness, dishonesty, asocial conduct) should not be corrected by force or authority but that the causes of these faults should be investigated and eliminated and then there will be a change in attitude. Since these causes are almost always found in social deprivation or the youthful traumas triggered by it, the decisive thing is to deal with the social roots of misconduct. If this is done successfully—the theory holds—then there will be a new and free spontaneity in which attitudes will automatically change. Wrong attitudes will no longer develop when measures are taken to deal with social liabilities.

We have conceded already that the anti-authoritarian principle can have a useful corrective function vis-à-vis certain patriarchal forms of education. The problem, however, is that once again a pedagogic method is ideologically exalted into a principle. We recall our earlier question whether the absolutized principle of self-development is not unrealistic inasmuch as it lays an intolerable burden on children and hence does not do justice to them. A spontaneity which paradoxically becomes a claim produces frustrations. (We have already given examples of this.)

At one point there can be no doubt, for we obviously accept the postulate that conditions should be created on the basis of which spontaneity is possible. If freedom, as we said, is a basic essential of humanity, spontaneity has to remain, or to become again, our goal as a form of direct self-development. If conditions, including social conditions, have to be created to this end, this means primarily that all obstacles to self-development must be removed.

To illustrate what is meant by this, we think again of young muggers and terrorists. It is obvious that their form of self-development is not the same thing at all as an expression of spontaneity. It is an expression of aggressive impulses that are triggered in them by outside forces, mostly the social conditions mentioned. These young people are under pressures that are exerted on them by conditions in their environment. If we want to lead them to the pedagogic goal of achieving true spontaneity and self-determination, then above all we must eliminate the enslaving conditions of their lives which corrupt them. But this can never mean opening up a sphere of premature or untimely spontaneity. To work against the previous distorting compulsion by an anti-authoritarian principle is nonsensical and will inevitably have catastrophic consequences.

These considerations lead to the truly crucial question whether we can in fact wait until the basic conditions are changed and the sources of false development are plugged. While we draw up plans for this and develop initiatives toward their implementation, our newspapers carry terrible stories of muggings, attacks, and acts of terrorism. Do we really do the guilty parties a service if we leave them relatively unscathed, imposing only minimal sentences, and seeking a long-term solution for the evil by dealing with its causes or roots? In reflecting on this question, we need to realize that it is not just a matter of method or tactics. We are up against a basic theological problem, the so-called doctrine of law and gospel. This is particularly significant for anthropological questions.

The gospel, too, speaks about a new spontaneity as human self-fulfillment, namely, love. Love cannot be forced; it can only be "there" as something self-evident. It is there when we are redeemed from the ties of natural humanity and become new creatures, when in the image of the neighbor a different image and dignity may be seen from what was there before. But alongside the gospel is the law. From the biblical standpoint the law has a kind of ancillary function in relation to the gospel. We shall try to explain this by what will be, I hope, a helpful illustration.

Using without hesitation a rather dated comparison, I picture the gospel as a good shepherd. The sheep love the good shepherd. They know his familiar voice. They follow him "spontaneously." They are drawn to him. But by the path there is a juicy tuft which is irresistible to the sheep's palate. One of them breaks loose from the flock and nibbles it with great enjoyment. Naturally it does not want to disobey the shepherd or stop following him. It does not think (if we may let a sheep think for a moment) that it can let the shepherd go ahead, or that the tuft is more attractive than he is. It neither thinks this nor feels this. It simply stops without thinking that there is anything contrary in this to following the shepherd. But then the sheep dog comes along and nips it in the leg. This nip tells it: *There* is the shepherd, and *there* you must go too.

The sheep dog symbolizes the law and its function. The law is not a second authority or court alongside the gospel, or the shepherd, as its personification. The law simply reminds us what the gospel requires of us and where the shepherd wants to lead us. It puts to us the question whether our spontaneity of discipleship, of love, is still in force when we see the tuft, or whether the tuft is not contrary to this. Do we not have here the self-contradiction that we previously diagnosed as hypocrisy?

Among other things, then, the law is a sign that in this fallen and doubtful world we cannot wait until everybody follows the good shepherd spontaneously, or is compelled to live according to some other idea of humanity. Only fanatics and enthusiasts can think this, and they are then tempted, under the slogan of anti-authoritarianism or with a program of permissiveness, to give to people a premature self-government which is too much for them and will destroy them. In this aeon, then, we rightly need legal and institutional safeguards. We need the law, the intervening sheep dog. It is for this reason that the emergency orders are set up about which we read in the story of the Noachic covenant (Genesis 9:1–11).

Institutions can drop away only when their disciplinary functions are "internalized," as sociologists put it. Only then can what they do be achieved spontaneously. If, for example, we love—and love is spontaneous—we do not have to be led by the hand in our dealings with others. Love is "there" in our new being, and through our new image of others. It cannot be the object of a command.

In contrast, the lawlessness of modern anti-authoritarianism is just another form of fanaticism by which the watchman office must see itself (as always) mobilized. It is fanaticism because a false, ideologically perverted image of the human lies behind it, namely, the image of people who are intrinsically good, and will be actually good if only they can be liberated from the corrupting power of social repression. But what frees them from their alienation plunges them in fact into new alienations, i.e., into the dictatorship of a lawless vacuum. This dictatorship does not have the blessings of the order which the Creator set up as a sign of his sustaining grace even for this transitory world.

Here again the church hears a summons from the very center of its proclamation. Over against the utopian dream of a freedom that becomes ideology, it holds up the redemption from the self that is promised in the gospel: redemption for the spontaneity of love, for the "liberty of the children of God." The church also speaks about the commands of God which are an indication of the blessing of established orders.

We do not say that the critical interventions of the watchman office in the political world (taken in the broadest sense) are in favor of older, long-standing orders. If they were, the church would have to be regarded as a defender of the status quo and it would be reactionary in principle. The orders that we have in view as structures of secular existence are not static and timeless constructs but temporal and historical constructs which constantly change even though there is an unchangeable core. Even these changing orders, however, have the dignity of institutions which cannot be promulgated one-sidedly and are thus secure from arbitrary manipulation. The theological criticism of ideology, then, means letting the reason that is freedom for objectivity work in such a way that it detects fear and hope as motives that are hostile to redemption in our political, educational, economic, and social thinking, planning, and action, and thus unmasks goals which hide behind humanistic slogans but are antithetical to true humanity.

Thus theological anthropology invades almost every sphere of life. But since objectivity and de-ideologizing are its driving force, it is protected against the arrogance of trying to speak as an expert in all matters and constantly interfering. Its critical task relates to the sphere of motives, to what takes place in the "heart." Even what it has to say critically against ideologies and in favor of objectivity is motivated and limited by its pastoral commission.[15]

G. HUMANITY AND TECHNOLOGY

HOMO FABER.
ANTHROPOLOGICAL PROBLEMS
OF THE AGE OF TECHNOLOGY

I. TECHNOLOGY AS SOMETHING "QUALITATIVELY" NEW

a. The Historical Gap Between Craftsmanship and Technology

The secular orientation of modern humanity that occupied us in the last chapter is essentially the work of technology. The term Homo faber expresses a technological determination to which we seem to be subject. We cannot define our being in the world without facing the phenomenon of technology and clarifying its significance for human existence.

Ernst Jünger in his *Arbeiter* says somewhere that among spectators in a stadium or movie theater one can find a deeper piety than at the foot of pulpits or in front of altars.

We should not be overcome by disquiet at this kind of statement. Naturally there is something wrong about trying to measure the intensity of devotion and then venturing to compare its different levels in the fields of religion, sport, and technology.

Nevertheless, there are two relevant points in Jünger's pronouncement.

First, he is right about the degree of strength to which we are affected today by secular phenomena, including, not least of all, technology. To illustrate this, let us suppose that a religious teacher wants to give relevance to matters of faith, and to do so puts them in the horizon of our technological age. He compares the Holy Spirit to an electrical current to which a bus must link itself by a trolley if it is to go. Creation, as he presents it, is a wonderfully well-thought-out and organized chemical factory. Faith is connection, little faith a loose connection, and no faith no connection. But in this didactic venture the teacher has a strange experience. For in the imaginations of his students these comparisons have such a dynamism of their own that the illustrations crowd out what they illustrate. In later tests he finds that his students have found the technical images very gripping but they have forgotten their application to faith and the Holy Spirit. This confirms Jünger's statement.

A second element of truth in what he says is as follows.

In his book *Das Heilige*, Rudolf Otto, who achieved classical status as a philosopher of religion at Marburg, describes religion as an experience of the Wholly Other. This experience is unique, transcending everything that we encounter in the world. It may seem paradoxical, then, that technology, which rests on dealings with the present world, should present us with experiences that are analogous to the religious experience of the Wholly Other. How is this possible?

Technology is not just a continuation of familiar craftsmanship. Looking at a modern production line, or automated construction methods, or computer technology gives us the impression of being in a very different and unfamiliar world. Thus it cannot be grasped in the same way as the older craftsmanship and at essential points stands in discontinuity with all previous historical epochs. Goethe in *Wilhelm Meisters Wanderjahre* already expresses disquiet at the new things that are coming whose consequences cannot be foreseen. He sees a threat in the development from work by hand to work by machines, for this will give rise to an artificial need purposelessly to protect superfluous labor. He was much exercized by the tendency of machines to take over. Mechanization was approaching very, very slowly, like a storm, but it would come and strike.

The older form of work was, in fact, something that was in our own hands. We had a direct personal relation to what we made. In technology, however, natural forces intervene, such as steam, electricity, electronics, and atomic power. A qualitatively new world of production has come. It is no longer in our own hands. Like Goethe's sorcerer's apprentice, we threaten to be reduced to the role of mere functionaries to whom the law of what we do is dictated by the powers that we have unleashed. What I have called the intervention of natural forces brings with it a relation of indirectness to what is made with the help of these forces. This indirectness, once operative, commences to trigger processes of its own. It begins to make history and to engulf the humans who for their part think they are making technological history.

Technological means evolve on their own. We are no longer asked whether we want the new developments, e.g., whether we want atomic technology. We have to want them because other nations or commercial concerns or ideological systems will achieve a monopoly over these forces and thus gain technological, economic, or military supremacy over those who lag behind.

b. The Revolt of Technological Means

The phrase "revolt of technological means" has been coined to show that in their further development the initiative has slipped out of human hands and these means are now evolving on their own. It is they that dictatorially govern human ingenuity and volition. Technological advances take place almost automatically. We humans have to chase behind and see to it that we keep up. *Homo faber* threatens to become *Homo fabricatus*.

As we are occupied with technological progress and the refinement of technological methods of production, we are thus forced to ask how we can assert ourselves against technology now that it has been unleashed and is taking over the role of a partner and opponent. This may be seen not merely in technology in the narrower sense but also in medicine, whose modern achievements would be inconceivable without the use of technological apparatus. The fight against infant mortality and infectious diseases is producing a population explosion which threatens to bring on a cosmic catastrophe. Medical skill in prolonging life artificially, which seems to be covered by the Hippocratic oath, threatens to take from us the right to die and to become the scourge of humanity. On every hand we have to take steps to deal with the results made possible by our abilities. What might have seemed in advance to be a utopian dream has turned into a shock utopia. (We have discussed this already in our section on utopias.)[1]

Along these lines Nikolai Berdyaev says somewhere that in this technological world utopias are in danger of coming sooner than we expected. We thus face the very different question how we can avoid their final achievement. The world of total technological, physical, and biological manipulation, a world in which all things are possible, would be an unwelcome one. We are thus beginning to fight for a nonutopian world that is a little less than perfect. We are trying, as one might put it, to jump off the vehicle which is leading us down the precipitous slope of means to an oppressive perfection.

In this way technology introduces into human life a foreign element which bedazzles us and can take on for us the quasireligious significance of the "Wholly Other"—the other which in a remarkable imitation of devotion evokes fascination and horror and can be for us a kind of fascinating and horrifying mystery.

Those who pursue technology are perhaps the least affected by this foreign invasion. Understandably they are under the optical illusion that can be produced by what is close and familiar. Biologists, however, have noted and discussed it all the more emphatically. Konrad Lorenz points out that in earlier periods changes in geology and climate were slow and thus allowed us to adapt to them biologically. As concerns the elemental force of change, the technological age is like one of the convulsions in nature. The difference is that it has drastically changed the conditions of human life in just a few decades. The suddenness of the change means that we have no time to adapt, to digest technology. We still toy with the idea of doing all that we are now able to do. Even cultural skeptics who have found a hair in the soup, and see in technology a threat to the quality of life, know of no way in which to put the brakes on the autonomous advance of technology or to mitigate its consequences. Our humanity is no match for our technological ability. Our maturing does not synchronize with technological progress. Our intellectual and spiritual makeup is pitiful in comparison with the splendor of our technological ability. To extraterrestrial spectators we must look like people of the bush in evening dress.

Antoine de Saint-Exupéry has given a visionary depiction of the lack of synchronization between technology and humanity.

What are the centuries of the machine age, he asks, compared to the millennia of human history? We have only just become at home in the land of deep shafts and gigantic power stations. We have only just entered the new and as yet uncompleted house. Things have changed so fast, including our human relations and the laws of work and custom. Even our values have been shaken to the depths. Words like separation, distance, alienation, and returning home mean the same, but refer to different realities. To interpret the world of today we use a language that was made for the world of yesterday. The life of the past seems more natural to us only because it fits our language better. We are exiles and have not yet found a new country. We are young savages, and are astonished at our new playthings.

II. THE ANTHROPOLOGICAL QUESTION RAISED BY TECHNOLOGY

The tension between our ability to plan all things, to achieve infinite technological extension, and our simultaneous inability to master our being in the world, our human existence, causes great anxiety. This anxiety finds expression in the question: Where is it all leading? It arises out of the unforeseeability of technological possibilities, but even more so out of an obscure and mostly unconsidered awareness that the gap between technology and human control might become even greater. The results of technology—the spread of big cities, the building of gigantic concrete apartments, the power of multinational corporations, which would be unthinkable without technological resources, the rhythm of industrial work, the consumer drive triggered by technological production—all these and many other results give us the disturbing sense of being subjected to forces that we cannot control and that plunge individuals into depersonalized anonymity. This fundamental sense of unease may be the cause of the many depressions and frustrations that caused young people to explode in the late sixties and seventies. The older generation easily forgets that it is the young generation that will have to control that unforeseeable future and is thus plagued by its apocalyptic possibilities. (As George Bernard Shaw said, old people are dangerous because the future is all one to them.)

As Christian Morgenstern says ironically in his *Butterbrotpapier,* this anxiety generates *mind.* It makes us think. What we think about are the questions of our final Whence and Whither, which were long since thought to be dead, buried in the passion to master the world. These are the significant questions in a world of technological ends. Following Saint-Exupéry, we might say that winning the territory of technological possibilities was a task for soldiers, but now is the time for settlers. These must know the soil on which they are to build and the foundation on which to erect their houses. The questions of the foundations of existence, of what is constant in a time of rapid and unforeseeable change, is a religious question.

For many people this question is no longer posed by the church's tradition. It arises out of the bosom of this present world which caused us, through our sober rationality and technological capacity, to regard it as settled, outdated, and antiquated. Technology itself, the most worldly thing of all, forces us to ask who we are and where it is taking us.

This situation is a special kind of *kairos* (hour). The religious question that arises is particularly relevant because it is posed by our life situation. Alongside the mature Christian tradition, therefore, new phenomena of the religious consciousness now take their place. They have many of the marks of a religious subculture, e.g., charismatic rapture and a liking for Negro spirituals.

All these movements, and more thoughtful discussion of the question of meaning among intellectuals, are characterized by the fact that they arise under the pressure of an age in which something alien threatens to lead us off and plunge us into alienation. (We have tried to show that technology is normally involved in this.) In such circumstances the resort to Negro spirituals is natural because they, too, arose under pressure and oppression. Whether the religious question that becomes relevant in a new form here will link up with the Christian tradition there can be no saying. All that I want to say at the moment is that this new phenomenon is of independent origin and has developed in the midst of a rationally and technologically dominated secularity.

Faced with the biblical symbols of the end of history in the Book of Revelation—the sea turning into blood and the stars falling from heaven—many contemporaries confess that these are strange to them. They are compromised as mythological notions that are drawn on by world-denying fanatics. But the atomic age has developed its own eschatology by carrying technological reflection to its limit and presenting terrifying visions.

On the one side this extreme possibility consists of the tapping of absolute power. This power is absolute because it is no longer confined to earthly limits but pushes on through thermonuclear possibilities to an imitation of the production of solar energy. It is not merely by the exploration of outer space but by atomic technology that we are breaking out of the planetary province of our earth. On the other side the extreme possibility is that as the subjects of this final exercise of power, summoning up all the energies of creation, we are also the objects of these measures. They carry us with them and often lead us where we do not want to go. We are suddenly handed over to the possibility, and even the necessity, that we might put a total end to ourselves and our world in a complete reversal of creation. The ambiguity of technology reaches a climax here. It takes on eschatological rank.

It is thus the most secular of all things—atomic physics and the biological manipulation of genes—that fertilize the soil on which the religious question springs up. This question is as follows: How can we master our anxiety, our fear of ourselves and our own possibilities? In intensity this anxiety may be compared with the earlier fear of the Last Judgment and the terrors of hell. The role of medieval preachers of repentance, who scared people with depictions of hell, is played today in a very secular form by illustrated magazines, popular papers, and horror movies. Those who produce such things know that horrors stimulate sales and that anxiety flees for refuge to the euphoria of a desire for destruction (Friedrich Sieburg).

Another form of the emergent religious question is this: Who are we as the people who see ourselves in these extreme possibilities— and subject ourselves to them? Are we masters of this world through the magical power of technology, or are we like Goethe's sorcerer's apprentice, for whom the powers that he released were too strong? Here again the question raised by technology has an anthropological thrust.

The attempt to master this world in disobedience, in a proud claim to lordship, in the desire for the self-adoration of human ability, leads to domination by this world. Who are we then? Are we Adam, who was told to have dominion over the earth, and who was thus entrusted with a technological drive? Or are we Prometheus, who tried to achieve mastery over the earth without any command from the gods, and thus wanted to worship himself as the author of an eighth day of creation? Who are we?

Technology, then, raises fundamental questions of human existence that we would least expect it to raise. It is a serious error to think that only rustic people who are close to the soil stand in relation to the final mysteries and the question of God because they still have to do with sowing and reaping in a (supposedly) sacred world. If that were so, then after World War II a new world savior would have perished with the liquidation of the Morgenthau plan. The indelible character of the religious question may be seen in the fact that even our age, with its extreme developments, must still provide the soil on which it may flourish anew. The essential significance of a theologian like Dietrich Bonhoeffer is that he drew attention to the secular relevance of the question of God.

III. THE AMBIVALENCE OF TECHNOLOGY AS A REFLECTION OF THE AMBIVALENCE OF HUMANITY

The core of our thesis in this analysis of the technological phenomenon is the demonstration of its ambivalence. But to say this is still to be short of the real problem. The real problem lies in the role and character of humanity itself. Who is this Homo faber or Homo fabricatus who is seen to be both initiator and victim of the technological process?

This question forces us to make an important statement, namely, that it is not technology itself that is ambivalent but humanity as the subject of technological achievements.

To understand this it will be helpful to recall the biblical command at creation: "Have dominion over . . . the earth" (Genesis 1:28). Here, if anywhere, technology seems to have a theological place. For it uses the forces and laws invested in creation. The use of these enables us (as Homo faber) not merely to take over the world but to work with it, to make it arable, to adapt it to our use.

The command at creation undoubtedly means that we should have this dominion over the world in God's name, as God's vicegerents, and, as it were, under God's eyes. But what happens when we no longer stand under God, when we want to be like God, and even to be God, when we think we can put all things under our own rule—when the "fall" takes place? The fall means quite simply that we want to break out of the role of creatureliness and usurp the throne of God.

But in this way we become a danger to ourselves. Without God— which means without the final commitment that we have called the premise of trust and the basic condition of communication—everything is permissible (Dostoevski). Hence everything is to be feared. The dispersion and confusion of languages at Babel is the result of this fear.

The ambivalence of humanity between commitment to creation and Promethean emancipation finds expression in the ambivalence of technology. To the degree that we develop our technological potential, our ability to destroy grows with our ability to construct. We can ruin the earth as well as shape it. We see a beginning of this with the pollution of our immediate environment. The thesis of Karl Marx that possession of the means of production, i.e., technological instruments, carries with it the possibility of expansive egoism and the enslaving of dependents involuntarily confirms the ambivalence that we have just noted. (We may say this even though the detailed prognoses on the basis of which Marx made it have inevitably fallen victim to the abstractness of his view of history.) The world of people who had only bows and arrows is much less sinister than a world in which people have atomic power and the ability to manipulate biologically their genetic heritage. As we have become questionable beings after the fall, the consequences of this questionability increase with the degree of its technological outworking.

We are thus faced by the question whether it is technology that is a danger to us and not we ourselves, whose arms have been lengthened by technology, who are a danger to ourselves. From what has been said, this is obviously a rhetorical question. It sets a limit to the fashionable phrase of many critics of civilization when they speak about the "demonism of technology." This is one of the evasive maneuvers that we continually find in human history. Guilt is given the function of fate (this dubious term is appropriate here!) and by mythicizing things and forces, we avert the judgment that should fall on our own heads.

In the last resort, the question is not how we are to restrain atomic technology—to take the extreme example—but how to restrain ourselves, or, better, how we are to correct ourselves. And since we do not change fundamentally, neither do the great truths about us change. They are as young as the stars of the firmament that have always shone over us. The statements about creation and the fall, about our destiny and its sabotaging, do not grow old even though the fashion of the world changes fundamentally (through technology), even though it does grow old and the new age, too, is destined for the scrap heap. "The world passes away, and the lust of it"

(1 John 2:17). It passes away with its lust and anxiety, with its lust to master the world and its anxiety in face of its powers. "But my words will not pass away" (Mark 13:31). They will not pass away, and are kept from growing old, because we to whom they apply will remain the same to the end of this aeon, and only the forms of grace and judgment will change, not grace and judgment themselves.

IV. A SERIOUS MISUNDERSTANDING OF THE ANTHROPOLOGICAL SIGNIFICANCE OF TECHNOLOGY

a. The Problem of Autonomous Processes Again

In thus describing technology as a problem of humanity and not a problem on its own, we seem to have gone too far. The doubtfulness of this anthropological focus may apparently be seen in an obvious short circuit. For it seems as though we are forced to the dubious conclusion that since we ourselves, not technology, are the cause of all the trouble, the apocalyptic dangers of the technological age would go away if only we would "straighten up" and change our historical role. If we would correct ourselves, we would adjust to our technology too. This trivial and very erroneous solution has only one good thing about it. Its refutation forces us to bore more deeply into the relation between humanity and technology.

To demonstrate the absurdity of that solution, we have to remember what was said about the revolt of means, about the pressures in social structures and historical processes, and about the autonomy of technological development. For this has shown that we are not just the autonomous, subjective authors of technological processes but that we are also brought into dependence on them. There can be no question of any simple causal relation between ourselves as authors and technology as our product.

The theme of autonomy has already occupied us in various connections. It is the decisive area in which the problem of freedom, and hence a basic question in anthropology, presents itself. In what follows we shall refer back to what has been discussed already, but we shall also apply it more closely to technology.

A specific model here is the situation of those who did research on the atom, for it has often been charged that they should have held off in view of the foreseen military consequences of their research. Immediately the question arises whether any human attitude or resolve could in fact have halted the progress of atomic research and application. Did human freedom really have any chance of intervening?

The workers in the field had in fact some arguments against the accusation. I will mention only two which have to do with the question of autonomy.

First, we recall what Arnold Gehlen said about the bondage of those who do research. They themselves do not decide to put certain problems. These arise in the course of questions and answers. Research and its technological application, as we have seen, are related by factual necessity and not by some resolve on the part of Homo sapiens or Homo faber. We have even asked whether the ship of scientific and technological progress does not sail with no one on the bridge. Only at the beginning and end of the process, in the decisions to investigate and to use, does Gehlen think that there is anything like free resolve. The intervening phase is governed by the ineluctability of laws and processes.

Second, a further form of autonomy may be located in the necessary relation between action and reaction, advance and retreat. This form is connected with what we earlier illustrated by the law of competition. It is rooted in the interaction of our historical situations. I am tied both to what others do on the basis of my action and also to what they have already done. The problem of rearmament and disarmament illustrates this.

A state, or alliance of states, is not free to disarm unilaterally. If it does, it exposes itself to the danger of giving others a superiority in power that will threaten its own sovereignty and continued existence. (The same applies in relation to economic power and in other areas of life.) Even bilateral and multilateral agreements do not remove the pressure, for in view of the mistrust that obtains around the tower of Babel there will always be the suspicion of cheating on the part of others. Let us use once again the example of two enemies facing one another with loaded pistols so that they might both be killed if they fire at the same time. They thus decide to pause, to count three, and then to throw away their pistols at the same moment. But since they both distrust one another—the nations they represent have no code of honor—each is afraid of being set up by the other, i.e., of throwing away his or her weapon while the other keeps it and thus achieves superiority. This expresses in a simplified form the problem of the pressures inherent in structural interaction.

The need, especially in politics, to take the law of action into one's own hand arises out of this pressure. In this way I can attain conditional, if not absolute, independence of action in relation to others even if the very next moment their reaction means that the game has to begin all over again.

We certainly cannot doubt that this law of interaction takes on an unheard-of sharpness when we have to do with technological competition in armaments. This is inevitable because the expense is much higher and technological planning and production take longer. Thus the action and reaction are not just for a moment but for all the foreseeable future. The science of futurology depends a good deal on this.

b. The Command of Love as an Interruption of Autonomous Processes

Only when we are aware of these ineluctable processes can we realize what is meant by the interruption demanded by Jesus in the Sermon on the Mount. For he asks no less than that we should refrain from hitting back when someone hits us on the right cheek, that we should show a love of enemies which does not let us engage in hostile reaction. We are thus taken out of the devilish circle of escalation, of giving more than we get, which is unavoidable in tense interaction. Love as Jesus understands it is not just a reaction to those who love us. What is there special about loving those who love us? The Gentiles do this too (Matthew 5:46 f.). Is not the law of reaction, whether in hate or love, a mark of the "world"? We, however, are to know whose children we are (Luke 9:55). Love for Jesus always means making a new beginning rather than basing our acts on what has happened or what we expect to happen. We should not base our acts on what *has* happened because they should be dependent on God's will rather than other people and their actions. And we should not base them on what we *expect* to happen because we should not be governed by what we think the reaction of other people might be. I am not to calculate but to venture. I must refuse to be just an effect or to stay within the figure of a dance of interaction. I am to break out and begin a new dance. Understood in this way, love is a "first cause."

A dimension of being is thus inaugurated in which the dictatorship of autonomy is overthrown. Does this mean, then, that when we turn in radical obedience to the command of love, a prospect opens up for total victory over that dictatorship even in this age?

I believe that that is a misunderstanding. The doctrine of the two kingdoms, which we discussed earlier, is an attempt to take issue with dubious, utopian expectations of this kind. It shows that the suprapersonal orders of life which are represented in such structures as the state, society, and the economy demand different forms of obedience from those that are characterized by the command of love. To that extent Bismarck's saying that one cannot govern the world with the Sermon on the Mount is right. The Sermon on the Mount is not meant to be a constitutional law for the present world.

The reason why it is not may be found when we look at those to whom it is addressed. It is addressed to individuals, especially the disciples as the eschatological community. Those who love as Jesus intends can do so only as they are addressed, only in personal discipleship. When we venture to love where we would normally defend or secure ourselves, we do so on our own responsibility. We act as saints, not politicians (Max Weber). Politicians have to weigh consequences. They have to ask what will happen next (Theodor Storm). They are responsible for the fate of others, for whole structures like states or economies.

We can avoid asking about the consequences, about what will come next, about expected reactions, only when we act in faith, eschatologically ignore the law of action in the present aeon, and take the consequences. We must then be ready to suffer and fail. We can accept this readiness for ourselves, but we cannot make it a law of political action because (though not only because) all public action in this world has to deal with people of very different philosophical backgrounds, especially in epochs of pluralism. We cannot suppose that they will have the same readiness as we have. Hence in the secular kingdom, the kingdom on the left hand, the will of God demands other forms of fulfillment than it does in the sphere of personal commitment to which faith calls us.

This is the reason why no promise is given us that the autono-

mies and pressures of this aeon will cease when faith begins. This
world will proceed according to the laws of the Noachic covenant
until the last day. No utopian change is promised for this world.
Only in a sign will the eschatologically new world shine forth where
the miracle of faith, love, and hope is enacted.

c. Autonomy as Suprapersonal Guilt and Not Fate. Radical Differences in Political Action Resulting from This Distinction

At this point we should recall some earlier considerations (pp.
259 ff) that seem to me to be of decisive importance if the idea of
the two kingdoms is not to lead to a non-Christian fatalism. We saw
that autonomous processes are not a fate coming upon us from outside and thus relieving us of guilt. The laws of self-assertion (sacred
egoism, action and reaction) that find outside expression are simply
macrocosmic reflections of what lives and moves in the microcosm of
the human heart. I cannot regard myself as an "I in myself" docetically isolated from the world, as though I were here and the wicked
world there. I myself "am" the world; I have to identify with it.

It might be thought that such things are all metaphysical speculations and theological trivialities that have nothing to do with real
life. The exact opposite is the truth. The question what rank I accord to autonomies (whether I view them as fate or identify with
them and see a guilty involvement in them) can produce very
different attitudes and programs in such spheres of life as politics and
technology. To illustrate this concretely and perhaps somewhat vividly, I will take an example from the political realm.

Giving free rein to fancy, I will imagine a discussion of these issues
between Lenin and Jakob Burckhardt.

After sounding one another out a little, the two adopt a good
opening gambit and begin to speak about the evils of the day.
Though with very different inner orientations, they are agreed that
increasing industrialization and technology are producing mass mediocrity, depersonalization, and egalitarianism. Though they agree
about this, dissent arises at once when they begin to evaluate the
movement. Burckhardt thinks it is all terrible. We should try to set
up barriers against it wherever we can. States must protect individuals and private spheres in their constitutions. The aim of education

must be to develop personal life and to nurture cells, such as the family, in which it can flourish. Lenin laughs and tells Burckhardt rather patronizingly that he is simply tilting at windmills. He cannot resist the law of history with its dialectical logic. He cannot possibly play off freedom against necessity. Freedom is simply insight into necessity with a view to exploiting it. Protest against necessity will only tear us in pieces, reduce our strength, and accomplish nothing.

Burckhardt then asks what is Lenin's solution. Lenin replies: "I accept the necessity of this autonomous process. I enter the stream and swim with it. In this way I yoke the dynamic of history to my chariot and multiply my own power. Against history one can do nothing. With it one can move mountains."

From this imaginary paradigm one can infer what decisions the various interpretations of autonomy carry with them.

Burckhardt, though he does not speak for Christianity, thinks that we are responsibly implicated in autonomous processes. He is clear that these do not roll on like fate beyond good and evil, that they are not just an indifferent law. He thus calls for personal protest. He thinks that it is only with a bad conscience that one can adopt an attitude of uncritical compliance, of indifferent laissez-faire.

Lenin, on the other hand, makes a virtue out of the necessity of history—its tendency to produce mediocrity and depersonalization. He intensifies the autonomy of history by personal acclamation and espouses the thesis that we should abandon what it seeks to overthrow, i.e., human personality. If the forest of the world is full of wolves, let us howl with the wolves; then at least we will not be their victims. Lenin lets the pressures or necessities of history be his own imperative, increasing his own effectiveness thereby.

We have seen where this way leads and do not need to say more about it here. If in contrast a statesman like Bismarck—in spite of his rather Machiavellian nature—defends the virtue of moderation to William I and the military after the defeat of Austria and France, this virtue rests by no means least or last of all on the fact that Bismarck knew the Sermon on the Mount and was disturbed by the contradiction of the necessities of his policies with it. The traces of a bad conscience that may be seen at this point have a restraining function. He was protected, at least, against exalting the necessity of the world—the pressures of politics—into a virtue.[2]

In these final considerations we have burst through the narrow theme of technology but engaged in a direct continuation of the discussion which it required of us. There is hardly a sphere of anthropology of which we do not get a glimpse from the plateau of the theme of technology. We have thus come up against political questions as well as the fundamental issue of the mystery of humanity itself, of its creatureliness and alienation, of the ambivalence of its existence. Even the interfacing of freedom and necessity has been vividly set before us by our depiction of modern Homo faber.

H. HUMANITY AND TIME

I. THE HISTORICITY OF HUMAN EXISTENCE

a. The Greek View of History as a Background

The relation of humanity to history has already occupied us in the chapter on "Humanity, History, and Experience" (D,I). Our interest then was in the question how far history is a kind of macrocosmic presentation of humanity that helps it to self-experience. Our present concern is with the problem as to which understanding of time and temporality underlies a Christian view of history.

The biblical understanding of history takes on a special profile for those who study it when it is seen against the contrasting background of the Greek experience of history. To this end the views of Herodotus and Thucydides, which thus far we have only hinted at, will be of great help to us, different though they are.

The gaze of intellectual Greeks is directed upon what is timeless and imperishable. The nontemporal unchangeability of the platonic ideas has paradigmatic rank in this regard. Yet the proof of experience that everything is subject to change raises the question why this is so and what are the causes of change. So far as we can see, the question receives no final answer. No goal of mutable occurrence is found; no teleological conception is developed. The sharp changes in life, the plunge from fortune to misfortune, the fall from greatness to destruction, are all unfathomable. Even the appeal to a divine basis of life leads nowhere; indeed, when Herodotus, who views history as an accumulation of reversals, speaks about the gods, he calls them jealous and inconsistent. They enjoy causing confusion and disorder. This theological reference to the caprice of the gods seems to suggest that the changeability of history is not regarded as an optical illusion grounded only in the subjectivity of the beholder but is viewed as a fundamental quality of being and its basis.

In contrast to what is timelessly valid and constant, history is thus judged to be a plaything of Tyche, or chance. Only those who escape the play of Tyche, and turn to timeless ideas, achieve their destiny in Plato's sense. Human existence does not have its basis in its historicity but in what transcends historicity, in the essentiality of the idea. Thus to regard human historicity as constitutive is absurd. History as a dimension of chance is alien to our true being. If we remain in this dimension, the result is fatal.

In spite of this declassification of history, the Greeks are not indifferent to it. They still produced great historians. We thus want to know what was the nature of their interest and how it arose.

To do this, we need not look farther than the very obvious fact that the Greeks, like all mortals, found themselves in the turmoil of history and were naturally interested in what was happening. But what made a historian like Herodotus, who considered only the changes and chances of history, attractive even to the disciples of Plato, lending philosophical value to his interest in history, was something different.

For if Herodotus found no movement toward a goal in the historical process, if he perceived no eschatological orientation in it, if he did not even raise this theme in the form of a question, his diagnosis of contingency did not exclude the fact that the storm of history brought the whirling bodies together in recurrent patterns and figures. Chance, then, does not rule out a certain regularity. We have here what we today would call the law of chance. If we throw the dice enough times, the element of unforeseeable chance in the individual throw is overruled by a law in virtue of which the number 6, for example, will come with a certain regularity. To get behind chance and discover its secret rules is pragmatically important for Herodotus, for one can then be guided by the rules, learn from history, and make it profitable for one's own action.

Among the fundamental patterns that Herodotus perceives, for example, is that arrogance carries its opposite with it. Hybris avenges itself; "pride goes before a fall." Along these lines, Polybius finds a regularity in history that is not unlike Hegel's historical dialectic. Political history takes the course of thesis and antithesis (although he himself does not use these terms). Constitutions come and go. States rise and fall. All this takes place according to recurrent patterns, so that if we know these we can predict what will develop in our own history. To have this power of prediction is obviously of the greatest importance in formulating political programs.

The essential point here is that this observing of constant and recurrent patterns does not make causal explanations possible. One cannot say, for example, that the wealth of Croesus is the "cause" of his downfall. In place of such explanations, all that one can say is that too much fortune usually avenges itself and provokes the envy of the gods. When Herodotus tells us how Amasis terminates his friendly agreement with Polycrates, he does so with the statistical certainty that the pendulum that has led him to extreme success will now swing to the other side.

Why, then, could Herodotus be read and accepted by disciples of Plato? Obviously because he was looking for something constant in the contingency of history, not, of course, the platonic idea that transcends events, but still an immanent law that is outside time and constantly manifests itself in it. In the march of events there are always patterns such as the relation between Hybris and Nemesis, pride and fall.

Once we grasp the special form of this regularity, we can understand why the Greeks could find no goal in history, why they perceived no time-line, why, indeed, they did not even want to ask about such a thing. The way in which they were impressed by recurrent patterns made them indifferent to the distinction of times. Past, present, and future lost any specific qualities for them and merged into the timeless identity of what is always the same. The graphic form in which to present their view of history is not that of a line but of a circle. The cyclical law of recurrence, of transition from the end to a new beginning, the constantly new actualizing of the basic patterns is the secret program of what is called history. The Greek yearning for what is beyond time, and therefore for what cannot be destroyed, finds a new variation here. The platonic idea finds precursors and successors. We have here the constant core around which new crystals form with their wonderfully varied colors.

b. History in Biblical Anthropology

When we put the biblical view of history against the Greek background and clarify it by contrast, we cannot develop an extensive Christian theology of history.[1] We shall have to be content to try to portray humanity in its self-understanding as an entity in time and history.

1. IMMANENT AND TRANSCENDENT STANDPOINTS

Illegitimate Transcendence: The Bird's-Eye View of the Spectator

To summarize what we shall be saying, we may advance the thesis that history is the world-process which God controls, which involves dialogue with humanity, and whose beginning, center, and end are based on his will and plan. In accordance with this, past, present, and future have their own specific and unconditional emphases, so that the course of history—both general and individual—is not that of a circle but that of a directed line.

Joseph Wittig says somewhere that strictly a biography ought not to begin at birth but at death. It can be written only in the light of the end, because only in this light can one perceive the whole. If history is viewed as a kind of biography of the world, we might arrive at a similar thesis and in so doing stay close to the picture of the directed time-line.

Before we test how far this thesis finds illustration in the Christian view of history, let us be clear that Wittig's statement works out empirically when we observe historical processes.

Thus if we isolate smaller sections of history or specific phases in a life, we cannot perceive any overall meaning. We achieve only glimpses. Momentary success cannot tell us whether a project or venture will be worthwhile or will last over the long haul, whether there will be any significant relation between achievement and reward over the whole of life (or history). The moment does not reveal whether a good act will receive its reward or a bad one will be avenged. The system within which there is reward and punishment, or, to put it more theologically, within which the higher will is manifested that distributes rewards and punishments, may be seen, if at all, only in broader fields and over longer periods. Chance rules the moment. It is the category of the moment. Chance as we understand it is not a statement about the content of events, as though lightning struck without any choice on our part, or we were on a blind flight into the void. Chance is merely a statement about a specific aspect in my approach to history and my viewing of it—the aspect of the moment.

Thus the poet in Psalm 73 notes that the rich and powerful and ungodly—those whose "eyes swell out with fatness" (v. 7)—take only a momentary view. They live for the moment of success, and are trapped in this. The same is true of those who "turn and praise them" (v. 10), in contrast to the righteous who are the object of unjust contempt. The rule of the moment ceases, however, when we look beyond the moment and consider their life as a whole: "I went into the sanctuary of God; then I perceived their end" (v. 17). Here the aspect of contingency is changed in two ways.

First, the psalmist looks beyond the moment by considering the whole course of their life, by looking back at it from its final frontier. Second, he looks beyond the moment by going into the sanctuary and thus viewing the moment from the standpoint of eternity.

Both ways of looking beyond the moment offer distance and a view of the limits. The limits bring to light the laws which embrace the individual moments in a continuous chain. One of these laws which represent the nexus in processes, the plan which effectively shapes them, is the law of guilt and retribution. This law, of course, is largely hidden. Theologically one must even say that it is hidden in a deeper sense even where it seems to be manifest. Yet it is true that certain contours of the regularity of guilt and retribution do appear. It was in this sense that Bismarck once ventured the saying that the accounts of history would be more exact than revisions in the Prussian senate.

We might illustrate this by some of the interpretations of German history that have been attempted after the collapse of the Third Reich.

If we ignore superficial writers (like those who proclaim a new stab-in-the-back legend), most of these work with the law of the "long haul." They do not explain the collapse by specific contingencies of the moment, e.g., the exhaustion of war materials or biological reserves, or tardiness in inventing the atom bomb. They seek instead to detect the more protracted operation of the law of guilt and retribution over longer stages of the historical process. The correct insight that such an attempt has to dig deeper into the past has led to the view that not merely Bismarck but Frederick the Great and even the event of the Reformation were mistaken developments which culminated and terminated in an apocalyptic figure like Hitler. An illusion of seeing the whole is created by going farther and farther back. But a partial stretch, no matter how long, is not the whole; it is still a part. It is also fragmentary inasmuch as it depends on the perspective of the beholder and thus loses even more of its representative force.

We cannot achieve a total view along these lines. In a kind of self-judgment of the illusion, we can only achieve a type of historiography that is "criminalistic." The field of historical beholders and writers is full of spies who all range far afield and try to track down the original criminal, because in the foreground of history an arrested criminal seems to be a victim or collaborator of an alienated and long since perverted spirit of the age. In this concern of "criminalistic" history to capture the head of the great conspiracies, and thus constantly to extend the radius of historical action, there may be seen a correct—if distorted—awareness that the theme of guilt and retribution drives us to the very horizon of history. Only at the very limit is everything law. But where is the limit of history?

Here again we come up against the law of chance. Chance is present only when our view is limited, as in individual electrons. But statistics, which deals with big numbers, sees that "irrationality," the random nature of individual things, is caught up in the regularity of the larger unit. So it obviously is with history too. What seems to be a matter of incalculable freedom—as in the case of what is euphemistically called "free death" (i.e., suicide)—can be determined with some regularity when a larger view is taken and the averages are worked out for countries or continents.

Clearly big numbers are needed in history if its law is to be manifest: the law that "over the long haul" certain things are rewarded or punished.

The only thing is that the whole of history in all its individual and universal relations will have to be available to us if we are to know this law with any precision. But the claim to have such a view of history would be a claim to know the whole of history, to be no longer within its confines, but to stand in a place of transcendence. Along these lines not only Kierkegaard has made against Hegel's philosophy of history the accusation that its author puts himself outside the process and tries to discover the plans of the World-Spirit, or God.

Any illegitimate attempt to achieve transcendence from within history carries with it the penalty that the upshot of the attempt is not insight but blindness. When some view of the relation between guilt and retribution seems to open up in some part of the field, the very next moment the view is more fully blocked than before. What results from a bird's-eye view, or, better, the transmundane view of the astronaut, the contemplation of the mere observer, is not the law of guilt and retribution but fate and necessity empty of all values.

Hence it is no wonder that Hegel has no sense of evil but regards it as a mere transition in the process.

One can see this from Oswald Spengler's morphological survey of history, within which moral or religious values, norms, and categories lose their authority. This morphology can finally do no more than set history in analogy to nature and interpret its regular courses. What betrays this changing of history into nature, its de-ethicizing, and the excessive way in which Spengler sees humanity robbed of the essentials of freedom, is his relating of the development of civilizations across the centuries to the seasonal rhythm of natural law, i.e., to events in which are no values. No place is found, then, for freedom and responsibility, within which alone guilt and retribution are possible. Hardly have we seen a law before that to which it applies changes in substance. It is no longer a law of history but a law of nature.

What we observe here is not just an empirical fact but an indication of a theological process. The way of the bird's-eye view arises out of a need to see as much of the field as possible. But the whole field can be seen only from the border, from transcendence, from a distance. We who still live *in* history have not yet reached that point. For this reason the bird's-eye view, theologically expressed, is an illegitimate transcendence. It is an attempt to lift oneself above history in order to view it and cross its boundary from inside.

The result is the same as when other boundaries are crossed. We do not get a clearer view but our vision is obscured. When humans first crossed the frontier to God in order to grasp at transcendence and become gods, they did not in fact become gods but lost their status as children and were driven out of Paradise. Instead of growing bigger, they sank below the level of their human destiny. Thus, whether or not Goethe's saying is true that those who act are always right, there is no doubt that those who observe, i.e., who cross the boundary to get a bird's-eye view, are always wrong.

Christian Transcendence: Christ as Center

In the formation of a Christian view of history, the decisive thing is that the transcendence which is needed to observe meaning, e.g., guilt and retribution, cannot be achieved from within history. Transcendence breaks into history from outside and is then present within it. This presence of transcendence in history is *Jesus Christ*.[2] Faith finds in him the fulfillment of the postulate that it is only from the frontier, in the light of the whole, that one can speak about guilt and retribution. The figure of Christ has thus been called the center of history. This term is helpful to us in our thinking about the totality of history, inasmuch as the center here is the higher center of perspective from which one can see both the forward and the backward horizon of history. In fact, the New Testament expresses this in many ways, and with it the related understanding of history.

The backward horizon of history may first be seen in the light of Christ when we are told that in him the world was made (Colossians 1:16). What this obviously means is that the history of the world aims from the very outset at salvation, that creation has a "motive." Adapting another saying of Goethe, one might also say that the secret of history is not so much the conflict between belief and unbelief as between salvation and perdition. History is the sphere in which we are summoned to return from the far country to fellowship with God. This and nothing else is the secret of the many individual and anonymous people who are still "known" to God. This and nothing else is the destiny of kings, dictators, and world figures and their kingdoms, which all, as Christoph Blumhardt once said, stand under the sign of "going," whereas God's kingdom stands under that of "coming." History from its very inception is oriented to something of which Christ is—again from the very first—representative, i.e., salvation.

But the forward horizon of history may also be seen from this center of perspective. Christ will come again to judge the living and the dead. He will close history. Negatively this means that the end will not be in the continuity of history itself. The real end of rogues who "swell with fatness" (Psalm 73) will not be manifested in immanence, in the course of this age. At the end of history, when the harvest is gathered into the barns, when the collapse of all things comes, when the great tomb of the world gapes open, everything will be made plain, for at this frontier the king stands with his sickle and crown, and he knows what is in us, and has not lost sight of the mystery of *any* of us.

Finally the judgment of history may also be seen at that center itself and not just on the horizons. Since we have here the Resurrection on the third day, death is not a biological law, an event of nature devoid of values. It is contrary to nature. It is an enemy. It is a rent in the design of creation. With the healing of the sick and the ending of sufferings, the hopelessness of the world is disclosed here.

It awaits the day when redemption will be consummated. With the forgiveness of sins and the authoritative miracle of this forgiveness, unbreakable bondage to guilt, to an inescapable law, is disclosed.

Is World History World Judgment?
Judgment and the Person of the Judge

The dictum that world history is world judgment applies here in a different sense from that found in the philosophy of history represented by Schiller's "universal moral order." World history does not carry judgments with it in the sense of a logical correspondence between guilt and retribution, as in the saying of the blind harpist in *Wilhelm Meister* that all guilt avenges itself on the earth. How often it does not do so! Judgment is not tied to the stringency of the historical processes in which it takes place. Instead, history itself is judgment. As such, and totally, it is under judgment. It is in bondage to what none of us, even by changing historical structures, can banish out of the world. From the time of the mysterious break that we call the fall, we are all guilty. We are enclosed in what Frank Thiess has described as the "torture chamber of history," i.e., in the process of wars and rumors of wars, of dominion and suppression, and the unalterable laws obtain that "some are in the dark and others are in the light" (*Beggars' Opera*), that we all become guilty and we all have to die.

What we have said about the relation between history and judgment misses the crucial point if we have only this generalization in view. We must be more specific and ask whether the question should not be put in a new and different way. Is there any possibility of describing individual events, such as the collapse of the Third Reich, as judgments?

If it is right that Christ is the center of history, if the secret of history is thus to be found in a person who cannot simply be objectified and brought under intellectual control but is present incognito and can be grasped only in the venture of faith, then we have to say first that judgment, too, cannot be an object of "sight" but has to be an object of faith. I can speak about judgment only when I know the Judge, when he is present to me as the person who decides.

The analogy to earthly processes of judgment fails us here. For in these I do not have to know the judge but the laws he is appointed to administer. In earthly courts I have to be acquainted with the order that the judge simply represents. But God is not the functionary of an order that is above him and binds him as a norm. God establishes all orders by his sovereign will. Just as I cannot work back from creation to the Creator (as though everything perishable were really a parable, a decipherable parable) but can know the mystery of creation only when I know its Creator and its heart, so I can know judgment only when I know the one who judges.

All this simply means that judgment is "invisible" so long as the Judge and the things of faith are "invisible," or, better, "hidden."

We shall now try very briefly to clarify from various standpoints this hiddenness of judgment, which is simply that of the person of the Judge.

Since judgment cannot be established objectively, from the standpoint of secular empiricism this means that it is in principle *ambiguous*. The song says of Napoleon's army, when it was crushed in Russia, that the Lord smote it man and horse and wagon. But was there really such an "unequivocal" divine judgment on Napoleon? Perhaps the French might not unjustly object that if we are to use the category of judgment and not just of tragedy, then it was Europe and not Napoleon that was really smitten by God's judgment, since Europe rejected the Napoleonic order in this way and lost all its benefits. It had had the chance, the French argument might run, to come under the life-giving force of a grand political idea, and after Napoleon's fall could only sink back into the decay of outmoded traditions. Was it not Napoleon, then, who executed judgment on Europe? The metaphysical roles as well as the characters of great figures in history are ambivalent. But does not this relativize what we say about judgment?

Even in regard to great disasters, on a general or individual scale, in which it is easier to say who the victims are than in the case of Napoleon, e.g., the downfall of Germany or lifelong sickness, our diagnosis that this is a divine judgment still comes up against a final frontier which shows how profoundly dubious it is. Can this suffering be—unequivocally—deduced "causally" from this preceding guilt? If we are to steer clear of banal contingency, might it not still be given some "final" significance in terms of God's educative purpose? Do not these two interpretations cancel one another out, since disaster and suffering may have the character of judgment in one case but that of salvation (or purification) in another?

In the story of the man born blind in the Gospel of John (9:1–3), the two interpretations come into dramatic collision in the dialogue between Jesus and his disciples. The disciples take it to be self-evident that some fault must be the reason why the man was born blind. His state has the character of judgment. ("Who sinned, this man or his parents, that he was born blind?") But Jesus turns the causal explanation of the disciples into the apparently opposing final explanation, replying that he was born blind so that "the works of God might be made manifest in him."

In this case, too, we seem to be confronted by the insoluble ambiguity of catastrophic situations. For who would dare to explain such a situation as authoritatively as Jesus did and wrest from it a disclosure of the unequivocal divine message? What is finally at issue here is not just the authority of the interpretation but the power to make the blind man see and in this way to bring to light the hidden purpose of his blindness. We have here, not just an interpretive word, but an active word. For this reason the story evades all attempts to exploit it hermeneutically and to derive from it any specific schema (e.g., teleological) whereby to interpret history.

The question arises here whether the apparent ambiguity, the hesitation between causal and final explanations, while not challenging the message of judgment itself, may not require instead that we should examine the nature of divine judgment more closely. Might it not be that what seems to be ambivalent offers a demonstration that we have here two complementary parts of judgment itself, that judgment is in fact *twofold*, retribution for what has taken place *and* education for what is still future, repelling *and* seeking, perdition *and* salvation?

This thought leads us again to the decisive thesis that the mystery of judgment (whether as retribution on the past or seeking for the future) is to be understood in the light of the person of the Judge, i.e., in faith. For according to the biblical witness, the person of the Judge has shown himself to be one who will not leave guilt unpunished, who will avenge wrong, but who also upholds his covenant and causes his saving counsel to rule in history. He is the Judge, but he is also gracious. The two aspects come together in the term "visitation," which signifies both a refusal to let evil go unpunished and an infallible intention of saving, of bringing to the goal, of bringing back home. The union of the two cannot be established empirically. Certainty can be achieved only by an act of trust in the person of the Judge, who is present in person, the person of Jesus of Nazareth, who opens his "heart," and who thus triggers the spontaneity of trust which also carries with it responsibility to his person.

"Silence" of the Judge

There is a further reason why judgment cannot be established objectively. This can be stated only theologically. It is the fact that God's judgments may consist of his *silence*.[3]

Our inability to establish correspondence between guilt and punishment (e.g., because God is silent and passive when according to our postulates he ought to unleash judgments and make clear examples) causes a great deal of difficulty and poses the problem of theodicy in all its severity. Yet it is not as though nothing were happening when God seems to be silent and passive. Judgment might well take place in his very silence and passivity. These might be the judgment.

In the language of faith this means that God "withholds his arm" and leaves people to the consequences of their actions, to self-judgment. He retires from the processes that people have set in motion and abandons them, if one wills, to the autonomy of these processes. Thus Paul says (Romans 1:24, 28) that idolaters who no longer see themselves as creatures, but exalt themselves above God, are delivered up (*paredoken*) to their own hearts' aspirations and thus left on their own. There thus develops a self-enclosed finitude that does not seem to be disturbed by any divine interventions. But in reality this finitude is a prison in which we are confined. The God who is banished out of our existence accepts this banishment in a dreadful way, and stays away from us.

Precisely at the moment when deniers of God are lulled into security by his silence and mock at God's judgments (because they confuse his act of withdrawal with his nonexistence), faith sees these judgments pressing on the world with oppressive force. It may feel this so strongly that it finds in the coming of open storms of anger, and the onset of a *dies irae* (day of wrath), a kind of redemption from the sinister quality of silent judgment. By way of example the author recalls that the sure path trodden by Hitler, almost like that of a sleepwalker, in the days of his success made an impression of this kind on many Christians. The silent onlooking of the Lord of history was apocalyptically sinister in character. It was thus a relief when God began to speak again in the storm of judgment, even though they became victims of the disasters that then ensued.

We see, then, that God's silence over the world, the apparent nonexecution of judgment, does not have to be taken to mean that we have no antennae for what is going on, or that the impression of silence is a case of bad acoustics, so that the silence of the Judge is due to our subjective lack of receptivity.

No, according to the biblical view of history and judgment, the silence of the Judge may well be a reality. It is part of the "style" of divine judgment. Even the angels about God's throne bear witness that God's silence is real and does not merely rest on impressions due to our hardness of hearing. The silent God does not judge only— or, better, he hardly ever judges—by reacting against wrongdoers with lightning strokes or other disasters *ex machina*. He judges by withdrawing and letting things take their course. He becomes the absent God. In this way, as we have seen, he gave up those who built the tower of Babel to the consequences of their own action. In doing nothing, he subjected them to the centrifugal force that they themselves had set in motion. To that extent his silence was supreme activity. What he allowed to happen was like a coming down and dispersing. By simply looking on, he was active in their self-confusing.

Paul takes this view in Romans 1:18ff. His development of the idea offers a model of what is open and what is hidden in judgment. To vertical disorder—the exalting of the self against God—there corresponds perversion on the horizontal level of life. Paul illustrates this distortion by use of contemporary material from Stoic lists of vices. Instead of seeing themselves as creatures, people make the divine their creature and worship gods of their own making. There is a corresponding confusion of the order and ranking of other values in their lives. Males free themselves from the created sexual relation and turn to their own sex. Lower elements triumph over higher elements, impulse over spirit, the irrational over reason, children over the authority of their parents, pitilessness over love.

Obvious though the results of this judgment and self-avenging seem to be in this diagnosis of life, they are hidden as well. The corrupt people about whom Paul is speaking would probably be quite astonished if one were to hold up this mirror to them, and even a thoughtful psychologist in an analytical test could hardly come up with any other conclusion than that they feel secure. They do not hear the thunder of judgment. It is unreal to them. Perhaps they even speak about the successful self-fulfillment that they have achieved in their lives.

Something similar might have been said about those who built the tower of Babel. Perhaps there was a philosopher among them who began to reflect on the dispersion and confusion of tongues, and found something positive in the experience. What would he say? Perhaps that the power of dispersion and mutual conflict, war and controversy, all that which shattered their original peace and unity of language, all that is the "father of all things" (Heraclitus), the original creative impulse of life. Perhaps they would even reply that a certain measure of Mephistophelian revolt is stimulating: We soon flag and seek total rest, so we need a companion who will entice and work on us; we need someone to act as a devil.

The ultimate concealment of judgment is perhaps that we make a virtue out of the final necessity of a world that is out of joint.

Course and End of the "Why" Question

All that we have said about the form taken by divine judgment has simply been in exposition of the thesis that only the Judge can unlock the mystery of judgment. Apart from encounter with the personal Thou of the Judge, who in Christ manifests himself paradoxically as our "Father," we have no hope of answering the question how, or how well, the order of this world functions. We really have no hope when faced with this question, not merely because the tormenting question "why?" gives us no rest, but because there is no solution for it. There are two main forms of its insolubility.

It may lead us into a dead end, leaving us only with the cheerless conclusion that it is unfathomable. The next step beyond this is the nihilistic insight that what is unfathomable has no bottom, that the world has no ruler, no father, that it is tossed around by Moira and Tyche.

Or it may end in the statistical perspective of the law of chance and the silence of nature. A combination of the first and second answers may be found in the attempt to interpret the finite world "tragically," i.e., to posit an order that is an unfathomable fate for both the gods and us, since we neither know by whom it is established nor to what end. This situation, which no longer understands judgment because the Judge is banished beyond the horizon, is itself a judgment.

For biblical thought the torment of the "why" question—and therefore the torment of the silence of the world's Judge—does not end with the solution of the question but with redemption

(*Erlösung*) from it. This redemption is based on trust in him who has revealed himself as the Judge but also as the Father. This trust yields the certainty that the Midgard serpent does not encircle the world but that the world has a fatherly basis. This is why, when the Christian faces the riddle of history and his own subjection to it, he does not say, "This is why," but, "Nevertheless I am continually with thee" (Psalm 73:23). This statement makes sense because of the person of the Judge. Only within the trust that he evokes is it possible to wait for the reason "why," to wait for the sight which is finally promised to faith. All attempts to achieve this end before the time end either in the dead end of the "why" question or in utopian dreams.

But as we must not replace faith by a desire for sight, so we must not fall victim to a trusting fatalism that makes faith the purely passive object of transcendent events. The Judge and the one who makes things happen form a personal binding force which summons to partnership and responsibility and involves a wrestling with destiny. Everything depends on the name in which I engage in this wrestling (e.g., as a doctor or patient with sickness). Do I do so on the basis of a supposed and presumed insight into the meaning and therefore the justification of what is happening, or do I do it in trust in the hidden one who gives meaning, i.e., sustained by that "nevertheless"?

2. PROPHETIC DISCLOSURE OF THE MYSTERY OF HISTORY

History Not a Logically Perceived Continuum but Grounded in God's Freedom

If God is understood to be the Lord of history, the diffuse multiplicity of individual events merges into a single whole. This merging cannot mean, however, that we can perceive its continuity logically and thus see the basis, goal, and meaning of the individual events. This would involve an insight into the why of things—which we have rejected. If the Lord of history is the object of faith, the same applies to the unity of history which is based on his world government. What we mean by this unity is not just that East and West will rest in the peace of his hands but that the times of history, past, present, and future, will be dissolved by the same hands.

The Old Testament prophets had glimpses of this whole and proclaimed it in their oracles. For this reason it is incontestable that the prophetic view of history was the decisive impulse in the formation of a concept of history. They still have an impact today even when, contrary to the thrust of their own message, the philosophy of history changes faith in the unity of history into supposed knowledge of the logical continuity of its course. Hegel's thesis concerning "reason in history" is a typical example of this influence and modification.

The primary tense of the prophetic proclamation of the unity of history is that of the future. It is as the author of the future that God is absolutely the Lord of history. The future is foreseen in his counsel or plan, and he fulfills this plan gloriously (cf. Isaiah 28:29). History in this sense is "all his work," his total work (10:12). Trust in his plan carries with it the assurance that God will make the future his own future, i.e., that he will overthrow the false and usurped thrones of earthly rulers. He "will punish the arrogant boasting of the king of Assyria and his haughty pride" (10:12). What may be seen here as world judgment with the punishment of wrong and the vindication of right is not the immanent logic of world history. No, what happens is grounded exclusively in the counsel of the "holy One of Israel."

It is the prophets' confidence in this counsel and plan that gives them the authority to make statements about the future. They anticipate this, though not in the form of speculative knowledge undertaking to think God's plan through to the end and thus falling victim to the arrogance of reading God's mind. If God is the author of history, they must be content simply to proclaim the glory of the end to which he leads all things while leaving the way to this end under his control and recognizing that the individual steps on this way are hidden from human thoughts (Isaiah 55:8). If the prophets venture all the same to predict certain future steps, this is only because they are "revealed" to them. Amos tells us expressly that there are revelations of this kind: Yahweh does not do anything without first revealing his plan to his servants the prophets.

If God gives this kind of revelation, it implies much more than mere prediction of the course of things. For things do not follow a course. They are done by the Lord of history and stand at his disposal. In this sense the *word* (Hebrew *dabar*) that contains the revelation does not merely have the verbal sense of announcing but the ontic sense of doing or commanding: "I will speak the word and perform it" (Ezekiel 12:25, 28). God does not merely declare the future; he brings it to pass. The faith that looks into the future is not just prediction but promise that God will keep his word and be true to himself.

The prophets, of course, did not just "prophesy" the future. They considered all the work of Yahweh and all the history that he brought about. This may be seen in the way in which they combine past, present, and future.

In relation to the past we have a kind of prophecy in reverse. The prophets do not just record facts. Their purpose goes beyond the objectivity of reporting. They regard what takes place as a manifestation of the plan of salvation. The facts are not important in themselves but as transparencies through which it may be seen what God has done in them. In this sense the stories of Israel, the theologies of history advanced by the Yahwist, Elohist, and Deuteronomist, are forms of retrospective prophecy. Tradition here is not simply historical recollection and continuation in what is thus recollected. It is the record of history as thus interpreted. Hence there belong to tradition, not just the things interpreted, but the interpreters too, the prophetic witnesses. These are the mediators of God's plan for history and have the rank of guarantors.

The linking of the three tenses of history is done in God's name. For *Yahweh*—the name God gives himself (Exodus 3:14)—means: "I am who I will be." "And," as one might add, "who I have been from the beginning." I am the bracket around past, present, and future.

The union of past, present, and future is thus in two senses personal. On the one side it is grounded in the person of Yahweh,[4] in his counsel, his active *dabar*. On the other side it is disclosed in the view of history that the word of Yahweh gives the prophets, and it points, therefore, to the persons of the witnesses (H. J. Kraus).

If the union of past, present, and future is personal in this way, and can thus be described only by personally nuanced terms like "counsel," "will," and "purpose" on God's side, or "faith," "obedience," and "interpretive authority" on ours, then one can understand that the relation between the tenses is not to be viewed statically nor regarded as a process established by law. History as seen in this way cannot be calculated in advance nor predicted as a process would be. It is full of surprises. The Spirit of God by whom the prophets speak cannot be contained, or changed into a scheme of interpretation that is given once and for all. He is present only at specific times, i.e., when Yahweh reveals himself.

This dynamic, nonstatic character of the prophetic view of history has both a theological and an anthropological aspect.

The *theological* aspect may be illustrated by the occasional use in the Old Testament of the expression that God "repents" of something. Thus he may repent of abandoning his guilty people to judgment, and therefore to the logic of guilt and retribution (cf. Exodus 32:14; Jeremiah 26:13; Amos 7:3, 6 et cetera). Here the prophetic statement itself is not afraid of massive and rather embarrassing anthropomorphism. It seems to relativize God's omniscience. Ironical glosses such as "God corrects himself," or even "God gives way," would not suggest themselves to the prophets or their believing hearers, though they might to platonically oriented or even modern readers. What seems at a first glance to be anthropomorphic is in truth only an indication that the plan of salvation is not a legally fixed program which boxes in God himself and to whose normative thrust he is subject. If his mercy is unending and new every morning (Lamentations 3:22), then up to the end one cannot see which way it will take. One must expect fresh surprises every day. If God changes his will and does not conduct history according to a set decree, this does not mean vacillation in the ordinary human sense. Behind every revision is the constant factor of his faithfulness: "Great is thy faithfulness" (Lamentations 3:23)—though it might take a fresh form each morning and we can hardly keep up with it. The transparency of history for its true goal of salvation may be seen in the prophets at this point. They look beyond what might seem to a human view to be the irrational turbulence of events—often contradictory events—and see the unchanging and constant factor that they call God's faithfulness.

The *anthropological* aspect of the fact that history is not a fixed process may be seen in us in the way we deal with history, and especially in the way we link past, present, and future. An example is the way in which the prophets—and the New Testament witnesses too—find a relation between prophecy and fulfillment.

In the history of theology almost all interpreters have dealt with this theme. The way the relation is defined reflects a theologian's view of history and understanding of revelation. To develop this basic theme, one must put all one's cards on the table. Since the various schools and denominations have produced so many different theologies, there is great variation in the—often controversial—solutions to the problem of relating prophecy and fulfillment. I mention this by way of excuse for the fact that in the present context I cannot present the material systematically but can only indicate some approaches which seem to me to be essential and to support my present position.

When the word of Yahweh that is disclosed to the prophets says in advance what is to come, when it offers promise or threat for the future, it puts its hearers in the situation of waiting for history (Isaiah 8:17). The word of promise and later historical events can then be compared. Have the promises been fulfilled? Has the threat materialized? The answer to this question either confirms and strengthens faith in Yahweh's plan and faithfulness, or it challenges and shatters it.

"Prophecy-Fulfillment" as Key to Human Historicity

Prophecy of what is to come may be found not only in the form of predictive words. Events or figures in history itself may have prototypical significance and foreshadow what is to come. (One may speak of "typological" history in this connection.) I will give a few examples.

1. Israel's exodus from Egypt is an event of liberation which is not only predicted by Joseph (Genesis 50:24) but which is also itself a prefiguration of the work of Yahweh. When Israel finds itself threatened by the Amorites, it is to remember the miracle of the exodus and trust that Yahweh's act of faithfulness will be confirmed in coming afflictions (Judges 6:8 ff.). In the same way disaster may be prefigured, i.e., when Israel no longer views that former act of liberation as a prophecy but instead gives in to hesitation, fear, or indifference (Deuteronomy 8:14; 13:11).

Thus decisions about what is coming depend on the people's attitude to the past: whether they let the prophecy be fulfilled or prevent it from being fulfilled and thus turn it to hurt. In both cases—in the salvation it brings or the disaster it triggers—the prophecy is in force. This is how Joshua presents the exodus as a prophecy at his last gathering with the people. They are to decide *how* it is to be fulfilled (Joshua 24:17 ff.).

2. Abraham has familiar prototypical significance as the "father of faith." It may be seen from his figure that the new covenant is a fulfillment of the prophesying Old Testament. "Abraham believed God, and it was reckoned to him as righteousness" (Romans 4:3).

This prophecy is regarded as fulfilled when Christ's redemptive act opens up direct access to God and frees us from the conditions that the law laid upon us with its demand for achievement (James 2:23).

Another Old Testament figure, the priest Melchizedek, is also viewed as a prophetic figure of this kind. In this sense he is a central character in Hebrews, which of all the New Testament writings has the most comprehensive view of prophecy and fulfillment and even uses allegory to present the old covenant as a foreshadowing of what is to come. Thus Melchizedek prefigures Christ, for he is a "king of peace," "a priest for ever," "without father or mother or genealogy," having "neither beginning of days nor end of life" (Hebrews 7:2–3). He bursts into history without being produced by it, in this way "resembling the Son of God" (7:3). He is a predictive analogy.

3. Hebrews interprets especially the sacrificial system of the Old Testament as a prophetic depiction of what is fulfilled in the passion and cross of Christ (Hebrews 8–10). Here again the past is "a shadow" of what is to come (Hebrews 10:1; cf. Colossians 2:17). The priests of the old covenant shed only the blood of animals, but the Crucified offered himself and shed his own blood.

The little word "but" is a decisive one here. It indicates for the first time that in the fulfillment something other may occur than one might gather from the word of promise or the prototypical event. This is indeed so. The fulfillment transcends the prophecy. The prophets, as it were, do not really know what they are saying when they give the words of promise. The words know more than the speakers. Only the fulfillment shows what is really contained in them. In the light of the fulfillment they take on a different aspect. They show their true face. The hermeneutical rule one has to adopt regarding them is that the promise is to be understood in terms of the fulfillment, the Old Testament, in its true sense, in terms of the New. Like Hebrew letters, then, the Bible has to be read backward. Only at the end can one see the beginning and the way. We pointed this out earlier when we said about biography (whether of an individual or the world) that it can be understood only in the light of the end, the completed development.

Transcending of Prophecy by Fulfillment:
The Path to an Open Future. Three Models

The fact that in the fulfillment something new emerges which could not be read off from the prophecy by mere interpretation is very significant for the biblical understanding of history. To gauge the importance of this insight I will at least hint at some examples that illustrate how the prophecy is transcended—or corrected—by the fulfillment.

I will look first at the sacrificial system of the Old Testament, which, as already stated, Hebrews views as a prefiguration of the sacrifice of Christ. Here we come up against that characteristic "but."

First Model: The Idea of Sacrifice

Since the Crucifixion took place in a world that was shaped by sacrifice, it was obvious that it should itself be explained as a sacrificial action. Hence a whole group of associations was available linking individual features in sacrificial worship to the event of Golgotha and thus presenting them as shadows of what was to come, as ritual prophecy.

As Hebrews sees it, however, this analogy cannot be taken to mean that what was fulfilled at Golgotha was simply a painting in of what the sacrificial system of the old covenant had already sketched. If it were, then we should simply have the timeless presence of an idea of sacrifice whose identity would remain the same through every historical variation. But this would be intolerable to a view of history which is oriented neither to a timeless idea nor to the logic of an evolutionary process but to the act and resolve of the "person" of God.

In fact, Hebrews shows that, while Christ's sacrifice on the cross fulfills the ritual prophecy, it also transcends it and introduces something new and unexpected. This thing is so new that even if one were to plumb the very depths of the sacrificial system of the Old Testament, one would never find it there. One could not find it, because it was not there.

What is this new thing? I will be content simply to indicate two typical aspects.

The first brings us back to the "but." Human priests simply sprinkle defiled persons "with the blood of goats and bulls and with the ashes of a heifer," which "sanctifies [them] for the purification of the flesh." But Christ offers himself "without blemish to God" (Hebrews 9:13 f.). We do not need to discuss the arguments of Hebrews here, but it obviously finds a new and radically altered quality in the idea of sacrifice. This self-offering of Christ is more and other than cleansing from ritual, bodily defilement. It purifies the "conscience from dead works" and frees it "to serve the living God" (v. 14). It thus goes to the very center of our existence and grants a new relation to God. "How much more?" asks Hebrews. This "more" indicates that the fulfillment is very much more than the promise. It brings a new and extra element in comparison with which the rite of promise is only a shadow, a hint of the picture, a scrap of the melody.

That prophecy is transcended by fulfillment, and thus receives from the future the light that reveals its true significance, might be proved by many quotations. One particularly striking instance is the way in which the Johannine Christ finds in the feeding of Israel by manna in the wilderness a predictive reference to himself. The manna was a promise, but the fulfillment, the true gift of God, is much more, namely, the "true bread from heaven." The prophetic gift of manna was a "thing" that relieved hunger in the desert; the true bread from heaven is a "person" who says of himself: "I am the bread of life" (John 6:30–35). In the manna God gives "something"; in Christ he gives "himself." This is the extra element in the fulfillment.

The giving of a new quality to the promise is even clearer in another illustration given in Hebrews in which the shadow of prediction stands in sharp contrast to the light of fulfillment.

The priests of the old covenant brought their offerings not only for the cultically assembled people but also for themselves (3:3; 7:27). They, too, were among the defiled persons. They were not differentiated from them by holiness. They were in solidarity with sinners. And because they and the assembly were defiled continually, hardly had they offered the sacrifice before they had to do it again. They did not deal permanently with the state of defilement. The offerings had to be constantly repeated. But Christ, who offered himself as a perfect sacrifice (9:14), did this once and for all (9:27 f.). He did something definitively new in the relation between God and us. The definitive element is as different from the provisional prefiguration as is light from shadow. The figure of the definitive One cannot be constructed out of the outline of the shadow. It cannot, then, be anticipated. It has to come, to find fulfillment, and to manifest itself, for its significance to be weighed. Only then, in retrospect, can the shadowy prefiguration be seen in its indicatory character as in a frame.

Second Model: Expectation of the End of History
and the Parousia

As a second illustration of the fact that the fulfillment does not stand in simple continuity with the prophecy but carries with it something new, and hence can understand the prophecy better than it understands itself, I will take the promise of the coming again of Christ (the Parousia). Here we see in a very striking way that the future (the fulfillment) is not an organic development of the past (the prophecy), that it does not correspond mechanically to what prepares the way for it as screw to thread. Expectation of the Parousia as we find it in the gospels heightens the tension between the times to an extreme point.

A glance at the relevant words of promise will make this clear at once. According to Mark (9:1), Jesus says: "Truly, I say to you, there are some standing here who will not taste death before they see the kingdom of God come with power." In the so-called "synoptic Apocalypse" we find in all three gospels another saying of Jesus along similar lines (cf. Mark 13:30): "This generation will not pass away before all these things [namely, the return of the Son of Man] take place." Finally, in a saying to the disciples in which he alludes to the incomplete mission in Palestine, Jesus says: "You will not have gone through all the towns of Israel, before the Son of Man comes" (Matthew 10:23).

That this word of promise did not come to pass, that history has gone on for millennia, and that Jesus was thus wrong in fixing the temporal end of the world, has not only bothered devout readers of the Bible but claimed the attention of scholarly exegetes as well. Resort has often been found in the exegetical device of treating the statements, not as original sayings of the Lord, but as later constructs of the community (cf. Oscar Cullmann). The generation that is to experience the return has also been construed, not as the people then alive, but as the Jewish people or the whole of the corrupt human race. It is not our task to collect specimens of such interpretations or reinterpretations across the centuries. We must be content simply to indicate in what direction such attempts have gone and still go. Some New Testament scholars, of course, do offer serious arguments for the authenticity of the sayings. If I accept this in what follows, this is not because of the frivolous need of the nonexpert to find those expert findings that suit his purpose, nor out of any pseudoconservative anxiety lest the hypothesis of "community constructs" should undermine the reliability of the biblical word and make it impossible to appeal to Jesus himself. Naturally I have well-considered reasons for preferring the thesis of authenticity. And even in face of the possibility that my lack of competence might have led me astray, I will take these as a hypothetical basis for the discussion that follows. I will do so because I am attracted by the task of pursuing as far as possible the above-mentioned tension between promise and fulfillment. If we have rightly grasped the biblical view of history, we must accept this tension. It is a test of our thesis. This tension is present in extreme form, however, when we have to accept it that Jesus himself promised the imminent end and then examine what the real or supposed nonfulfillment of this promise means. In this sense I judge that the hypothetical acceptance of authenticity has fruitful heuristic significance.

Although it seems that people soon realized that the promised imminence of the Parousia was not right, and that all things remained as they were, the nonfulfillment never produced a crisis in the sense of seeming to compromise the authority of Jesus. As noted regarding the interpretation of history by the prophets, what happened was that the events following the promise, though they might not fit in very well as a fulfillment, were evaluated as a new experience of faith, and attempts were then made to reinterpret the promise in the light of this experience. Thus in the Lucan writings the unexpected stretch of time between the Resurrection and the return is found to be the time for the work of the Spirit in the primitive community and hence for a new mode of the presence of Christ. As new and surprising forms of fulfillment were found which gave the promise an unexpected twist, the sayings of Jesus were seen in a new light. At least, they were so little called in question that at a time when it was clear that the bridegroom would be absent, the community handed down unchanged the sayings of Jesus about the imminence of his Parousia instead of suppressing them as a source of offense. In virtue of the acts of the Spirit in the primitive community, the prolonged interim makes good sense.

The question why there is a delay in the fulfillment can also cause us to look in other directions and explore the laws of God's kingdom. One of the answers given consists of a reference to the ungodly power that "holds up" (*katechein*, 2 Thessalonians 2:6 f.) the salvation event. The world that is dominated by this force is not yet ripe for the consummation. God's plan has never been carried out automatically as though it were a cause and history its effect. In making humanity his partner, God exposes himself to human freedom and the episodes this causes. (One has only to think of the fall.) The time between the Resurrection and the return does not simply run off but is exposed to episodes of this kind. One of them, and perhaps the most determinative, is that we are under the control of that ungodly power, so that there have to be further battles before God's final "victory day" can be proclaimed (cf. Luke 8:12).

Are all these considerations mere shifts and dodges to comfort believers in their disappointment at the nonreturn of Jesus? If they were, we should surely be able to detect the shattering impact of the problem. But there is no sign of this. How, then, are they bold to speak about fulfillment in spite of the problem of dating?

They can do so simply on the basis of another saying of Jesus about the Parousia: "But of that day or that hour [the end of the world and his coming again] no one knows . . . nor the Son" (Mark 13:32). In the light of this saying, which ascribes such knowledge to the Father alone, the question of the date cannot be the point of the promises of Jesus; the point is imminent expectation as such. And even here there is a question whether imminent means immediately on the brink. This question has to be clarified from the ensuing period, which enables us to read the promise backward. In other words, the question for the primitive community is as follows: "What in the promises of Jesus has been fulfilled?" Or: "Why has it been fulfilled in this way, and what light does this form of fulfillment throw on the saying?"

This approach, we must maintain, is possible only within the biblical understanding of history, for which a prophecy is not a simple prediction or a foreknowledge of the goal toward which the historical process is pressing. The schema of prophecy-fulfillment in which this view of history may be found, lives by the certainty that what comes is not limited to history and has not simply to be discovered in it for the goal and future to be found.

History itself has no will or end of its own. Its course is grounded in the resolve and freedom of the Lord of history. As he is faithful to himself, in that freedom he will do new justice to each new hour. He can even "repent." Hence those who have received the promise can only *wait* for the fulfillment. Waiting does not denote mere psychological patience to endure the interim. It does not point to a simple problem of time. It is an attitude of questioning. It is an expectation of something whose how and why cannot be perceived at the moment of promise, so that they will always be surprising. The question that is put to the future is thus as follows: "How am I to understand the promise in the light of the fulfillment? What did it really say to me?" When the primitive community, in the light of what happened, puts this question to the sayings of Jesus about imminent expectation, it finds a double answer.

First, it finds a reference to the sudden, unannounced, and noncalculable nature of the Lord's Parousia. We are already surrounded by his advent and do not know from what direction he comes. This makes our waiting into supreme watching. The nearness of the Lord gives an unconditional accent to every moment of life. We cannot postpone discipleship until later and claim today as *our* day. If the day of the Lord comes like "a thief in the night" (1 Thessalonians 5:2; 2 Peter 3:10), then the summons is in different forms: "Today, when you hear his voice, do not harden your hearts" (Hebrews 3:7), or: "Watch, therefore, for you do not know on what day your Lord is coming" (Matthew 24:42). The steward who knows his master's timetable and can be sure that he will not surprise him will have a good time and let things take their course. He will say: "My master is delayed," and "begins to beat his fellow servants, and eats and drinks with the drunken" (Matthew 24:48–49; cf. Luke 12:45). But the steward who knows the nearness of his master and the uncertainty of his coming remains sober and watches "with loins girded and . . . lamps burning" (Luke 12:35). Thus imminent expectation divides people into wise and foolish virgins (Matthew 25:1–13).

If, then, everything goes on as usual in apparent contradiction of the sayings of Jesus, if the course of the world is unchanged, and it is in this light that the primitive community has to ask about the different interpretations of the promise, it arrives at this answer: The promise of an imminent Parousia could not mean that a date could be fixed. The indifferent steward was asking about dates, and so were the foolish virgins. This question is a sign of noninvolvement. We recognize that Today, the Here and Now in the midst of ongoing time, is qualified by the nearness of the Lord and the noncalculability of his coming. Hence we no longer ask, "*When* is his future?" but, "*What* does it mean for us?" It means: Watch. And this in turn means that the values of life are transvalued when seen in the light of his coming. The relation between big and small, important and secondary, the many needs and the "one thing needful" (Luke 10:41), is fundamentally changed. God's history can be understood only in connection with my own history, his coming only in connection with my watching.

History is neither an isolated human dimension nor an isolated divine dimension. Biblically seen, it is a union of the two. Hence the history of the future, hence Christ's Parousia, is also my own history, the history of my watching, my soberness, my re-evaluation. The two spheres of history are connected.

But the question of the meaning of the imminence of the return in the light of events found a second answer from the primitive community.

The certainty that God's kingdom has drawn near is based primarily on the fact that in the person of the risen Lord the decisive breakthrough has already taken place and the end is anticipated. Adapting a metaphor of Luther, one might say that the serpent's head has been wounded and all we now have are its body's death-throes. Compared to this event, remaining history has no specific weight. It is an interim.[5] The direct connection between the event of the Resurrection and God's final triumph, the anticipation of the end, shrinks this interim. The prophets bring the end close as with a telescope and see across the interim. This phenomenon of prophetic style and vision is so familiar that there is even a technical term for it in theology; the prophetic foreshortening of perspective.

This foreshortening is not based on a psychological urge of the prophets, whether in hope or fear, to dwell more in the future than in the present. It is based on an understanding of history which experiences it as a salvation event, i.e., as an event in which the decisive thing has already taken place and the end is already anticipated. The interim between is no real gap. The end is close, God's kingdom is at hand. How can it fail to be when it has already been in the midst of us (Luke 17:21)?

In this light we can understand a remarkable phenomenon of church history which might otherwise pose an insoluble psychological riddle. We come across many occasions when expectation of the Parousia has reached fever pitch. Christian communities have seen themselves confronted by the imminent end. In World War II, as I myself heard and saw, this expectation was based on John's Apocalypse. Hitler was the beast from the abyss and the party sign was the mark of the beast without which no one could buy or sell

(Revelation 13:16 f.). All the signs seemed to indicate that the great tomb of the world would soon open. At such times of certainty about the end, which may be found across the centuries, there is then an inclination to draw up a timetable of the final events and set a date for the Parousia. Even such a respectable and sober biblical theologian as Johann Albrecht Bengel (1687–1752) did this, and believed that the thousand-year reign, the final phase of world history, would begin on June 18, 1836. What might seem to be a psychological riddle is as follows.

The expected end has never come as calculated. Many times people have gathered on hills to see the Son of Man come down on the clouds of heaven at the predetermined time, and to hear the trumpets of the Last Judgment. They have awaited these events with chorales devoted to the Second Coming. But while one might have expected a reaction of great disillusionment, the exact opposite has been the case. There has been neither a crisis of faith nor a rebuking of the prophets. People have just gone back home and begun to wait and calculate afresh.

How are we to understand this strange result? We can do so only in the light of the understanding of history expounded above. Under the impact of the striking of the decisive blow, the perspective of expectation shortens. The end is seen directly ahead. If there has been an error in dating, the certainty remains that the decisive thing has already taken place with Christ's Resurrection and that the remaining time of this world is qualified as a mere interim. Thus one can go on watching unembarrassed.

The reader will perhaps excuse the author if he offers a personal anecdote by way of illustration.

In World War II, I was in the group around Carl-Friedrich Goerdeler, who was expected to be Chancellor after Hitler's fall. This courageous and intellectually gifted man gave us excellent analyses of the situation, with prognoses for the immediate future. His prognoses were marked by two features. First, he predicted economic, political, and military events, which usually ran as he foresaw, as we could see at the next conference. Second, he tried to fix a date for the final collapse, but in this he was always wrong. He usually gave the regime only about three months, but it always survived, and we still had to meet as an opposition group. But none of us ever thought of denouncing Goerdeler as a pseudoprophet. He might have been wrong about dates, but the accuracy of his objective prognoses still impressed us.

What is the bearing of all this? The decisive turn in the war was the battle of Stalingrad. Only death-throes followed. The agony could be protracted. But this did not alter the fact that it could result in nothing historically "new" until the end came. It was an interim that stood under the sign of the end and simply brought this on. Here again, then, we had a kind of prophetic foreshortening of perspective. The error in dating was only incidental. Indeed, it validated the intrinsically accurate diagnosis and prognosis. Those who saw the real historical significance of the battle of Stalingrad had to assume that the end was near. Those who did not, who accepted the interpretation of Joseph Goebbels, had to experience the refutation of their reading of coming events.

This relation to the future is an illustration of the biblical understanding of history.

The difference, or, phenomenologically, the contradiction between the promise and the new quality brought by the supposed fulfillment, has always left the impression, outside the high stance (or borders) of faith, that the promise has not found any fulfillment. The hermeneutical principle that the promise has to be understood afresh in the light of the supposed fulfillment, that the shadow of what is to come has to be interpreted in the light of what does finally come, inevitably seems to be an evasion whereby faith tries to argue its way out of its disenchantment.

In fact, this impression of nonfulfillment is easy to understand. It is the necessary result of a view of history which is content to document immanent processes and to try to see the logic behind them. But here in the biblical view of things we have a different level of observation. The heuristic principle which directs it is confidence that the Lord of history stands by his word, that he remains true to himself, and that all events come from his counsel, from the actuality of his controlling will.

If God's "higher thoughts" (Isaiah 55:8) hold sway in history, and if we do not yet grasp what he is doing, but will only learn this later (John 13:7), we have to let our own thoughts be controlled by what he plans as his consummating goal and his path to this goal. We are thus thrown back upon waiting and persisting.

Only on this presupposition—and really only on this—does the thesis of a transcendent fulfillment make sense. It thus attains the rank of prophecy only because God is understood as the one who is in charge of his word and acts and direction of history. In contrast the comparisons that a purely phenomenological history might make between prophecy and fulfillment can only lead to contradiction. Even a deistic view of history can do no more than turn in a negative report here. If God is a kind of clockmaker who has set the world clock at the beginning but now lets it run its course, then obviously the conviction holds sway that we can understand this course once we grasp the causality. The principle of causality, however, conflicts with prophecy and fulfillment. Hence a painful difference between prophecy and fulfillment is noted. The prophets are compromised by this. The tormenting distinction between "timeless truth of reason" and the "accidental truth of history," as the worthy Lessing formulated it, finds one of its bases here.

Deism is a good example of the difference between the two views of history. Its clockmaker thesis means that we can infer the divine Inaugurator of events from their causality. For the biblical view of history, however, God is concealed in events whose interconnection we cannot see. Only the Inaugurator himself is certain. And it is because of him, of his "higher thoughts," that we are confident that history, too, is his work. In this confidence history is then his likeness even though we cannot equate the picture of events and that of their Inaugurator. We wait until what we cannot know is disclosed. We do not ourselves know the interconnection (not even that of prophecy and fulfillment), but we know the one who plans it. We do not infer God from history but history from God. This is the decisive difference.

Third Model: Prophecy of Disaster as a Reference to the Abiding Patterns of Historical Situations

In final elucidation of the relation between prophecy and fulfillment, I want to discuss the prophecies of judgment in the Old Testament. Here we not only have the gap between the threat and its apparent nonfulfillment. We also see another and very significant aspect of the theological understanding of history.

Historical judgment (e.g., in Joel 3) is not just an anticipation of the final reckoning. No mistake is seen if the prophets proclaim the end itself, and then, when the judgment is past, things go on as usual. On the contrary, as Joel perceives in his vision of the plague of locusts, the Last Judgment is seen to be present in the temporal judg-

ments of history. It is as a likeness or prefiguration of this kind that
Joel's "Alas" makes sense: "Alas for the day! For the day of the Lord
is near, and as destruction from the Almighty it comes" (1:15–20).

One of these visitations will be the last one, though there can be
no saying at the moment which it will be. (The "last" in this context is the total overthrow and destruction of Jerusalem, the end of
Israel. But in the light of New Testament eschatology this, too, is
only a prefiguration of the "Last" Judgment, the end of the world in
the full sense.) Earlier fire and brimstone rained on Sodom and
Gomorrah in a catastrophic judgment, and the kings of the East
also killed and plundered (Genesis 14:1–12; 19:24–29). Similarly, when Joel announced the coming of the "Northerner" under
Antiochus, who for a time stopped the temple services, this, too,
might be regarded as a prefiguration of the final disasters that over-
took Jerusalem in A.D. 70 and 135. The averted assault of the Northerner was for Israel a kind of foreshadowing of the final attack of
peoples from the North that Ezekiel foretold.

To put it in the form of a metaphor (whether borrowed or my
own, I am not sure), one might say that the great hand of the world
clock is always reaching twelve and then ticking on. But the little
hand keeps moving forward until it will finally signal "twelve, the
goal of time." This metaphor shows us that the judgments are not
just symbols of timeless disaster but also denote the unrest that
pushes the world clock forward until it will finally have run its
course. Time will have an end, history will reach its limits.

The biblical view of history interprets the present as this interim.
We stand between an Already and a Not Yet. The ungodly power
has "already" been dethroned: "I saw Satan fall like lightning from
heaven" (Luke 10:18). But "it does 'not yet' appear what we shall
be" (1 John 3:2).

On this view of things human existence does not find its basis,
meaning, or destiny in history, or at least in what history seems to
tell us about its origin and goal. Causality and finality as immanent
categories of orientation do not display what human existence is really all about. This links up with what was said at the beginning of
this book, namely, that we cannot learn the true nature of our being
from the objective sphere. What finally characterizes us is our standing between the Already and the Not Yet, our temporality, which is
more and other than simple movement in time and history. Temporality in the biblical sense means being thrust into time, accompa-

nied in time, and summoned out of time. Temporality points to that which transcends all time. "My times are in thy hand" (Psalm 31:15). This is why temporality cannot be understood in terms of itself and why our relation to it is grounded in trust and in expectation of the unexpected. The correspondence between prophecy and fulfillment throws light on this background of history and thus discloses our place in history.

Appendix: Erich Auerbach's Figurative Interpretation of History

So as not to lengthen this chapter unduly, I will reluctantly refrain from working out for its presentation of history the implications of Erich Auerbach's great work *Mimesis* (1946) and simply allude to some of the more important points.

According to Auerbach, it is a dominant rule in ancient classical literature that a more ordinary style should be used for everyday practical reality, either in the form of comedy or of pleasant and elegant light reading. Since everyday life is not really worthy of literature, social forces are not clearly depicted in ancient realism. Society simply consists of given and permanent institutions as a background to what takes place. Its structure (aristocracy, democracy) may be mentioned indirectly, but it is not a true literary theme. It is an established a priori model. Thus the presentation of history has a static character. Events take place over a timeless basis. This changes only when, with the rise of realism, which Auerbach pursues up to the modern period, everyday life becomes a worthy literary theme. Then the holdup ends and history begins to move and truly becomes "history." Its static character, as in the categories of Greek and Roman historiography, is replaced by a dynamic character.

Medieval realism in particular, Auerbach thinks, is based on the story of Christ with its ruthless mixture of everyday reality and supreme and lofty tragedy, which transcends the older rules of style. An incident like Peter's denial, which externally is just a police action and its results, would have been conceivable in antiquity at most only as a farce or comedy. The popular fishermen and tax collectors and Samaritans and harlots and the rich young ruler are taken out of their ordinary situations and brought directly before Jesus, and how they behave at this moment is necessarily a very serious matter and often very tragic.

Thus we have a world which on the one side is real and ordinary and familiar as to place, time, and circumstances, but which on the other side is shaken to its foundations, being changed and renewed before our very eyes. This temporal event at the heart of the everyday world is for the New Testament authors a revolutionary one in world history. It is the grand model of all history.

The essential thing according to Auerbach is that everyday events, e.g., the offering of Isaac, are not tied to a single point in time but transcend it. They have the significance of world events, of decisive situations in our own existence, and therefore they have significance for us.

This transcendent element, which is not to be found, Auerbach thinks, in either Homer or modern literature, leads to the figurative interpretation of history in the biblical sense and thus makes the schema of prophecy-fulfillment into a category of historical experience. Hence it is characteristic of the Christian view of history that for it an earthly event has concrete reality here and now but has also a meaning beyond itself, either proclaiming or confirming another event. Thus the connection between events is not regarded as primarily one of temporal or causal development but as one of unity in the divine plan of which all events are members and reflections. Their direct connection on earth is less important, and perceiving it is sometimes dispensable in interpretation.

These very important references seem to me to make it plain that our own presentation of the biblical understanding of history agrees at essential points with Auerbach's literary researches. They can give us no idea, of course, of the wealth of comparisons between the various forms of realism and the incomparable riches of the work in materials and reflection.

II. THE REACHING OUT
OF HUMAN EXISTENCE TO THE FUTURE.
THE MEANING AND LIMIT OF PROGRESS

a. Hope and Anxiety as Anticipation of the Future

Humanity cannot be understood without the principle of "hope" and the resultant relation to the future. It denotes a significant difference from animals that we can—and must—project ourselves into the future. Ernst Bloch's teaching is an ontology of the Not Yet. To be human, for him, is to be on the way to something else. Asked to put his philosophy in a single sentence, he can say: "S is not yet P." Considering coming possibilities, the potentiality of the future, releases the impulse not to be content with the present but critically to overcome it. In this sense the promises of which we spoke have the function of challenging our present situation and that of the world. The fact that we are not content, that there is no friendly harmony between us and reality constitutes unquenchable hope. This keeps us dissatisfied until the great fulfillment of all the promises of God (Jürgen Moltmann).

It would be a distortion to see the future only in a positive light. For William Faulkner, looking at the future kindles no hope, only resignation. None of our experiences can last. The future is the time of cessation. It is the epitome of transitoriness.

The hope kindled by the future can also be a mirage. It can expose us to the bewitchment of various schemas, e.g., creative evolutionism, scientific humanism, or communism. These tie our aspirations to the future, to the innermost core of temporality. Almost all vices are rooted in the future. Gratitude looks to the past and love to the present, but fear, greed, lust, and careerism look to the future. A whole generation is in search of the rainbow—neither honest nor kind nor happy in the present, spurning the true gift that is given it now, heaping it up as fuel on the altar of the future (Clive S. Lewis). The Russian proverb that "many fools feed in the pasture of the future" points in the same direction.

Orientation to the future not only kindles the light of hope or the will-o'-the-wisp of false hope, but is also the true cause of anxiety. The future is present in anxiety, which is a tragic existential factor for Heidegger. Lack of anxiety as well as lack of hope is something we find to be nonhuman, or a symptom of being still at earlier stages of human development. In Africa I have found primitive peoples whose climate and vegetation allow them to live without care or concern in the immediate present because they have enough for their needs. But because the future is no challenge for them, they are reduced to the moment and remain undeveloped. The human drive toward culture and self-fulfillment has not yet been triggered in them at this stage. Civilized or awakened peoples are always those that are open to the future, particularly because they bring it into the present by way of anxiety or anxieties. Climate and natural environment should not be overlooked as factors which either promote or hinder this.

Hope and anxiety are related in face of the future. Hope is often the desperate hope that what is feared will not happen. And anxiety, especially in the form of care with its changing masks, accompanies hope like a shadow and calls it in question.

The by no means arbitrary metaphor that hope is light while anxiety is shadow brings out already the supremacy of hope. This is the true theme of orientation to the future. Hope is to be realized; what threatens is to be held at bay.

Radical hopelessness is in fact lifelessness. It is the death of humanity. In psychological statistics the extinction of the will to live among adults can often be traced back to infancy. In homes in which unwed mothers are allowed to visit their children regularly, growth is faster and the mortality rate lower than in homes that do not permit visits. Hope has stimulating force even in the early stages of life.

The art of leading others, especially in politics and most especially in times of crisis, has always been understood to be the art of arousing hope. A master of ingenious propaganda like Goebbels made frantic efforts, toward the end of World War II, to kindle hope, and therefore to promote the will for self-preservation, by talking about miracle weapons. The eschatology of the Marxist system also shows us how effective utopian hope of the future can be. Passions released by utopian dreams can have enormous historical force.

b. Belief in Progress as a Paradigm of Hope for the Future

Among human expectations for the future, hope of progress has high and, in some sense, representative rank. The Enlightenment gave decisive impetus to the idea that the future is the time of advance, of going beyond the present. A view of history like that of Lessing in his *Education of the Human Race*[6] illustrates this. To the degree that reason frees itself from the distortion of reality that necessarily develops under the sway of myths and superstitions, the possibility of a rational organization of the world increases. Under the rule of autonomous humanity, and with the release of all its possibilities, the world is moving toward a bright future.

Yet the naiveté of the first hours of hope has worn off. It has yielded to a skeptical view of humanity also produced by reason. In the historical process of education the Enlightenment has been enlightened about itself. The fervor of the emancipation of reason is now accompanied by the experience that if reason can take us beyond ourselves, it can also make us more beastly than any beast.

The path of even well-founded hope for the future has been constantly taught sobriety. Caesar Augustus, lauded as the shepherd of his people and the prince of peace, and even venerated as the mediator between the macrocosm and the microcosm and as a type of Zeus, did indeed create the Pax Romana and seemed to fulfill what Vergil predicted in his Fourth Eclogue around 40 B.C., namely, the coming of a world savior who would rid the earth of fear and war. Nevertheless, this hope of peace led to its own shattering by self-scrutiny and self-enlightenment. For the Pax Romana did not turn out to be a restoration of some original state of peace. It was a violent form of pacification (what a paradox!). It was simply the armistice enforced by the subjection of the world to Roman rule. It was a peace of threat and force. It is significant that the *ara pacis*—the altar that Augustus set up to his cult of peace and therefore to himself—was erected on the field of Mars. The Pax Romana was established under the pitiless conditions of the Pax Babylonica (Hans P. Schmidt). But once examined and sobered, hope inevitably ceases to be a driving impulse. There arises a history of disappointed hopes.

It is obvious, then, that fear of the results of progress dogs belief in progress like a shadow cast by this light of hope. The emotions stirred by the Club of Rome with its statement on the limits of growth are not the causes of this fear but its reflection.

Since our present attitude to the future will be essentially determined by whether we affirm the promises of progress in hope or doubt them with skepticism, I should like to deal with the belief in progress (both individual and collective) as a typical instance of our attitude to the future. As a part for the whole, it will serve as a model.

c. The Antithesis of "Conservative" and "Progressive." Unmasking of a False Alternative

How can we really fail to be progressive and open to the future? The alternative is to be retrogressive, and who would be prepared to accept this kind of label? It is part of the tactics of unfair polemics to force one's opponents into the corner of retrogressiveness. In an objective, even if sharp, debate, these opponents will know how to defend themselves and perhaps to take the offensive. But if we object that they are out of date, that they are not in touch with the spirit of the times, that they are victims of their age, it is of little avail for them to have either the eloquence of a Demosthenes or the brilliance of an Einstein. For whatever they say is no longer judged from the standpoint of its truth or falsity. It is discredited in advance as outdated, as long since discarded, as no longer "with it," as modern young people, and adults who ape them, might say.

The issue here, then, is not whether a thing is true or false but whether it is conservative or progressive. At this level of argument, or, rather, of nonargument, the intellectual rigors of debate are avoided and slogans sprout. As Arnold Gehlen has finely said, a faith that moves mountains is put in phrases. Terms like "reactionary" and "fascist" and "hostile to progress" can obviously be bandied about without any intellectual effort. Charming words are carried in front of one like a foil.

It has been our custom to put painful or doubtful terms into Greek, Latin, or French. This has the advantage of putting them at a distance and making them less offensive. However well-trained or robust we might be, many phrases are more palatable when left in their original tongue. Thus pornography, or porno, is less shocking than a translation would be. Leaving it in the Greek accustoms us to it so that it ceases to give us a kind of verbal goose flesh. Along the same lines people nowadays might prefer to speak about "avant-gardism" rather than progress. This has a good ring and abounds with youth and aspiration for the future. Even older people who do not want to be thrown on the scrap heap—and who does?—use this kind of terminology so as not to lose touch. But a wrinkled neck sticking out of colorful clothes is ridiculous to young people. Alexander Solzhenitsyn has rightly spoken out against those who, instead of resisting, will lick up anything so as not to appear conservative.

The term "conservative" *seems* to describe a position that is opposed to a vital and progressive openness to the future. It has become a term of abuse and is generally assumed to stamp those to whom it is applied as reactionaries, to denounce them as squares whose only concern is to maintain the status quo. The association that the word has for many of our contemporaries is perhaps that of "conserves," i.e., foods that lose their freshness through being kept.

Thus the terms "avant-gardist" and "conservative" have become alternatives that are almost equivalent to "good" and "evil."

In an effort to correct this linguistic confusion, we shall first claim that the alternative is one that is totally unfair. For the word "conservative" has nothing whatever to do with retrogressive or hostile to progress. Its opposite is not "progressive"—for a conservative may be progressive—but "desirous of novelty," i.e., making change an end in itself. Perhaps this is putting it too simply for sociologists to understand if they have been spoiled by our customary jargon. Let us say, then, a "mania for innovation" instead of a "desire for novelty." Then they will know what we are talking about.

The word "conservative" arose in opposition to the French Revolution and its abstract and ideological idea of history. It could not be a synonym of "ossified" because it represented the rights of living history in contrast to an artificial, abstractly constructed state that was proclaimed to be correct.[7]

The conservative wants to preserve what has developed historically, or to restore it when it is overwhelmed, not in deference to the law of inertia or for the upholding of the status quo, but for the simple reason that it has proved itself. The question whether it has really done so cannot be answered, of course, without finding a place for reason and conscience in the inquiry. Hence the conservative has to be a mature and involved person to do justice to this intellectual claim.

It is one of the marks of conservatives that they are oriented to life as it is lived and thus remain aloof from views of humanity and history which are preconceived, ideological, or utopian. If we assume in advance that all existing structures are wretched and deserve only to be condemned, and that only visionary structures for the future can be good, then, in view of the disillusionment that will inevitably come, this can only do harm. The statement that everything that exists deserves to perish can only be uttered by a Mephistopheles.

All this forms a kind of prelude to what we have to say about the term "avant-garde." If this word simply meant that we ought to make the world better than it is, that we should enhance the possibilities of peace and justice, that we should fight hunger, avert the population explosion, and lessen the gap between rich and poor by appropriate economic and social structures, then avant-gardism and progressiveness would be so breathtakingly and self-evidently right that no one could possibly reject them. But unfortunately their advocates are not content with the comparative—to make "better." Avant-gardism feeds on remote utopian visions of what the world ought to be. It is nourished by the dream of a finally anarchist world that will bring perfection, not merely to the structure of the world, but also to humanity itself when all alienating structures have been cast off and humanity can at last emerge as it is in itself, in its original goodness. This is the secularized dream of a heavenly Jerusalem —secularized because it is not God but humanity itself, the genius of Homo faber, that will bring into being this new and different world.

If, of course, we measure today's world by this ideal, visionary world, it naturally goes down with drums and trumpets. Hence one can make the metaphysical diagnosis that it deserves to perish. The twentieth-century Mephistopheles can also add the rather impressive thesis of "the dialectic of the negative," which in popular parlance means that when something is destroyed, a phoenix will be found that will rise up out of the ashes.

Clichés are easily believed—but they are also transitory. Avant-gardist ideas have short lives. They date more quickly than electronically guided antimissile systems. They are so short-lived that the cameras needed to record them have to be focused quickly to catch them. The visions are enwrapped, as it were, in a perpetual twilight of the gods. And the earlier gods, seen in restrospect, have a macabre or ludicrous appearance.

If, then, we reject certain forms of avant-gardism or progressiveness, we do not have to indicate thereby that we are reactionaries clinging to the past or even the remote past. Our rejection *can* mean, on the contrary, that we are more progressive than avant-gardism, that with our eyes on life we see approaching bankruptcy, and are looking ahead to the remote future, to what will follow the great collapse.

Furthermore, that kind of avant-gardism fails because it can never be achieved in a context of continuous teamwork. Its champions divide into solipsists and little groups that are inevitably inefficient and impotent. The constant schisms and divisions and clusters bear witness to this. The story of the revolutionary student movement of the later sixties and early seventies might serve as an example.

Why this is so, is not hard to say. For when everything is challenged, there is no common basis of values or norms on which to operate. Hence we have to begin afresh continually with Adam and Eve in order to set up a structure of norms.

We can quickly test this out. Why does a leader, if possible, choose as his closest aides those who are tied to him by common convictions? He probably has very pragmatic reasons for so doing. But he also does it because he does not want to discuss these convictions afresh each day. He does not want them to be constantly challenged. He does not want to be subjected afresh each day to the strenuous and time-consuming need to justify himself. In other words, homogeneous companions are important because productive cooperation is possible only on a common basis. If there is no consensus in basic principles to start with, each day has to begin again at the beginning, with Adam and Eve. And in the evening, because there is still debate about principles, ten hours will perhaps have been spent discussing a free market against government controls, and no business letters will have been written. The result is a blocking up of every creative impulse. Without the conservative salt of a common basis of values and norms, a tasty supper cannot be cooked. In this regard "the dead ride fast" (Gottfried August Bürger).

d. Technology as a Stimulus to Belief in Progress

Although the term "avant-garde" flourishes and is regarded as chic today, in the spring night of the belief in progress the bloom is already off the word "progress" itself. Environmentalists, traffic experts, town planners, and cultural philosophers suspect that there is something awry with it. Only psychologists and sociologists, who in these younger disciplines are less prone to self-criticism—or some of them at least!—still look ahead undisturbed to the dawning realization of their projects. But for them, too, the hour of truth is coming.

Before I speak about the crisis in the belief in progress, however, I must first show how the belief arose. I will resist in this regard the professorial instinct to plunge into its history. One might begin this in the thirteenth century with the first use of the term "modern." I myself will simply ask what it is in *our* day that stimulates confidence in progress or shatters it. In so doing I shall be taking up much that I have said already and adopting the thesis that the autonomy of technological progression is what has triggered a certain belief in progress in us. As earlier, we thus ascribe representative significance to philosophical processes. By their irreversible forward thrust, which knows no halt, they suggest to us a progressive mood of optimism (at any rate in the earlier stage, which we have called naiveté). I should like to illustrate this by an anecdote which I think will serve as a didactically fruitful model.

As promising young teachers in the Third Reich we had to visit an academy in Kiel-Kitzeberg which was under the philosophical direction of Alfred Rosenberg. Representatives of all the faculties were present. In such cases there would usually be lively debates and discussions, and inevitably these would end up with such ultimate questions as the meaning of life or history or the nature of the forces promoting and sustaining life. While we were exploring these issues without coming to any conclusions, one of us made the remarkable statement: "It is strange that the pre-Socratics hundreds of years ago dealt with all the questions into which we are rummaging, questions of the meaning and basis of life. Philosophy is obviously marking time and making no progress."

At the very time when we were led to this melancholy conclusion, an admiral took us aboard a warship in Kiel harbor. The constructive rationality of this technical product, e.g., the clever coordination of the different weapon systems, made a deep impression on us. As we were talking on the way home, suddenly the young colleague who had made the remark about the pre-Socratics put to us the question: "Dear people, which is the greater achievement, Kant's *Critique of Pure Reason* or this warship?"

This question was almost like a blow that for a moment took our breath away. Can the two things really be compared? Can we even put them in the same sentence?

The two things—on the one side the statement that we have made no progress in ultimate questions, and on the other the product of technology which makes an impression of progress—give us every reason to think. And in fact, if we compare these paradigms, we might get some new insights.

In ultimate questions, humanity is always, and with each new generation, asking *afresh*. The old questions crop up unchanged in new editions. We find this as parents. The answers that we arrive at by struggle, our faith or philosophy or experience of life, we cannot just bequeath or transmit to our children so as to give them a foundation for their own findings or new construction. They will not take such things from us. They do not want a prefabricated parental foundation. They search the horizon with their telescope and ask where there might be a spot where they have never been. They want to probe all truths and rules of life for themselves and in their own experience, and they are willing to pay the price if only it makes them wise. But they want to be wise themselves and not just to be the heirs of wise parents.

Technology, however, presents us with an aspect of life in which things are very different, indeed, the exact opposite. Here each generation does not begin afresh; one generation stands on the shoulders of the other. This is why there is no generation gap in technology or the exact sciences. Since technology is so pervasive and influences our lives in so many ways, this law of one-way progress obviously has a great suggestive effect on us, so that we naturally apply it to other spheres and generalize it. But while mankind continually progresses, individuals, as Goethe says, remain the same. Justinus Kerner recognized this when one and a half centuries ago, before the technological age was fully under way, he had dreams about the technical phenomenon of flying: "Launch out, O man, move up from the steamship to the flying ship, fly with the eagles and the lightning, you will still get no further than the tomb." The fact that our finitude has to be recalled in this emphatic way shows that technology carries with it a temptation for us to overlook our subjection to death and to view ourselves as self-transcending creatures who erroneously transfer technological progress to our own beings.

If the concept of progress unleashed by the technological age produces increasingly friable feelings of dissatisfaction, this blight on progress is due to the fact that we ourselves are the great obstacle, we who are obviously outside the mechanism of progress for reasons that are undoubtedly theological. It is in reference to us in this sense that Kierkegaard says that, no matter what one human generation may learn from another, it never learns what is truly human. In this regard each generation makes a new beginning, has the same task as that which precedes, and makes no more headway. Thus no generation can learn from another how to love; in this respect each must begin again at the beginning. If it is not content just to love (as earlier generations did), but wants to do "more," to "progress," this is idle and foolish talk.

e. The Change in Form of Utopias

How little we fit in with the progress suggested by technology may be seen when we note the change in utopias and reflect on the reasons for the change. At the very latest from the time of Berdyaev and Orwell we have begun to fear what technological achievements might put at our disposal. The world of total technical, physical, and biological manipulation—a world in which all things are possible— seems to us to be a sinister world. We have already seen why. For theological reasons, we are sinister to ourselves. Our fear of ourselves grows with our growing power of manipulation. Thus utopian desires that were once dreams of total mastery of the world have become shock utopias. Woe to a world in which humans have a total say, which is condemned to be totally *their* world!

But there is a second way of looking at the change in utopias— those darling idols of the belief in progress—at the mutation which they have undergone. Originally utopias were ideal portrayals of the end of history. At this final point a classless society was expected, or a world without hunger, injustice, or violence. These visions forced us to ask how they could be realized. Alternative solutions were offered which show a good deal of constancy and still recur, namely, the revolutionary and the revisionary solutions. The former says that to achieve the eschaton of final harmony we must intensify the class war, increase confrontations, even by force, and in this way propel history toward its goal. The latter operates with the postulate that we must put the desired final state into provisional practice even now by settling all conflicts and pursuing consistent pacifism. The one, therefore, forces history dialectically to its end by way of antitheses, the revolutionary principle being integrated into the dialectic. The other anticipates already the vision of peace at the end of

history. Both deal with the same question, namely, how the desired
goal of history is to be reached.

Today, however, there has been an essential change. Utopias have
undergone a radical change in form. Usually people today do not ask
first about the utopian goal and only then about the means or ways
to reach it. They do the exact opposite. The technical means are already present. But they offer less delight in the new possibilities of
achievement than fear lest we might not be able to control them. In
place of final dreams, which we no longer have, the primary concern
is how Homo faber, the sorcerer's apprentice, will be able to handle
the means that seem to make a cosmic goal attainable but have broken loose and are leading us where we do not want to go.

We have already diagnosed the reason for this anxiety, arguing
that humanity in its innermost being, ethically, is not yet a match
for what it can do technologically. We do not have mastery over the
instruments at our disposal. Konrad Lorenz has pointed out that our
inner development does not synchronize with the uncanny rapidity
of change in a technological civilization. We have not kept up.

Before we can think about the final stages of history and dream
utopian dreams, the technological means are already available. This
is a reversal of the previous situation. I will give three instructive examples.

The first is atomic power. This is at our disposal, but it does not
give us visions of an end of history filled with its blessings. On the
contrary, we are worried about how we can handle it. All that we can
do with it for the moment, and for any foreseeable future, is to produce an equilibrium of terror.

The second is the biological means to sustain and prolong life. But
this offers us no ideal picture. We are faced with its by-product,
a population explosion, over which we must gain control.

The third is the medical ability to prevent conception in the form
of the pill. This has brought with it completely new ways of understanding sex ("completely new" if one considers the public and universal character of the change). But again this means does not lead
to a final state of free sex with no repressions. It does not even
lead in this direction. We rather have the sense that an alarm is
sounding that finds expression in the question how we can prevent
the complete neutralizing of sex, its decline into a mere matter of
hormones, its loss of all human qualities.

Utopias today seem to be compromised by our inability to have any final dreams and our total preoccupation with stopping what we are able to do and are even forced to do (in virtue of the autonomy discussed earlier). We no longer have visions, then, of the consummation of a process of perpetual growth. Our gaze is fixed on the limits and crisis of growth.

f. The Ambivalence of Progress

This brings us up against a phenomenon that is much discussed today—there have been echoes of it here and there in this book—so that I shall hardly be able to introduce the reader to anything new. I have in mind the Janus head of progress—its ambivalence. To stir our imaginations a little, I will simply give three illustrations or models which come from the very heart of our present experience.

The first is the automobile, the darling child of civilization, a status symbol, a sign of far-ranging travel. Yet this very automobile pollutes the atmosphere and chokes the roads and streets that were built for travel. Thus progress seems paradoxically to consume itself. In other words, the technological means provokes a revolt against the very ends whose instrument it was supposed to be.

The second illustration is the general problem of travel. This provides us with a kind of sketch on which we can find almost all our problems. If, for example, we can cover distance quickly by car or jet, we seem to save time. But we constantly find that this is not really so. For the time saved lays new and additional duties on us by way of recompense. Thus in the old days, when a friend died in London, a person in Hamburg or Berlin was not expected at the funeral. The notice of the death would come too late and the journey would take too long. Today the two flights needed can be done easily in the time available.

The third is life in what we call today, with a fashionable if stupid abbreviation, a "consumer society." There is a partial truth in the term, as in all such slogans. Technology sees to that with its enormous range of consumer goods for eating and drinking and for homes and travel and leisure. All these things have to be claimed and used if the economic process is to roll on without disruption. Even so-called ordinary people are blessed with comforts of which the great lords of the Middle Ages could hardly have dreamed when, troubled with gout and rheumatism and toothache, they looked out of their unheated alcoves upon the countryside and found poor consolation in the fact that it was all theirs.

But there is a limit to consumption. The maximum is reached when we need more time to consume and enjoy all the goods provided than we have at our disposal between work and sleep, as a clever person once put it. One might add that the maximum is also reached when the strained organism cannot handle any more. Once upon a time it enhanced the social prestige of guests in a luxury hotel to have a dinner of six courses, but today if they are content with a glass of tomato juice, the head waiter will probably be whispering to colleagues that they must have at least three hundred employees.

This is not a digression. It helps to show how ambivalent progress is when it takes from us with one hand what it gives us with the other. Progress does, in fact, seem to feed on its own children. More precisely one might perhaps describe its ambivalence as follows (in characteristically sharp but by no means arbitrary paradoxes):

The computer is the instrument that solves problems of its own making.

The airplane poses new variations of the problem of time that it is supposed to solve.

The automobile is the traffic problem which it was designed to solve.

g. The Future as a Substitute for Transcendence

The point of these assertions obviously cannot be to furnish us with gloomy portraits of a universal cultural pessimism. We make two inferences.

First, we are shown how hollow a naive belief in progress is. We are warned not to give in without reflection to avant-gardist dreams.

Second, we have to put the crucial question, What is the reason for this strange structural law of ambivalence?

In thinking about this, we may be confused by something that hardly seems to harmonize with this ambivalence and the resultant skepticism regarding the future.

Although utopian desires and dreams have been increasingly compromised and have increasingly become the causes of frustration, anxiety, skepticism, and even shock (of which we have given some symptoms), nevertheless there is evidence of a very remarkable flight into the future, an almost unintelligible expectation that in it there will still be fulfillments that will snatch us out of our present troubles. In illustration one need only think of the boom that is enjoyed today by futurology, e.g., in the form of peace institutes, oriented to the future, which have sprouted like mushrooms since the beginning of the seventies. These flourish in expectation that something new in principle will emerge out of research into areas of conflict, and that knowledge of the reasons for conflict will enable us to bring them under control.

Skepticism about the future seems in a very paradoxical way to carry with it an almost boundless hope for the future, of which Ernst Bloch is a typical representative. To become a futurologist, or to propose a theology of hope, is ipso facto to be up-to-date.

The slightly ironical tone with which I say this should not be taken as an attack on legitimate futurology, although the scientific claim implied by the word does have some ridiculous features. (I admit to a certain measure of unholy glee when I see how many futurological economic and monetary projections were wiped out overnight solely by the unexpected energy crisis of 1974—and we had looked on them with veneration, almost as if they were a verbally inspired text! And how about some of the theories that only yesterday were the last word in pedagogy?)

There is nothing against futurology when it takes the form of long-term prognoses and projections in such fields as the planning of roads or buildings or cities, or in areas that are subject to statistical measurement. Here the alternative to planning is dilettante improvization, unsystematic patchwork, muddling through at the level of symptoms instead of systematically dealing with the basic problem. No one wants this. Hence its opposite, futuristic calculation and planning, is legitimate. For in this way, without utopian dreams, we can tackle the structural problem and master it, not in the sense of producing a perfect world, but at least in that of making the present world less imperfect and subjecting it so far as possible to our own self-determination.

My objection, then, is not to this partial and rational future expectation but simply to the ideologizing transfiguration of the future, to flight into the future. We have mentioned certain forms of this flight and recall especially the prognoses of some Marxist-oriented sociologists (like Marcuse), who claim no less than that social structures which eliminate repression will produce new people living like lemures with no aggressive instincts and going about in a world without any crime.

If such flights of fancy disqualify themselves for people of a sober mind, other forms of expectation begin to take root in those who suffer less from a lack of rational self-control. I have in mind the fascinating talk of a future world-state in which there will be no major wars and disputes will be minimized as purely internal matters. To me this avant-garde dream is not primarily doubtful (in a good sense) because it seems to be unrealistic and unrealizable. That might be debatable. Another objection—a theological one—has greater weight for me. For this dream overlooks what humanity is, and that it will always be the same, that it is a very dubious phenomenon with the fall behind it. Here again awareness of the story of the fall is the strongest antidote to every form of utopian sickness.

The medieval plays about Antichrist, and W. Soloviev in his *Story of Antichrist*, had in fact a better grasp of the situation. Here the dream of a great and peaceful world society is unfolded—but the dream, in self-contradiction, is a "consistent" one. Absolute power corrupts absolutely, as Lord Acton put it. Fallen humanity cannot handle the possession of uncontrollable power over the whole earth. Its Promethean or Cainite nature becomes virulent.

In these visions of Antichrist, then, the world emperor does not have the face of a redeemer but has demonic features. There are no institutional safeguards against the devil and the pact that humanity has made with him. The human potential for evil will find access into all the structural forms of world organization and translate itself into kinetic energy, no matter whether the structures are bad or less bad. It is the final blindness to reality which the Bible calls "folly" that people will not accept this but fall victim to the illusion that they can overcome evil, that they can, as it were, structurally outwit it.

I regard it as the worst misunderstanding of the permanence of evil if the inference were made from it that we should let things be, that nothing can be done about the old Adam and Eve. Naturally, in opposition to such defeatist deductions, we ought to seek out the least evil and manage human nature as best we can in the circumstances. Along these lines democracy with its sharing of powers and control of force is one institutional possibility.

What we are against is the misleading and truly unrealistic dream that there is some future form of the world in which we can approximate once more to the harmonious state of Paradise. For this reason the progressive-sounding thesis regarding domestic world politics seems to be on the side of illusion.

The author admits to a constant feeling that this flight into the future is simply a pointer to a loss of transcendence.

When the present, in Leopold von Ranke's words, is no longer seen in its "immediacy to God," it becomes mysteriously empty. This emptying out of time can lead to the Mephistophelian thesis that it deserves to perish. It can thus result in capitulation, in the cry: "After us the flood!" But it can also lead to a latching on to future expectations and a falling victim to utopias: Today everything is so dreadfully fixed. We are subject to material pressures. The technological society does not let us play a determinative role. The upward way is blocked. Heaven is evacuated. We are trapped in self-reposing finitude. We are in the hell (Sartre) in which we are "below ourselves." Only the future is open. *There* is fluid lava that can be molded. *There* nothing is fixed. *There* is room for open possibilities —and for dreams. For secularized humanity the ideologically transfigured future is a surrogate for lost transcendence.

h. What to Do?

We shall now attempt a concluding evaluation of the many aspects of our human relation to the future.

Have we not received a new confirmation that what has impressed itself upon us as the ambivalence of progress is simply a reflection of humanity's own ambivalence? In our discussion of technology it was already obvious that what is called progress is no other than the ongoing self-realization of humanity. With the loss of the basis, goal, and meaning of existence, loss is increasingly clear in this area too, as if projected on a giant screen, namely, as lostness in the mass, as helplessness in the midst of social pressures, as impersonality in subjection to anonymous machines. One might describe the picture on the screen at considerable length.

What progress brings is certainly very imposing when it plows up the world and leaves its traces until the world becomes a "secondary system" and a copy of itself, until it finally confronts itself (to quote Heisenberg again). In face of this imposing creative power one recalls the saying of Sophocles that life knows many powerful things but nothing is more powerful than humanity. (The word "powerful" hardly does justice here to the Greek *deinon*, which carries with it the sense of something sinister.)

Nevertheless, it is remarkable that the closer we approach the great tapestry of human culture and civilization, the clearer is the red thread which runs like an artery through all its forms and phenomena. Mother earth, on which cities and cathedrals and factories and power stations stand, has drunk the blood of Abel. This blood of the mistreated and murdered brother runs in every rut and gutter. Cain, the great brother and father of the human race, mysteriously proclaims his presence in every place. In every symphony the note of suffering and death may be detected. This sign is printed on every Doric pillar. Are not slaves and the deprived, the miseries of peasants and laborers, part of the greatness and Apollonian splendor of Greek art? Is not the greatest that humanity can produce based on an earth that has drunk the blood of Abel and the sweat of those deprived of their rights? Do we have to learn this from Marxism? Can we not find it for ourselves, in a much profounder form, in that old story of Cain? Was Heinrich von Treitschke really right when he once said, rather daringly, that one statue of Phidias outweighs all the misery of the millions of slaves of antiquity? Who is right, Treitschke, or the old story of Cain and Abel?

Since humanity itself is the true problem of the world and the real question mark in all progress, everything depends on its changing itself when it seeks to change the world. But this insight is of little use unless it is also seen that humanity has no power to change itself. This is the negative side of the old belief that a new being is based on grace alone and cannot be the product of our own work.

It is at any rate a dangerous illusion to think that we can redeem ourselves by furnishing the world with new and better structures. This illusion is simply another form of trust in "work-righteousness." This outmoded term, which has taken on some patina with hundreds of years of use, simply refers to the mistaken belief that humanity has the power to shape itself. In the days of the New Testament and the Middle Ages what was usually in mind was moral and meritorious action whereby self-mastery could be attained. In the social ideologies of the modern period, self-mastery is sought by collective action, i.e., by changing the social structure. In changing that, in thinking we can change it (and believing that it is absolutely determinative), we have to accept the possibility that we can shape humanity itself.

Now certainly we ought to try to improve these structures. To argue to the contrary would be as foolish as saying that, since we cannot be righteous before God by doing good works, we are dispensed from doing such works. We could go even further, as some people did with whom Paul had to deal when, from the correct statement, "Where sin increased, grace abounded all the more" (Romans 5:20), they drew the fatal conclusion, "Let us continue in sin that grace may abound" (6:1, 15). We thus come up against problems that are anything but new. They are simply variations on those that are old and familiar.

It is not, then, that we oppose the task of changing social structures. My objection is simply to the false hopes that are connected with these structural improvements, and especially the hope that in this way humanity can escape its own problematical nature. Such escape, redemption, awaits it elsewhere.

If it is true (as we said) that all individual and group egoisms, the sacred egoism of the state, conflicts of interests, competition, and repression are all a macrocosmic reflection of what haunts the human heart and mutters in it, there can hardly be any question to what point in the world the theme of redemption applies. Those who think they can change the world without changing this heart, without making this heart the theme of their plans for change, are putting things backward and reckoning without their host. Perhaps no one has put this more forcibly than Ingeborg Bachmann in her story *Das dreissigste Jahr*, where she says at one point: "If you put off the person, the old one, and put on a new one, then . . ."

What a Christian should say about changing the world from this angle seems to me to be as follows.

There can be no doubt that we have the task of making this questionable world a little juster and freer and less complacent.

If I put this very modestly, and use only weak comparatives—"a little more or less"—instead of high-flying utopian terminology, I am indicating thereby the limits of what we can do and calling for a little modesty. In particular I am giving a warning to ideologically bloated hopes: Those who promise heaven on earth have always made this world into hell.

But if we should undertake this task of shaping and changing the world, if it should be our goal to make it a little juster and freer, then everything naturally depends on the ordering of our priorities. And here the question is: How are we to control the human heart, or to whom are we to entrust this control? If the younger generation today is shaken by revolutionary waves, by many forms of unrest and rootlessness; if it is perhaps seeking escape from the desert of meaninglessness in the imaginary world of drugs, then we interpret this situation much too superficially if we find in it no more than outrage about certain authoritarian wrongs, or about imperialism in the near or distant east, or about the indifference to misery in the developing countries. Young people themselves do not really know how to "articulate" (as they put it today) the cause of their unrest, and they mostly look for it only in the foreground. But their real problem is to be sought in a deeper dimension. They suffer—more instinctively than reflectively—from the incongruence between that for which we are destined and to which we are oriented on the one side, and the reality of life on the other. This is the pain of a great betrayal. Using current terminology, they call it "alienation." Christians call it sin. And because this problem contains the question as to who we are and where we can find ourselves and our identity, this pain has its value even if it often expresses itself in repulsive forms. The younger generation is looking for a track that the older one has often enough lost sight of because it is interested in another animal, a different prey.

The track to which I refer is a religious question in cipher form. One of the essential contributions that Christian proclamation should render today is that of helping to decipher latent religious questions and in this way bringing these questions and the message into contact instead of letting them pass by one another like lines askew in space. The religious question is growing among us to the same degree that the question of ecclesiastical institutions is plunging into crisis. But two processes that ought to be concurrent cannot continue counterrotating—unless a final judgment has already burst upon us.

III. HUMANITY AND FINITUDE.[8]
THE BEGINNING, END,
AND CENTER OF EXISTENCE

a. The Question of the Whither

1. THIS WORLD AND THE NEXT

The seal of human finitude is death. Death is the boundary between this world and another which we either can or cannot see, which is understood either as eternal life or as pure non-being. As the boundary limits our temporal existence and thus gives it the appearance of a totality, the decisive thing for an understanding of this totality is how we view the boundary, whether what lies beyond it is nothing or eternal life. Not only history as a whole but individual life as well has to be read backward, as we have seen. Hence the understanding of death is related to the understanding of life, and vice versa. Where will we go when we go forward to death, and where will we arrive when we cross its threshold?

In all systems of government, rulers have constantly played the shabby trick of consoling the poor and exploited with a better future so as to turn their eyes from their present misery and make them accept it. This is a sorry fact. So is the further one—the idea of a momentous historical process in the course of which God is merely a transcendent figure who in his heavenly world has lost all contact with concrete humanity, with its conflicts, with the pressures and frustrations to which it is exposed, with the happiness and terror of this present world.

Annoying though these misunderstandings and abuses are, including the severing of the vertical and horizontal dimensions, it seems to me to be quite illegitimate to deduce the nonexistence of the next world from botched concepts of it. I do not like the term "the next world," since it smacks of occultism. It is also compromised as the supposed preserve of the church, as this-worldly ideologists like to show, and it is theologically suspect. For now that "he whom the whole world could not encompass has lain in Mary's lap" (Luther),

God has left that other world and in solidarity with us exposed himself to the pressures of history in this world.

That other world no longer seems to be relevant now that God is in this world. But this statement at once raises a new problem. Did God shut the door behind him when he came into this world? Has he moved his dwelling for good from the heavenly sphere to the earthly sphere? Has this world become a self-reposing, externally sealed-off finitude into which God is now "integrated," so that he can now fulfill himself through the world's fulfillment? This would be a massive misunderstanding of what the New Testament means by "incarnation." A classical example of this misunderstanding may be seen in Hegel, and especially in the left-wing Hegelians. This view inevitably seems to lead not merely to secularization but to secularism as a consequence of the Christian theology of incarnation.[9]

As stated, I do not like terms like "the next world" or "the hereafter." I am also uncomfortable with the theology which knows all about the extraterrestrial sphere and can offer a guidebook to hell and purgatory and all the streets of the heavenly Jerusalem. But the term "the next world" is a necessary if inadequate cipher to express the fact that our existence is not self-grounded. With this fact is connected the constant need of human existence (already noted) to transcend itself, to put the questions of its Whence and Whither. Such questions cannot be chased out of the world by an epistemological veto. We may illustrate the need to put such background questions by the following examples.

First, an atheistic newspaper in Moscow recently printed the following statement from a reader:

> If my life on earth is filled with ideas and emotions, and then it all simply disappears, this life is an intolerable absurdity. Why should we develop our mind and feelings if we came out of nothing and will return to nothing? Why, then, should we have a fleeting consciousness of existence in which we can see myriads of stars in a moment, learn to add and divide to infinity, explore the heights and depths, experience delight and horror, rejoice in beauty, find intoxication in creativity, and love unselfishly? Why, one asks, was all this given if I am not eternal, but the next moment will vanish into a non-being in which there are not even any dreams? Why all this?

The question, "Why all this?" is the question of the meaning of life. It asks, then, about something that can never be an object of objectifying thinking. For it has in view that which encompasses and sustains all objects and even the act of knowledge itself.

Second, Adolf Holl in his book *Tod und Teufel* raises this higher question in the form of a comparison. Alluding to the fact that we must die, he says, "We have to leave the theater before the end of the play. We cannot wait until the end. But if the end has not come, we do not know the outcome. Hence we cannot pass any conclusive judgment on the piece." What the author obviously means is that from the few notes and snatches of melody in my finite life I cannot know the whole composition or the meaning that sustains and constitutes it. But the question of this meaning, the question which asks about more than partial ends and teleological functions, the question of the ultimate theme of my life cannot be expunged. It occurs even in thinkers and writers like Albert Camus and Gottfried Benn, who speaks about the absurdity of our Sisyphus existence. If human existence is not an automatic evolution or unfolding of itself, if it is based on decisions and can fail because of wrong decisions, there is a need to ask about the meaning of the whole which is its theme. This can—and usually will—be done in an unreflecting way. One cannot expect hedonists to establish their position philosophically. They will live in the name of an instinctively established basis about which they may then be questioned within their capacity for reflection.

Because the reference to the whole is part of our basic human constitution, we have to ask about that which cannot be answered with an appeal to immanent connections. It would be intolerably banal to explain this need by mere curiosity or speculative desire. An eradication of the question would not simply mean an overcoming of the vice of curiosity but a cessation of humanity itself. Robots, organization people, consumers, playboys, and other caricatures of Homo sapiens would obliterate the human image.

2. HUMAN AND ANIMAL DEATH[10]

As humans, in distinction from animals, we have to ask about the basis, goal, and meaning of life; thus death is also a question for us. This distinguishes us from all other creatures. The most obvious mark of this distinction is that, unlike animals, we know about death. We know that we have an allotted span, and that this span is limited. As Friedrich Hölderlin sings, the birds of the wood breathe freely, but we see the dark future, and hence we have to see death, and we alone fear it.

Nietzsche refers somewhere to Christianity's misuse of the hour of death. Parsons try to make people receptive to their message by threatening them with their last hour and its ineluctable approach. Certainly the terror of judgment and the next world has always been present, along with a good deal of sentimentality about death. But this misuse of the appeal to the last hour is not the same thing as the knowledge of death and the future which we have in mind. Otherwise it would be of interest only to the elderly. They alone would be suitable recipients for the related messages of horror. For they have now drawn near to the last hour; it is actual for them. In fact, however, there is another kind of awareness of death. We all of us find this special human knowledge in ourselves and in literature, from Rainer Maria Rilke to Camus and Heidegger.

At each moment of life, and not just on the point of death, we realize that we are finite and are moving on to death. We accept this even though we may never think about it. We hasten to fulfill our plans, to meet demands, to build houses, to pass examinations. We know that time is running on and wasted hours will not return. Even the young have this enciphered awareness of death. They say, "I am only young once; I must not miss anything." Youth will not come back. With every hour we lose a part of ourselves. Athletes are well aware that around thirty years of age the curve will irrevocably and irreversibly begin to turn against them. They thus achieve as much as they can in the moment that will not tarry. Life is a winning of time, as Shakespeare says. All this testifies to a knowledge of our finitude, of death.

It is also apparent that the clock is a deceptive symbol from which to gain an understanding of time and finitude. The circling hands which constantly go around afresh, making of each end a new beginning, nourish the illusion that things go on forever and we can always begin anew. As our theology of history has already shown us, the Bible teaches an understanding of time that presents the period between birth and death as a straight line and not a circle or spiral that constantly comes back to itself.

This suggests another metaphor. We are going along a long corridor with many doors that have no handles on the back, and all close behind us of themselves as we pass. There is no going back. We cannot undo the past. We have to keep going until our future ends. We thus drag our past with us. It cannot be reversed until death. We are this past. This is why the forgiveness of sins may be said to mean that in God's eyes I am no longer identified with my past.

3. THE RESURRECTION OF THE FLESH

Over against this irreversible course up to our end, this being for death, the Bible sets the grandiose antithesis that our mortal existence is enclosed and sustained by eternal life. It also gives us to understand that our life, while a one-way street, is not a dead end that leads only to death. Death is a going home—a transition to incorruptible life.

The Nicene Creed expresses this victory over death in the phrase "the resurrection of the flesh." This sounds alien to modern ears. It has nothing whatever to do with airy whisperings of immortality, or the sentimental romanticism which speaks about the home of the soul being up there in light, or other flimsy coverings for the dark abyss of death. Contradicting all the arts of homiletics and apologetics, it is like a bull in a china shop. I will thus abandon any attempts at tactical maneuvering and let this statement stand in all its stiffness and strangeness: "I believe in the resurrection of the flesh." What does this mean?

Luther said already, with some concern, that it sounds shockingly physical and might easily make us think of a butcher's shop. In reality, however, the biblical term "flesh" does not refer primarily to our corporeality but to a specific quality of being. Flesh here signifies our transitoriness, the fact that we must perish. All flesh is as grass that withers (Psalm 103:15). We are made of earth, dust, and we shall return to dust. No redemption will spare us the way of the seed into the earth where it must die and become dust, so as to be awakened to new life. "What is sown is perishable, what is raised is imperishable" (1 Corinthians 15:42). For the rest, what is said about eternal life, or being in the resurrection, is very discreet and reserved. It is limited to metaphors. Everything will be totally different from what it now is. This is the heart of the matter. "Flesh and blood cannot inherit the kingdom of God" (15:50). It is too different.

There is a story told of two medieval monks who were talking about death. They hit upon the idea of promising one another that whoever died first would come to the other the next night, and in answer to the question *Qualiter?*, (What's it like?) would reply either *Taliter* (As we thought) or *Aliter* (Different from what we thought).

Well, finally one of them did die and the next night he appeared briefly as a ghost to his brother, and when the anxious question came: *Qualiter?* he gave the answer: *Totaliter aliter* (Totally different).

Those who have experience of this *totaliter aliter* are immune from utopian dreams that might deceive them into thinking that there is a kind of kingdom of God on earth, a possible world of perfect justice, an identity of the world with what it ought to be. Belief in eternal life and the kingdom of God as Jesus proclaimed them has nothing whatever to do with this. Utopias follow our own desires and expectations and postulates. They are continuations of our own time-lines and projects. God's eternity as the "wholly other" is beyond our own planning and thinking and imagining.

This does not mean, of course, that it has nothing to do with our historical life. The new heaven and new earth that are not of this world are still goals of this world and also its critical limits. They are goals inasmuch as God's kingdom shows us what it is all about here and now, i.e., that we should fight the suffering and crying and tears that are still among us, that the love of this kingdom seeks to establish power already here and now, and that the sabbath, representing institutions, must not be lord over those whom God has made in his image and whom he wills to perfect as this image in his kingdom (Mark 2:27 f.).

But critical limits are also set to this kingdom. They affect the political dimension. Recognition that God's kingdom will not be produced by us makes us proof against the idea of utopian orders which will themselves produce a new humanity. Instead of abandoning us to such dreams, the coming kingdom of God demands, as we have seen, that we should take small steps to make this dubious world of ours a little better and juster, a little less complacent, if we may be content with comparatives instead of illusory absolutes that impede specific, steplike advances. Along these lines Karl Barth said somewhere in his *Final Testimonies* that he could not be without hope when he looked on a world in which people can take small steps with the prospect of all things becoming new—*all* things. "When we view the whole we can view the parts too without despair or agitation" (ET, 1977, p. 26).

Another limit is set by God's kingdom. Eschatological dreams refer only to fulfillments for later generations, granting no share in these blessings to the thousands who live earlier. The message of the resurrection of the dead, however, says that all—the dead and the living, the first generations and the last—share the same proximity and fulfillment. Time and finitude have lost their mastery. Past, present, and future, they are all immediate to God.

4. THE DREAM OF IMMORTALITY

How can we be certain that death is not the last frontier? What basis is there for this certainty? Is it based on the belief that there is an immortality of the soul, an indestructible substance, as Plato taught and as we hear again and again in Christian funeral sermons?

As a rule such theories of immortality[11] rest on the wishful thinking by which we try to outwit death. Formally, they always make use of the same trick of thought. This consists of dividing the self into a perishable and an imperishable I. In all such anthropologies, whether mythical, philosophical, or scientific in provenance, the perishable I is the physical part of the individual. In death this is destroyed and reduced to dust. The imperishable part of the I is variously understood. There is a broad range of interpretations. Thus Plato has in view the immortal substance of the soul, which is unaffected by death, which existed long before the body, and which survives it. Another view is that the immortal part of the I is its "general" side, which survives all individual existence, e.g., the suprapersonal tree of the people, which continues even when individual leaves fall. We are thus immortal inasmuch as our being belongs to suprapersonal social spheres into which it is integrated and in whose areas of operation it has continued life. Traces of this kind of idea may be found even in Hegel and Marx, where the universal element, represented now by the species, is the indestructible substance of the historical process which takes up the individual into itself.

I ask myself whether behind these notions of immortality the true motive is not that of a desperate reaction against the absurdity expressed in the Soviet newspaper, namely, the absurdity which makes the extinction of life, its annihilation, tormentingly incomprehensible. Understandably the threat of that absurdity mobilizes wishful thinking and causes us to look around for zones of the I that will be beyond the grasp of death.

Profounder minds have not been content to oppose this wishful thinking with rationalistic arguments, especially of a psychological kind. They have refrained from saying that all these doctrines of immortality are unreal and unprovable imaginings and that we should cling to what is demonstrably real, that what we see is the absolute end, and that it is intellectual honesty to accept this. No, they have brought against the belief in immortality a very different objection that I find most impressive. I have in mind Christopher Marlowe, the author of the first Faust tragedy in the sixteenth century, just before Shakespeare and long before Goethe. After his twenty-four-year pact with the devil, Faust here was afraid of immortality. He begged the mountains to fall on him, the earth to swallow him up, and the cosmos that he might be dissolved in it. For immortality without God's grace and in the sphere of perdition is a terrible thing. Hell is having to go on when the eternal ground of being is lost and nothingness encircles us. Thus Faust longs to be absorbed in Nirvana, just as the Buddhist wants to be released from the eternal cycle, from continually having to start a new existence.

The resurrection of the flesh has nothing whatever to do with this dream-wish of immortality. This has to be said clearly because these non-Christian teachings have only too often found their way into our pulpits and burial addresses. Over against them the Bible sternly sets the corruptibility of the flesh and the burial of the seed of wheat. We do not have eternal life in virtue of some inextinguishable spiritual spark that will glow on under the ashes of perishability. We have it because we are called out from death and there is an awakening from the dust.

5. THE CERTAINTY OF ETERNAL LIFE

But now the decisive question arises in true earnest: How can we have certainty of eternal life if death is seen in the New Testament so realistically, without illusions, without being softened by dreams of immortality? The suspicion that we have here just another dream, with different trappings and in a different dress, is a natural one.

If we pursue this idea that the wish is again father to the thought, we come across a point that withstands it and cannot be harmonized with it. For we can say that in the New Testament death is not an independent theme and hence cannot be the subject of a real debate. We no longer have to gaze at it as a rabbit does at a snake, for we know him who has bruised the head of the snake and robbed it of its deadly power. Thinkers who believe in immortality wrestle continually with the mystery of death and forcefully try to lift the veil that lies over it. In contrast, the people of the New Testament are fascinated by the certainty that Jesus lives, that he has won through death to life, and that we can have fellowship with the "prince of life."

All that is then said about death can thus be no more than a by-product of this primary trust in the Kyrios who will not leave us when the torch of life flickers out. Dying, we die to the Lord (Paul). In my experience Luther confessed this certainty of life, or ongoing life, most profoundly in a passage to which we have referred already, saying that once God has begun to speak to someone, whether in wrath or in grace, that person is immortal. What he means is that God will not let a conversation that he has begun with us be interrupted by death; hence death will not have the last word for those whom he addresses.

What lives on according to this saying of Luther is not, then, some quality of our own soul that survives death intact. The point is that God has begun a history with us and that this history cannot cease to all eternity. The power that prevents death from laying its hand definitively upon us is the faithfulness of God. What survives death is not a quality of the human soul but the alien dignity which is central to our anthropology.

This certainty that God will always be faithful to us did not arise —this is decisive—merely in face of the experience of death and the shock of mortality. If it had done so, we should have every reason for distrust, for suspecting wishful thinking. But no: The faithfulness of God is experienced first in innumerable life encounters from the times of the patriarchs to our own. A cloud of witnesses, patriarchs, prophets, and saints stands above us. They all confess that this God released them from their chains, freed them from anxiety, pardoned their guilt, and made possible for them a totally new beginning of life.

Those for whom all this is certain then ask—but only then and incidentally, "What about death? What can it do when this very different hand is upon me?" And difficult and painful though dying may be—through cancer or multiple sclerosis or an earthquake or a plane crash—even this most difficult thing acquires a new sense and becomes a going home. We are expected there. More than by the witnesses this certainty is given by Jesus himself, who tasted death but did not remain its prisoner. "Where I am, there shall my servant be also" (John 12:26) enables us to understand the Christian laughter and defiance of death that rings out in Johann Franck's chorale "Jesus, my joy," where from the fragile walls of our decaying world (just shaken by the Thirty Years' War) there sounds the echo: "Though sin and hell affright me, Jesus will hide me." And Paul Gerhardt, too, bears witness that we are companions of a living Lord who will not let any power, even death itself, snatch us from his hand: "He rides through death, the world, sin, need, and hell itself, and I am his constant companion." The church's songs of eternity enable us to see how triumphant is the sense of victory, how sweeping the certainty of ongoing life.

From this standpoint one can understand why the Bible is so very reserved and discreet in its references to what we call the next world. Many atheists think that the next world is the center of all Christian thinking, but in fact it is of little interest in the deeper sense. Instead, Christian involvement is primarily with communion with the Kyrios who leads us from faith to sight, from the dark mirror to face-to-face encounter (1 Corinthians 13:12). The nature of this condition, the scenery of the world to come, is of little interest.

The parable of Dives and Lazarus (Luke 16:19–31) makes it particularly clear that the message of eternal life does not direct our attention to the hereafter that we cannot see but forces us to look at the here and now of the present world.

To be sure, it seems at first to give us some details about the next world. There is reference to Abraham's bosom, on which the poor man finds relief from his pains. We are also told about the fires of hell in which the fat capitalist roasts, suffering in his own body something of the torment which, when alive, he had so hardheartedly ignored in others. Here, then, the theme of the next world seems to be struck, and theologians have constantly tried to deduce a kind of topography of the hereafter from the details given.

But if they do, they go off at a tangent and miss the true point of the parable. This is to be found elsewhere. For in hell, and in torment, the rich man begins to experience for the first time something like love. He suddenly thinks of his five brothers who are still alive and perhaps give no more thought than he did to the question whether their lives have any foundation which will endure beyond death. Perhaps they were just as unmerciful to the poor Lazarus at their gate as he was—the rich man who now has to suffer the consequences of his bungled life.

Now, when it is too late for himself, he is concerned about the dangerous thoughtlessness of his brothers. He thus asks father Abraham to send someone who can give a report on the next world so as to make clear to them, by reliable information, what the issue is. But Abraham refuses. There will be no firsthand report from the realm of the dead. "Your five brothers, poor rich man, have Moses and the prophets. They have the word of God." If they will not listen to this, how will it help them to receive an eyewitness account from the next world? They will know how to hold aloof from this too. (Perhaps they will treat it as a spiritualist fake, or persuade themselves that they have merely dreamed it.)

This, and this alone, is the theme of the parable: The fate of the five brothers who are still alive and who threaten to bungle their lives too. The topography of the hereafter is not the theme. This is simply called in to help to clarify metaphorically the problem of life. It is not itself the drama but the scenery or setting of the drama. As pictures of the next world are given, the present world is at issue. It is here that God comes. The five brothers and our relation to them are the theme.

Among younger Christians there has been for some time a slogan that I like because it seems to point in the same direction. This is the slogan: "There is also a life *before* death." It undoubtedly contains some criticism of certain forms of Christian fixation on the next world at the expense of this world. The question is put: Does God only want to meet us beyond the frontier of death? Has the here and now nothing to do with him? Is it solely a matter for our human, our only too human programs? How foolish is this separation of this world and the next, of life before death and life after death, when in fact death has had to give up its function as a frontier and can no longer divide us from a love that encompasses both the living and the dead in the name of the risen Lord.

In Christianity the conquest of death is not tied to material things (such as a substance of the soul which is immortal). It is "personal," if one will. We have to use personal terms to describe it. As noted already, we have to talk about a conversation or history of God with us, or about a name by which we are called and which cannot be blotted out to all eternity, or about a hand that is laid upon us and will not let any power snatch us from its grip.

The fact that it is not a matter of powers that overcome death, but of the person of him who does so, helps us to understand why the Bible focuses its statements on the human relation to this person and is very sparing in its references to the nature or scenery of the hereafter, hardly ever lifting the curtain which hangs before it. State-

ments about the next world are not an end in themselves. They have
to be, and want to be, interpreted in terms of what they mean for
our existence as it is seen in the light of God. We cannot understand
them, then, if we do not see their anthropological relevance, even
though they have more than this and are not just mythical "ciphers" for anthropological statements.[12] When the father of the
great biblical theologian Adolf Schlatter was dying, some devout
brethren stood around his bed and, in a touching and edifying way,
tried to comfort him: "You will soon dwell in Zion's golden halls
and see the crystal sea." They were not leaving out any apocalyptic
symbols, for they knew their Bibles and especially the Revelation of
John. But the dying man suddenly turned to them and said,
"Enough of that hereafter rubbish. All that I need is to cling to the
neck of the Father." He wanted only a single (personalistic) image,
that of the way in which the father welcomed the prodigal son and
kept faith with him. In so doing the dying man had his gaze fixed on
the essential point. He did not want to know anything about the
heavenly setting, the detailed scenery of the world to come, the
streets of Zion. The vital point for him was direct fellowship, a face-
to-face encounter with him whom thus far he had known only in
faith. The well-known epitaph of Kierkegaard is to the same effect
when he describes eternal life as a state in which he can "speak eter-
nally with Jesus."

It is not, then, because I dream about a hereafter, and try to take
refuge from present misery in this dream, that I believe in the life of
the future world. I believe in this simply because I am now a "companion" of him who will not let me slip from his faithfulness or
allow death to interrupt my fellowship with him. Holding his hand,
I go confidently into the dark, into the unimaginable and totally
different world of the future. He who awaits me—again a personal
category—will not be strange or different. I shall recognize him even
in his *totaliter-aliter* as the one whose voice has for a long time been
familiar to me as the voice of the shepherd is to his sheep.

What awaits us beyond the boundary of death is not unknown territory but the immediacy of what our temporality allows us to see
now only in a dark mirror (1 Corinthians 13:12), i.e., in the faith
which has to wrestle with contradictory appearances and is thus an
embattled faith.

Eternal life, then, is not a mere hereafter, a postmortal epilogue
whose relevance is by no means evident so long as we are occupied

with the text of our present life. No, eternal life is mine even now. It determines me here and today. The reason for this is the self-transcendence which has occupied us from the very beginning of our deliberations.

As we have seen, what our empirical and objectifying knowledge of humanity grasps is basically particular and fragmentary. We never hear the whole melody, only snatches of it. As those who in the midst of life are in death, we never see existence as a whole. We see the play without the last act. We do not hear the author's commentary in the epilogue. Eternal life, however, has to do with the totality in which temporal existence and its eternal destiny come together and reach fulfillment. As eternal life is also the state of sight and immediacy, we see our true identity, the I-Thou relation to him who has made us for himself, so that our heart is restless until it rests in him (Saint Augustine).

This true identity cannot be seen by empirical self-observation or by any external analysis, no matter how penetrating it may be psychologically. In what we call eternal life, it is the power that sustains our lives and determines our Whence and Whither. The absence of this power comes to expression in the need to seek beyond and beneath ourselves, to transcend ourselves, to let ourselves be unsettled by the question of the basis, goal, and meaning of our existence.

If eternal life can be understood only in personal terms of him who is known as the eternal and living One, this is no less than the point of the gospel. The metaphor of the homecoming of the lost son or clinging to the Father's neck expresses all that needs to be said about the fulfillment of human existence or congruence with the image of what we ought to be. The likeness of all things transitory, including what we ourselves are, can be understood only when we know the author of the likeness, the one who made what is transitory and called us as his own image and likeness.

b. The Question of the Whence.
Borderline Questions Between the Biological and Theological Interpretations of the Whence[13]

I might conjecture that readers will be surprised when they note the order in which we have dealt with the theme of humanity and finitude, i.e., discussing the Whither first and only then the Whence.

Should we not have done it the other way around and thus discussed the beginning before the end?

What may seem to be logical, however, is not anthropologically true to fact. The question of the limited and finite nature of human existence is known to us only from the boundary of death and the irreversibility of the time-line established thereby. Only this "being for death" raises, not only the question of the meaning of death, but also the counterquestion of our Whence, our origin.

I find an impressive reference to this order in the fact that "the most extensive statements about Yahweh's creation of the world occur only in later texts" (Gerhard von Rad). We can hardly assume, of course, that Israel discovered only later the theme of creation and genesis. This is barely conceivable, for Israel lived in a world whose rich store of creation myths not only forced this question on it but also compelled it to mark off and maintain its belief in Yahweh and hence to make "origin" a theme. If this theme occurs only in later texts, this can hardly be explained as due to a later turning to the theme by Israel. More likely is the theory of von Rad that Israel needed relatively more time to bring into a right theological relationship its older belief in creation and the real saving acts of Yahweh in history. These saving acts in history are the acts of Yahweh which aim at the future, at goals, and which thus move toward an unknown Whither, from Egypt to the wilderness, and from the wilderness to the Promised Land. The history of the people with its covenant God is that of a permanent exodus by puzzling ways to a promised Whither. Only in this light, on the basis of experience of this history, can the concept of creation be defined. The historical dating of the creation stories already makes it plain, however, that the question of origin is a later one. It can be put only when the prior question of the Whither has been answered.

But what is the nature of this question of the Whence, especially when we have to take into consideration biological answers to it as well? One might start with the fact that more recent biology, as Morin says, derives the life of the cell from its substratum in acids and proteins. Since human existence, including self-transcendence, is tied to these "atoms of life," there obviously seems to be a close connection between logos and bios, personhood and brain, biochemistry and self-consciousness, as the subject of anthropological investigation.

It would be beyond our competence and ability to discuss borderline questions of biology and theology in *this* sense, especially as nonexperts can only comment on secondhand information. My more modest but fundamentally very decided concern is to work out the decisive issues in the discussion of these borderline questions. At this point we are faced by a chaos of cross-purposes.

To clear the ground a little, we do best to start at the historical point where the most striking clash took place between theological and biological anthropology, namely, the controversy between Darwin's evolutionary theory, which we cannot discuss in detail, and the belief in creation. On both sides irreconcilability was assumed, by Darwin sadly and resignedly and nonpolemically, by church orthodoxy with the theological fury which is usually aroused when there are real or supposed attacks on the substance of doctrine and the faith.

1. THE MEANING OF THE BORDER BETWEEN THE TWO VIEWS

In the biblical creation story we do not have a pretheoretical view of human origins expressed in mythical ciphers. If we did, it would necessarily be outmoded by theoretically based and more mature conceptions, or at least would be in competition with them. The point of the creation stories, their kerygmatic goal, is different. They seek to establish a specific relation of human existence, namely, its relation to the Creator. Establishment of this is independent of the genetic question that is the central point for the theory of evolution. The distinction between the genetic and ontic questions is strictly preserved here even though there is (naturally) no reflection on it.

Once we are clear that our relation to the Creator is the point of the creation stories, they are reconcilable in principle with *any* biologico-genetic theory, whether it is the theory of an evolutionary ascent from prehuman forms of development, as it presented itself to Darwin, or the rather daring and more speculative conception of Wilhelm Preyer, Max Westenhöfer, and Edgar Dacqué that, in a complete reversal of Darwin, animals are not precursors but degenerate forms of humans, and the organic world does not arise out of the inorganic but the inorganic world is a degenerate form of the organic.[14] I intentionally oppose to one another two such antithetical genetic theories in order to make it clear (and it will become even clearer in what follows) that the creation stories, which are not governed by any genetic view, can be neutral toward all genetic theories. The question of our relation to God is not affected by these debates. Wherever it is seen or thought to be in opposition to them is due to misunderstanding, whether on the part of natural scientists who think they can derive ontic statements from their genetic theories, and who thus come into collision with the belief in creation and its relationship thesis, or on the part of theologians, who miss the kerygmatic point of the creation stories and thus erroneously think that these are giving binding teaching about human development which they must defend against all rival teachings.

This gives us already a first pointer to the decisive issue here.

We are forced to choose between the theory of biological evolution and the biblical doctrine of creation only when scientific theories cross the border and become ontic dogma or when, rightly or wrongly, it is thought on the theological side that this has taken place.

This observation leads us to the key question: How do borderline questions between biology and theology arise?

We can understand that there should be such questions, such points of friction, when we realize that the two disciplines have a common subject. In both biological and theological anthropology this subject is humanity. By way of example I will mention three specific zones of overlapping.

First, both disciplines have something to say about the origin of humanity. For the moment we may ignore the double sense of the term "origin," i.e., genetic cause and ontic basis. Theology speaks about our origin in God and defines our nature with the help of this basic relation. Biology speaks about origin in the sense of descent.

Second, both disciplines have something to say about the human body. Since the related debates have always centered on the bodily phenomenon of sexuality, we may note in regard to this common subject matter that biology discusses the physiological side and finds analogies to the sexuality of mammals, whereas an ethically oriented anthropology sees in sexuality the vital medium for the personal relation of an I to a Thou. Personal fellowship never takes place in the abstract but always between specific individuals, between persons who belong to specific stages of culture, who have different philosophies and vocations, who are of different ages, and finally who belong to one or other of the two different sexes. The physical sexual level is very important, but it is only *one* of the levels at which the I and the Thou meet, enter into fellowship, help one another, incur obligations, and serve one another or exploit one another. Again, everything is very concrete. There is no such thing as serving or exploiting "in itself." Both are possible only within one or more of the existential relationships mentioned. Hence these relationships and levels of encounter, e.g., that of physical sex, can never be ends in themselves. In an ethical anthropology sexuality can be understood only as that which we have called the vital medium for true personal relations.

Third, death is a theme that the two disciplines have in common. Biologists define it as the extinction of all vital processes (heart, circulation, brain). Theological anthropology, while obviously not denying the physical processes, again regards them as a medium for a very different event, the judgment of God. "You are dust, and to dust you shall return" (Genesis 3:19), says the story of the fall. Paul has this in view when he says that "the wages of sin is death" (Romans 6:23).

What the story of the fall has in mind with this understanding of death is that our guilty act is one of pride, wanting to be "like God." In death we who want to be unlimited are assigned our limits. Trying to rise above dust, we are reduced to dust. Snatching at eternity, we run up against the barrier of our temporality. This judgment at the level of our relation to the Creator takes place under the cover and in the medium of the natural law of death. Our being is thus in the full sense a "being for death."

At all these points we can see how conflict can arise between the two views, and how it arises because one or the other crosses its proper border. In illustration we shall use just the first and third examples.

As regards origin, biology crosses the border, as indicated, when it tries to infer our ontic nature from our genetic descent and is thus forced to adopt Nietzsche's idea that we are animals. As a rule this extension of the scientific view is no longer called biology but biologism or vitalism. The "ism" suffix denotes an absolutizing tendency, the elevating of a partial view into a total philosophy. The border is crossed on the theological side when theology says that humanity did not develop genetically but was brought into being by a single act of the Creator, which can be documented historically. Biology replies to this by pointing to the established evolutionary stages and the long stretches of time needed for them. It thus believes that it may validly refute the creation stories when these are taken to be literal history.

As regards the understanding of death, biology crosses the border when it thinks that its statements about the physiology of death describe "being for death" as an existential phenomenon. This can only mean that no difference is seen between human and animal dying; they are regarded as one and the same. This is no less than an attack on the humanity of dying and necessarily involves its depersonalizing.

No special theological criteria are needed to recognize this and to guard against it. Thus Rainer Maria Rilke constitutes himself an advocate of the humanity of dying. Its humanity emerges in the fact that it is not just a universal biological process that is seen on the surface. Dying fulfills the life we have lived. It is part of its unique content. Thus Rilke prays that we may all be given our "own death," the death that proceeds from the life in which we have known love and meaning and need. As the span in which we have known these ends in death, the content of life is manifested. Thus death brings the true meeting with the self. It is more and other than a purely natural event. It is highly personal. Strictly we cannot say, "There has been a death," but, "I die."

Rilke calls human dying in this sense the "great death," and he distinguishes it from the "little death" which sinks below the human level and is like the end of animals. This "little death" takes place when we are not ready for death, so that death is "green and sour" like unripe fruit. This kind of death is no longer my own but an alien death which comes upon me like a biological fate and means no more than this. In *Malte Laurids Brigge* we have a ghostly vision of this little, alien death which is not "paid" by God: "There has just been a death in bed 559. Factory style. Individual deaths are not so easy with this mass production, but that does not matter. The bulk counts. Who cares about a well-made death? . . . The desire to have one's own death becomes increasingly rarer. Soon it will be as rare as one's own life. . . . We die the death that is part of illness, for once we know all the illnesses, we know that their fatal outcome belongs to them and not to the people who have them. The sick, as it were, need not do anything."

If in this sphere biology crosses the border by overlooking the individuality of human dying in the name of a generalizing process, theology does the same if it uses Paul's statement that "the wages of sin is death" as an argument with which to contest the biological view and to say that death came into the world with the fall understood as literal history. On this view the irruption of death into the human world may be dated chronologically. Prior to this break in time, i.e., in the case of Adam and Eve before the fall, there was no death. Sin brought with it a kind of physiological mutation. Not always, but not infrequently, does crossing the frontier take such a grotesque form. We shall have occasion to consider some other bizarre inferences.

2. CROSSING THE BORDER: REASONS AND FORMS

If biology can exceed its terms of reference by giving normative rank to its genetic findings, a similar crossing of the border can take place in theology too. And we can say precisely when this happens. It happens when theological statements about human nature are not expressly distinguished from the thought-forms in which they are clothed in Scripture. Thus the Bible presents the earth as a disk arched over by the glass globe of the firmament. Again, the time-bound concept is found that human beings were formed out of clumps of earth. Once these parts of the biblical story are seen, not as time-bound *forms* of the statements, but as the *content* of the statements, so that they are made an obligatory part of the faith, conflict inevitably arises with the findings of science which function as elements in a scientifically responsible view of things.

How crass and grotesque the collision may be can be seen from the spatial thinking of Johann Kaspar Lavater (1741–1801) regarding Christ's Ascension, when he says that a cannonball would need millions of years to reach the closest of the fixed stars, and from this one may deduce how rapidly Jesus ascended into heaven. (We need not here go into the related problems of "de-mythologization" raised by Rudolf Bultmann. It is enough to say that the problem is an acute one irrespective of the way Bultmann has posed and answered it.)[15]

If we reject the distinction between the *point* or content of the statements on the one side and their time-bound *form* on the other, we cannot see the decisive reason for the border crossings. This reason is that biologically and ethically oriented anthropologies have completely heterogeneous spheres of validity. The same things look very different as we approach them differently. It is thus a basic epistemological mistake not to make a sober distinction between spheres and approaches. I shall illustrate this from two very different fields.

In so doing I regard it as important that they should really be of different provenance. If they are, the suspicion cannot arise so easily that I am using a theological trick to try to explain the fatal collision course between biology and theology as due to a failure to distinguish their different spheres and validity and the resultant differences in their statements.

Our first example is this. In his work *Die Grenzen der naturwissenschaftlichen Begriffsbildung*,[16] Heinrich Rickert refers to the different methods used by natural science and history. He finds the difference in the fact that the former has a generalizing tendency, the latter an individualizing tendency. Wilhelm Windelband makes a similar distinction between the nomothetic intention of natural science and the idiographic intention of history.[17] What he means is as follows.

In a phenomenon, natural science notes what it has in common with other phenomena of a similar kind. It observes the laws that govern these phenomena. In hens it notes the capacity to bear eggs and is not interested in the peculiarities that might result from a "deranged" hen. A scientist who is interested in the exceptional should become the director of a museum rather than a biologist! He or she could then validly set up a cabinet of rarities. But if the interest of such a person is exclusively in the particular that cannot be generalized, this involves a movement outside the sphere of natural science into the zone of the historical. For in contrast to the method of natural science, history, as Rickert sees it, focuses on the individual and particular. It observes that which distinguishes one phenomenon from another. In Napoleon, for example, it notes the special features of this person as compared with other members of the species. Hence I have not described Napoleon well, or in a historically relevant way, if I simply collect the general, natural features that enable me to subsume him under the master concept of the human species.

If, then, I transplant a historical or scientific statement from one sphere to the other, which is an alien one, this has results whose grotesquely ridiculous character shows dramatically how nonsensical such transpositions are. Paul de Lagarde makes this clear by a satirical depiction of the historical figure of Helmuth von Moltke, who, he says, "was born at Parchim in 1800, often gave cause for complaints at his dirtiness when in the cradle, served in the Danish and Prussian armies, was sent to Turkey, lived for a time as adjutant of Prince

Henry of Prussia in Rome, and was finally appointed head of the Prussian General Staff. He now owns the estate of Kreisau, where he spends part of the year. Such blatantly misleading accounts as these, which contain nothing but true statements, are printed and read by the thousands." The misleading element that Lagarde has in view is that Moltke is not presented from the appropriate historical standpoint but in a generalizing and nomothetic way, first as a biological being in the cradle, then as the representative of a military career. There are today magazines and newspapers that mislead us with the help of true statements.

The ridiculous nature of such statements, which are objectively true but are put in an alien sphere, shows how significant the appropriateness of the mode of statement is, whether historical or scientific. In spite of objective correctness in detail, a truth is changed in substance, and is thus untrue in a deeper sense, when it is pushed across the border into alien territory. Comedy is a phenomenon of contrast.[18] And the comical caricature in such transplantings is a sign that there is such an antithesis in spite of detailed correctness. In their distortion the individual elements in such a picture give an untrue impression.

The second example also involves a confusion of spheres which necessarily has bizarre consequences. We have in view the relation between musical and physical statements.

Naturally a work like Johann Sebastian Bach's *St. Matthew's Passion* has a physical side. From this angle the oratorio is made up of a regular series of vibrations of sound whose examination is just as valid as is the musical or religious interpretation of the work as a work of art. We have to be clear, however, that we have here two completely different categories of seeing, hearing, and evaluating, so that we cannot just add them together, and we certainly must not confuse them. The object of study is the same, but we are looking at very different things. As it would be wrong to say that the statistics of the sound vibrations *are* the Passion, or, even worse, that they are its essence, so it would be a mistake to contest the quantitative and physical side of the work in the name of its musical quality. This would be just as absurd as denying the timeless validity of a mathematical principle on the ground that we cannot conceive of it without the quantitative operation of certain mental functions.

The two aspects do not merge, and their distinction has to be firmly upheld. This may be seen from the absurd results of confusing them. For example, as T. Bovet says ironically, it would mean explaining Goethe's *Faust* by certain glandular peculiarities in Goethe's *fissura sylvii*.

When I interpret a work of art, I am speaking about a quality in describing which I cannot adduce the very different spheres of quantitative measurements because these do not get at the heart of the matter. I would be a kind of physical materialist (there are such in the zone of "isms"!) if I were to say that a symphony by Beethoven "consists" of certain vibrations, or that a painting by Rembrandt "consists" of certain surfaces covered over by oily substances. Eduard Spranger brings out the scandal of such distortions when he tells the story of a mathematician who, after attending a Beethoven concert, commented, "Fine! But what has he proved?" Similarly, I would be a speculative idealist (there are also such in the zone of "isms"!) if I were to deny that works of art have this quantitative side, this physiology, and regarded myself as justified in talking only about their timeless validity and musical worth. Perhaps one may rightly find an analogy to this distinction of unmixable aspects in microphysics, in which the wave aspect and the corpuscle aspect stand in an exclusive relation to one another.

3. THE ATTEMPT TO PROMOTE A "SCIENTIFIC" PICTURE OF HUMANITY (EDGAR MORIN)

In our deliberations we have taken various opportunities to show why the nature of humanity is not just an objectifiable datum and thus evades the grasp of science. This question now arises in a new form, namely, from the standpoint of where exactly the border lies between scientific and ontic statements about humanity, and how we come to know this border.

Before we tackle this, we will take as vivid an example as possible of the attempt to arrive at ontic statements about humanity by scientific means. A good illustration is Edgar Morin's attempt at a new biological anthropology dealing with the riddle of the human.

Typical here, it seems to me, is the intention to fill the gap left by discarded traditional beliefs and philosophical conceptions. Those who in another way and with another thrust want to say what these traditions once said but can no longer say, thus desiring to take up again an abandoned task, can only be saying that what they are dealing with is thus the riddle of human nature. Since they have at their disposal no prior metaphysical or theological findings, they are forced to start empirically with objectifiable facts. Thus they have to summarize the results of research in the brain, in behavior, in information theory, in cybernetics, in ecology, and, of course, in the biology of cells, so as to try to assemble a comprehensive anthropology out of the mosaic of individual sciences. We shall refrain for a moment from asking a question that will occupy us later, namely, whether a mere synthesis of individual aspects can give us an anthropology in the absence of a picture of humanity already gained from other sources.

Morin seems sometimes to approach this question without ever putting it. He shows that it is obviously not enough that some biological theories trace back the life of cells to their substrata in acids and proteins and then try to reach in this way an understanding of life, and ultimately of human life. Instead of an inductive procedure from below, from the atoms of life, another task, or at least an additional one, is urgent. We have to work back to principles of order that are unknown in chemistry, i.e., to the concepts of information, code, message, program, communication, restriction, repression, expression, and control. The very fact that the concept of the machine can be applied to the cell, and hence to the basic unit of life, is extremely significant. For a machine is an organized whole and cannot be reduced to its component parts. A higher unit like a machine cannot be dissolved in elementary units or deduced from them. It alone explains the properties of these units. In this new anthropology, then, there is an opening upward. Information, code, message, program, communication, restriction, repression, and so on, are concepts won from the experience of human relationship and thus far seem to be indissolubly bound to psychosocial complexity. In contrast, they appear to be irrelevant in the basic unit of life, the cell.

At this point, it seems to me, Morin contradicts his original intention of solving the riddle of the human by adding different aspects together. Instead, he posits a higher system of organization represented by the complex machine. This system is already there at the basis of life, since the cell is a complex society of molecules directed by a government.

I think that this opening upward necessarily raises a question that is critical for Morin, namely, the question what this underlying total system, which cannot be broken up into its individual elements, really is and signifies. Can its being and significance be deduced from its immanent structure? No demonstration is needed that it cannot.

Do we not learn it from a very different source, namely, from self-experience? And do we not do so in such a way that we understand ourselves as beings who have to ask about themselves, who may succeed or fail in this, but who yearn for an experience that looking at the organized whole from the standpoint of an upward opening can never give? But this means that we cannot gain ultimate criteria for the human question in the field of what may be investigated objectively.

On the one side, in face of the no longer wholly new biology and its focus on the substrata of life, Morin rightly sees where the limit of this view of things lies. On the other side, however, he does not seem to note the limit of his own conception. At any rate, he does not discuss this question of the limit. He obviously believes that the upward opening to the higher teleology of the total system elucidates the riddle of the human. There is no doubt that this discovery makes an essential contribution to our view of the human. To that extent it is a model of broad cooperation between natural science, the social sciences, and theology in the anthropological realm. Morin himself, however, does not regard his thesis as merely a material contribution to the elucidation of humanity but as the decisive insight. Although he has in fact gone beyond a mere biologism, he has not overcome the scientific perspective in principle, but simply extended it.

This gives urgency to our own question how we can know where the border of science lies in the area of anthropology. Since theology, whether with dogmatic certainty or with the self-critical awareness of a faith that is seeking intellectual clarification,[19] points with some keenness to this border and constantly finds it being crossed when attempts are made to understand humanity apart from our relation to God, the question may be put as follows.

Does natural science have to be told by theology that it has this border, or can it see it for itself?

Although the author is well aware that even putting the question exposes him to the suspicion of clerical arrogance, he still thinks he must emphasize that there is a real point to the question. For to know a border, we have to know what is on the other side. It is of the very nature of a border to separate two spheres. We can understand what the East-West border in Germany really means, not if we simply see our own sphere limited by it, but only if we also know the type of government to be found on the other side. Obviously we have to have some knowledge of both sides of a border when we speak about it, even if beyond the border of Oceanus, like the Greeks, we see only inconceivable chaos. For the concept of the inconceivable beyond the border has to be formed if the border of Oceanus is to be possible. In the same way, do not scientists have to know that which transcends humanity, bursting through the limits of what can be grasped objectively, if they are to know the border of their sphere of inquiry in anthropology? Do they not have to come up against this fact of the transcendent which may be seen in the human need to give the self responsibly to the search for a meaning that lies outside the competence of science? Does not the mere problem of freedom give them some awareness of this?

What is at least true is that scientists have to know humanity as an object of faith, that they have thus to use a theological category, if they are to see that interpreting the nature of humanity biologically is an illegitimate crossing of the border, an act of dogmatism. We have to know the norm if we are to recognize breaches of it. The norm for what humanity is by nature is posited by what lies beyond humanity. It is fixed by our fundamental relationship.

On the other hand, biologists do not need theological categories, e.g., a concept of revelation, to have a *general* awareness of crossing the border of science. Without theological help they can obviously stake out very well the boundary beyond which their scientific statements about our human genesis become philosophically dogmatic statements about our nature; when they move on, as it were, from Darwin to Nietzsche. The only thing is that without an awareness of the nonobjectifiable dimension of existence, of the nature which can only be believed, they will regard crossing of the border as legitimate and even demanded. They will understand it as a kind of philosophical enhancement of detailed empirical research, as a metaphysical completion, or as a working out of the deductions from the standpoint of natural philosophy.

4. JACQUES MONOD AS AN ILLUSTRATION

One of the latest prominent attempts at a metaphysical completion of anthropology with the help of molecular biology is to be found in a book which became a best-seller and which profoundly expresses the spirit of the age. I refer to the work by the Nobel prize winner Jacques Monod on "chance and necessity."[20] Just because Monod presses on from scientific findings to philosophical inferences, he finds himself involved in conflict with positions which try to grasp the nature of humanity that transcends empiricism, no matter whether these take the form of philosophical ideologies or religious convictions.

It is not surprising that Monod finds himself engaged in a war on two fronts. On the one side he is fighting the Christian belief in creation, which he tries to prove absurd, while on the other side he opposes dialectical materialism, whose assumption of a goal-oriented historical evolution falls under the same verdict.

As regards Marxism, he thinks that microbiology makes the movement toward the goal of a classless society impossible. For natural and historical processes have no program. They go by leaps and are ruled by chance. As regards the belief in creation, he thinks that blind chance leaves no place for any meaningful idea of the divine overruling of things. This is a consoling thought, but it is invalid and illusory.

Over against these convictions Monod sets his own decisive thesis. In necessarily abbreviated and popularized form, this is to the effect that the development of life, and especially human life, cannot be traced back to an evolution that follows the law of necessity or the plan of a Creator. Human development, to which we may restrict ourselves, is due to pure chance, to a kind of lottery that might have brought up other winning numbers. For the tiny mutations and leaps in molecular biology are unforeseeable and accidental, like a game of dice. Humanity might not have developed. Hence it cannot be traced back to any prior conception, whether this be regarded as necessary evolution or a divine Logos established in the world.

All this has for Monod both a scientific and an ethical implication.

As regards the former, we know that life appeared on earth. But how great was the probability that it would do so? On the basis of the present structure of nature, the hypothesis is not ruled out—but is very probable—that the decisive event (the decisive leap into the first constellation of matter) has taken place only once. At the present hour we may neither affirm nor deny that life on earth is unique and that the chances of its occurrence were almost nil. The theory of an isolated incident, a chance mutation, as that to which we owe our life and being, is an offense not only to believers but also to most natural scientists, although for different reasons. But this is how it is.

The ethical implication is far-reaching. It is very close to what Monod's friend, Albert Camus, made his confession. We humans, he thinks, have a deep-seated need to explain the cosmic nexus, to put ourselves in a cosmic order, to know that we are embraced and sustained by meaning. It is an unheard-of relief to see our existence entrusted to a saving plan of this kind. But the longing for this derives from an ultimately cowardly need for reassurance which cannot face the real truth. The real truth is that humanity is a chance product cast into an alien, indifferent, and silent universe, like a foundling that is not related by blood to the family in which he or she lives and grows up. We are like gypsies on the edge of the universe. And this universe is deaf to our music and remains unaffected by our hopes and sufferings and misdoings.

In theological language this means that there can be no question of any footsteps of God in a so-called creation, of any spermatic logos, or scattered remnants of reason and planning, in this lordless and ungoverned universe. All the signs that we have of the basis of the world tell us to the contrary that we are alone in an indifferent and incalculable universe, in which we have developed by pure accident. Nothing is decided concerning either our destiny or our duties. There is no eternal law to enlighten us, no natural law to be practiced on us. The conclusion is that it depends wholly on ourselves to choose between light and darkness and to accept responsibility for the norms and laws to which to subject ourselves. No one can escape the impression made by the pitiless severity of this conclusion. It compels respect.

It is worth considering, and may give us pause epistemologically, that the paleontologist Teilhard de Chardin, whom we shall have to discuss in a special section, interprets the same phenomena very differently. He, too, is naturally aware of the mutations and leaps and incalculable factors in the sphere of evolution. But he views this process in the light of its end, of the meaningfulness of human life, and of the final point, Omega. In so doing, he finds in the leaps an opportunity for the spiritual energy invested by the Creator in the cosmos to work itself out and to change the dead necessity of a process into a meaningfully directed movement.

What gives us pause, epistemologically, when we see these contrary interpretations of the world is the obvious question whether Monod and Teilhard really derive their rejection or affirmation of meaning from strictly empirical factors, so that in view of the contradiction one or the other of them must be guilty of an error, whether in relation to the empirical data that serve as premises for the conclusions, or in the interpretation of these data. According to Kant's law of antinomies, however, it would be absurd to find the reason for the contradiction in an error of this kind. If there can be no question of an error, then obviously both of them are drawing from the objective facts of experience inferences which transcend experience and are thus beyond the competence of experience-bound reason. Then there have to be "antinomies" of this kind.

Epistemologically one suspects that both thinkers have really imported as presuppositions what they think they have deduced empirically, and have then found a confirmation of these presuppositions in the facts. Their imported presuppositions have thus acted as a category directing their way of looking at the facts. (Marx, among others, has a view of history that serves similarly as a philosophical category which causes him to look at the historical process in a particular way and to make the corresponding associations and selections.)

In fact, the two thinkers do not owe their cosmologies and anthropologies to their investigation of evolutionary processes but carry with them a load of philosophical and religious goods when they embark on their investigative excursions. What they hear from the woods is simply an echo of their own cries. Monod owes his view of the world, expressed in the image of the gypsies, to the literary message of his friend Camus. At any rate, Camus expressed the very thing that pushed Monod in this direction and thus placed at his disposal the philosophical category for his investigation with its aim to interpret as well as amass information. Teilhard de Chardin, in contrast, was a Roman Catholic and a Jesuit. The presupposition that evolution is under spiritual direction lay ready to hand for him. Looking at experience, he found in it a confirmation of the inheritance of faith which had already been given to him prior to all experience.

This leads us to the conclusion that scientists can indeed know the border that separates their exact findings, e.g., in molecular biology, from their evaluations based on a particular anthropology. But they may regard the extension as legitimate, we have said. And we have tried to understand why they are so sure of its legitimacy. What empiricism seems to proclaim as a philosophical message offers itself in confirmation of something that is known already, of a conviction that is already present. This coinciding of premise and conclusion gives the effect, or at least offers the suggestion (?), of supreme certainty.

If, then, scientists cross this border, if they derive from factual findings articles of faith concerning all reality and the nature of humanity, they can do so only at the cost of the transcendent element in human existence. Teilhard is not a good example here, because the transcendent element is contained in his Christian premise and is thus retained in his empirical findings as the spiritual component in evolution—or is at least imported into them. Here, then, the particular is interpreted by the totality, not extended into the totality.

Monod, however, produces an extension of the particular into the totality along the lines of the world view of Camus. But in distinction from Teilhard with his Christian faith, Monod does not advance this kind of knowledge as revealed knowledge prior to experience. It is supposedly taken from experience as the impact of life. Only when the empirical particular is extended into a totality does knowledge of the totality react dialectically on interpretation of the empirical details. Thus the impression that we are gypsies on the edge of the universe is confirmed by insight into the chance nature of the realm of mutations.

In this way Monod does in fact banish the transcendent from view. We are not perceived as beings who grasp themselves, and have to do so. With a moral rigor even more impressive than that of Camus, Monod does say that we have to choose between light and darkness. We have not only to lift ourselves out of the realm of chance; we have to give ourselves the meaning that the universe refuses to confer on us as a gift.

Here, then, we might seem to have a remaining trace of transcendence. This simply goes to show that no view of humanity is possible in which the need to grasp the self is totally eliminated. But this is transcendence of a very different kind from that which we have found (or sought). Here, when we look at ourselves, we find the puzzling brute fact of our freedom, as in Sartre. But we find nothing corresponding to this freedom out there in the universe. We may set goals of self-fulfillment for ourselves, but what takes place outside in evolutions and mutations before us, around us, and in us, has no goals of this kind. We do not meet anything there or find anything analogous to our striving for meaning. This is what Monod has in view when he says that the universe is deaf to our music and unaffected by our hopes and sufferings and misdoings.

If what we have tried to show in this book is true, namely, that we are never isolated entelechies but are always to be understood in a cosmic reference, then the absence of cosmic transcendence is bound to have the effect of making anthropology a victim of this lack. What does a world look like, and humanity within it, if there is no Whence or Whither? Can humanity really set goals for itself if the world denies them to it, or if they are denied to the world? Can it set goals for itself, and thus transcend itself, if the world in which it acts has no goals? In this case, will it not be solipsistically thrust back upon itself and become a docetic shadow, as in Max Stirner's *Individual?* Ought not Monod to ask *how* he can arrive at the demand that we should choose between light and darkness and hence remove ourselves from the play of chance? Is not this demand for self-transcendence itself a matter of chance? Can it be anything else? With a tiny mutation might we not have been insects, spared the burden of freedom and simply living by reflexes?

To what absurdities are we driven here? Is it not an absurdity, then, to trace back the freedom that is supposed to serve specific goals to a play of chance that has no goals?

Obviously my freedom contains the postulate of a world nexus in which it is foreseen and makes sense as freedom for a goal. Salvador de Madariaga alludes to this when he asks Monod, "Even if we grant that things are as he describes them, where does the initiative come from, the envisaged goal, the energy (which is not that of heat), that drives evolution forward? The choice and persistence to reach such heights as the Sistine Chapel and the *Ninth Symphony,* where do they come from? This is the true secret of life." If we speak about the spirit that is to make use of freedom, and thus allude to something transcendent, we can hardly ignore the spirit that guides evolution toward the moment of our freedom. For this spirit, as Madariaga again says, "determines evolution, undertakes selection, suggests projects, writes messages, fixes and transmits codes, rolls the dice on the green table of time, and gives necessity its pitiless weight." The very fact that our human world is not the necessary product of evolution, that it might never have developed, might very well suggest faith in a Creator who called us out of non-being into being, out of the inorganic into the organic and spiritual.

Readers should not regard this last remark as an attempt to appropriate Monod for Christianity. In this battle of scientists it would be too easy to side with Teilhard or Madariaga simply because one welcomes the support that seems to be given by scientists of Christian views. All that I am trying to draw from the conflict is a conclusion that might be put in the form of a question: Does not this debate about the interpretation of nature, which cannot be decided on empirical grounds alone, demonstrate the ambivalence or ambiguity of all natural and evolutionary phenomena? And does not this confirm precisely what we have seen earlier, namely, that the belief in creation, as a view of the totality, does not arise merely out of the investigation of nature, any more than does the atheism which Monod seems to regard as self-evident? Some find the footsteps of God here; for others these footsteps are obliterated in a waste of sand with no exit; for yet others, including the Psalmist, faith does not need footsteps: "Thy way was through the sea, thy path through the great waters, yet thy footprints were unseen" (Psalm 77:19). Faith, including faith about humanity, cannot be decided by whether or not God's footsteps can be detected.

We have shown, then, by the example of Monod how dubious is the attempt to use empirical data as a source of philosophical statements or ontic definitions of humanity. Neither theological nor epistemological arguments enable us to infer from evolutionary processes either goals or lack of goals, or from the genesis of humanity its nature, or from its quantity its quality. Hence we cannot cross over from one area to the other as though they differed only in degree and were built upon one another.

5. ANTHROPOLOGICAL SIGNIFICANCE OF
QUANTITATIVE AND QUALITATIVE ASPECTS

The first thesis here is that the qualitative essence may be stated in quantitatively measurable presuppositions but cannot be deduced from these.[21]

In illustration we shall use again some examples that we have considered already from various angles.

Bach's *St. Matthew's Passion* can obviously be studied from the standpoint of its physical structure, i.e., its sound vibrations and their mutual relations. But this investigation cannot explain why some of these vibrations have the character of worship or the quality of beauty. Much more important for us is how this applies to ourselves. One might show that in order to make the Cartesian statement: "I am," in order, then, to make a personal utterance, certain physiological conditions are necessary (corresponding to the physical condi-

tions in music). There has to be a head that thinks. The functions of
the brain have to be intact (for schizophrenics might think that they
do not exist). To make possible the undisturbed functioning of the
brain, many other physiological conditions have to be met. All these
presuppositions make possible, but they do not explain, why a specific set of such factors can be marked off from all other being and
described as an "I."

P. Lecomte du Noüy in his book *Human Destiny* (1947) conducts an impressive experiment in thought which sheds important
light on the impossibility of mounting up from what is quantitatively measurable to the quality of the human. He assumes that a
conscientious and clever observer wants to study the laws of human
society. Having visited all the countries on earth, he concludes that it
will be useful to study what is common to all societies, humanity itself, for it seems only logical that the laws of common life should
rest on the qualities and characteristics of individuals. But in turning
to the study of individuals, the observer unwittingly crosses a threshold which he cannot recross, since the psychology of the masses cannot be deduced from that of individuals. Convinced of the unity of
science, of the mutual relations between all phenomena, and of the
thesis that a full knowledge of basic phenomena will automatically
lead to knowledge of those that are more complex, he concludes that
ignorance of the human body is a first obstacle, and that the causes
of human behavior will be found through a study of human anatomy
and physiology. But here again he unwittingly crosses a threshold
which can no more be recrossed than the first one. Physiology leads
to biochemistry, a third irreversible crossing. To know biochemistry,
he has to study inorganic chemistry, which leads him to cross a
fourth threshold. He then has to study molecules and atoms and
subatomic elements—electrons, protons, et cetera. This is the last
threshold. When this point is reached, it is impossible for him to put
things in reverse and retrace his steps to the original problem, that of
society and human individuality.

Why—and this is precisely our problem—can the process of analysis not be reversed? Why cannot we move from an analysis of the
individual elements to the synthesis with which we started? Why
cannot we move on from the ultimate constituents of matter to the
living organism, from the organism to the psyche, and from the
psyche to the person? How is it that we cannot work up from the

vibration to the note and from the groupings of notes to the qualitative synthesis of the work of art, e.g., Bach's oratorio?

Some basic anthropological considerations that we have already presented might help us to find an answer. At the higher level a qualitatively new factor arises which is non-derivable. One of the most important breaks constitutes a boundary here beyond which the quality of the human begins that can no longer be understood in terms of what is quantitatively measurable. Strictly the comparative idea of a "higher" level is inappropriate in this context, because it suggests an added point at which the vibrations become notes and the notes become a work of art. For the vibration *is* the note, presupposing there are ears to hear it. And a musical work *is* a synthesis of sound vibrations, assuming that there are people to understand it; a dog might howl when it hears a fugue by Bach!

We thus come up again against something that we found earlier. Whether I perceive the quantitative or the qualitative side of a phenomenon depends on my approach. Do I approach it with instruments of physical measurement, or with an ear to hear it, or with the possibility of musical understanding? The one thing cannot be derived from the other.

This leads us to three theses which are particularly relevant to the problem of human genesis and which are best discussed, therefore, in that context.

6. THE QUESTION OF THE GENESIS OF HUMANITY IN THE LIGHT OF CREATION

The Modified Question

The first thesis is that we must distinguish between presuppositions and causes. In the case of causes I can arrive at effects with the help of an a priori synthetic judgment. From the causes of the movements of the stars I can calculate what their movements, the effects, will be. In the case of presuppositions, however, I cannot make this kind of deduction. Presuppositions are not causes that have to have certain effects. They are conditions on which a certain effect is made possible and *may* ensue. We are on the level of possibility here, not necessity. Thus certain physical conditions have to be met if Bach's *Passion* is to be written. There have to be certain physiological presuppositions if someone is to be the author of the *Critique of Pure Reason*. Yet people who have the requisite physical or musical information, as any expert has, are not thereby qualified to write or compose such works. Mephistopheles alludes to this when he speaks ironically about philosophers who come in and prove that things have to be thus, a third and fourth thing following on a first and second in such a way that without the first two they would not be, for while their students applaud, this knowledge gets them nowhere. It simply orients them to basic logical structures and their interconnections. But from these elements they cannot construct a nexus, a qualitative synthesis. In this way Mephistopheles presses further the experiment in thought suggested by Lecomte du Noüy.

In other words, we have to achieve on our own the quality of *St. Matthew's Passion* or the *Critique of Pure Reason* if out of the quantitative presuppositions there are to arise the qualities represented by these two works. But only Bach and Kant can do this. Hence there has to be the nonderivable quality of genius if those qualities are to develop out of the quantitative presuppositions. Without this intervention of genius, the leap from the given conditions to the effect of the work is inconceivable. An element of the inconceivable is, of course, introduced when we take genius into account, for genius is inconceivable and non-derivable. It is thus an extreme representation of the human itself, an expression of the human spirit in crystal purity. Quality, as these examples very impressively show, can never be deduced from quantity; only its quantitative presuppositions can be demonstrated.

The second thesis is that, when this is applied to humanity, it means that humanity itself cannot be deduced from measurable, objectifiable, quantitative presuppositions, nor can its nature be explained genetically. If I still attempt an explanation of this kind with such an unsuitable object, if I try to deduce humanity from its genesis, what I am doing is making the presuppositions of physical existence, the preconditions of the modern form of life into "causes" in terms of which I calculate the resultant "effects," whether I view these as the climax of an evolutionary ascent or as the product of chance in a genetic lottery. Either way I treat the human element as though it were an objectifiable entity and thus subject it already to a heteronomous principle.

The third thesis is that everything depends, therefore, on putting the genetic question in the correct order.

If it is true that quality cannot be derived from calculable quantitative conditions, we are forced to conclude that we have to begin by knowing what humanity is. Only this prior total and ontic view of humanity enables us to fix the anthropological position of the genetic question and to know the framework within which it arises. Only then can we be clear that humanity itself is a non-derivable quality and that we are not to look in the genetic sphere for information about it. We can see the limited nature of genetic conditions and presuppositions only when we already have a picture of the final goal of humanity and do not expect this as a later answer that genetic research will provide. Only thus can we be free of the temptation to make this picture derivable, and illegitimately to construe biological and genetic presuppositions as causes, or, metaphysically, to interpret them as the ontic basis of the human.

In an explicitly and intentionally restrained way, I want to say that if we understand this, the fall into anthropological error *can* be blocked, that there is a real *possibility* of avoiding it. The case of Monod has shown us, of course, that the genetic problem may still be put first and ontic statements may be expected from its solution. To be sure, along the lines of Camus, there was a prior picture of humanity in this case too. According to this picture, humanity is marked by chance and absurdity. It stands under the sign of Sisyphus. But this picture, which presents us, not in transcendence or forward projection, but in naked factuality, cannot afford protection against an overextension of the genetic question. On the contrary, it finds itself confirmed by the chance play of mutations in the sphere of microbiology. It is not enough, then, to say that there has to be a prior picture of humanity to give the genetic question its proper place and rank. The decisive question is: What is the nature of this picture, and does it regard humanity as a transcendent entity or not? That this transcendent element is not restricted to the Christian view of humanity, even though it has enhanced thematic significance here, is something that we have stated again and again in the course of our deliberations.

Biological Analogies (Adolf Portmann)

In his *Biologische Fragmente zu einer Lehre vom Menschen* (1944, 1956) Portmann considers not only ontogenetic facts but also their anthropological significance.[22] In this work of interpretation he lays claim to criteria which in an astonishing way, rare in his discipline, are analogous to the evaluative approaches that we have worked out in considering the relation between genetic and ontic factors. Portmann does in fact keep in view the limitation of genetic conditions that we have held to be so important.

This finds expression in the fact that he does not derive his view of humanity from evolution in the sense of an ascent from the animal kingdom, but postulates the final picture of humanity as something to which to orient himself. My knowledge of evolutionary processes does not teach me what humanity is. The converse is true: My knowledge of humanity, present in the form of self-understanding, enables me to understand the evolutionary conditions. (The *priorities* are then right even though the two processes of knowledge interact and fructify one another.)

We can understand human development, says Portmann, only if at every stage we see the development of an organism with a unique upright stance, a peculiar openness to the world, and a social culture shaped by speech (*Biologische Fragmente*, p. 80).

Thus the picture of humanity is not constructed out of a synthesis of objective facts but is already there to guide researchers in their inquiries. The clearer our view of the human form of existence, the stronger the certainty that the question of human or any other origins cannot be answered today by the method of research. Only an overextension of the sphere of (genetic) validity deceives us into thinking that the doctrine of evolution can answer the most difficult questions in research, especially in anthropology.

Since, according to Portmann, we must orient ourselves to human totality, to the full range of humanity, physical, mental, and psychological, the following methodological implications are to be noted.

1. Evolutionists want to understand humans in terms of their animal ancestors, and so they draw special attention to the *similarities* between us and animals. (Thus they point out that the human child passes the chimpanzee stage toward the end of its first year.) Portmann, however, asks us to look at that which transcends the organization of plants and animals and thus to find the form of human life that is unique, close though it may be to that of higher animals. In this concern for the unique factors which break through every analogy there is expressed, according to Rickert, the individualizing tendency that is proper to historical study, in contrast to the generalizing of natural science. Categories may thus be found already in Portmann which are not available within the limits of biology but have to be accepted from outside these limits.

2. This individualizing aspect is expressly found by Portmann in the fact that we transcend bios and are open to history. But since the unity of our being is based on the interdependence of all the individual regions of our existence, neither the historical nor the biological sphere can be considered apart. Only a cooperation of different disciplines can correspond to our multiple unity.

This unity, says Portmann, demands a combined disciplinary approach which will allow for our historicity, for the special nature of our development of hereditary factors, both their organic basis and their unique openness. In this approach culture will be recognized as our "second nature," and terms like "openness" and "culture" will not be mere expressions for solemn occasions but ontic features to which our forms of development correspond. Portmann's use of the phrase "second nature" for human culture is a brilliant and ironical relativizing of a purely biological view of nature. For him "nature" embraces all the essential aspects of humanity. He thus has a frame of reference similar to that which the neurologist Rudolf Janzen adopts when he calls the relation between brain and personality the central theme of his work.

We should not think that the priority accorded to the indivisible totality of humanity is so one-sided in Portmann that he simply begins with philosophical and historical considerations and only then looks for the biological conditions for this prior picture of humanity. Research into human ontogenesis might rather be described as the primary motif of Portmann's biological work. In the course of this research he then came to see the uniqueness of humans, e.g., in their fetal and post-uterine development, their brain structure, and other physiological features. He discovered the privileges and defects that distinguish us from all the primates. But this postulated historical priority of his research-motif does not have to mean that he put the ontic question only in the light of his biological findings and answered it in terms of those findings. This would imply a derivation of the human from objective data, which neither Portmann nor anyone else can accomplish. Even though biologists may not assume that they will discover human uniqueness, they are not without something of this assumption, inasmuch as they bring with them some awareness of this uniqueness "at the back of their minds." This awareness serves no less a role than that of a "hermeneutical principle" which helps them to interrelate the biological facts. This is true, as the example of Monod shows, even when we enjoy only the meaningless existence of gypsies on the edge of the universe. Here, too, a prior picture of humanity "at the back of the mind" provides an organizing schema for the biological data. For Monod the data simply confirm, as it were, what he knows already.

In other words, those who do research on humanity are themselves human and cannot be without a self-understanding that precedes all their research.

As Portmann says, we realize that we none of us study humanity without presuppositions or build up the results of our research stroke by stroke on a white sheet of paper. We integrate these results into a picture whose outlines, often barely visible, are already there, provided by the intellectual work of past and the pressure of current opinion. This prior self-understanding changes with the epoch we live in, sometimes Christian, sometimes materialistic. Scientific work, like artistic creation, begins with an initial sketch that changes with further work but many of whose basic features remain the same. By this "initial sketch" Portmann means what we have described as the assumption "at the back of our minds."

In drawing his view of humanity, not from evolution, but from other sources, especially self-consciousness, and then examining its biological presuppositions, Portmann makes the distinction we asked for between "causes" and "conditions" of humanity. He even makes it linguistically by speaking about the organic "presuppositions" of human and animal behavior.

What are these organic, evolutionary presuppositions?

One is that humans are like birds that have to leave the nest. If we compare human pregnancy to being in the nest, infants are comparatively helpless and unprepared when they are thrust out into the world. They are physiologically "premature." Only after the first year do they reach the stage of development that most mammals have to have at the time of birth. To be in the same position they would have to be in the womb a year longer than they are. A twenty-one-month pregnancy would be needed.

This "premature" birth means that in distinction from calves or young giraffes, which can stand the first hour and are ready to follow the herd, human infants seem to be defective. They are not only helpless and in need of care, they also lack the qualities which direction by instinct makes possible. The reason for this lack may be defined in terms of the physiology of the brain.

In lower mammals the centers of the hypothalamic region of the midbrain are much better integrated than in anthropoids and humans. This morphological fact has to be related to the impoverishment of the sphere of instinct and the location of the centers of several important functions in the sphere of the cortex of the cerebrum. In humans the relative weakness of instinct is balanced by a big increase in other central motive systems. This consists especially of an enlargement of the hemispheres which determine the rank of vertebrates. Measurements of these hemispheres confirm this, having the value of 170 in humans, 49 in chimpanzees, 70 in elephants, and from .7 to 32 in other mammals. This extraordinary increase is obviously related to the weakening of instinct. It shows how unique are the motive possibilities that seem to be related to the human style of life.

This is simply one among many examples of Portmann's physiological method. Examining the physiological conditions of human development, he is concerned about the main question how far these conditions make it possible for humans to have unique privileges surpassing those of any other creatures.

The very deficiencies of humans—their impoverished instincts and their helplessness the first year out of the womb—are in fact the preconditions of their special privileges.

Even before discussing Portmann's physiological research into the brain, we had occasion to refer already to the lack of instincts in connection with Herder and Gehlen. Since we humans, to quote Goethe again, are not taught by our instincts but have to teach them, we have to look for norms and values by which we may orient ourselves and thus teach our instincts. We thus have the opportunity to fashion civilizations in freedom and responsibility.

The helplessness of physiologically premature birth points in the same direction. The first year outside the womb allows the normal processes of maturing, which do not take place in the mother's body, to be advanced by contact with the outside world, by the forced experience of many sources of stimulation, and in the form of development for the upright stance, for speech, and for the ability to perform judicious acts. Thus natural processes in humans take place under unique conditions in the first year of life, instead of under universally valid conditions in the womb. These presuppositions are normative for what counts as specifically human. Openness to the world in human maturity is made possible by the early contact with the riches of the world that is peculiar to humans. What first seems to be subjection to a physiologically premature birth, and hence a defect, is in truth our human opportunity. We have here physiological preconditions for the possibility of becoming historical beings who can deal with the world and master it as subjects.

Furthermore, the first year itself is already under the law of history at a time when, if we were true mammals, we would still be in the darkness of the womb under purely natural relations. Already in this very early period in which we have moved out of the embryonic state, in addition to general processes, many unique events take place which often enough determine our destiny. (The description of the historical echoes here, even linguistically, Rickert's distinction between individualizing and generalizing.) The first stage of life in this physiologically premature birth not only prepares us for historical existence but already has a historical structure. We are also given a tendency toward a unique flexibility in our attitude to the world. It is part of our lesser development of fixed instinctual modes of behavior that no specific environment seems to be appointed for us. We do not have a particular setting like animals, e.g., steppe or forest, river or mountain. It is in keeping with our particular mode of existence that we can make any natural sphere our own world, that we can construct this world out of natural conditions that are changed by human action.

This flexibility in relation to the world is for Portmann the decisive difference from animals. It underlies our possibility of becoming historical. Animal behavior, in distinction from human, is tied to environment and fixed by instinct. Human behavior is open to the world and is marked by freedom to decide. Signs of this mobility and openness are the upright stance, speech, and the ability to perform judicious acts, i.e., autonomy and self-determination. The conditions which make these possible are also foreseen in our genetic disposition.

Our ability and need to transcend ourselves, and not to accept the status of predetermined objects of natural processes, are not facts that we can perceive only as *spiritual* beings, i.e., that we can affirm only as we neglect our *nature*. In his book *Die Rückseite des Spiegels*, Konrad Lorenz advances and develops the thesis that all that epistemological theory takes to be the structure of human experience is anticipated in our development, i.e., in the sphere of nature. Lorenz, Portmann, and J. Illies too, agree—in spite of their differences in some respects—that when we look at the constitution of human *na-*

ture, we can see how prepared we are for what we know about ourselves pre-theoretically, namely, that we must grasp ourselves responsibly and be open to the world as subjects, that we are beings with open possibilities, that we do not reel off our lives "automatically" like creatures that are bound by instinct but have to make decisions.

In discovering this, and thus finding our pre-theoretical self-consciousness remarkably confirmed, we have an "aha" experience such as naturalistic anthropologists who are supposedly free from presuppositions can never have. For the latter think that they have no prior knowledge of who or what they are. There is thus no knowledge to be confirmed or refuted. They hope to learn who or what they are from biological laws. They live in an illusion of complete freedom from presuppositions which cannot be challenged even by their pre-theoretical self-consciousness.

Theologically considered, Portmann's view does not have to lead to the biblical understanding that we are beings with a destiny as God's partners. The Christian *appropriation* of such a view (which in earlier cases we have steadfastly rejected) does not arise, for Portmann's thesis would fit in with very differently oriented pictures of humanity as well. A secular humanism might find in Portmann's ontogenetic conditions of human life a substructure for its own understanding of humanity. Nevertheless, the *counter*question of the conditions of creaturely evolution is particularly significant in the light of the biblical view of humanity, and especially its creation (Genesis 2).

As in the name of this *counter*question we consider Portmann's doctrine of our openness to the world and historical existence, and our ability to perform judicious acts, we are discharging what we take to be the task of theology today, namely, interpreting empirical facts, taking up a position in relation to them. Since the biblical story of our creation contains a statement about our destiny, the question is indeed relevant what disposition the Creator gave us for the reaching of our destiny as creatures. As the Creator speaks to his creatures and fixes their destiny, he is not addressing an indifferent chunk of universal nature but a specially prepared part of nature—humanity. Here, too, the word of the Creator is a creative word which brings about the capacity of the creature—*one* creature—for the word, and thus places the conditions for this capacity at its disposal.

Perhaps we might add that, just as little as Portmann derives hu-

manity from its evolution, so little should we derive the biblical view
of humanity from Portmann's. We have here a prior self-understanding, provided to us by the Bible, which examines the physiological
preconditions in the form of a *counter*question. Those who have
read the biblical accounts of creation and studied Portmann's biological fragments will thus have much the same aha experience as Portmann did in his own way.

Background of the Modification:
The Biblical Account of Creation

The biblical account of our creation confirms in its own way the
fact that we are to be understood, not in the light of our genetic evolution or biological origin, but in the light of our goal, of what transcends us. The biblical story knows no causal but a definitely final intention. It does not ask where the hand comes from, but why it is
there.

This may be elucidated by the concept which most pregnantly
describes our special position in the cosmos and our privileges
vis-à-vis the animal kingdom, namely, that of the divine image. All
the basic anthropological questions come into focus in this concept.
This is why the debates between Christian denominations and theological schools are reflected in it. Increasingly sharper distinctions
have thus developed. Necessarily we are unable to go into all this
here.[23] We will restrict ourselves to presenting the basic feature of
the divine image that is common to every interpretation. This consists of its *final* character and comes to expression primarily in two
typical traits.

First, according to the J account,[24] God blows into us the breath
of divine life and gives us a share in himself. He directs us to himself
(Genesis 2:7).

Second, in our relation to God and our destiny, we are privileged,
according to both accounts (2:16 and 1:28), to be addressed by
God's command and hence to be called a Thou. In distinction from
all other creatures we are thus more and other than mere objects of
the creative fiat: "Let there be."

Other parts of the narratives confirm that we are addressed in the
second person. Thus we are given authority to have dominion over
the earth and all life as God's representatives (1:28; 2:19 f.). It seems
to be important that we are not given this dominion because of any
superiority over animals, i.e., because of any "downward" relation.

We receive it because we are seen in analogy to God's government of the world, i.e., in an "upward" relation.

If we try to formulate this upward relation, this final view of the divine image, we might say that humanity enjoys its privileges vis-à-vis animals and its special position in the cosmos, not because it is "above" animals, but because it is in a unique way "under" God.

Only in this light can we explain why in Psalm 139 our origin, i.e., our basis, is not viewed from the genetic standpoint but exclusively from the standpoint that God has known us from the very first and called us to fellowship with himself. I will quote once again in a modern version some verses that claimed our attention earlier (vv. 13–16):

> For thou didst form my inward parts,
> thou didst knit me together in my mother's womb.
> I praise thee, for thou art fearful and wonderful.
> Wonderful are thy works!
> Thou knowest me right well;
> my frame was not hidden from thee,
> when I was being made in secret,
> intricately wrought in the depths of the earth.
> Thy eyes beheld my unformed substance;
> in thy book were written, every one of them,
> the days that were formed for me,
> when as yet there was none of them.

The emphatically final approach in this psalm rules out any rivalry with biological or genetic statements about humanity, or, better, it rules out any interpretation of the psalm as witness to an early, unenlightened stage of such statements. The particular standpoint of Psalm 139 makes it possible for us to view its message of human origins against the background of any biological understanding of human development. The psalmist considers development in his own way, but he does so within our final destiny. He thus speaks about the processes of conception and birth, about embryonic development in the womb. But through the means—and it is only a *means*—of biological development God says, "Let there be," and there is; "I" am. God knew me, says the psalmist, even as an unformed substance, at the prehuman stage of my development, and he called me by my name (Isaiah 43:1).

This placing of the genetic question within a prior knowledge of our nature, namely, of our divine likeness, is decisive. For it gives the biological process the rank of a means in and by which God's creative work is done. This ranking is presupposed when Christian parents speak about God *giving* them their children. The term "gift" does not mean that children fall from heaven in the form of a supernatural gift, so that there is no need to ask about their immanent genesis. Parents have a good knowledge of the genetic process of conception and birth. But they also know that the real thing about becoming and being human goes beyond the genetic process. The real theme here is that the Creator uses this process as the means of his "Let there be." The process represents the physical events on whose basis alone our personhood, our partnership with God, and our projection toward the goal of our destiny are possible.

In this light it is easy to see an analogy between our individual development in the womb and human development in general, as a type. For this reason, without doing violence to the sense, we might say that God knew humanity as an unformed substance, in the preform of Homo sapiens. God is its continuity inasmuch as he had the project of humanity in his mind long before actualizing it, and he then called it into being by ways which the law of created bios already held in readiness. In saying that God is our continuity I mean that the transition to the human in evolution is a secret of creation which objective thought cannot pierce even though the biological side of human genesis may be worked out without any gaps. The impossibility of deriving human personhood from any immanent continuity reflects again the diastasis between quantity and quality, or means and content, to which we have already drawn attention.

To ward off the suspicion that in referring to an insoluble mystery of creation in the transition to humanity we are simply engaging in the kind of apologetic trick of thought that theologians sometimes practice, I should like to point out that I can offer a philosophical parallel in Kant's investigation of the relation between the sensory world and the intelligible world. Since we have discussed this already in relation to the problem of freedom, I need only recall the main points here.

The world of objective experience does not in principle display the phenomenon of freedom or human personhood. Freedom is not a gap in the causal nexus. (We need not repeat the reasons for this.) Experience of it takes place in a different dimension, that of practical reason, which confronts me, as a willing and active being, with an unconditional "You ought." From the standpoint of objective thought, the two worlds of theoretical and practical reason are not logically related, and cannot be. They are joined only by the personal union of the I which both knows and acts responsibly. In principle, there can be no demonstrating either the boundary between them or the transition from natural being to personal being, i.e., to humanity in the full sense of the word.

As stated, this is only an analogy. But at the decisive point it brings out our problem with all the sharpness one could wish. The immanent continuity of our development is only a biological means within which true humanity emerges as a non-derivable fact. Personhood does not have its basis in the efficient or final causes of evolution but in our relation to the practical logos that transcends us, or, theologically, in our relation to the determinative divine ground of our being.

How final in *this* sense is the orientation of the idea of the divine image, and how strongly it resists a purely genetic understanding of humanity, is ultimately shown by the fact that our divine likeness is never presented as a mere *gift* of creation but always also as a *task*, the reference to a goal, an appeal for self-actualization.[25] In Pauline theology the indicative of gift (you "are" God's image, you "are" a new creature) is always coupled with an imperative, a task. I have to become what I am, what is already promised to me. I have to actualize my being on my side. The summons to become what we are applies here too.

If we finally consider that in the New Testament the divine image necessarily finds a norm in the express image of God that is presented in Christ, so that our human divine likeness is integrated into the order of redemption rather than creation, the final character of the image, or, better, its eschatological character, is something that we cannot possibly miss.

7. THE POSSIBILITY OF "DEHUMANIZING"

An exciting question arises here whether we can lose our privileged position as God's image, whether we can thus give up on ourselves. To put it more directly and dramatically: Can we, by giving up on ourselves, sink back into the animal realm and lose our specific quality? Is it possible that we can become mere digits in an antlike state, that we can fall victim to depersonalization through consistent collectivizing? It need hardly be pointed out how relevant this question has become in an age of ideological techniques of government.

In asking whether the divine likeness can be lost, we must distinguish between losing and forfeiting. What I have lost, I might regain. But forfeiting means renouncing something I have not myself achieved, e.g., that I am God's image, so that I cannot "get rid" of it. I am stuck with a divine likeness that I have forefeited but cannot set aside. I have thus to stay within the circle of God's terrifying and consuming holiness. I should still have to do this even at the lowest level of collective humanity and its depersonalizing, even if I lived by the thesis that a human being is nothing but a phenomenon of glands, or a bundle of nerves, or a mechanism of reactions. No "wings of the morning" (Psalm 139) will carry me away from the prison of my identity; no Promethean defiance will free me from the golden chain of my noble destiny. If I could lose my identity in such a way as to render it null and void, to eliminate it, I should be excused, having reached the zone beyond good and evil. I should have escaped the sphere of influence of him who made me in his own likeness. I should again have the innocence of animals or inanimate objects. But since I cannot lose the divine image, but only forfeit it, I have to stay within his searing splendor. I am still one who is asked concerning the basis, goal, and meaning of existence—and therefore concerning what is forfeited.

All that has changed is that the radiance of divine majesty has ceased to be a fiery symbol or sign directing my life. It has lost the warmth that radiates concealment and protection. It has become a searing glory in face of which I am aware of my own nothingness. It does not shed its light into the darkness to dispel it. It is simply a No above night and darkness. What was deliverance is judgment. What was gospel is law. This judgment does not just strike the individual existence that has to confess its guilt of forfeiture. It strikes above all the suprapersonal forces, governmental systems, and social structures which set us on the way to that forfeiture. But even in these it strikes the people who unleash and control these processes.

In conclusion, I should like to adduce two thoughts which press home the point of what precedes. This point stands out against the dark, apocalyptic background of possible and ultimately impossible dehumanization which threatens when we are understood as mere particles and products of evolutionary processes, when a material origin is made the key to the riddle of humanity.

First, Thomas Carlyle, addressing a congress of biologists devoted to the problem of descent, once stated that while they regarded us as a little higher than tadpoles, he preferred with the psalmist (Psalm 8:6) to regard us as a little lower than angels. This gives very pregnant formulation to the problem of relationship that we have constantly encircled. Naturally Carlyle was not contesting our derivation from tadpoles and their predecessors. At any rate, he had no interest in attacking evolutionary theories in the name of a biblically based anthropology. What he was concerned about was the impossibility of grasping what is distinctively human with the help of genetic findings. This distinctive element is addressed only when we are put in the hierarchy of God's creatures and their relationships to God, or, more sharply, only when we are set in relation to the beings that are at the top of the hierarchy and hence closest to God, i.e., angels. This relation can be in force with *any* theory of biological descent. We are to be defined only in terms of our Whither and not our Whence. The more this distinctive and final theme of our existence is kept in view, the more freely and the less dogmatically the Whence can be investigated. Redemption is always redemption for objectivity.[26]

Second, the indestructibility of the divine image, and therefore of humanity, does not rest on our immanent qualities. We can lose all these. There are monsters, human hulks, who have nothing recognizably human. From our discussion of those who are supposedly worthless we know what inferences can be made from the loss of human qualities. The indestructible character of humanity cannot be based on these qualities. It rests instead on an external factor, namely, that we are called by name, that we are addressed, and that another has brought us into a history with himself.

The certainty of the divine likeness is thus grounded in our final relationship, in what we called our alien dignity. If we base our dignity on our biological origin, we are simply made into more highly organized animals. If we base it on our immanent value, on our functional abilities, we are sacrificed to animality. For when we lose our usefulness, we lose our right to life. Only that relation establishes the inviolability of our humanity—only the fact that we are the children of God, the apple of his eye, bought with a price.[27]

I. CRITICAL ENCOUNTER WITH ANTHROPOLOGICAL CONCEPTIONS

I. HUMANITY IN DEBATE WITH THE UNCONSCIOUS (FREUD, FRANKL)

The theses of this essay on anthropology have always been developed in such a way as to bring us into critical—and, we hope, self-critical—dialogue with other positions. We have repeatedly discussed sociologically oriented anthropologists, especially Marx, but also Gehlen and Schelsky, as well as the New Left. In the last chapter we tested our view in encounter with natural scientists—Morin, Monod, and Portmann. All our deliberations have involved philosophical and literary references, as is hardly avoidable when the theme is anthropology.

It seems to be important that in conclusion we should enter into debate with paradigmatically important forms in which the main points in our own view are tested by the human sciences, whether these pose a challenge, as in the case of Sigmund Freud, or seem to offer analogies in approach or material findings, as in the case of Teilhard de Chardin and Viktor Frankl. This dialogue can be carried on only with critical alertness, even in relation to our own position.

a. Survey of the Material and Information on the Problem

We recall that in examining the modern age, and especially secularization, we have found that it approaches knowledge empirically and thinks it is confined to the horizon of experience and of what is objectifiable. It has also become clear that when this aspect of things is made absolute, it necessarily leads to a crisis, especially in anthropology. For humans are self-transcending beings that have to comprehend themselves and see themselves in the light of a theme, of a directing norm. They cannot just let things be, or be led by instinct. If this need to see the self from the standpoint of a theme, whether this theme be given by God or not (as in Sartre), is what is distinctive in humanity, then it is obvious why human nature cannot be plumbed by empirical soundings.

That we are closed off against such attempts at objectification is obvious, for the point to which we are referred cannot be objectified. Neither God nor the norm of the good (in Kant's sense) can be found empirically. Hence a consistent empiricism is forced to explain such norms—God or the good—in terms of its own categories and criteria. It can do this, for example, in the way that Herbert Spencer does by regarding the good as a cipher for the useful, and thus understanding conscience as a store which preserves and documents experiences that have shown the good to be useful and the useful to be good.[1] Sociological empiricism can regard the good— or what society calls the good—as a pragmatic postulate which serves the goal of stabilizing a class situation, as in Marx. Finally, God and the good can be regarded as projections of fear and hope, as in Ludwig Feuerbach. Fear and hope are physical sensations which can be registered objectively and empirically. Here the supposedly empirical causes of what seems to be transcendent are analyzed and the transcendent is thus given the appearance of a metaphysical spook. It is incorporated into the self-reposing immanence which can be grasped by us.

The consequences of this kind of anthropology are obvious. The picture of humanity is brought under the rule of axioms which prejudice and limit what is said about it from the very outset. They do so in the sense of not considering what is really distinctive, the orientation to self-transcendence, the fullness of the dimensions of human existence. They all arrive at a reduced or one-dimensional existence.

Although anthropology owes an incomparable debt to the psychoanalysis of Freud for uncovering hitherto unknown rooms in the house of the I—the cellars of the unconscious—and thus extending considerably the horizon of anthropological problems, Freud himself seems to have been an advocate of the reduction indicated. He integrated humanity into his philosophically understood psychoanalysis and forced it into the Procrustean bed of empirical axioms. For this reason he might serve as a good example of one-dimensional anthropology.

This is particularly true because Viktor Frankl cannot be understood apart from the background of Freudian psychoanalysis and its anthropological consequences. Frankl's debate with Freud is from a standpoint that is close to ours. Our essay might support his view with some arguments which Christian tradition has placed at our disposal after discussing humanity for hundreds of years.

When I speak of a philosophical psychoanalysis, i.e., one which is consistently empirical, I mean that it does not perceive the purely provisional nature of empirical perception and has no sense of its limitations. It cannot have such a sense because it absolutizes the empirical aspect and thus thinks it can gain a total picture of humanity with its help. Although we cannot present Freud's view with any fullness here, I should like to give a simplified sketch of it. My aim will be to emphasize what is anthropologically relevant and what contains the nub of the controversy which led to the logotherapy of Frankl. It would be an exciting task, but one we must forgo, to develop the anthropological problems of psychoanalysis in such a way as to form a choir out of the voices of those who were taught by Freud but who also abandoned him, especially Alfred Adler and Carl G. Jung, but also Erich Fromm, Karl Menninger, and many others. If instead we must be content with the duet of Freud and Frankl, we might also draw attention to the basic theme that would be dominant in the full choir, at least within the confines of the anthropological theme.

b. The Anthropology of Sigmund Freud

At the heart of psychoanalysis stands the failure to control a psychological conflict or to work out a traumatic experience. The harmful effect of the conflict is due to repression, i.e., the banishing of the conflict from the conscious realm to that of the unconscious. Healing comes with the actualizing of the conflict (or neurosis) and transfer to the doctor-patient relationship.

What is uncontrolled and repressed is brought to light especially by the analysis of dreams, since dreams are outside conscious control and thus present uncensored pictures of what is held down in the unconscious. By analytical uncovering, what is uncontrolled can be fruitfully worked out. The sick person receives guidance. The self regains its lost autonomy.

With this theory Freud opposes voluntarist psychology and its purely rational appeal to the conscious ego. Suggestion and persuasion cannot help us to conscious moral volition, for the true basis of motivation is left out of account. Only the actualizing of what is operative and repressed in the unconscious can do it, i.e., a new and satisfying solution to the conflict.

Freud viewed the psychological processes that he analyzed from a dynamic, economic, and topical standpoint, i.e., from that of impulses, the amount of stimulation, and the location. He thus conceived of a psychological apparatus with spatial extension, an as yet unknown regularity, and a division into various courts, the id, the ego, and the superego.

Freud characterizes the id as that which is inherited and constitutionally established or achieved. This is the layer of unconscious impulse. In distinction from it is the ego, which mediates between the id and external reality. The ego controls access to the possibility of movement. Somewhat independent of it is the superego, which exercizes a kind of censorship over the claims of the impulsive life to the ego. As a court deriving from the ego, it continues the influence of the traditions of parents, family, race, nation, and society, playing the role of an authority with a judicial thrust. The polar antithesis of the superego, which controls the ego, to the impulsive claims of the id upon the ego, gives rise to conflicts that can lead to psychological illnesses, or neuroses. Thus the overstrictness of the superego, functioning as conscience, is a leading cause of neuroses. Early fear of parental authority lives on as fear of conscience and is preserved and kept alive by the superego as this assumes parental authority.

The most hotly contested part of Freud's theory, and the most important for his theses, is his teaching on impulses. Impulses are the tense needs of the id, and especially its bodily demands. Two basic impulses are eros and the impulse of destruction. Eros embraces the tension between preservation of the self and the species, love of the ego and love of objects. It seeks to bind, to establish and maintain greater unities. It is opposed—after the manner of attraction and repulsion in the inorganic realm—by the impulse of destruction, which seeks to dissolve, to destroy, to reduce life to an inorganic state again.

Freud thought of this death-impulse relatively late, when he had been attacked by many thinkers, even some of his own students, because of the one-sidedness of his original teaching on impulses. He found in the destructive impulse an aggression turned against the self. This reversal was understood as a redirecting of blocked aggression into a passion for self-destruction. Thus no one will commit suicide who has not first wanted to commit homicide. The individual perishes through inner conflicts.

The total energy of eros at our disposal is called libido by Freud. It is at first so stored up in the ego that it becomes primary narcissism, or introverted self-love. This state persists until the ego finds objects for the libido and thus the original narcissistic libido changes into object-libido. This means that the ego develops a relation to some object in the form of a desire for goal-oriented action. The ego is thus both a reservoir and a dispenser of the activities of the libido. At this point the doctrine of impulses seems to be unclear. It is left open by what criteria libido is dispensed, and how it can shift objects (one is reminded of the plasticity of urges in Gehlen), but can also seem to be fixed on the same objects for the whole of life. (Freud himself dealt with the facts that are under discussion here, but did not examine them from the standpoint of our present investigation.)

In this context of the work of distribution, the activity of the ego in repression is also unclear. In his book *Die Stellung des Menschen im Kosmos*, Max Scheler puts a critical question to Freud on this very point, asking what is the true origin or subject of the act of repression. What is it in us that negates, that denies the will to live, that represses impulses? Freud's doctrine with its guiding principle of tension, which he borrowed fatally from nineteenth-century research into electricity, is developed in an empirically physical framework within which there can be no answer to this question. It would contradict his basic attitude, determined by this framework, to feel qualified either to put the question or to give an answer. At the most he merely admitted that exposition of the workings of the libido can only partially describe the conditions of eros, for the sexual function, or sexuality, is not the same thing as eros. United with the libido are forces from various parts and organs of the body which come together in the ego. Eros, then, represents a complex of many partial impulses. The libido is the related quantum of energy.

The role that Freud assigns to sexuality here as the decisive part of eros is viewed more soberly and with greater restraint today. In Freud's psychoanalysis it seems to be the most natural paradigm. This is due not least to his criticism of contemporary society, which was controlled by prudery and the collective repressive processes of the Victorian age. The reason for the criticized overestimation of the sexual function is to be found here.

This time-bound side of Freud is what causes Herbert Marcuse to hold aloof from some of his premises. The anthropological definition of the relation to society plays a role here. In Freud, selfish desires for pleasure, which are governed especially by the sexual libido, result in an ultimately invincible tension with any form of social life, with any order of society, and therefore with all the opportunities of progress in it. This basic tension produces the host of permanent tensions inasmuch as society and its guiding tradition, if they are to survive, demand a high degree of repression, or at least sublimation, of those impulses. This demand cannot be met even in a socialistic order. No order can change selfish and aggressive impulses into impulses that are committed to society and promote it.

Marcuse, however, thinks that a welfare society with its repressive toleration has dismantled these complexes, or at least put them in a state of incubation which prevents their open outbreak. For one thing, there is no impulse for such conflicts in Western society, for there is no ruling father figure and hence no need for the Oedipus complex (an essential feature in Freud's teaching). Sexual repression has also been reduced by widespread liberalizing and the discarding of taboos. Again, Marcuse thinks psychoanalysis is outdated inasmuch as the assumed antagonism between individuals and society has been ended by an identification of individuals with their peers and by the principle of reality that controls society. Marcuse can explain the possibility of this only by an important correction of Freud. We are not, as Freud thinks, a constant bundle of impulsive energies (relatively) independent of time and space. We are plastic and can be molded. Hence society can pervert us. It can destroy or impoverish our psychical structure. It can make us weak. It can subject us to itself. It can integrate us and alienate us from ourselves by this assimilation.

With this assertion that new relations resist an unmodified appropriation of the psychoanalytical view, Marcuse obviously thinks advance can be made only by postulating a true humanity that is conscious of itself and not alienated by assimilation. But since this is only postulated and is not objectifiably present, we must develop an exemplary elite which will proleptically achieve the absent processes of consciousness. By such an elite Marcuse has young intellectuals in view—students.

I have introduced this digression on Marcuse because it is an impressive illustration of what may be found to be time-bound or Victorian in Freud. If I understand Marcuse aright, he thinks this element was unwitting (which is ironical in the father of psycho-analysis), for with his overemphasis on sexuality Freud was not de-liberately or specifically reacting to his age. This may have disposed him, without noting it, to regard us as a bundle of (primarily) sexual impulses and to regard us as ultimately independent of society, or at least of its changes.

Connected with the empirical framework that controls his psycho-analysis is Freud's development of a regular psychological mecha-nism. At this point he retreats a step from conscious law to natural law in psychological processes. (It is no wonder that he is near to Feuerbach's anthropology!)

The claims of impulse well up from the unconscious into the ego, become pre-conscious—a preliminary stage of consciousness is pre-supposed here—and come under the censorship of the superego, which guards their access to full consciousness, either repressing them, or permitting them only if by being changed or covered over they no longer have their original form. To what is repressed there is now constant resistance, a kind of institutionalized repetition of the original act of repression.

In repression there is usually substitution, i.e., the transferral of the wish to an available object so as to provide at least partial satis-faction. Sublimation is a kind of transferral of this kind, and serves as a safety valve, especially when the impulse is too strong. The claims of impulse can never be fully repressed or weakened by substi-tute satisfaction. Such transferrals do not succeed if the impulse is originally too strong or is inflamed by the external world. If the superfluous psychical energy is not let off somatically, there is trans-position or weakening in the form of an unhealthy substitute, i.e., a neurosis. Neurosis is a sign of the defective working of the psycho-logical apparatus. It is a red light for the observant doctor.

Neurosis has deep roots in the development of the personality. The conflict between the superego and the id, which takes place on the soil and at the cost of the ego and has pathological effects, is an-ticipated in childhood. Uninhibited sexuality in the boy—Freud di-vides it into oral, anal, and phallic phases—turns in the phallic phase to the mother as a first object of love. It then finds a limit in the ri-valry of the father, who asserts himself by prohibitions and threats of punishment. This first removal from an object of love produces a psychical trauma, the Oedipus complex. At this stage the superego emerges as a court which normatively governs our mode of existence.

Earlier the ego accepts the claims of the id more or less unfiltered. Now it emancipates itself from the id.

At the beginning of the development of personality—or, shall we say, of becoming human?—there is thus a complex, a conflict with the external world. If the superego arises in this initial conflict, it does so by identification, i.e., by the adjustment of the ego to an alien ego which serves as a model and ideal in the development of the superego. As a rule the father is the model with which the child begins to identify. The father can be both rival and model at the Oedipus stage. We do not have alternatives here. The child has ambivalent feelings toward an external world which resists its wishes and which may be seen for the first time in the person of the father.

The imperfect overcoming of the Oedipus complex, often caused by an early increase of childish sexuality (Freud presupposes abuse or seduction by siblings or adults), forms the basis of all future sicknesses. Our development depends on the way we master this complex. The child is father to the man.

Human life begins, then, with a dramatic exposure. The dependence of this dramatic introduction on the biological constitution and social disposition of individuals leaves plenty of room for conjectures as to the outcome. Freud deliberately avoided such conjectures. The drama of personal development was of interest to him only insofar as he thought he found a certain regularity of development in it, namely, the restriction of sexuality. He tried to find a regular framework for the apparently accidental nature of this development.

c. Critical Considerations

1. THE BLINDNESS OF PSYCHOANALYSIS TO NORMS

It is easy to see that in this understanding, as in that of Marx, there has to be a division into substructure and superstructure, though here the psyche is not determined by its material, economic base but by the biological pressure of the libido and the resultant conflict with society. Intellectual products, e.g., philosophy and religion, are sublimations of this conflict. Thus Ludwig Binswanger can say that for Freud, philosophy is nothing but one of the most eminent forms of the sublimation of repressed sexuality. As in Marxism, philosophy, an ontological discipline, has the significance of ideology. It is not a normative science with a Whither in the truth but is to be understood in terms of its genetic Whence and seems to be the product of the impulse-mechanism of the libido. Its results can have the significance only of projections and sublimations of these impulses. The objective value of its statements is thus close to nil. These statements are relevant only as symptoms of a certain process of impulse, sublimation, and repression.

From this standpoint, Frankl thinks, philosophy simply becomes the theorizing of a muffled neurosis. The question whether the reality might not be the reverse and neurosis the practicing of an inadequate philosophy (or anthropology) is never considered. Karl Jaspers develops a first implication of this view when, in his *Allgemeine Psychopathologie*, while admitting that Freud often sees admirably what results from the repression of sexuality, he never finds him asking what happens through the repression of the psyche. But might not the banishing of philosophy to the ideological superstructure—an ironical self-deception in the great teacher of repression—be based on this kind of repression of the psyche? Frankl's belief that it was led to his concept of logotherapy, in which he tried to bring the psyche back into psychology.

Now there can be no doubt that every science, and therefore every attempt at psychological analysis, has the task of unmasking. This may seem to be put rather strongly and polemically, but it is familiar to us, more mildly stated, in epistemology. Thus Kant unmasked all forms of metaphysics and showed that they overlook the radius of action of what may be perceived. Any attempt, in the name of the axiom that we must shun presuppositions, to display the unrecognized and latent presuppositions in any theory, is an act of unmasking of this kind. Finally, all ideological criticism, all efforts to unveil the secret philosophical or pragmatic background of a theory, are attempts at unmasking. It is thus legitimate to have ideological doubts of philosophical or theological views and to look for psychogenic impulses behind them. (Thus, for a psychiatrist, a thinker like Kierkegaard naturally poses the question what significance the powerful figure of his conflict-torn father had for his deliberations. The author remembers a debate he had on this theme with the psychiatrist Hans Bürger-Prinz.)

Nevertheless, this ideological criticism or psychogenetic analysis is valid only so long as it seeks the truth in the chaos of alienation, only so long as it is in the name of truth, and, out of concern for it, that it engages in its critical explorations. These explorations are only the means to an end. When unmasking becomes an end in itself, it serves only a desire to "debunk" and becomes nihilistic. As Frankl says, the unmasking psychologist no longer sees the forest of life itself for the trees of deceits, and then unmasking results in cynicism, and finally becomes a mask itself, the mask of nihilism. Letting unmasking become an end in itself, Freud tells his age that he will show it the real springs of its thought and action.

What are these? In his treatise on sexual theory, Freud says that the production of sexual stimulation provides a stock of energy that is largely turned to other than sexual ends, and by repression constructs later sexual limits. This potential of sexual energy not only meets our own needs but has reserves for additional constructs—the superego—which channel the elemental stream of basic energy, hold it in check, and make it a creative force in other fields. With the help of sexual barriers this potential both limits and extends the self.

Sexual barriers—what are these? Among other things, they can be artificially produced mechanisms of control along the line of Victorian prudery. And undoubtedly this puritanically restricted milieu, as often noted, had no little influence on the development of Freud's own theory. But sexual barriers are not to be viewed only from this standpoint of perverted domestication. In them we also discern the self-transcendence which has stood at the heart of our own anthropological discussion. We humans are not a passive part of nature that is simply shaped by nature (*natura naturata*). We are also that part of nature that does the shaping (*natura naturans*). In our quality as persons we have to wrestle with natural impulses. We are in a battle between will and impulse, between personal determination and animal trends.

Our decisive observation, then, is that our protest against ourselves which is the mark of humanity, our basic existential contradiction is not interpreted here—any more than such intellectual products as philosophy—in terms of a normative Whither but solely as the product of a misdirected impulsive energy (or at any rate one that exceeds mere sexuality). This is the nihilistic depletion here. It does not stop at the true reality of the human but eliminates it by merging it into objectifiable impulses and their processes. In the writings of Freud there are many examples of this banishment of mind or psyche by mechanistic principles. According to Schopenhauer, this dissolving of the moral world in psychological laws and procedures is the true perversion of mind; at root it is what is personified by the belief in Antichrist.

That Freud in consequence neither has nor can have any feeling for the question of meaning, that this can be for him only a pathological symptom, is something that Carl G. Jung finds fault with in his work *Die Beziehungen der Psychotherapie zur Seelsorge*. As he sees it, the fact that many theologians seek psychological support or pastoral help in Freud's theory of sex or Adler's theory of power seems very strange, for both theories are at root hostile to the spirit because they are psychologies without soul. They are rationalistic methods which hinder the development of spiritual experience. Among his patients past the middle of life, i.e., the age of thirty-five, Jung did not know one whose ultimate problem was not one of religious adjustment. What he meant by this was that psychoneurosis was a suffering of the soul that had not found its meaning. The reason for this suffering was spiritual arrest or unfruitfulness. A letter of Freud to Marie Bonaparte is revealing in this regard when in it he says that the moment we ask about the meaning and value of life we are sick.

2. THE PERVERSION OF THE PICTURE OF HUMANITY

We think we can call it perversion when Freud describes that which makes us human, our orientation to meaning, as a symptom of sickness. If we put the counterquestion what is then regarded as health, we seem to be entangled in contradictory tendencies in Freud's structure of thought. For a first answer to the question of health might be that it is proper to us to be unaffected by the question of meaning and value and to live in an unabashed laissez-faire of spontaneity. How else can we picture a life that has no concern for meaning? But Freud will not accept this natural alternative to the eliminated question of meaning. For if we are abandoned without direction to spontaneity, we begin to live in the uncontrolled sphere of the unconscious and are left helplessly at the mercy of the blows of this unconscious, if one may speak a little frivolously. Psychoanalysis is supposed to free us from this very helplessness! Tormenting complexes and errors derive from the unconscious. We thus need to become aware of it, to bring it under control, to cease to be passengers on the helpless ship of life, to become captains on the bridge, to begin to steer the ship consciously. But this leads to a situation in which, if we are steering, we have to ask about the destination, i.e., about meaning and value. Is this secondary question the epitome of health? Is it no longer under the suspicion of being pathological, like the primary question? Can we really take control of ourselves and steer ourselves (as Freud desires) if we do not know or want to know where we are going? Without information of this kind, might not those who are cured of their complexes be doubly helpless, and, after wrestling with their past, need help to master their future? It seems to me that this kind of question was one of the impulses that led not only to Jung's criticism of Freud but also to Frankl's development of logotherapy.

The perversion of the picture of humanity that is signaled by this unsolved contradiction seems to me to be essentially that in Freud, humanity is as it were bisected from the standpoint of its relation to time. Psychology—in the act of liberation—nails us to our past. As the psychiatrist Friedrich Braasch correctly observes, the relation to the future, which is equally important for human development, does not receive anything like the same attention. Relationship to the future, as we said in Chapter H on the relation of humanity to time, is a specifically human quality. Animals have no future. But the human relationship to the future cannot be solved apart from the question where it wants me to go, and where I myself want to go. It is thus very closely bound up with the question of meaning.

This perversion or distortion, however, expresses itself not only in the relation to time, in fixation on the past and mastering the past, but also in spatial symbols. Humanity as a box of functions is inverted inwardly. The animal substructure, the stratum of impulses and emotions, is regarded as the dominant factor. The human element—the ego filtered and ruled by the superego—is simply the tip of an iceberg whose base, which governs the tip, is below the water.

The question naturally arises here whether this anthropological construction does not pose the problem from what zone of unconscious situations it derives. It has to put to itself the question which it puts to philosophy. Jaspers draws attention to the significant fact that Freud himself was not "analyzed." We cannot try to make good this lack in the present context, but we can do something along that line in the form of the question whether this psychomechanical picture of humanity is not the expression of a specific situation in life and time. In other words, does it not derive from the situation of a loss of meaning, a lost relationship with God, so that it does not really *lead* to a surrender of the question of meaning but is originally *based* upon this?

Joachim Bodamer conducts an inquiry of this kind in his essay *Die Krankheit der Psychoanalyse*. It seems to him that a psychology which perverts humanity in this way can develop only when we no longer see ourselves as divinely determined but lose our balance and thus produce a psychology which corresponds to this loss of balance, which disguises itself as scientific truth, and which according to the customs of the day is unassailable and unquestionable as such. Where God no longer transcends us as a mystery, there is nothing mysterious about us. We can be examined like machines. Psychology is the secular simplification of humanity . . . which it has cut off from its source. It obviously corresponds to our modern self-understanding. The two things condition one another and mutually evoke one another.

3. THE PRAGMATIC CONDITIONING OF PSYCHOANALYSIS

The relation between psychoanalysis and an industrial society which has cast off religion and is oriented to the secular may well bear some responsibility for the mechanical structure of its picture of humanity. This leads us to the conjecture which Bodamer expresses, namely, that the analogy of the machine has an impact in another respect, namely, in the goal of therapy, the restoring of our functional capacity in this industrial society, the understanding of our smooth adjustment to its processes as good health. The author can confirm from his own observation what Bodamer illustrates from American life. A society which insists so strongly on conformity, especially in the business world, though not in that alone, cannot use people who are burdened with obstructions to their functional efficiency or with personal problems that either hinder or make more difficult their full integration into the process of production.

Thus eros, the irrational antithesis of technology, has to be fitted into the industrial landscape and "functionalized." This is the decisive reason why psychologists and psychiatrists have a national role. They are omniscient and omnipresent figures. Few people do not lie on their couches. Their terminology (inferiority complex, Oedipus complex) crops up freely in discussions and on committees. Eros with its desires and torments is regarded as a divergent force. It is sand in the machine—a hindrance to its smooth operation. Its awkwardness prevents those smitten by it from achieving full and unrestricted performance. From a pragmatic standpoint, eros is a weakening factor. It may develop motive forces in us but on the job it can only act as a brake, as the opponent of all rationalization. Hence psychiatrists and psychologists are needed to counterbalance the friction and release a maximum of potential for achievement.

Competition, not the capacity for love, is the real test of vitality. An unregulated and unbroken sexuality spoils our chances in this race for external happiness in which there is no friction. The only remarkable thing is that with the spread of psychoanalysis, neuroses increase—a proof that they condition one another, according to Bodamer. Perhaps Bodamer is saying too much when he speaks about proof. To me this is more like a guess. But even if one says about this inflation of neuroses that it has come about "in spite of" psychoanalysis rather than "because of" it, the thesis still stands that psychoanalysis is an expression of the age and its sickness.

What is a humanity, one might ask, whose conflicts can be pragmatically evaluated and genetically explained (e.g., as youthful traumas) after the manner of psychoanalysis? What are conflicts which, except when they are pathologically exaggerated, are understood as no more than an essential sign of humanity, as a need to protest against the self, to be at odds with the self, and to force oneself by the introduction of mind and will? Is not this the very heart of what we have expounded as self-transcendence? If Freud had in view only sick, distorted, neurotic conflicts, no one would question the need to treat them therapeutically so long as the therapy does not increase the conflicts, turn against itself, and, instead of eradicating the conflicts, make real and lasting ones out of those that are merely sham. The core of conflict itself has the indestructible character of the human.

It is a merit of Frankl's logotherapy to work on the basis of this respect for conflict and hence to do justice to the human. In contrast, Freud is forced by the dominant category of the genetic to question the conflict itself. This prior decision regarding conflict is based on the fact that it is seen in the light of its evolutionary Whence instead of its Whither. The fact that conflict is a sign of human openness, of the task of self-transcendence and the capacity for it, is thus overlooked. Even pathological conflict may sometimes serve to develop rather than distort the human picture and be a creative force in intellectual and artistic achievement. An anecdote from my own experience illustrates this.

I was once present when two famous doctors, the Heidelberg internist Richard Siebeck and the neurologist Victor von Weizsäcker, were annoyed at their common colleague and friend Karl Jaspers and said that what had happened could only be due to some neurosis of his. Since I knew Jaspers well, I joined in the discussion and with some levity asked why, seeing that Jaspers had the good fortune to have two such famous doctors as friends, they did not cure him of his neurosis. With one voice, and with no irony, they both replied that he would then cease to be a great philosopher.

In his autobiography (*Ein Psychiater berichtet*) Hans Bürger-Prinz gets to the heart of this matter. He tells us of artists and poets whose conflicts he cured—homosexuality in the case of one writer—but with the result that he damaged or totally extinguished their creative powers. In this connection he confesses that conflicts are a constitutional mark of humanity and have, therefore, a lasting meaning and are teleologically planned. Without referring to Freud, he is obviously tilting against the great Viennese psychiatrist at this point. This is even clearer when he says that conflicts, including neurotic tendencies, must not be regarded only genetically but expounded in terms of their Whither. We constantly meet with the wrong idea, he says, that we are at our best when without problems. Nothing is more false. Our rents and cracks provide the impulse for leaps, for understanding and comprehension. If we were smooth like billiard balls, we would be pushed aside and would not be able to move out to others and ourselves. Everything significant in life, including the power one develops and the things one masters, has its origin in problems, in the rough surfaces of life. This *is* life.

Conflicts, then, are not a liability—at any rate when we avoid passing a negative verdict on humanity itself, although frequently we are illogical enough to bracket the negation of conflict and the affirmation of humanity together. If instead we regard conflict as a constitutional mark of humanity, we shall be ready to accept conflict even if sometimes it reaches the border of the neurotic or passes this border.

4. ALBERT GÖRRES ON THE "PSYCHO-PHYSICS" OF FREUD[2]

If Freud cannot understand conflict as a constitutive mark of the human but explains it in terms of trauma, this is finally because he does not see us in any superior context of meaning and never thinks that our anxieties or conflicts, instead of being mere products of immanent defects in psychological development, might be based on the absence of this context of meaning.[3] His concept of a psychic apparatus thus forces him into a kind of physics of impulse which finds only the operation of an entelechic interplay of psychic powers. According to Görres, a human being is for Freud a hormonally directed impulsive being whose organism as a physico-chemical system is in constant change through processes of material change within it. These changes will necessarily bring disintegration unless there is a regenerative process of breaking down, rebuilding, and renewed breaking down. Every organism has regulative mechanisms that keep the building up and breaking down in balance, so that a unity and totality is maintained and increases. What Freud calls a psychic apparatus depicts us as systems which are characterized by a distinctive regulative mechanism of our own.

This sheds a fresh light on what we think we must call the alienation of psychoanalysis to spirit and its blindness to norms. The idea of a regulative mechanism automatically means that the life of the soul or intellect, and all experience and activity, are simply designed to maintain that balance. Humanity and the human spirit are not the keepers of being, as Heidegger says, but only keepers of that material interplay. Their only task is to be faithful stewards of the claims it makes upon them.

In this light it is understandable why Freud can only interpret conflict negatively—and especially the basic conflict between what we are and what we should be, between concrete reality and meaning. The economy of that material interplay can only cause us to seek the least possible friction in all reflection and aspiration, in all experience and behavior. To put it rather sharply, the only norm is the law of least resistance. We have seen earlier that this law of the conservation of psychological forces, as in America, corresponds strangely to the economy of functionalism which is the goal of the industrial society. According to Freud, desire and happiness describe this state of balance which is free from conflict or tension.

It would be wrong, and in a thinker of this rank absurd, to say that the spirit is necessarily denied in this physics of impulse. Freud claims the spirit in a high measure. In his life, as the book by his doctor recognizes,[4] he hears the claim of an exalted ethos. He could never call the spirit nonexistent. Many quotations could be adduced to show his reverence for it. He can even agree with Aristotle in defining us as rational animals. We must remember, however, that for him the rational consciousness does not have the significance of a directing norm. It is simply a tool which the impulses had to make to satisfy the needs of that interplay of forces which in humans, unlike the rest of nature, cannot achieve the peace of balance without it. Thus spirit, as Görres puts it, is a luxury tool of animal life. This contribution of spirit to life is not in the least contested by Aristotle and his disciples, but with them the service is compared to that of rider and horse. The rider does not serve the horse. The rider is not there for the sake of the horse.

In the instrumental understanding of spirit which is demanded by the psycho-economic model, we find the reason why the concept of God can have only *functional* significance for the development of the state of mental balance. It helps us to achieve an equilibrium of impulses. Under the pressure of danger, depression, or feelings of guilt, we can be like frightened children who are helped by the idea of God when we need protection. The idea of God's forgiving love softens the pressure of guilt complexes. A desire for power is satisfied by the certainty that we enjoy the support of an omnipotent partner. Thus the idea of God can be a means to alleviate impulse-tensions of every kind. God is no more an independent reality than spirit. He has the rank of a projection which serves the conservation of impulses, just as spirit is an instrument which animal life uses in the case of humans because these do not have the automatic self-regulation of animals which are governed by instinct. The life that is laid upon us is too hard, says Freud himself. Hence, to make our lot supportable, we look around for help. This may take forms ranging from primitive intoxication to the more sublime narcotic of religion.[5]

It is connected with Freud's fixation on the impulsive mechanism of the psyche that he never considers the question which we put earlier to Feuerbach's theory of projection and which is brought against Freud in logotherapy. Is there not a perversion here (or, more cautiously expressed, a philosophical presupposition), inasmuch as God is not the original father-image but the human father is an image of God? Might it not be that the father is not the original of all deity but God is the original of all fatherliness? Where does the truth lie, in the discovery of the *anthropomorphism* of the idea of God as a projection of the father-model, or in the confession of the *theomorphism* of reality in whose creaturely features the image of the Creator may be discerned?

5. PSYCHOANALYSIS: WORLD VIEW OR INDIFFERENCE TO WORLD VIEWS?

Naturally the choice between anthropomorphism and theomorphism, between Freudian and Christian anthropology, cannot be made on objective grounds. This is why we intentionally gave it the form of a question. Two confessions confront one another here. The one calls God the original, the other calls him a copy and projection. But we cannot be content simply to break off the dialogue between these two irreconcilable but unverifiable positions. We must make two vital statements.

First, we must emphasize that at this point Freud is *confessing* something. He is operating on a prior axiomatic assumption which is not subject to the criterion of truth. In its presuppositions, then, psychoanalysis is a kind of belief. It is a belief which is ultimately nihilistic inasmuch as it views humanity in terms of its Whence and not its Whither.

The result is that in the Christian debate with Freud we do not have a clash of belief and science but a clash of belief and belief. Jaspers is exaggerating when he says that Freud avoids any philosophical appeal and does not claim to be a prophet. This is true only to the degree that he is not sectarian and does not speak in imperatives (and what a self-contradiction it would be for a psychoanalyst to do that!). In his main works on criticism of religion, *Totem and Taboo* and *The Future of an Illusion,* Freud nails his flag to the mast, just as in his moving correspondence with the Evangelical pastor Oskar Pfister he—ironically—calls himself a "wicked heretic" for whom the Christian circle of ideas is a remote one. Even Jaspers allows that all theories have a tendency to be espoused with the enthusiasm of world views. Thus Freud became the starting point of a world view which went far beyond him and yet was still nourished by his spirit. What lives on and develops here is the confessional character of the axioms which we have tried to establish.

Second, our Christian statement involves more than this reference to Freud's philosophical axioms. Its belief that God is the primary reality and prefigures human fatherhood (instead of vice versa) is in keeping with its anthropological principle of human self-transcendence. Thus the issue is whether humanity is indeed of such a kind that it transcends itself, that it has a relation to the basis, goal, and meaning of existence, and that it must take up some attitude toward this. In the last resort, as we have said, we are naturally an object of faith ourselves inasmuch as the transcendent reference of our existence cannot be objectified. Yet in this human object of faith we have to do with our own most authentic reality, which is constantly required to recognize itself in this picture of a self-transcending being. Even though this picture cannot be verified objectively, it carries with it the claim that it can prove itself to be true in the encounter with life. For this reason we do not have in this object of faith a transcendent authority or the rabid demand of an obligatory dogma.

The question whether and in what sense we are beings who have an open attitude to life along these lines is not considered by Freud (except inasmuch as the possibility of such a question is implicitly rejected). Yet it is only on the basis of this question that the theological statement that God is the final reality and not a projected illusion makes sense. Even what one might describe, in heavy quotes and with tongue in cheek, as "modern nihilism," even Sartre, Camus, and Gottfried Benn, and not just Christians, live by the dogma of self-transcendence. Thus the decisive question to Freud has to be whether his criticism of religion as an illusion does not show that he overlooks or betrays the fundamental reality of human existence. In speaking about heaven, he has to give up his understanding of earth. The evacuation of heaven might well be related to the denial of meaning to those who live on earth. Those who speak about God betray their human secret.

In this sense the final debate is whether Freud has seen true humanity or deals only with alienated humanity, with humanity in its unnatural form. This is the real issue. But this is also a question of phenomenology, of an inalienable regard for reality, and not just a concern of Christian theology. Hence I might say that at this point the theological picture of humanity contains the obvious truth about it from this standpoint.

For this reason Erich Fromm, whom one cannot really claim as a Christian anthropologist, alludes to the decisive question when in his *Analytical Social Psychology and Social Theory*[6] he says that to change the state of those who are afflicted by the sickness of the age, i.e., anxiety and unrest, we must have some conception of what it is like not to be alienated, of what it means to live a life that is centered on being and not on having and using. What he obviously means is that we need an anthropology which does not merely establish negative things (alienation, repression, neurosis) but knows something about the original picture and true being of humanity which goes beyond having and using and functioning.

Fromm is telling us that Freud does not take note of the basic relation to the world and to being. For this reason he has to dissolve the being of humanity in psychological processes and projections. Hence he cannot (and on his premises must not) put the question of truth or fact to his superego as the representative of meaning, norms, and values. He simply explains how the superego comes into being but not whether it has ontic or normative rank, not whether it is based outside us, not whether it is not the product of psychological processes, but is simply reproduced and brought to light. This superego is compromised at once by the fact that one can explain its genesis and thus show that it is a mere product. The diagnosis follows that it is no more than a projection. The original sin of philosophical empiricists, if one will, is that they think that they have explained away a reality if they can explain its genesis. An example may be found in Darwinists (more than Darwin himself) and in Spencer. Explaining the Whence instead of the Whither leads people to miss the anthropological point because it detaches us from the relations that make us subjects of decision. The result is a shockingly one-dimensional understanding of humanity and new neuroses, as Frankl thinks. It is perhaps due to this relationship that the ironical dictum has arisen that psychoanalysis is the sickness it claims to cure.

I know of no more brilliant criticism of this mistaken conception than that of Fromm in his essay on Marx's contribution to anthropology,[7] in which he says that modern academic and experimental psychology is to a large extent a discipline in which alienated researchers are studying alienated people with alienated and alienating methods. Every word is important here:

1. The alienated people who are the objects of this research are those who suffer from boredom, emptiness, and meaninglessness, and are thus subject to neuroses;

2. The alienated researchers are diagnosticians and therapists who begin with a distorted plan of human existence, with the one-dimensional humanity to which we referred, and who find no place in this plan for the ontic question;

3. The alienated methods are procedures which are governed by this wrong anthropology and which claim only the category of the genetic, of empirically observable psychological processes,

and the category of the pragmatic, which looks at people from the standpoint of functional adjustment;

4. The alienating methods, finally, are those which by mistaken diagnosis and therapy intensify and escalate the pathological alienation, leading to what Gertrud von Le Fort, in her story *Das Schweisstuch der Veronika*, calls the "dreadful peace of the psychiatrist."

Though one cannot miss the elements of philosophical atheism in Freud's psychoanalysis, one must be careful when the question arises whether psychoanalysis can be used as an impartial instrument[8] which takes up a neutral attitude toward the beliefs and philosophical positions of patients. The answer would probably be that any form of psychoanalysis of any philosophical provenance must lay partial claim to Freud's discoveries (especially his awareness of the unconscious, some of his teaching on neuroses, and much else). Along these lines Frankl's logotherapy bears clear traces of the Freudian school, though it holds aloof from its philosophical premises, and indeed turns them upside down, since Frankl finds the true and dominant cause of sickness, not in the repression of impulses, which he does not deny, but in the repression of the spirit, in the refusal to tackle the question of meaning, in the elimination of norms and values. Jaspers already had rejected Freud for overlooking this aspect of repression. Nevertheless, though the philosophical banner might change, and the corresponding neutrality of the psychoanalyst might be contested, the issue in every case is repression and the task is to actualize in the consciousness something that lies beneath its threshold. This is obviously an imperishable legacy of psychoanalysis. In view of the possibility of transfer, however, it would be beside the point to speak of the philosophical indifference of psychoanalysis. The different convictions can bear only an eclectic relation to it.

Freud himself hardly gives us any clear data on the issue. If appearances do not deceive, the correspondence with his pastor friend Pfister[9] betrays a marked uncertainty in this matter. His statement that psychoanalysis is an impartial instrument that can be used in the Christian pastorate seems at a first glance to be hardly compatible with his writings in criticism of religion. In one letter he refers to the successful psychoanalytical work of his friend and expresses the conviction that (formally) his therapeutic results have been achieved on the same path "as ours." "But you are in the happy situation," he continues, "of leading on to God and at this one point of restoring the happier condition of earlier days in which religious belief stifled neuroses." In itself psychoanalysis is neither religious nor the opposite, but an impartial instrument which both pastors and lay people can use so long as they do it to liberate sufferers. Freud is struck by the fact that he himself has given no thought to the extraordinary assistance that the psychoanalytical method can give to pastoral counseling. He has overlooked this because this whole sphere is so distant from him as a "wicked heretic."

Did Freud really make the philosophical impartiality of psychoanalysis believable? Could he not make this admission to his friend even while retaining his atheistic reservations, which did not just accompany psychoanalysis but had their origin in it? Do we really have to assume that he was under the impression that God might be a reality because his friend Pfister could champion him in spite of psychoanalysis? Freud seems to have thought that faith in God, which, without irony, he described as the "happier condition of earlier days," could act as creative therapy vis-à-vis neuroses. But could it not have produced this effect even if it was an illusion? How many illusions have achieved notorious power in history and released all kinds of forces and counterforces! One need only think of the role of utopias. And might it not be medically required to conceal the severity of a sickness so as to lighten the momentary burden by the illusion of hope and bring patients across the critical threshold by the mobilizing of their vital powers? Freud did not have to retract anything of his atheism to be able to laud in this way the belief in God.

Just because belief in Freud's view vacillates between being a pathological symptom and a possible means of therapy, just because it may have a helping function, Freud the doctor does not want his patients to "analyze away" any belief in God they have. He cultivates the tolerance that he advocates. If psychoanalysis shows that in a given case belief has a therapeutic function and is not a traumatic derailment of the superego, he deals with his patients, it seems to me, along the lines of H. Vaihinger's philosophy of "as if," acting as if this function were right, as those in "happier days" assumed.

But can Freud seriously think that patients do not see through the "as if" game of their therapist? They must have had very little skill in discerning spirits (1 Corinthians 12:10) and had a very superficially conventional faith if they could be credited with this degree of blindness. Would not more sensitive patients have noted

Freud's own uncertainty as this came to light in his vacillating understanding of faith?

Is it true, then, that psychoanalysis can be used untruncated in various philosophical situations? Is it really an impartial instrument?[10] Did not even Pfister have to proceed eclectically, along the lines mentioned, when he—successfully—united psychoanalysis and pastoral counseling? Did he really—we do not know—subordinate the repression of the spirit to the repression of impulses, as his master obviously did? As a disciple of Freud he was certainly concerned as a therapist to eliminate the Oedipus distortion of faith in God, its degeneration into a "father" complex. But unlike Freud, he could do so as a pastor only by trying, in the name of the true God who has appeared in Christ, to topple the popular idol, not by eliminating faith itself as the root of all evil. The true God is appealed to here as the normative factor. This appeal is the decisive means whereby to unmask the traumatic perversion and pathological excesses and thus to differentiate between the original organ and the cancerous cells.

Can psychoanalysis pass unchanged—a neutral construct—through this kind of filter? Freud does not tell us in what he writes to Pfister. He remains the prophet, although fortunately without the gestures and zeal that we usually associate with prophets.

Perhaps another note may also be heard—that of uncertainty in face of what his friend believed and the nature of what he called his "happy situation." A breath of self-doubt may possibly waft through these letters—doubt about his anthropomorphic conception, doubt whether the image of God is produced or reproduced. Those who stand under the impress of the ethos in whose name Freud lived (as the recollections of his doctor movingly illustrate) can hardly imagine that he found the normative criterion of his life only in the fiction of his superego.

But it would be idle and speculative, and perhaps even lacking in taste, to continue guessing in this way and to subject Freud himself to a more than questionable psychoanalytical test.[11] However that may be, self-transcending humanity resists all the one-dimensionality that is ascribed to it. One form of this resistance—along with many others—is the logotherapy of Viktor Frankl. All the same, the unconscious that Freud discovered will still find a place in all future anthropology.

d. Transcending of the One-Dimensional Character of Psychoanalysis by the Logotherapy of Viktor Frankl[12]

1. THE CRITICAL STARTING POINT:
AGAINST THE REDUCTION OF HUMANITY

Frankl takes self-transcendence seriously. He is thus an incomparably fruitful partner in the debate between psychology and theology.[13] His new point of departure is historically conditioned. He begins by presupposing that our frustration today is no longer *sexual*, as in Freud's time, but *existential*. To a large extent we find ourselves in an existential vacuum which manifests itself in despair as to the meaning of life, in the failure to find any Whither for it, in emptiness and boredom.

As many writers from the Soviet sphere affirm, this sickness is widespread.[14] The loss of meaning among young people leaps unasked across the boundaries of the capitalist and socialist orders of society. It is a universal syndrome. Frankl recalls that Paul Polak foresaw this development in 1947 when he said that the solution of social problems will really free and mobilize the spiritual problem. Only then will we study ourselves correctly and recognize our real problem.

Our liberation from many of the basic worries of life in the welfare state has been a tremendously fruitful one, even though it has brought its own challenges. We now have time and available energy to confront ourselves. We have to put up with ourselves. We are in a state of collective relaxation such as we know on vacations when we are exhausted by our jobs. This relaxation may be challenged, of course, by the ghosts of unmastered things which everyday stress normally holds at bay. As Ernst Bloch says, when we are alone and undirected we are afflicted by the anxieties that we otherwise experience only at the hour of death.

This is perhaps one of the essential reasons for the bigger generation gap which became evident during the student revolt in the sixties. The older generation has lived through one or even two world wars. It has known the terror of the Hitler period and its aftermath. It was so occupied with the elemental needs of life that it had no time to experience an inner vacuum. At any rate, external worries hardly caused any internal pain. Hence this generation was poorly equipped to do justice to the demands of young people who, brought up in the comfort of restored civilization and under the protection of many caring hands, had unabsorbed energies at their disposal with which to face the questions of the basis and meaning of existence. What they could not receive from the earlier generation—or could do so only in much too niggardly a form—was experience of an answer to these questions, or an answer made credible by experience. They naturally found a vacuum here, or tried to force their way to an answer in dramatic ways. This exposed them to utopias and the resultant fanaticism. They were helpless in face of demagogic speeches. All this is understandable. Yet it would be ungenerous of older people to lecture the young with the pharisaical argument that they are sowing their wild oats because life is too easy for them, and that they should take an example from those who have survived disaster and destruction and done the work of rebuilding.

Who finally have the harder time and experience the greater torment—those who struggle to survive or those who despair of life—is a question we cannot decide, but it really is a *question*. A Dutchman, who was both witty and candid, perhaps hit on the truth when he told the rebels in Amsterdam, "You have no problems—*that* is your problem." To have no problems because external problems are solved and internal ones are so hopeless that we suppress them, or flee from them into an imaginary world of drugs, can be a more tormenting state than that of hunger or fear of overnight bombing. A generation which in spite of the severity of what it has been through has never suffered from frustration through boredom or lack of challenges must be on guard against pharisaical arrogance.

The observation that the basic questions of existence break out all the more vehemently when there is greater social security is one of the things that helped a psychiatrist like Frankl to see the relevance of these questions for his own field and to find in them realities and not just projections of existence. Thus there developed in Frankl, through innumerable conversations with his patients, a strengthened conviction that there are noogenic as well as psychogenic neuroses, i.e., neuroses which arise in the realm of the spirit through loss of meaning or disruptions in the process of self-transcendence. Along these lines, too, there can be complexes which develop through repression of the spirit.

This loss of meaning is connected essentially with what Frankl calls reductionism. He means by this the intellectual situation which reduces us to a present, objectifiable, and therefore one-dimensional reality. Psychoanalysis is for him a symptom of this one-sidedness, but by way of a chain reaction it also brings about an intensification of it. The process of anthropological reduction comes to expression in a recurrent phrase: "Humanity is nothing but . . ." Life is nothing but a process of burning up, of oxydation; values are "nothing but defense mechanisms and reaction formations" (in an American journal); "humanity is nothing but a biochemical mechanism fed by a system which energizes computers."

When Frankl gives examples of reductionism, his spontaneous reaction to them is an important force in the production of his new conception. He was never prepared, he tells us, to live for the sake of reaction formations or to die on account of defense mechanisms. Borderline situations which test us to the uttermost, which are a matter of life or death, usually have the ability to bring out realities and unmask fictions as mere shams. When Frankl puts the question of life and death, the reductionism experienced in his dissatisfaction involuntarily becomes for him a plea for the question of meaning which reductionism discards. It is one of the hard, exposed realities which cannot be explained as mere emanations of the superego.

Typical is the way that Frankl reacts to the reductionistic statement that we are nothing but computers. We are indeed computers, but we are also infinitely more. The works of Goethe and Kant are made up of the twenty-six letters of the alphabet like those of Hedwig Courths-Mahler and E. Marlitt, but this is of very little importance. The *Critique of Pure Reason* cannot just be called a collection of the same letters as Marlitt's *Das Geheimnis der alten Mamsell*. The extra quality in the works of Goethe and Kant, over and above the quantity of letters, is the nonobjective meaning or content or form of expression. The same self-transcendence may be seen in our works as in ourselves.

2. THE SIGNIFICANCE OF THE QUESTION OF MEANING IN EXISTENTIAL ANALYSIS

If in a psychological view of humanity the issue is that of the meaning that we give ourselves by self-transcendence, we have to realize that meaning cannot be provided or ordered simply because we need it for therapeutic reasons. This would challenge again the reality of meaning and threaten to bring us back to the philosophy of "as if" that we observed in Freud. As the internist stimulates the glandular system, so the therapeutist would be stimulating the superego to produce certain hormones of meaning. But because meaning, as a nonobjective reality, can neither be objectified nor manufactured, it cannot be ordered. Trying to give or order meaning along these lines would lead, Frankl thinks, to moralizing. And morality in the older sense will soon be played out. In the future we shall no longer moralize; we shall ontologize morality.

What does this mean? Negatively it means that morality cannot be reduced to casuistic definitions of what we ought to do or not do. In the sense of Pauline theology, this is a legalistic understanding of morality. It involves compulsion. In contrast, an ontologized morality will regard as good that which is required by the fulfillment of the meaning that is laid upon a being and demanded of it, and it will regard as bad that which restricts such fulfillment.

It is certainly no accident that this definition of ontology reminds us of Anselm, for whom everything has its place in the order of being and meets the claim of right and wrong only by achieving its relation and thus achieving meaning. Thus the truth (and goodness) of fire is that it burns. The same type of claim is met by us as we relate ourselves to God as the final cause.

In ontologized morality, then, the terms "good" and "evil" are identical with "meaningful" and "meaningless." They can be defined only as we relate our existence to being itself and fit ourselves into a comprehensive framework. This framework is what is given. It has, as it were, ontological priority. For Frankl, then, we cannot "give" meaning. This would be in conflict with that priority. Our task can only be to "find" meaning.

But if meaning is not under our control, but has to be found, this means that it may also be withheld. The question what happens then is an important one for therapists. For essentially, as Carl G. Jung recognized in his practice, they have to deal with people in this situation. Since existence in meaninglessness is painful, there are at work in those who can neither find it nor invent it forces which drive them into flight from the tormenting sense of meaninglessness. In this flight they try to find surrogates for lost meaning. Surrogates of this kind are diversion and dissipation, which try to cover over inner disintegration with the help of outward attractions, to fill up the vacuum with imports. Other surrogates may be found in the production of nonsense (as in the theater of the absurd) or in the attempt to extend or muffle the consciousness in intoxication,[15] which is supposed to create "subjective meaning."

LSD shows that this subjective meaning is not only a surrogate for the true meaning that has been lost but simply makes the night of meaninglessness even darker and alienates us even further from real tasks in the outside world, from the demand for life and work that are full of meaning. Frankl said that it always reminded him of the research animals in which scientists placed electrodes. Whenever the circuit was closed, the animals experienced satisfaction, whether of sex or appetite. They finally learned to close the circuit themselves, and they then ignored the real sex partners and food that they were offered. They lived remote from life. Exactly the same thing is done by many who evade confrontation with real life and the challenge of meaning, withdrawing to the sphere of an imaginary or surrogate life, whether through pot or in the form of utopias.

If our modern sickness is that of existential frustration, of being trapped in the futility of meaninglessness, then education, as a kind of therapeutic prevention, must have as its primary goal our liberation for responsibility. Responsibility means relating ourselves to our Whither, seeking our true being, appropriating our humanity. The opposite is being content to be the mere plaything of outward attractions or a mere function of the spirit of the age. One might say that education for responsibility is largely identical with education for emancipation, at least to the degree that we must achieve autonomy in relation to the outside world. We take our ontic rank seriously only when we do not merge into our environment or yield to its claims without choosing.

In this regard the contemporary background again proves to be a motive force behind logotherapeutic considerations. For some of the basic tendencies of our age oppose the legitimate task of liberation—a term we do better to avoid in view of its fashionable misuse!—for they involve us in a confusing and intensive mass of claims and thus try to absorb us into themselves.

Frankl illustrates these claims by the attractions provided by the mass media and the pill.

If humanity is more than the enclosed entelechy of the individual, if it has a reference to being and hence to a place in the nexus of all being, it is obvious that the chief threat to humanity arises at this point. For the danger of outward distraction, if we yield to it, threatens to destroy our place in being. Since nature abhors a vacuum, it is evident that this danger increases as the growing lack of meaning leaves a vacuum in the psyche. Indeed, in the form of a chain reaction we then evacuate the psyche even more. We repress the spirit and its receptivity to the claims of meaning in order to make room for the imports from the outward world.

How are we to counteract these destructive tendencies therapeutically?

Certainly not by bombarding our threatened contemporaries with purely moral appeals to pay heed to the question of meaning. They have already immunized themselves against the claim of the human. Under the spell of attractions they have lost their sense of this and are no longer in a position to listen. This is why the therapeutic prevention that education can give must come earlier. In face of the confusing pluralism of attractions and claims and possibilities, it must teach us how to choose, how to be selective. The ethical task is not to fight against attractions but to choose the one to which to expose ourselves. If we are not to perish in the flood of attractions, in total promiscuity (which the pill makes possible), we must learn to distinguish what is essential and what is not, what has meaning and what does not, what demands response and what does not.

For the moment, Frankl thinks, there are only some preliminary signs that we are beginning to see this. He finds such signs in the many acts of protest, especially on the part of young people. But usually the protesters are simply lashing out blindly without having any positive model of humanity in the name of which to make their protest. It is undoubtedly one of the tasks of therapy to bring to light the hidden and suppressed theme of the human as both a gift and a task.

3. THE QUESTION OF THE PHILOSOPHICAL NEUTRALITY OF LOGOTHERAPY

Readers will perhaps have expected us already to put to logotherapy the question that we put to Freud, namely, whether this existential analysis and its dominant question of meaning have to be tied to some philosophy or whether they can be "impartial"—which we doubted in Freud's case. Does not the answering of the question of meaning demand some philosophical or religious commitment? And if so, can therapists be neutral toward other views of meaning that they might find in their patients? Will they not rather see themselves as missionaries or pastoral counselors who, to be objective, will certainly avoid indoctrination, but will not refrain from saying on what basis they speak. Not refraining means imparting or suggesting. One might argue that this is legitimate on the ground that counselors are full of the conviction that they can offer nothing more helpful than that which they have found to be a cure for themselves.

We must examine this question more closely. Freud regarded values, meaning, and norms as projections of the superego and thus interpreted the mere occurrence of the question of meaning as a sign of sickness. Frankl, however, begins with the reality of the normative. His task with patients, then, is either to free this lost and repressed reality or to eliminate its neurotic excesses (e.g., in the form of the Oedipus complex). He has to deal with either too little on the one side or too much on the other. But the philosophical question arises again at this point. Can one speak neutrally about the normative court of conscience? Can one do so especially when, like Frankl, one knows so much about its relativity and fallibility? Can one speak about responsibility without saying what it implies?

These questions seem indeed to be open ones. Though Frankl himself does not say so, I can imagine patients looking for psycho- or logotherapists whose personal convictions are in tune with their own system of values. There will then be a common basis which will mean that conviction need not be challenged from the outset and the organ itself as well as the cancerous growth regarded as the root of all evil (as religion was for Freud). This might be true at least for patients who are not harassed by a nihilistic vacuum but suffer from distortions of some conviction already present. In a sphere which involves such intimacy as psychotherapy, and which thus relies on communication between patient and therapist, I find it hard to imagine how there can be any fruitful therapy without this basic consensus.

Frankl himself seems to have no worries on this score, and one has to grant that he has arguments from experience that nonexperts do not have. In answer to the question of philosophical impartiality he advances the motto which is quoted at the beginning of this book, namely, that no psychiatrist or psychotherapist—or even logotherapist—can tell sick people what the meaning is, only that life has a meaning, and that it has this in every condition and circumstance, thanks to the possibility of finding meaning in suffering.

Frankl is certainly right when he finds one of the most striking differences between humans and animals in the fact that humans can suffer ethically. This is the decisive argument against some of the postulates of euthanasia and mercy killing. Yet we enter a jungle of open questions at this point.[16] Is there a degree of suffering that cannot be mastered by reflection, so that the question of meaning is excluded? Is there a degree of mental primitiveness which is immune to logotherapy? Finally, does not the conversation of the three friends with Job show that one might postulate meaning and still fail to find it? Job does not find salvation by coming to see a meaning that is already there but when he is told what meaning it is. This answer is beyond the competence that Frankl ascribes to the therapist.

What Frankl means by the givenness of meaning may be seen from his illustrations. Thus he spoke to some hardened criminals in a prison near San Francisco, including some who had been sentenced to death. He told them that the experience of value in very simple people had helped him to see how this was related to the meaning of life and work and love and, last but not least, suffering bravely borne. The inmates understood him.

Two features, it seems to me, are particularly important here.

First, Frankl assumes that there is a naive sense of meaning in simple people, without going into the question in which philosophical systems of coordinates it occurs. In one case it may obviously be the product of sound common sense, in another it may be Christian, in yet another it may be produced by ideology. Frankl leaves all this on one side, not even mentioning it once. In so careful a thinker this has to mean that he deliberately excludes such systems because they are not essential to therapy. His task is simply to express the fact of meaning, to free it from the rubble, and then to let the patient give it its special nuance, whether by understanding it in terms of some ethics or meeting it in the concealment of the Nevertheless of Christian faith. Does this support the neutrality of logotherapy? The second feature will show how hard it is to give an unequivocal answer.

Second, when Frankl addressed the prisoners in San Francisco, he tells us that they listened to him closely because he himself had once been close to the gas chamber. In telling them this, he undoubtedly wanted to establish solidarity at a critical point. He had not only been in an extreme borderline situation but in this situation he had seen himself confronted by the task of answering the question of meaning. The theme of meaning arose for him in face of open meaninglessness and even the contradiction of meaning. He thus regarded himself as a credible witness to this audience for the possibility of not repressing the question of meaning even in such situations but of facing it and even finding an answer.

Naturally this solidarity is very helpful. It awakens trust and meets the demand for communication in therapy. But is it conceivable unless Frankl tells the convicts how he *personally* dealt with the question of meaning, where he found the meaning that enabled him to survive the terrors of that period? We can hardly think so. But in going beyond the mere fact of meaning and becoming *personal*, is he not imposing his own convictions and crossing the border that is obviously set for the doctor's competence?

The example is a little sharp, for a prison address is not professional therapy. If, rather boldly, we transfer it to the doctor's office, we can imagine that there would have been restraints. Frankl would have nailed his colors to the mast, but only in the sense of the *fact* that one can find a way to meaning even in extreme friction, and in so doing one can have courage to tread the same path within the framework of one's own convictions.

If I understand Frankl aright, logotherapy takes us only to this point. This means that it has a Socratic tendency. It does not aim to indoctrinate patients philosophically but to set free what is repressed and covered over in them, to eliminate what is excessive, and to straighten what is crooked. An express confession would then be relevant only to the degree that the doctor says that he himself has tested the matter, so that he is not like a blind person speaking about colors with no existential experience, but recognizes some solidarity with the patient. The Socratic element here lies in the claim to the patient that the temptation of transference can be avoided and there can be cooperation in forming the patient's own convictions instead of simply copying those of the therapist.

These considerations bring us to the zone that Freud forbade us to enter. In our concern to understand Frankl, we have put questions that he himself does not raise. But we had to put them if we were to deal with the anthropological background of logotherapy. It is of the very essence of this approach that it necessarily raises the question of conviction and commitment, though not of the content of the conviction and commitment.

In illustration of Frankl's Socratic procedure whereby he does not enforce his own views but helps patients within their own structures of life and thought, I may refer to a passage in his recollections.[17] Thus he tells us about two men in the concentration camp who were resolved on suicide, using the stock phrase that they had "nothing more to expect from life." He had to produce in them a kind of Copernican revolution so that they would no longer ask what to expect from life but what life expected from them, namely, that someone or something, a person or a work, was still there for them. It soon seemed that life was, in fact, expecting specific tasks from them. One was publishing a series of geographical texts, but this was not yet complete. The other had a daughter abroad who idolized him. A work was waiting for the one, a person for the other. Here we see vividly what Frankl meant when he said that no single, universally valid meaning can be prescribed but there is a fact of meaning which will take different forms for each of us. All these forms are related by a transcendent factor which is proper only to humans. In distinction from animals, we humans can hope. We can anticipate the future. We know how to love and be loved. Awareness of meaning can make life supportable even in borderline situations. This corresponds to the wisdom of a saying of Nietzsche that Frankl quotes: "Those who have a Why in life can put up with almost any How."

4. CRITICISM OF FREUD IN THE LIGHT OF LOGOTHERAPY

The marked difference of this view from that of Freud is obvious. It raises the question of reality that Freud regards as merely a projection of the superego. If healing is a bringing back to order, a return to true identity, to what existence ought to be, it is in the last resort a mistake to suppress this goal and theme of healing by degrading the self-transcendence that is laid upon us in the name of meaning, by treating it as a ghostly projection, as a self-posited superego.

We confront here the question of the truth of human existence. The psychology that is so prevalent today is so destructive, and as a rule accepts so complacently innumerable breaches of taboos and a freedom which is not directed by any meaning—one need only think of the attractive word "liberation"—precisely because it suppresses this question of truth. In this connection we should note again the profound saying of Fromm that alienated researchers are treating alienated people with alienated and alienating methods. One can only ask with concern what new Caudine yoke these psychological engineers will impose on people who are already suffering from alienation.

We may sum up the change that logotherapy signalizes as follows. It is to be regarded as an answer to the challenge of Freud's psychoanalysis and it is thus related to this both by continuing and contradicting it.

Freud's anthropology, as we have seen, is characterized by reduction. It limits the self to a bundle of impulsive energies which create successful or unsuccessful self-regulations in the consciousness.

It is worth noting that, since this reduction misses the truth about humanity, the suppressed dimensions of human reality come to light in contradictory and incompatible anthropological statements. I will mention two of these incompatibilities.

(1) We have referred already to Max Scheler's criticism of Freud. To Freud's thesis that the impulsive energies are censored and then repressed or sublimated by the superego, Scheler puts the critical question who or what it really is that does the censoring. Or, more sharply, who or what is it that sets up this censorship in the ego? Freud—necessarily—does not answer this question. The gap points to a contradiction that cannot be resolved on his view. For, as Frankl says, one cannot derive the repressing, censoring, and sublimating court from the impulses; these provide the material to be repressed, not the court to do the repressing. Frankl offers a surprisingly simple formula for this contradiction. It has never yet happened, he says, that a river sets up its own power station.

(2) The second fundamental contradiction in Freud is this. On the one side he stresses the impotence of the conscious ego, which is driven by the id, hampered by the superego, and repulsed by reality. As the psychosomatist Paul Christian says, the greatest part of the soul is unconscious, alone, and unrecognized. It is an elemental being deep within us. Ideas, acts, and thoughts are essentially determined by the unconscious, by forces deep down. What is done and thought and said at the human level is only in the foreground. Being only on the phenomenological level, it is improper. It merely represents the unconscious struggles between the id and the superego.

Nevertheless—and this is the contradiction—there is no proof in Freud of any predetermination by fate or biology. That he does not advance any such proof but even argues against predetermination may be seen in the premise of psychoanalytical therapy. Therapy can help patients to know themselves and to choose who they will be. This responsible choice presupposes the freedom that Freud claimed for himself in his research. But this freedom was not for him an object of scientific research. It could not be so, for it would have raised at once the theme of self-transcendence, the question of the Why and Wherefore of this freedom. This theme had no place in Freud's reduced anthropology or in the epistemological tasks limited by this reduction.

The contradiction that I want to exhibit comes out plainly here. Freedom of choice was not an object of scientific research, and could not be so, but it was the precondition of this research. Freud simply claimed it without thinking much about it. If he had done so, he would have been led to the absurd thesis that he would have had to regard his own psychoanalytical work as a mere projection of his unconscious while still trying to confront this unconscious in undetermined freedom and to bring it under control. To use again the metaphor of Frankl, he could hardly assume that the river of his own impulsive energies had produced the power station of psychoanalytical theory. At this point Freud "believed" without being able to verify what he believed and without even realizing what his premises were. He "believed" in the power of reason and its ability to free us from superstition and the production of illusions.

5. DOCTORS AND PASTORS AND THE SUBJECT OF ANTHROPOLOGY

In these contradictions dimensions of the ego appear which are veiled by psychoanalysis and even repressed by it. There comes to light the phenomenon that we have expected, namely, that human totality asserts itself against one-dimensional truncation. Frankl makes himself the advocate of this totality in his concern for a psychology of the spirit and not just the soul, as in his medical counseling. The psychotherapist daily confronts philosophical questions which have to do with the meaning of life and with the denial of meaning or the failure to find it. Out of philosophical fairness we have to arm ourselves with the same weapons. Doctors who are versed in epistemology will refuse to prescribe an arsenic cure for people wrestling with spiritual despair. With the help of a psychotherapy that is oriented to the spirit, they will try to provide their patients with spiritual support, to find a spiritual anchor for them.

Logotherapy takes "logos" seriously, i.e., the sphere of truth, value, meaning, and conscience. It reckons with the fact that mental illnesses, e.g., neuroses, might have their basis in unsuccessful wrestlings with the sphere of logos, or even with its repression. Negatively, this means that it refuses to slip psychologistically into inadequate criticism and heterologous argument such as occurs when, e.g., feelings of guilt or despair, or even philosophical difficulties, are diagnosed at once as the result of complexes and are thus robbed of their own worth, of their own specific weight. Instead, doctors must engage in an immanent discussion of philosophical questions and enter into a spiritual debate with those who are suffering at the spiritual level. This means that the spirit must be distinguished from the soul or psyche. It must not be psychologically or psychopathologically derived from the psyche. We have here two different spheres. The world of the spirit is a world apart whose nature and values cannot be psychologistically projected onto the psychological level. Hence logotherapy seeks to engage in existential analysis as an analysis of humanity in responsibility.

As we said in our section on the ontologizing of ethics, the resultant obligation must not become a legalistic demand. It is to be understood in terms of the meaning that it claims. The question of meaning can overpower us in all its radicalness, e.g., in puberty. One of its pathological forms is ethical nihilism, which maintains that pleasure, and the securing of pleasure, is the whole point of life. This leads morally to a leveling down of all goals and hence to indifference, apathy, and a damaging boredom. From this standpoint it does not matter what we do. The giving of money to charities might serve to remedy the absence of pleasure just as much as the giving of the same money to culinary enjoyment. Since all life is confronted by death, all pleasure is meaningless. Frankl makes it plain in this way that a one-dimensional reduction of humanity to pleasure and impulse brings down upon itself the revenge of a betrayal and damaging of the dimension of values, e.g., the value of meaning itself. This revenge then takes a psychopathological form.

If we take the world of values seriously and do not merely treat it as the result of psychological processes, some important conclusions follow for the therapeutic attitude of doctors. They must enter into an immanent philosophical debate about meaning with their patients. They must show them that they may be determined by meaning even in relation to an irreversibly reduced (an incurably sick or crippled) life. We must give those who are condemned to die, says Frankl, the chance to die their own deaths (the "great death" of Rainer Maria Rilke), i.e., to fill their life with meaning up to the very last moment, even though the question may be how sufferers will face their sufferings at this supreme and final point. It need hardly be pointed out that we have here an argument against suicide and euthanasia as solutions.

In this connection Frankl refers to a psychologically sound person who was about to commit suicide but was cured of this intention when another doctor showed him that he had a wrong view of freedom. He knew only freedom "from" and not freedom "for," but with a right understanding of freedom he would not be able to throw his life away. Frankl ends this story by asking who of us can deny that this doctor was not only justified in dealing with his patient in this traditionally not very "medical" way but was in fact obligated to do so.

At this point doctors are again in that final solidarity with their patients, vis-à-vis questions of human destiny, to which we have referred already. They are not dealing with them as driven people over against whom they stand in superior detachment. They are treating them as they do themselves, as people who relate to themselves, and are summoned to do so.

One might describe as follows the final implication of the position of doctors as Frankl proclaims it. The nervous specialists to whom people are going in droves instead of to their pastors must also be *pastors*. They must be persons who are in solidarity with their patients regarding the question of meaning. Otherwise this exodus to secular counselors will have destructive effects.

Frankl, then, arrives at the idea of medical counseling, at a metaclinical interpretation of suffering, at existential analysis as an ontological explication of personal existence, and finally at a psychotherapeutic picture of humanity.

What he has in view is the personal union of priest and doctor, of pastor and psychotherapist, or at least their cooperation inasmuch as they ultimately work in the same dimension. If I understand Frankl aright, this common dimension is not one of common faith in the narrower sense, e.g., a common denominational confession. It is that of the recognition that there is a dimension of values and norms, that existential and social conflicts—and to that extent the dimension of faith—are taken seriously. Negatively this agreement is characterized by the fact that destructive conflicts are not just interpreted psychologically but are regarded as an unmastered wrestling with some true reality.

For the rest, there can be no doubt that Frankl—taken as the representative of a new type of psychotherapy—has mastered all the techniques of analysis and therapy and at this level does his work in much the same way as the Freudian analyst. (To that extent he can be "eclectic," in the sense mentioned, vis-à-vis Freudian analysis.) For Frankl, however, the thing that matters is the sign under which, and the framework within which, one does all this. This framework embraces the picture of a humanity that grasps itself, transcends itself, and is oriented to responsibility.

Without this picture, everything is *falsified*, for therapy has no goal. As education is not just a matter of skillful didactic manipulation or of techniques in dealing with people, but has in view something for which education is given, so the aim is normative in psychotherapy too. Without a guiding plan of humanity, psychology is destructive and simply promotes the neuroses it intends to fight, and may even become an expression of these neuroses. I believe that we are witnesses of this melancholy spectacle to an extraordinary degree today.

But can doctors measure up to the claims that Frankl makes for them? We must not overlook the seriousness of this question. These doctors have not only to be very good medically, especially in psychiatry and neurology, having a full command of the art of healing, but they must also be "wise," having reflected on the ultimate problems of life, and wrestled with them in person. They must also be motivated by solidarity with their patients and hence, as we may quietly say as Christians, by *love*.

One can hardly maintain that modern doctors, especially psychologists with their traditional training, are even approximately qualified to fill the bill. An important task of curricular reform is posed here. Where no chairs exist in the field, the hour demands that arrangements be made to teach medical anthropology and ethics. The need here is for interdisciplinary and interfaculty studies, since anthropology spills over into every area (even into such very modern disciplines as information theory and computer technology). Thus budding doctors need to be brought into touch with philosophy and theology. Theology for its part needs to know the essentials of psychotherapy, at least to the extent that these will enable it to recognize its own limits and be an able partner in the dialogue between psychotherapy and pastoral counseling. The imperious demand is that our universities should reenter the lost terrain of general studies in order to see again the anthropological affinity of all the sciences and to put the question of meaning. The dialogue between psychotherapy and pastoral counseling is only one example of what is required.

II. HUMANITY IN SELF-TRANSCENDENCE (TEILHARD DE CHARDIN) [18]

a. Sketch of Teilhard's View

1. TEILHARD AS A REPRESENTATIVE OF CONTEMPORARY QUESTIONS

Hardly a single representative of the intellectual world—and certainly no theologian—has in the last decades exerted such a fascination in educated circles as the Jesuit paleontologist Teilhard de Chardin. Scientists, or at least some of them, object that he weakens his exact findings by metaphysical speculations. The cardinals in Rome, or at least many of them, fault him for integrating Christian dogma into evolutionary theory, for changing it thereby, and for thus bordering on heresy. Many of his works have still not been published and lie in the mausoleum of Paris archives.

It is a temptation at this point to tell the story of Teilhard's life, and especially his scientific travels, so as to give some impression how profoundly his thought is related to the drama of his personal existence. But necessity compels us to plunge at once into the material and to choose as a starting point the question what makes his thought so fascinating. Two suggestions might be made in answer.

First, the unrest of the younger generation is due not least of all to the fact that it finds the unity of life broken. On the one side it sees the steady progress of the sciences and their technological application. It sees the developing rule of computers and the increasing mechanical and material exclusion of the soul. It sees the dreadful possibilities of biological manipulation. It sees ecological problems and the threat posed by means of mass destruction. It realizes that the future which is menaced in this way is its own future. The resultant question—we have touched on it before—is whether we are humanly a match for what we know theoretically and can do technologically.

Can we master these things in the name of some superior meaning? Or will we be helplessly trampled by technological developments? Is there not a sinister cleft between our ability to master the world and our inability to be "human"? Teilhard, however, offers us a new and grandiose framework which holds these two contrary things together. This is why we listen to him.

The second reason for his fascination is related to the first.

The cleavage in the world makes fear of the future a widespread sickness of the age. An unknown X, which comes to expression in many shock utopias, seems to be creeping up on us. Teilhard, however, offers a view of the world in which the future is the time of fulfillment. God's government of the world sees no recall of creation; on the contrary, it is leading what is created to its fulfillment. At the end there will be an epiphany of meaning, traces of which may be detected even now by those who are open to them. Natural science in particular is helpful in pointing us already to this movement of God toward the future. If a scientist and thinker of the rank of Teilhard can counter our concern about the future with such hopeful diagnoses, we are ready eagerly to accept his consoling message.

2. TEILHARD'S AIM: SYNTHESIS OF SCIENCE AND FAITH

One of Teilhard's concerns is what one might call a theodicy of life. All of us need something to justify life. Such justification demands proof that it will not be lost in nothingness but converges on some superior meaning. What use is it knowing details and their sum if we do not understand the whole? As a paleontologist Teilhard has to do with exact facts and findings—the details—but these are "symbolical" for him, that is, they are ciphers for a universal meaning which embraces all life, even pre-life, and especially human life. Even more, this universal meaning first achieves self-consciousness in the noosphere of the human brain.

Teilhard has a second concern. A science that does not stop at objectifiable details but thinks symbolically, and thus gives objects their meaning, impinges on the intentions of religion. For obviously there is an impartation of meaning in every religious statement. Creation itself implies a meaningful plan of the world whose structure withstands, and indeed includes, all opposing evil and accident. Human thinking, planning, and acting may assume that they can intercept and autonomously replace the idea of creation. But in truth they are foreseen in this plan. They involuntarily become an instrument and must finally serve the aims of the Lord of history. "You meant evil against me," said Joseph to his brethren, "but God meant it for good" (Genesis 50:20). A scientist who thinks within the framework of a structured world nexus of this kind represents in personal union the functions of both knowledge and faith. At any rate, this is how he understands his calling.

In seeking such a synthesis, Teilhard has necessarily to fight a war on two fronts.

His scientific colleagues object that he is saying more than is objectively verifiable and that this extra element is not well defined. The border is indeed a fluid one, if it is not erased altogether, because for Teilhard the process of knowledge does not involve a first act, in which we say, "Here are the exact facts," and then a second one, in which we say, "This is my interpretation; here are the symbolical and transcendental elements; you must accept the facts but you may ignore the interpretation." The situation is in fact very different, for the constructive nexus is there already before Teilhard ever begins. Inevitably, then, this system of coordinates helps to determine what the facts are that are ordered within it. For the initial hypothesis has to have an impact not only on the secondary interpretation of the facts but also on the facts themselves and their arrangement.

It works selectively. Along these lines Jakob Burckhardt and Karl Marx, for example, not only offer different interpretations of Greek antiquity but their different philosophical presuppositions cause them to see different facts and to arrive at a different arrangement of what is dominant and what is mere consequence.

Objections are made on the ecclesiastical and religious side as well. Does not the attempt to hold a consistent doctrine of evolution, to advocate this theologically, to reconcile Darwin and Aquinas, carry with it an attack on the doctrine of creation? Does not Adam, for example, cease to be "the first man" in whom—as regards creation and the fall—the destiny of the whole race is prefigured? In the eyes of science, says Teilhard, totalities and not individualities are seen in the distant past. Hence the first man is inevitably a group. One has only to contrast this with the encyclical of Pius XII, "*Humani generis*" (1950), to appreciate what a dogmatic disaster Teilhard seems to be heading for. Here the interpretation of Adam as a group is rejected as polygenism, the main argument being that if all of us do not descend from the one Adam, the doctrine of original sin is impossible. (Original sin is rather naively construed here as inherited sin, which cannot be harmonized with Teilhard's thinking.)

But we shall return to the theological problems later. For the moment I want to give some impression of the way that Teilhard's spirit is contested in the two spheres. "It is not surprising to me that he sees demons," says Conrad Ferdinand Meyer about Ulrich von Hutten, whose spirit was similarly embattled. Perhaps Teilhard sees them too. But he does not notice them in those who oppose him. (In relation to his secular colleagues he is confessional and argumentative; to Rome he submits in all humility.) If it is a matter of demons, he finds them especially where faith and science are put in opposition, where this schizophrenia in our consciousness no longer causes any pain, where there is no understanding that Teilhard's spirit is dominated by an irresistible demand for organic unity and coherence.

For Teilhard a cosmic sense and a Christian sense are not two different things. They are two axles which for the moment seem to be radically independent, and only after a long time and with much effort does he reach the point where through and beyond the human he sees a convergence and finally an underlying identity.

Our contention is, then, that the union of the two, the discovery of the coherence of all being, is not there for him at the outset, at least not in the form of reflection, at most only as a postulate which determines the direction of research. Nevertheless, the pressure toward harmony is there in his spirit from the very beginning—simply because he has such a strong cosmic sense and such a strong Christian sense, and the two call for adjustment. Here, perhaps, the Roman Catholic idea of the analogy of being plays the part of a promise that assures him of success in achieving the synthesis.

It seems to me to be important that we should note at the outset that Teilhard's concern is not to achieve theoretically a unifying cosmic formula. (This disinguishes him from Hegel, whose approach is otherwise similar.) His concern is rather to unite two divergent views, or, one might say, two passions which cannot be left unrelated. This gives to Teilhard's thought, for all its concern for detailed scientific questions, an existential nuance, an element of confessional commitment, which cannot fail to move anyone who reads him.

3. EVOLUTION AS THE LINK BETWEEN THIS WORLD
AND THE NEXT, THOUGHT AND BEING,
THEORY AND PRACTICE

Teilhard's passion for unity takes effect in the embracing of all forms of beings under the slogan of a comprehensive development. Both this world and the next participate in this development—the new magical word. This world participates inasmuch as it contains biological phenomena which develop out of one another either in ongoing processes or in leaps or mutations. The next world participates inasmuch as powers of divine direction, intelligent and spiritual inwardness, are at work in these phenomena.

But this concept of development has further implications. As it embraces both worlds, it also comprehends subject and object, thought and being. Thought and knowledge do not confront this development at an objective distance. They are part of it.[19] For at one of its stages matter takes on soul and spirit. It becomes conscious of itself. Teilhard calls this stage that of the noosphere. Thought is thus brought into the development. It has a specific place in the cosmic process. It belongs to one of its stages. It is thus set within the horizon of temporality. This distinguishes Teilhard's view from that of Kant, for whom thought was related to timelessly fixed categories and forms of perception. Altering Descartes, one might say that Teilhard not only does not see the *res cogitans* (the thinking thing) and the *res extensa* (the extended or objective thing) confronting one another, but the latter actually becomes the former and both are based on the same identity. To give thought a place in the world, Teilhard says in his anthropology, he had to internalize matter, so that spiritual possibilities and self-awareness might arise out of it. He had to conceive of an energy of the spirit, a mounting noogenesis which, in opposition to entropy, would give evolution a meaning, a thrust, a critical point, and finally cause all things to return to Someone.

As the duality of this world and the next, subject and object, is resolved in the unity of evolution, so the opposition between the church and the world, redemption and the cosmos, is also to be overcome. The same concept of evolution, which through Darwin's theory of descent caused deep alienation between biology and theology and made faith an extraterritorial stranger in the modern academic world, will bring the two close together again. The anxiety which results from the falling apart of the different spheres of being —nature and spirit, God and world—is an essential reason why many members of the present generation find their secret longings fulfilled in Teilhard's unitary view.

We must consider a final point, however, at which Teilhard's thinking satisfies this longing. In addition to the dualisms already mentioned, that between thinking and action, theory and practice has already been overcome in principle. Teilhard summons us to bring creation or the cosmos to fulfillment, not to be mere passengers going along with evolution, but to want this evolution and to advance it.

Here there is a formal analogy to Karl Marx and indirectly to Hegel. Our will is certainly confronted by the ineluctability of development and its historical processes. But at one of its stages development produces a being that has consciousness and can perceive the laws governing its processes. This fact confers upon that being the freedom to relate to these processes, to want them, and by doing so to promote them, so that necessity becomes volition. This is the point of the dictum of Hegel and Marx that freedom is insight into necessity.

To be able to fulfill the world in this sense, we have to have a comprehensive and systematic perception of it. Knowledge of the cosmos is thus the condition of our being able to trigger the processes which will complete it. This being so, intellectual discovery and synthesis are no longer mere speculation, thinks Teilhard, but creation. More precisely, one should say that they are active intervention in the event of creation. They change an attitude of mere contemplation into an effective cause. In any case, the consummation of things is tied to their exact perception by us. Those thinkers are partly right, then, who take it that a supreme act of collective vision will be the crown of evolution and that this will come about through the concerted work of human thought and research. The initial motive may be that we want to know for the sake of knowing, but at a higher level ability is made possible by knowledge, and we thus enter the active sphere. But mere entry into this sphere does not fulfill our human mission in the service of the spirit. For with increasing ability we have to *do* more, and doing more means *being* more.

Here again there is some association with the Marxist demand that it is not just a matter of understanding the world but of changing it. Yet there is also an obvious difference. For what we have here is not merely the pragmatic goal of improving the world but a submissive relation to creation with our human *being* more as its goal. In spite of this distinction, it is understandable that there should be some uneasiness under the cardinals' hats in Rome. Within these all-integrating syntheses, are not the familiar battle lines blurred and the traditional fences treated as nonexistent? Are not all enemies and rebels seen as friends who are all without exception embraced by the one unit and foreseen in the same divine conception of the world?

4. THE SPIRIT OF LIFE AFFIRMATION

It is not just the synthesis as such that is fascinating. So, too, is the spirit of affirmation which emanates from it. We know the thesis of many secular and Christian pessimists that the technology which derives from atomic physics is destructive. Even more so is the possibility of biological manipulation, the interference with genes. To know more than we can master, than serves to make us *become* more, leads to mischief.

In contrast, Teilhard's work represents a strong and enthusiastic affirmation of what is elsewhere feared. Teilhard finds in the idea behind creation the opportunity for knowledge to lead to true ability. The results of atomic physics, the discoveries of virus research, and the ever more penetrating understanding of genetic processes are for him signs of a coming mastery of the very processes of life. The approaching synthetic production of proteins will one day enable us to do things which it seems that the earth alone cannot do, i.e., initiate a new wave of artificially made organisms. Teilhard refers in this regard to the human "recranking" of evolution, i.e., to an act in virtue of which and through which humans take the initiative in completing creation instead of letting it come to a final halt by letting it take its own course. The task of being an impulse which creation itself has generated for its own further advance is one that is providentially assigned to us.

Theologically one might say that at a certain stage of evolution, when matter achieves self-awareness in the human brain, humanity is given the role of cooperating with the Creator, of co-creating. That it is by creation adapted to this role is a defense against its Promethean misunderstanding. Obviously the motive which leads us to grasp the helm of creation is not blasphemous aggression as in the case of Prometheus but a humble claiming of grace.

The secret dream of human research extends beyond atomic and molecular energy to an achievement of mastery over the basic energy which all the forms of energy serve. We can then together take the helm of the world by laying our hands on the true driving force of evolution. The bold who admit that their hopes extend thus far are for Teilhard the most human of all of us. In this sense there is a smaller difference than one might think between research and worship.

That the research which leads to worship is in antithesis to Prometheus is shown by what Teilhard said about the giant cyclotron at Berkeley in California, which he visited in 1952. Writing in 1953 about this giant instrument of research, which was for him a symbol of the noosphere, of what is superhuman, he said that what we simply call research commended itself warmly and colorfully to him, with special force, like faith and worship, which hitherto had been regarded as alien to science. Research and worship come from a common root, and it was his life's work to give intellectual expression to this synthesis.

Where had there ever been anything approaching this technological adoration among previous theologians? Francis of Assisi's "Hymn to the Sun" is applied here to the world of technology. This world is no longer excluded from God's kingdom as a world of demonic revolt. It is no longer made an antibody in creation. The cosmos is the body of him who is and is to come. Matter can be called the flesh of Christ.[20]

5. STRUCTURE AND IMPULSE OF DEVELOPMENT

What are the features of evolution, which has such a decisive impact on Teilhard's view of the world? In reply I will simply list its stages.

The first stage is that of inorganic nature prior to the coming of life.

The second stage is that of vitalizing. It is marked by the self-propagation of organisms, by a process that was not present in gases or fluids or the crust of the earth, including crystals. It stands in contrast to the destiny of the purely material world, which will end in a fiery death.

The third stage is that of the development and differentiation of organic matter. From the single-celled creatures which cover the earth like humus, there arises the branching tree of life with four main branches. From one of these come the mammals, reptiles, and amphibious creatures, and from the mammals come the primates, the group with the future. Teilhard depicts this as a rocket with many stages, humanity being the tip.

This leads us already to the fourth stage, that of cerebration. Here the boundary is crossed from the biosphere to the noosphere, to the realm of consciousness and reflection. Consciousness, which is present already in other higher creatures, condenses in humans into self-consciousness. As thinking beings, humans are marked by the highest stage of complexity thus far attained, as may be seen from the structure of the human brain. The furnishing of living creatures with a highly differentiated brain, and consequently with consciousness and thinking ability, brings the universe to self-consciousness at this one point. Hence humanity is no other than evolution coming to awareness of itself. The opportunity is thus afforded for knowledge of evolution and hence for the responsible willing and advancing of its thrust.

The fifth and last stage for Teilhard will be the final point of development, when matter will be completely transparent for the spiritual inwardness which illuminates and ensouls it, as signalized already in the noosphere. At this endpoint, Omega, the whole development will reach its culmination. It is leading to a mystical union with God. At this point all things will come together, find their explanation, feel secure, and possess themselves.

How will this development come about? What is its driving force?

In describing the rise and development of new forms, Teilhard largely makes use of views and concepts current in biology. He is aware of the accidental leaps that are called mutations and that are commonly assumed in evolutionary theories. But these mutations, as solely the results of accidents, cannot explain all phenomena. Teilhard believes that we cannot dispense with a directing factor if we are to interpret orthogenesis. What he has in mind is the movement of evolution toward a goal. This orientation to a goal may be seen most clearly in the privileged lines of development that lead to the noosphere, in the flight of the tip of humanity and its visionary culmination at point Omega. The impulse at work in orthogenesis, the guiding factor, finds its opportunity precisely in the fact that evolution is not causally determined but points of mutation are open to changes in direction.

This brings us to the core of Teilhard's view. Its fundamental thought is that of cooperation between the material factor and a system of inwardness, or a spiritual factor that is built into the world and is at work as the power that directs evolution. If Hegel says that being is rational as history, Teilhard would say, perhaps, that it is spiritual. This cosmic power of spirit has been at work in the world from the very first, even at the pre-life stage. At the most primitive stages, matter has a crude and rudimentary psyche. Nothing through all the different stages of evolution could emerge one day as the final goal if it were not obscurely present from the very outset.

We are reminded here, perhaps, of the type of monistic development that one finds in Origen. The original unity contains all the stages of development, splits them up into polar dualisms, and then, after this interlude, brings what is discursive back to original unity. Even in Norse myth, the contrary forces Odin and Loki have the same basis and finally come back together again.

Teilhard's concept of the spiritual endowment of matter, which comes out with increasing clarity in the course of orthogenesis, may also carry other associations. One might think of the logical embarrassment of a begging of the question by the prior smuggling in of what is later disclosed. The secret presuppositions are hidden like larvae in the ground and in the spring will produce a host of magically colored butterflies. Undoubtedly what might be regarded as a trick can hardly be deliberate manipulation in so respectable a figure as Teilhard. But one can hardly refrain from at least raising the question.

6. HUMANITY IN THE PROCESS OF EVOLUTION

The decisive point is that orientation to a goal, or the character of evolution as orthogenesis, is hardly conceivable for Teilhard unless one takes into account a spiritual factor which is at work in matter from the beginning. It is because of this that the mutations have the significance they do. They offer this spiritual principle room for development. A world process which is causally determined along the lines of Laplace—running off like a film—leaves no place for interventions or changes of direction. This room for development enables the spiritual principle to work as an "inherent preference," an authority which prefers and selects. This inherent preference may be seen most clearly in the future-oriented group of primates, which has been chosen out of the general biological process and leads on to humanity. It is in this connection that humanity is called the tip of a rocket with multiple stages. Humans, as the only creatures to reach the noosphere, are a symbol of the power of selection which elevates them from among the innumerable varieties of bios.

Since the process of evolution does not end with the development of humans, the question arises whether we can say where humans stand today in the total process, whether we can fix the point on the cosmic clock, between morning and midday, which is our present minute. All universally inclined thinkers, e.g., Hegel and Spencer, feel an impulsion to look back from the breadth of the dimensions of the cosmos to the point and moment which belongs to them as a mirror of the cosmos.

For this epochal determination of our present existence Teilhard's symbol of the globe offers an important illustration which helps to clarify the past, present, and future stages of evolution. The South Pole represents point Alpha, from which the privileged human race spreads out. In this movement the various human groups, the types and races, diverge. This divergence reminds us of the greater distance between the lines of longitude at the equator. There is, of course, intercommunication at this stage of divergence. Nevertheless, the basic character of this stage—on the way to the equator—is that of divergence and differentiation. The present distinctions and antitheses of the race are its result. One might think of the dispersion and confusion of languages at the tower of Babel. When the equator is crossed, the thrust of evolution is reversed. The lines of longitude come together again until they merge at the opposite pole, point Omega. A convergent trend replaces the divergent trend. The essential marks of this new trend are the increasing number of people, greater communication between groups, and the mutual interpenetration of cultures and civilizations.

It is not as though the way of convergence is as smooth and free from problems as the mathematical path of lines of longitude. Where there are people, there are no mathematically calculable straight lines. As Teilhard sees it, this second phase is marked, not by harmonious interfusion, but by severe conflicts, by attraction and repulsion, by expansion and suppression. In the war between China and Japan, Teilhard himself learned to know too much about the depths of human nature to be seriously tempted by any utopian visions of universal harmony. He realized that the gift of reason corresponds to a debit of unreason. The noosphere is the very opposite of a homogeneous structure. It is a converging phase full of threats and pain. Hence the prognosis of coming evolutionary developments goes hand in hand with the task of being a watchman and adviser who can help to guard against aberrations.

If we try to fix our own place in this twofold movement, we can say that we are already in the phase of convergence, that we have thus passed the equator, that we are on the way to point Omega. The lines of longitude are getting closer. International exchanges and economic relationships have reached an intensity never known before. Systems of commerce and information are reducing the distances between us. To an increasing extent humanity is seen to be a unity which faces common dangers in solidarity and is developing a collective consciousness. This psycho-biological megasynthesis is not a state but it enables us to see the goal when all humanity will be one. Individuals will remain such in body, but their spirits will become integral parts of the brain of the noosphere, an organ for the operation of the collective consciousness of all humanity. Here again the analogy of the monistic schema of thought reminds us of some of the visions of Marxism, especially the expectation of a new humanity with social organs which will think and feel and act as a collective being.

The final stage *prior* to the beginning of this convergence is that of the excessive estimation of the individual in the West. This expresses the greatest distance between the lines of longitude at the equator. But it is yielding to a phase of increasing socialization. In depicting this phase Teilhard is not afraid to use a dubious term like "totalitarian social life." He is well aware of the doubtful associations of the phrase, but his spiritual optimism is more than a match for these, for even in the distortions of totalitarianism he sees the deflected line of convergence. Furthermore, as we have seen, he makes it plain that the path to point Omega is not a harmonious one. (But does he not give us here a formulation which might be used just as well for the Marxist path to the classless society?) Humanity moves toward point Omega with tentative and often unsuccessful experiments. The path is not direct. We have to take the failures into account. Hence we are not to think that they contradict the convergent movement. One of the most striking differences between humans and animals is that the former are not automatically guided by evolution. They see what they are doing. They make programs. They have to grasp creation consciously and willingly as those who do things. This area of freedom carries with it a corresponding risk, so that Teilhard is not deceived by totalitarian caricatures of convergence.

7. SYNTHESIS OF NATURE AND GRACE
AT POINT OMEGA

As the cosmos moves in this way to point Omega, the final and most powerful synthesis comes to light, that of nature and grace. Roman Catholicism, this Jesuit thinks, is narrow-minded if it stays with medieval cosmogonies instead of integrating the kerygma (the Christian message) into the new understanding of the world and using the tremendous opportunities of expression that this affords. When we make this integration we give the appearance of Christ a new cosmic meaning which cannot be seen in any other way.

As Teilhard sees it, his scientific view impinges upon what Christian dogma also says. This dogma has, indeed, a firm place within evolution, so that the stages of this might finally be described as cosmogenesis, biogenesis, noogenesis, and Christogenesis. The universe comes to completion in a synthesis of centers, in a perfect agreement with the laws of union. God is the center of centers. Christian dogma culminates in this ultimate vision.

With an incomparable kerygmatic correlation, then, the results of scientific analysis are stated and anticipated in dogma. The analysis would not have shown this, or, better, Teilhard would not have carried its implications so far, even to point Omega, if the kerygma had not supported and confirmed biological discovery from a different angle. Along these lines Teilhard says that the final goal, God as the center of centers, corresponds so exactly to point Omega that he would never have dared to grasp and formulate the Omega hypothesis rationally if he had not already had an ideal vision of it in his believing consciousness, indeed, if he had not already had there its living reality. Thus the final goal is the synthesis of the believing and the knowing consciousness, of noogenesis and Christogenesis. Naturally this raises the question whether the categories of dogma were not at work already when Teilhard began to investigate the cosmos, whether he did not first put into the cosmos the things he later saw there. The problem thus faces us again whether a begging of the question does not lie at the root of this whole conception.

At any rate, Christ is for Teilhard the point of junction for the two elements in his thinking, God and the universe. What is more tempting than to assume that the inherent preference which gives development its direction is the Christ-factor which is built into the cosmos from the very first? This gives a new meaning to the doctrine of the incarnation, of Christ's entry into the cosmos. Dogmatic statements about Christ's pre-existence also acquire an unexpected content. They are no longer interpreted merely by the figure of Christ himself but also by cosmological findings. Here again two series of statements coincide which at first seem to be far apart and completely heterogeneous.

Understood this way, of course, the incarnation is still hidden, if not completely so. It cannot be completely hidden because the soul of the world which Teilhard discovers, the spiritual factor which is built into it as the Christian element, cannot be a brittle creation of his own thinking but forms the content of a long historical revelation. Hence even those who believe least cannot fail to see here one of the essential driving forces of human progress. To that extent the powers of the incarnation are not totally concealed.

If observation and interpretation reveal traces of it in this way, the understanding of evolution becomes almost a proof of God which seems to add the evidence of sight to blind faith. These traces, or the spermatic logos, will be unambiguously manifest only at the end of the process, i.e., when the eschatological point Omega is reached. Only then will Christ reach his fullness. Only then, if one may put it thus, will his incarnation *in* the world become his identification *with* the world. Only then will his cosmic character be revealed. The total Christ comes to fulfillment, and will be achieved, only at the end of universal evolution. Hence we do not get close to this full eschatological figure of Christ when we believe contrary to appearances, and therefore in a Nevertheless, but only when we merge totally into the universe. When we do this, when we become "worldly," we necessarily draw near to the spiritual or Christian components of the world. "I know," says Teilhard, "that I can be saved in discipleship of the incarnate God, whom he reveals to me, only when I merge totally into the universe."

Thus Christ becomes the cosmic Christ instead of the Redeemer related to individuals and individual salvation. He becomes the Pantocrator and the center of universal history. Undoubtedly this sheds new and fascinating light on certain christological passages, e.g., Colossians 1:16 ff. At the same time one hesitates to accept a speculation which makes of Christ a cosmic principle that can be perceived apart from faith, the Christian message being understood only as a confirmatory kerygma which fits exactly into prefabricated epistemological forms. The suspicion that this may be just an apologetic trick—a begging of the question—cannot be silenced. The harmonizing tendency of Thomistic thought, which tries to relate nature and grace in a schema of analogy, is pushed to an extreme here and made into an eschatological congruence of nature and grace, or, even more sharply, the two are fused into an identity. One can thus understand why the church's teaching office feels that this doctrine is both close to its own and yet also alien to it.

What prevents us from treating Teilhard's view as an apologetic device, what makes it, indeed, so attractive, is the impression that we have here of something more and other than mere speculation. In Teilhard the union that is perceived between faith and science, or grace and nature, is the goal of a breakthrough in the history of life, a breakthrough from suffering from the dispersion of being to its overcoming in unity. Teilhard thus begins at the same point as we all do. This makes all that he says so familiar. The harmony here is not a music of the spheres that he heard from the beginning. He is stuck with the same dissonances as we are, and the harmony is the object of a *search*. In a new way, and in face of a changed world situation, he wants to find in modern biology and atomic physics the unity of the medieval view of the world in which heaven and earth and hell are finally related to one another. Is this merely a sublime form of nostalgia? At any rate, the unity will be completely different from what it once was. Nevertheless, Teilhard thinks, it can be achieved. This conviction is what makes his thought so fascinating. The great event of his life, he could say, was the gradual identifying of the two suns in the heaven of his soul. One of these was the cosmic climax as seen from the standpoint of evolution or cosmic convergence. The other was the risen Jesus of Christian faith. These two suns are identical. Hence we move in a wrong direction if we separate them, if we see science and faith apart or in antithesis to one another.[21]

b. Critical Considerations

1. THE STARTING POINT OF CRITICISM

Certain criticisms were implicit in our presentation. All we need to do now is to develop them systematically. Two points will fix their direction.

First, the charm of a total view of the cosmos and Christ, of science and faith, of development, creation, and eschatology, is obviously purchased at the cost of keeping the frontiers between exact findings and speculative interpretation open and fluid. Thus one cannot objectify a decisive premise like the cooperation of the inherent preference, which advances what is complex and spiritual, with the material world and its autonomous development. It seems as though this may be read off from phenomena, but there is uncertainty as to whether it was not first read into them in a way that prejudices their investigation.

Second, certain vital questions remain open even on the side of speculative interpretation. I will mention only the most important.

Teilhard finds one profound and momentous break in the span of evolution. Up to the presence of the earth, of the geological-anthropological phase which determines us, the noosphere with the development of the human brain has gone as far as orthogenetic evolution can take it on its own. Here evolution reaches the point where it becomes conscious of itself. It does it by creating the organ that makes this possible—the brain. This exhausts the evolutionary possibilities inherent in the *self*-development of bios. In fact, there has been no essential development in the size of the brain since the quaternary period. Teilhard's interpretation of the evolutionary halt is that now the Creator has delegated evolutionary advance to the human consciousness awakened by him. From now on humanity does not evolve but shapes itself by consciously and willingly moving toward its goal, by becoming more spiritual and unified, by creating more inward forms of collective communication. The development and fulfillment of the human race are now the content of a *program* and not a mere trend in a process working *on* it.

Apart from the theological implications of all this, to which we shall return, these theses of Teilhard contain problems which other scientists have solved in very different and even opposing ways. I am not thinking only of philosophies of nature (like that of Monod) which are also speculative and thus necessarily involve antithesis. I am not thinking, then, of the mere clash of confession and counter-confession but of scientific challenges to Teilhard's view which bring out its philosophical overhang. One such arises when with exact research it is proved, or at least made probable, that this self-transcendence of modern humanity in the final phase of the march to point Omega has no support in established evolutionary theory.

This kind of criticism may be found in H. K. Erben's work *Die*

Entwicklung der Lebewesen. Spielregeln der Evolution (1975), although the author does not deal expressly with Teilhard and refers to him only incidentally in other connections. Precisely because Erben regards the noosphere as a break in evolution in much the same way as Teilhard, the very different inferences which he makes on the basis of the facts should give us pause. Many sociologists, and even some biologists, according to a widespread view, think that our scientific and technological progress has put us in a position to influence and even direct our own evolution. By self-domestication we have finally freed ourselves from the environment and natural selection. Thus secular evolutionary research, with no theological presuppositions, can come to the same conclusion as Teilhard, namely, that humanity, as a product of evolution, can take control of it, this creative role being assigned, however, not to Homo religiosus but to Homo faber as he makes use of his capabilities. Nothing, however, is more superficial, shortsighted, and doubtful, thinks Erben, than the utopianism that might derive from wishful thinking in this regard.

The exact data that resist this idea of self-directed higher evolution, and prove the ancient dream of a superhumanity to be unrealistic,[22] include especially the extremely high degree of specialization that Homo sapiens, the latest product in the human series, has achieved. For reasons that need not be presented here, this specialization carries with it a degenerative element, so that the development of an ultra- or superhumanity, a new type of humanity superior to all that has gone before, is most unlikely. As a very progressive and specialized line, the species Homo has almost certainly become sterile from the evolutionary standpoint. Expectation of an ultrahumanity is a "waiting for Godot." One might even go further and say that modern prosperity will soon end with rising population and be followed by a decline. There will be no superhumanity. We ourselves, the products of progress, are this ultrahumanity.

Instead of a self-transcending leading to point Omega, instead of a spiritualizing of the universe, Erben thinks the direction is toward the extinction of humanity, though there can be no calculating when this will come. What lies ahead of Homo sapiens is a gradual decline. The end has to come, for overpopulation will exhaust the raw materials that are at our disposal in the natural world around us, and this will lead to a breakup of civilization, of the megaprothesis that the species needs to survive.

The picture of humanity itself in this declining phase is not a pleasant one and forms a kind of caricature of the expected superhumanity. According to Paul Lüth,[23] who bases his view on Erben's depiction of evolution thus far, our descendants will become "egg heads," with large, round, and smooth heads, prominent foreheads, and underneath small, pointed faces which will look old because of loss of teeth and the retraction of the jawbones. Hands may only have three fingers, and if Homo sapientissimus can still go on foot, the walk will be anything but gracious because of the fusing of the heel and ankle. The enormous rise in intelligence will also be accompanied by the loss of the senses of smell and touch, with most unpleasant consequences. Superhumans? Superintellectuals at most! And even if we find this diagnosis rather wild, it is at least entertaining, and should be respected as a caricature of what is in principle a serious prognosis.

If we accept the fact—and Erben in no sense disputes it—that evolution has reached a point at which humanity interferes with it, one may well imagine that the development for which it now has co-responsibility will destroy its status rather than enhance it. In place of Teilhard's spiritualizing of the cosmos, Erben speaks of a technological penetration that will produce an artificial environment. The extreme specialization which rivets us to this environment, and the using up of the raw materials on which it depends, can lead only to destruction rather than to a final consummation. The nonobjectifiable element in this view relates solely to the ethical problem how we will handle this fate, how we will wrestle with it, and how we can retard it. (Formally there is some similarity here to Oswald Spengler's *Decline of the West*, which predicts degeneration on the basis of some natural structures in the course of history, and allows us the ability only to discharge the ethical task of meeting our fate in the same way as the soldier at Pompeii.)

It is beyond the author's competence to evaluate Erben's view with the only criteria that he himself accepts, namely, those of science. There can be no doubt that he himself does all he can to avoid philosophical and ideological intrusions and to let the facts speak for themselves, even though in the early chapters he tries to show what are the limits of this kind of objectivity. In any case, this involuntary scientific counterpart to Teilhard's vision of the future has great heuristic value for us. It can help us to see where Teilhard's view passes over from evolutionary processes into metaphysics, or has metaphysics as its starting point.

2. TEILHARD'S ANTHROPOLOGICAL CONCLUSIONS

Our own interest is less in the scientific problem than in Teilhard's anthropology, to which we shall now turn. (The two are, of course, closely related, and cannot be isolated the one from the other.)

Assuming that Teilhard's thesis is correct that our evolutionary status has put us in the position of being able to direct the process of development and push it on to its goal, will we accept this task and discharge it? Teilhard raises this question, but only inasmuch as he sees some possible failures and aberrations connected with human freedom. But should not all those who are forewarned by the story of the fall consider, too, the possibility that there might be a basic perversion of humanity, that freedom might be misused, that dubious utopian ideals and idolatrous conceptions might become our program? Might not the evil, titanic, and dangerous element in us be released and become virulent by being made the goal of human self-fashioning or included at least in the project? Are the excessive forms in which things like titanism, pride, and terror have constantly recurred in history really no more than experiments in freedom which have failed for various reasons? Have they not failed for essential reasons, and predominantly because the sinister element in us is our model, and we have made a virtue out of the necessity of our questionable nature? In face of the ingenuousness of Teilhard, which leads him to miss the seriousness of this problem, do we not have to ask whether he really takes the mystery of iniquity seriously? (This will occupy us later.) The Jesuit seems not to be aware of the question whether the evolutionary status of human self-government might not be the way to the human crippling which Paul Lüth caricatures.

We must press the inquiry even further. Does not the postulate that we must now project and fashion ourselves make sense only if we know what we are meant to be instead of having to construct our own model of superhumanity, only if we are thus under the guidance of revelation (or whatever we may call the authoritative communication)? But since Teilhard does not allow for this, except to an insignificant degree, his visions take on utopian features.

Certainly, as noted, he can sometimes raise the question of aberrations in freedom and in the direction of evolution. But he renders this question innocuous by saying that even massive forms of aberration, e.g., totalitarianism and its system of terror, simply point to the legitimate line of development in the form of a new communicative sense, and are failures, then, only for secondary reasons, i.e., as early and premature experiments. Thus there might be the most terrible forms of slavery in the chains of communism and nationalism. The crystal instead of the cell, the termite structure instead of brotherhood. Nevertheless, the totalitarian principle is dreadful just because it is the distortion of a wonderful concept and is so close to the truth. One cannot contest the fact that the great machine of humanity is meant to function. It has to do so; it has to produce a surplus of spirit. If it does not function, or produces only matter, it is working in the wrong direction.

But is not this the real problem—the wrong direction? How can one oppose the truth that when the machine of humanity is used in a perverted way it produces instruments of destruction and not of advance? And how can it be improved if we do not know our goal, if we fix our own goal, and if evil has a part in the fixing of this goal? Faith, of course, can meet this doubting question with the confession that while we intend to do evil (Genesis 50:20), the Lord of history is master of this evil and will not let his plan be thwarted by it but will give it a function in relation to this plan. The author himself will make this confession. But this is not the problem. For Teilhard does not use the arguments of faith to render the evil interludes of history innocuous. He uses the arguments of his insight into evolution. It is precisely at this point that his teaching seems to be so doubtful.

That he is advancing the results of thought (with faith only as a heuristic stimulant or confirmatory reference, but not reducing the autonomy of thought); that Teilhard really speaks in the name of thought and research, comes out with particular pregnancy in the final passage of his work *The Appearance of Man*. Here he summarizes the three phases of evolution from simple organisms to eschatological union, and he does it all in the name of science, logical deduction, and thinking things through. All science, he tells us, shows that at the stage of simple organisms there is a differentiation of the union of elements which brings them close to one another, i.e., unites them organically. But at the stage of reflective life, this union is personalized. By way of co-reflection, we must logically infer, the union totalizes the elements into an unknown entity at whose upper limit the difference between the universe and the person disappears.

This is the law of the complexity of consciousness when it is thought through consistently.

3. THE HOMELESSNESS OF FAITH

One may well hesitate to take a system of this rank, which is so existentially rooted, and fit it into general rubrics by labeling it "Hegelian" or "Gnostic." Nevertheless, one can hardly avoid stating that there are some monistic and pantheistic traits in Teilhard's thought. Connected with this, and illustrating it, is the fact that the Jesuit has no real home in his thinking for faith. The word "faith" can have many different connotations in the Christian tradition, but its main emphasis—and this is not merely the Reformation view—is on an act of trust, of a contested trust. This trust is contested because it has to maintain itself against appearances, in which the reality of God is by no means evident but is hidden and challenged a thousandfold.

When tempted in the wilderness, Jesus refuses to perform a demonstrative miracle which will bring him out of concealment and make him evident to appearances. That he should jump down unharmed from the pinnacle of the temple, or make bread out of stones, or present himself as the open ruler of the world, thus proving objectively to the eyes of all that he is the legitimate Son of God, is for him no less than a satanic temptation which he rejects (Matthew 4:1 ff.). Instead he takes the path of hiddenness to the cross, and, according to the oldest gospel, he comes to his end with the cry, "My God, my God, why hast thou forsaken me?" Christ is not manifested to the eyes of all as the Pantocrator. There is no syllogism by which we may say, "Therefore he is the Christ of God." He discloses himself only to a trust which withstands the hiddenness, the concealment of the cross, and the counterargument of appearances. "Nevertheless, I am continually with thee," even though everything speaks against it (Psalm 73:23). It is of a piece with this that faith can be understood only in terms of two dimensions, namely as faith "in," but also as faith "against."

Faith, then, stands in contrast with sight, in which we may see God as he is and know him with the immediacy with which we are known by him (1 Corinthians 13:12). To want to make God already an object of sight, perception, or thought, is to anticipate the eschatological state (in a Promethean or pious way) and necessarily to alienate the concept of God, making it a reflection of one's own spirit and adapting it into one's own system. The idea of a heavenly alter ego of our own creation, or Feuerbach's theory of projection with all its modern, e.g., psychoanalytical, variations, might well find confirmation in the resultant concepts of God.

Teilhard (not, of course, in his personal Christianity but in his systematic construction) can hardly avoid coming close to concepts of this kind. His thinking has more affinity to sight than to faith. The self-actualizing God who is the principle of orthogenesis seems, at least, to be less of a personal object of faith and more the object of a divinatory power of apprehension linked with empirical observations and rational analyses. How can a thinking in which evolution awakens to itself, and which is thus based on a final identity with its theme, still be the place for a Nevertheless?

The identity of researcher and theme produces a necessary epistemological analogy between being and consciousness. This is ultimately based on the fact that the two are two sides of the same reality. It is evolution that produces consciousness and gives rise to the noosphere. This is why we humans can *see* the cosmos, its development, and the spiritual background of this development. This is why, seeing, we no longer need faith.

One might adapt Goethe's statement and say that the eye which sees the sun derives from the sun and is thus "sunlike." We see here a reality which is identical with us, and we do so with the help of an organ, the brain, which this reality made. We are reminded of a saying of Hegel (in his *Lectures on Religion*) to the effect that the infinite spirit knows itself in finite knowledge, and conversely the finite spirit knows its knowledge as the infinite spirit. This is the general concept of religion. An embracing monon is present here in which we are not merely close to the spiritual background of being (Hegel's absolute spirit) but regard ourselves as in ultimate identity with it—so much so that the subject-object relation is removed between absolute spirit and finite spirit.

This brings us to the most profound reason why Teilhard can find no systematic home for faith. The Christian antithesis between faith and sight cannot be understood apart from the story of the fall. The original state in Paradise enjoys immediacy to God. But this is lost. Taking the forbidden fruit, seeking to be as God, has brought with it backsliding and alienation—an alienation that we cannot understand without the symbol of the original state. Now God is indeed the Wholly Other. He is not manifest. He is not available as a possible object of experience like trees, stones, or stars. He has withdrawn from sight. The abyss which has opened up can be bridged only by the "Nevertheless, I am continually with thee."

In Teilhard, however, there is no such fate of alienation.[24] Hence there is no bridge of a Nevertheless. A philosophy of identity links us with the spiritual basis of being and make this manifest with the immediacy which in biblical thinking is called sight.

4. THE DOWNPLAYING OF EVIL

The difficulty of giving evil an appropriate place in Teilhard's system, or understanding it as sin, is connected in his thinking with the problem of the homelessness of faith. In the epilogue to his anthropology Teilhard reacts with some sensitivity against the objection that in the landscape of his thought there is only light and no shadow. His sole concern, he says, is to display the positive essence of the biological process of the development of humanity. He does not regard it as necessary to expound the negative side or to draw attention to the shadows in the landscape. Pain, guilt, and tears are only by-products of noogenesis in its operation. They are not characteristics of humanity itself but accidental accompaniments. Even so, they do not have the negative accent of liabilities. They are often valuable and may be put to fresh use. They thus form meaningful steps in the teleological process. As one might say with Albrecht Schaeffer, on the tree of humanity there are only blossoms of two different colors. The darker hues are shadows, but they are not darkness, and certainly not the power of darkness.

This relativizing of evil is not surprising, for it results from the autonomy of the monistic schema. In every form of monism, evil is dialectically integrated into a process which needs it and makes it a creative impulse. Mephistopheles wills evil, but at the end he can only produce good. In Hegel evil becomes a transition, a principle which is finally creative. It can no longer be understood as an opposing force, as an ultimate estrangement, as an independently active power.

The interpretation of totalitarian tendencies in Teilhard's understanding of history, which we have mentioned already, offers a good example. The place of freedom, which the noosphere, produced by evolution, puts at our disposal, involves risks. Human beings can miscalculate. Our own navigation may steer us away from the real current of evolution and send us on detours. It may even lead to a distorted view of Omega similar to the totalitarian caricature of unity.

It is typical of Teilhard's thinking that such deviations do not seriously affect the optimistic expectation of a happy ending. How is it that even in the distorted concept of totalitarianism he can still see traces of the true consummation of history, so that even the aberration can be a meaningful phase in the advance toward this? Teilhard is certain that the inexorable movement of evolution can handle it. The deviations automatically contribute to the proper thrust. They are interludes, no more. Evolution has at its disposal a power of self-correction.

This is why evil is not a serious opponent of ours, or a demonic force. As in all monistic systems, it is viewed negatively. It is simply a lack of good which can always be made up, or a vacuum which mobilizes the abhorrence of a vacuum and therefore seeks to be filled. One might say that it acts as a brake. It prolongs things. But even this function can be a productive one. To use an illustration, one might say that the propulsion which drives the hand of a clock forward is related to a checking mechanism which gives the movement meaning. Evil in the mechanism of the world's clock is not just sand in the machine. It does not simply destroy or disrupt. It is the checking mechanism in forward propulsion which is built into evolution and has, therefore, a necessary function.

Teilhard has no sense of evil, no sense of the demonism of human pride which finds expression in the fall and displays a misuse of human freedom that can corrupt creation and with a certain amount of technological power can lead to self-destruction. This is why Teilhard is always a little embarrassed when he comes to speak about these questions.

I fear that precisely this weakness is what is attractive to many people of our generation. In fashionable utopias, in the visions that kindle revolutionary passions, we see again and again that the host is not reckoned with, namely, those whose wickedness sabotages ideal constructions of the world. They can do this so effortlessly that the constructions leave them out of account and thus enable them to work anonymously and in disguise. People do not detect the devil.

At any rate, it is a huge mistake to assume that if we achieve perfect social structures, crime, envy, hate, and other inferior impulses will automatically disappear. For those whose gaze is sharpened by the biblical outlook, the exact opposite is the case. Utopian orders will fail precisely because we ourselves are faulty and are thus the saboteurs of creation.

For this reason we must not put the cart before the horse. In plain terms, it is not enough to seek merely the perfection of the world's order, whether in the revolutionary sense of trying to achieve it with the passion of a Promethean activist, or in Teilhard's sense of dreaming of point Omega, when beyond all the confusion and mistakes the happy end of history will come with evolutionary ineluctability.

For Christians the true and central task is still to keep in view the crisis of the human heart and to offer the power of renewal which the Christian message promises. Only when we have seen the darkness of the heart and considered the promise that light will come into it, that the power of grace and redemption will offset it, only then, I think, are we secure against utopian dreams and can achieve the balance that will enable us to work realistically and soberly in the world and to make it a little more just, a little closer to the plan of creation. God's future is not the dream of a perfect world. This future is the situation of the father waiting to welcome the prodigal home. This son will not find his way back from abroad, and be received, by some automatic process, in a dialectical reversal. It will always be the miracle of a grace for which the calculations of thought are never a match.

5. TEILHARD'S ANTHROPOLOGY SQUEEZED BETWEEN THE HOLY SPIRIT AND THE SPIRIT OF THE AGE

There can be no doubt that Teilhard is a Christian deeply rooted in the Roman Catholic tradition and that essential features of his system are influenced by Scholasticism, especially the principle of the analogy of being. Nevertheless, he breaks through this tradition to the extent that, expressed in academic terms, the Renaissance achieves dominance over his scholastic foundations and brings him close to the spirit-monism of Hegel.

This is particularly evident in his anthropology, where the autonomy of his monastic approach compels him to leave no place for the doctrine of the fall. This is a blot on the map of his world picture. It gives the central doctrine in Christian anthropology, that of the divine likeness, a totally different form, so that it diverges considerably from the scholastic dogma.

Scholastic statements about the divine likeness of humanity cannot be understood apart from the story of the fall. This reference sees to it that a distinction is made between the natural and the supernatural components of the divine likeness. The natural side (reason, conscience, the upright stance) comes through the break of the fall only lightly affected, but the gracious or supernatural side, by which we are set in a personal relationship with God,[25] is lost with our revolt, with our "liberation." Only a new creation effected by grace can bring a restitution to the original state.

The Renaissance, which we take here as the symbol of the transition to the modern age, does not contest our character as God's image. C. Trinkaus has made the divine image the subject of a comprehensive depiction of Renaissance anthropology.[26] What happens is that there is a decisive modification. The *de facto* elimination of the doctrine of sin makes a distinction between nature and supernature superfluous. There is suddenly no point in a goal of redemption which means the regaining of our lost destiny and which therefore stands in need of grace.

Nevertheless, this cannot imply that the Renaissance has no lofty destiny for us. It, too, knows the tension between what we are and what we ought to be, between the present state and the awaited fulfillment of humanity. The reason for the tension, however, is no longer the fall, whose consequences must be overcome by redeeming grace. The tension lies in our human nature as such; we have still to *become* what in design we already *are*. The seed in us has still to come to fruition. We must be brought out of the state of incubation and become virulent. As Ebeling puts it, the fact that the rational soul is our form means that we are unformed, that we have to create and fashion ourselves into whatever form pleases us. The Renaissance is well aware of the self-transcendence which forces us to lay hold of ourselves. In distinction from Scholasticism, however, it sees here an ascent which has its basis in our natural endowment and which is achieved within the framework of our nature. There is no place in this schema for a fundamental disturbance which threatens the basis, goal, and meaning of our endowment and makes an act of redemption necessary. In this regard Goethe's *Urworte. Orphisch* offer us the clue when they describe the human entelechy which must unfold itself in life as a stamped form.

Teilhard's view, it seems to me, moves in this Renaissance direction. We do not need to be healed of a deep wound in our existence. We do not need restitution. We achieve fulfillment as the divine universe achieves fulfillment through us and our evolution. Hence there is no regeneration of something shattered, but the development of a seed to the final form envisaged for it.

The Christian vocabulary remains, but it now seems to be given a new intellectual and spiritual content. Hence we can at least understand the fears of the Vatican that the partisans of a Christian spirit of the age might hide behind the robes of a truly pious Jesuit and use the costume of the familiar terms of tradition as a mask which will enable them to occupy the temple unobserved. The call for a discernment of spirits thus becomes an urgent one (1 Corinthians 12:10).

At the same time we have here a constant problem which cannot be solved by any patent formula. This is the problem of uniting two different tasks. The first task is that of giving relevance to the Christian message by linking it with contemporary models of thought (in Teilhard's case by bringing dogma and evolutionary theory into mutual relation). The second task is that of not integrating the Christian doctrines into such models but leaving their own particular content unaffected.

Teilhard's spirit is a battlefield for these two forces. Perhaps one might speak of a tragic conflict which is constitutionally inherent in theological thinking. I myself cannot believe that Teilhard is opportunistically concerned about conformity to the age and is thus a culpable heretic. It seems more likely to me that he is the victim of a conflict, of a tragedy of thought (although I am venturing to use here a term that is not of Christian origin).

Only a Pharisee would evade the task that Teilhard has set himself, that of making dogma relevant and relating the two suns of the cosmos about which he speaks. It is easy to be orthodox in the ivory tower of the esoteric, on the level of purely dogmatic reflection. But by human standards, even those of the church's highest teachers, we can hardly judge here who will be on the side of the goats, and who on the side of the sheep, when it comes to the Last Judgement.

We have to risk running into heresy in order to win the truth.

Epilogue

Luther advanced the following theses in his *Disputatio de homine* of 1536.[27]

In this life we are for God only the material for life in its future form. Similarly creation as a whole, which is now subject to vanity, is for God the material for its future, glorious form.

As heaven and earth were related from the very first to the form they would have when completed after six days, namely, as the material for this, so we in this life are related to our future form when the image of God will be restored and completed.

In the meantime we are in our sins and are increasingly justified or deformed day by day.

Notes

(REFERENCES TO THE AUTHOR'S OWN WORKS ARE ALSO REFERENCES
TO THE BOOKS MENTIONED IN THEM)

A. HUMANITY—AN OPEN QUESTION

1. We shall deal with this issue later, especially in connection with Teilhard de Chardin.
2. This question plays a vital role in Wolfhart Pannenberg; cf. *Was ist der Mensch?* Kleine Vandenhoeck-Reihe, vol. 139/140 (ET, *What Is Man?*, 1970); "Die Frage nach Gott," *Grundfragen systematischer Theologie*, 1967, pp. 361 ff. (ET, *Basic Questions in Theology*, 1970, vol. II, pp. 201 ff.); cf. also Rudolf Bultmann, *Glauben und Verstehen*, vol. I, 1933, pp. 26 ff. (ET, *Faith and Understanding*, 1969, pp. 53 ff.)
3. We shall deal expressly with Monod and Morin in H, III, b. Cf. Jacques Monod, *Chance and Necessity*, 1972; E. Morin, *Das Rätsel des Humanen. Grundfragen einer neuen Anthropologie*, 1973.
4. On the relation between myth and history, cf. my book *Der evangelische Glaube*, vol. I, 1968, pp. 74–94, 120–31 (ET, *The Evangelical Faith*, vol. I, 1974, pp. 70 ff., 100 ff.).

B. HUMANITY—AN INSECURE QUESTION

1. Arnold Gehlen, *Der Mensch*, 1950; *Urmensch und Spätkultur*, 1956; Emil Brunner, *Der Mensch im Widerspruch*, 1941 (ET, *Man in Revolt*, 1939).
2. Cf. Alexis Carrel, *Man the Unknown*; Konrad Lorenz, *Das sogenannte Böse*, 1963; *Die Rückseite des Spiegels*, 1973.

3. Cf. my book *Wer darf leben?*, 1970 (ET, *The Doctor as Judge*, 1976).
4. Peter L. Berger, *A Rumor of Angels*, 1969.
5. Heinrich Henkel, *Einführung in die Rechtsphilosophie*, 1964; Richard Lange, *Das Rätsel Kriminalität*, 1970.
6. *Whatever Became of Sin?*, 1974.
7. Hugo von Hofmannsthal, *Prosa*, vol. II, 1959, pp. 7–20.
8. Cf. *Theologische Ethik*, vol. II, 1, 1615 ff.
9. Cf. my book *Das Lachen der Heiligen und Narren*, 1974.
10. For illustrations, cf. Dries van Coillie, *Der begeisterte Selbstmord.*
11. Cf. my *Theologische Ethik*, vol. II, 1, pp. 298 ff. (ET, vol. I, 1966, pp. 643 ff.).

C. THE NEW QUESTION OF HUMANITY IN INSECURITY

1. For what follows, see my *Wer darf leben?*, 1970 (ET, *The Doctor as Judge*, 1975).
2. R. Kaufmann, *Die Menschenmacher. Die Zukunft des Menschen in einer biologisch gesteuerten Welt*, 1964.
3. Cf. *Wer darf leben?* (ET, *The Doctor as Judge*).
4. Cf. the chapter on abortion in *Theologische Ethik*, vol. III, pp. 749 ff. (ET, *The Ethics of Sex*, 1964, pp. 226 ff.).
5. Cf. *Wer darf leben?* (ET, *The Doctor as Judge*).
6. *Op. cit.*
7. Cf. the discussion of the problem of punishment in *Theologische Ethik*, vol. III.
8. For the anthropological background, cf. Lange, *Das Rätsel Kriminalität*, 1970.
9. Cf. *Theologische Ethik*, vol. III, §1578 ff.
10. Cf. my book *Leiden an der Kirche*, Furche-Stundenbuch No. 52.
11. For the relation between the modern understanding of sex and anthropology, cf. especially Armin Mohler, *Sex und Politik*, 1972.
12. Cf. *Der evangelische Glaube*, vol. I, pp. 561–63 (ET, vol. I, 1974, pp. 383 ff.).
13. Luther developed this distinction between God's alien and proper will and work, and I have made it a normative principle of Christian anthropology in my *Theological Ethics.*

D. HUMANITY, HISTORY, AND EXPERIENCE

1. We shall discuss the question of autonomy more fully in "Humanity and Norms" (F).

E. THE IMPACT OF THE MODERN UNDERSTANDING OF REALITY ON ANTHROPOLOGY

1. For a more detailed analysis, cf. *Der evangelische Glaube*, vol. I, pp. 305 ff. (ET, vol. I, 1974, pp. 276 ff.)

2. It may seem to be a contradiction that at various periods of his life, even that of his *Romans*, Barth was by no means indifferent to political ethics but took up definite positions, e.g., in his disputes with the mill-owners in Safenwil, his cooperation with the Social Democrats (unlike Friedrich W. Marquardt, I intentionally do not speak of his socialism, though this is not the place to say why), and, finally, his utterances in *Eine Schweizer Stimme* (1948), especially his advice to Czech Christians. But (as against Marquardt) I do not think that these positions were theologically based in the strict sense; they derived instead from the judgment of reason in a situation of "Perhaps, and perhaps not" (cf. my *Theologische Ethik*, vols. I and II, 1, Index; ET, vol. I). The political decision itself is not theologically based, but Barth's criticism of ideology, which is immanent in it, is. This alone—though it is not the only reason—would compel me to criticize the attempt of Marquardt to derive a theological justification of socialism from Barth's thought. Marquardt, it seems to me, is interpreting both Barth's theology and socialism with a suspicious one-sidedness.

3. Since I cannot go into this here, consult *Theologische Ethik* (Index) and *Der evangelische Glaube*, vol. II (Index) under Analogy, *analogia entis*.

4. Cf. *Der evangelische Glaube*, vol. I (ET, vol. I) under Gogarten.

5. For Anselm's understanding of truth and his ontology, see op. cit., pp. 397 ff. (ET, pp. 276 ff.). On the difference between the Greek and the Hebrew understanding of truth cf. Klaus Koch in H. R. Müller-Schwefe, ed., *Was ist Wahrheit?*, 1965, pp. 47 ff.

6. On Descartes, cf. *Der evangelische Glaube*, vol. I, §3 (ET, vol. I, ch. 3).

7. He distinguishes between *intelligere* and *cogitare*, the former having some similarity to what we mean by understanding.

8. I owe this formula to Joseph Ratzinger, *Einführung in das Christentum*, 5th ed., 1968.

9. This is true of Vico, too, with some nuances.

10. Cf. Werner Leibbrand, *Der göttliche Stab des Äskulap. Eine Metaphysik des Arztes*, 1939; Paul Christian, *Das Personverständnis im modernen medizinischen Denken*, 1952; Arthur Jores, *Menschsein*

als Auftrag, 1964. Cf. also the works of Viktor Frankl, whom we shall discuss later.

11. Cf. *Theologische Ethik*, vol. III, §2877 ff.

12. Cf. G. Scherz, *Pionier der Wissenschaft—Niels Stensen*, 1963; *Niels Stensen*, 1964.

13. One might not unjustly expect a developed doctrine of sexuality and eros in an anthropology like this. I hope I can hit the right accents in restricting my presentation to their relevance for the change in modern consciousness. For a more detailed account, cf. *Theologische Ethik*, vol. III, pp. 507–812 (ET, *The Ethics of Sex*). On the biblical view of eros and marriage, cf. H. W. Wolf, *Anthropologie des Alten Testaments*, 1974.

14. Interesting in this regard is the Pietist view of marriage; cf. *Theologische Ethik*, vol. III, p. 648.

15. On the bearing of individual eros on the problem of monogamy and polygamy, cf. *Theologische Ethik*, vol. III, pp. 579 ff. (ET, *The Ethics of Sex*, pp. 86 ff.).

16. On divorce in the Christian tradition, cf. *Theologische Ethik*, pp. 695 ff. (ET, pp. 163 ff.).

17. The great thinkers of Lutheran orthodoxy (Johann Quenstedt, Abraham Calov, Martin Chemnitz, and Johann Gerhard) show how this restricts the range of anthropological themes. They overlook all empirical data, e.g., in the human sciences, and their chapters on humanity deal only with human rectitude, sin, and the problem of freedom of the will. For a survey, cf. Heinrich Schmid, *Die Dogmatik der evangelisch-lutherischen Kirche*, 7th ed., 1893, pp. 153 ff. (ET, *The Doctrinal Theology of the Evangelical Lutheran Church*, 1889, pp. 217 ff.).

18. I recall the first and extreme form of this positivism in Max Stirner's strange book, *Der Einzige und sein Eigentum*, 1845.

F. HUMANITY AND NORMS

1. We cannot discuss here the implications of this for a theological interpretation of Kant. I refer the reader to *Theologische Ethik*, vol. I, §1441 ff., 1643 ff.

2. Loc. cit.

3. There are many valuable examples of this in the cultural revolution that swept the universities during the sixties; cf. my book *Kulturkritik der studentischen Rebellion*, 1969.

4. *Der Neid. Eine Theorie der Gesellschaft*, 2nd ed., 1968.

5. Cf. my book *Offenbarung, Vernunft und Existenz*, 5th ed., 1967.

6. Cf. *Theologische Ethik*, vol. II, 1, §1067 ff. (ET, vol. I, p. 646).
7. Cf. *Theologische Ethik*, vol. I, §1852 ff. (ET, vol. I, pp. 383 ff.).
8. Cf. *Theologische Ethik*, vol. II, 2, §401 ff. (ET, vol. II, p. 67).
9. On Marcuse, cf. *Kulturkritik der studentischen Rebellion*, pp. 40 ff.
10. Cf. the exposition and criticism of the two-kingdoms doctrine in *Theologische Ethik*, vol. I, §1783 ff. (ET, vol. I, pp. 359 ff.).
11. The death penalty is a paradigm here, but this does not mean that it has the same obligatory ranking as law itself, and is thus to be a permanent form of punishment on God's authority.
12. For a detailed interpretation of the Marxist theses, cf. my book *Die geheime Frage nach Gott*, pp. 41–90 (ET, *The Hidden Question of God*, 1977, pp. 35 ff.). On Marcuse, cf. my book *Kulturkritik der studentischen Rebellion*.
13. For a more detailed account than is possible here, cf. my book *Notwendigkeit und Begrenzung des politischen Auftrags der Kirche*, 1974.
14. For another discussion of this theme, cf. *Theologische Ethik*, vol. II, 1, §1321 ff. On secularization and its Christian origin, cf. *Der evangelische Glaube*, vol. I, §16 (ET, vol. I, ch. 16). On the implications for the church's relation to politics, cf. the work cited in note 13.
15. For further discussion, cf. my book *Die geheime Frage nach Gott*, 1972, especially pp. 71 ff. (also pp. 41 ff.) (ET, *The Hidden Question of God*, pp. 59 ff. and 35 ff.). For reason in Luther, cf. B. Lohse, *Ratio und Fides*, 1958.

G. HUMANITY AND TECHNOLOGY

1. For details, cf. my book *Wer darf leben?* (ET, *The Doctor as Judge*).
2. On Bismarck, cf. *Theologische Ethik*, vol. II, 2, §520 ff. (ET, vol. I, p. 500).

H. HUMANITY AND TIME

1. Cf. my books *Geschichte und Existenz*, 1964; *Offenbarung, Vernunft und Existenz*, 5th ed., 1967.
2. How faith sees itself grounded and how Christ as the incarnate Word transcends history are matters we cannot go into here; for a detailed discussion of Christology, cf. *Der evangelische Glaube*, vol. II, 1973, pp. 322 ff. (ET, *The Evangelical Faith*, vol. II, 1977, pp. 263 ff.

3. On this idea of silence as judgment and the general typology of history as judgment, cf. *Theologische Ethik*, vol. II, 1, pp. 580–622.
4. On the personal God, cf. *Der evangelische Glaube*, vol. II, pp. 123 ff. (ET, *The Evangelical Faith*, vol. II, pp. 102 ff.).
5. See Paul's eschatological ethics (1 Corinthians 7).
6. Cf. my book *Offenbarung, Vernunft und Existenz*, 5th ed., 1967.
7. On the terms conservative, modern, and progressive, cf. *Der evangelische Glaube*, vol. I, pp. 12 ff. (ET, vol. I, pp. 30 ff.).
8. On death, cf. E. Jüngel, *Tod* (ET, *Death*, 1974); E. Kübler-Ross, *On Death and Dying*, 1966; H. Thielicke, *Death and Life*, 1970. On the future in general, cf. J. Moltmann, *Theologie der Hoffnung*, 1964 (ET, *Theology of Hope*, 1966); W. D. Marsch, *Zukunft*.
9. For a discussion, cf. *Der evangelische Glaube*, vol. I, pp. 372 ff. (on Hegel) (ET, vol. I, pp. 259 ff.); vol. II, pp. 189 ff. (ET, vol. II, ch. 11, 3).
10. On these matters, cf. my book *Death and Life*, 1970. A revised version of this work is now available (*Leben mit dem Tod*, 1980) (ET, *Living with Death*, 1983).
11. Cf. op. cit. for a fuller treatment.
12. For an interpretation of myth, cf. *Der evangelische Glaube*, vol. I, pp. 67–143 (ET, vol. I, pp. 66–114).
13. A fuller dialogue with K. Lorenz would be desirable in view of his stimulating (and provocative) relating of zoology and theology. For a discussion I had with Lorenz, cf. E. Stammler, *Wer ist das eigentlich der Mensch?*, pp. 90 ff. Cf. also J. Monod, *Le Hasard et la nécessité*, 1970; T. Löbsack, *Versuch und Irrtum. Der Mensch: Fehlschlag der Natur*, 1974; E. Morin, *Das Rätsel des Humanen*, 1973. For documentation, cf. also Klaus Funk, *Der Mensch im Schnittpunkt von Biologie und Theologie*, 1975. I also use here my chapter on the place of humans in the world in *Theologische Ethik*, vol. II, 1.
14. *Theologische Ethik*, vol. I, §770–73 (ET, vol. I, p. 396).
15. Cf. my book *Theologie in Anfechtung*, 1949, pp. 135 ff.
16. 5th ed., 1919.
17. *Präludien*, vol. II, 9th ed., 1924. I regard the radical distinction made by Rickert and Windelband as very doubtful. The use of sociological categories in historiography (cf. Marx) has shown that some generalizing and nomothetic aspects are valid here. Nevertheless, Rickert's distinction has a good heuristic and didactic significance for us, so that we need to take note of it.
18. Cf. my book *Das Lachen der Heiligen und Narren*, 2nd ed., 1975.
19. I am borrowing here from Anselm's slogan, "Faith seeking understanding."

20. For a brilliant account of molecular biology, a subject that is hard for nonexperts to understand, cf. Salvador E. Luria, *Leben—das un-vollkommene Experiment*, 1973. This raises the issue of our control of nature and its risks. The author, unlike Monod, refrains from drawing philosophical inferences.

21. This confusion of quantity and quality is typical of Marxism-Leninism, with its materialistic basis.

22. Cf. Portmann's *Entlässt die Natur den Menschen? Gesammelte Aufsätze zur Biologie und Anthropologie*, 2nd ed., 1971.

23. On this point, cf. *Theologische Ethik*, vol. I, §690–1174 (ET, vol. I, p. 426).

24. The Yahwist (J) and Priestly Codex (P) are the sources of the biblical creation stories.

25. Cf. *Theologische Ethik*, vol. I, §763 ff. (ET, vol. I, p. 458).

26. What we here call final causes is naturally to be distinguished from the teleological considerations that may also be found in biology. Thus Lorenz asks why coral fish are colored, and adds that when biologists ask this they are not concerned about the ultimate reason for the world but only about simple things that may be investigated, the answer being that the bright colors are for protection and concealment. The final causes are, in principle, outside this kind of investigation; they belong to a different dimension.

27. 1 Corinthians 6:20; 7:23; Revelation 5:9.

I. CRITICAL ENCOUNTER WITH ANTHROPOLOGICAL CONCEPTIONS

1. On Herbert Spencer, cf. *Theologische Ethik*, vol. I, §1465 ff.

2. Albert Görres, "Physik der Triebe—Physik des Geistes. Psychoanalyse und klassische Anthropologie," *Gott in der Welt. Festgabe für Karl Rahner*, vol. II, 1964, pp. 556 ff. The quotations in the section that follows are from this essay.

3. In his important work *Grundformen der Angst* (6th ed., 1971) Fritz Riemann has shown how the relation between anthropology and cosmology is significant in the understanding of anxiety.

4. Max Schur, *Sigmund Freud. Leben und Sterben*, 1973 (ET, *Freud. Living and Dying*, 1972).

5. On the criticism of religion in Freud, cf. Ernst Stadter in *Wahrheit und Verkündigung. Festschrift für Michael Schmaus*, vol. I, 1967, pp. 285 ff.

6. Fromm, *Analytische Sozialpsychologie und Gesellschaftstheorie*, Suhrkamp ed., 1970.

7. Op. cit.
8. Freud in a letter to Oskar Pfister (see note 9).
9. *Briefe 1909–1939*, 1963.
10. The author found Görres' thesis that psychoanalysis may be adopted all the more surprising in view of his stress on its philosophical character.
11. Jaspers also draws attention to this handicap. We should have to psychoanalyze Freud himself to grasp his personality and illuminate his world of thought, but we cannot do so since, unlike most great psychologists, he kept himself hidden.
12. Some important works of Frankl are *Der unbedingte Mensch*, 1949; *Ärztliche Seelsorge*, 6th ed., 1952 (esp. Chapters 1 and 2) (ET, *The Doctor and the Soul*, 1955); *Theorie und Therapie der Neurosen*, 1956; and various essays in *Universitas*.
13. On this dialogue, cf. Uwe Böschemeyer, *Die Sinnfrage in Psychotherapie und Theologie*, 1976.
14. Cf. H. F. Steiner, *Marxisten-Leninisten über den Sinn des Lebens*, 1970; H. Rolfes, *Der Sinn des Lebens im marxistischen Denken*, 1971. Frankl refers to two Czech psychiatrists in this connection, S. Kratochvil and O. Vymetal.
15. The second and third examples are taken from Frankl.
16. Cf. my book *Wer darf leben?* (ET, *The Doctor as Judge*) and *Zwischen Gott und Satan*, 1955 (ET, *Between God and Satan*).
17. *Die Kraft zu leben. Bekenntnisse unserer Zeit*, 1963.
18. Of the books by Teilhard de Chardin, cf. especially *Letters from a Traveller*, 1962; *The Phenomenon of Man*, 1959; *The Appearance of Man*, 1965; of books about him, cf. N. M. Wildiers, *Teilhard de Chardin*, 1962; S. M. Daecke, *Teilhard de Chardin und die evangelische Theologie*, 1967. In provocative supplementation, cf. H. K. Erben, *Die Entwicklung der Lebewesen. Spielregeln der Evolution*, 1975, which traces the evolutionary story in the same way as Teilhard's works but without the metaphysical and religious hypotheses, though not overlooking the suprasensory basis, and finding in Teilhard himself a possible mediator between religion and evolutionary theory.
19. An epistemological question arises here that Konrad Lorenz addresses in his essay "Naturgeschichte des menschlichen Erkennens" in *Die Rückseite des Spiegels*, 1973.
20. Cf. L. Scheffczyk, "Der Sonnengesang des hl. Franziskus von Assisi und die 'Hymne an die Materie' des Teilhard de Chardin," *Geist und Leben*, vol. 35, 1962, pp. 219 ff.
21. Reformation theology, like any other that is open to the world, sees a need to define the relation between science and faith and not to

leave an impression of heterogeneity, contradiction, or indifference. Cf. our own discussion in H, III, b, and Werner Heisenberg, *Der Teil und das Ganze. Gespräche im Umkreis der Atomphysik*, 1969 (esp. pp. 116 ff., 279 ff.); P. Jordan, *Der Naturwissenschaftler vor der religiösen Frage*, 1963; A. K. Müller and Wolfhart Pannenberg, *Erwägungen zu einer Theologie der Natur*, 1970; G. Ewald, *Naturgesetz und Schöpfung*, 1966 (a commendable introduction).

22. On these visions, cf. E. Benz ed., *Der Übermensch. Eine Diskussion*, 1961 (note esp. the contributions by Benz, L. Müller, H. Mislin, and Adolf Portmann).

23. Paul Lüth, *Schöpfungstag und Mensch der Zukunft*, 1965.

24. In spite of his appendix on the rank and role of evil in an evolutionary world.

25. On the scholastic doctrine of the *imago dei*, cf. *Theologische Ethik*, vol. I, §948 ff. (ET, I, pp. 197 ff.).

26. *In Our Image and Likeness. Humanity and Divinity in Italian Humanist Thought*, 2 vols., 1970. Cf. Gerhard Ebeling, "Das Leben —Fragment und Vollendung," *Zeitschrift für Theologie und Kirche*, vol. 3, 1975, pp. 310 ff.

27. Weimar Edition, vol. 39, I, p. 177. In analysis, cf. Ebeling, ibid., pp. 315 ff.

Indexes

I. NAMES

II. SUBJECTS

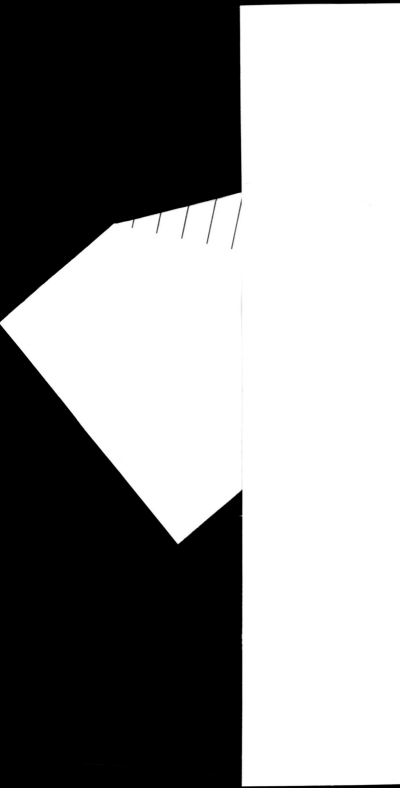

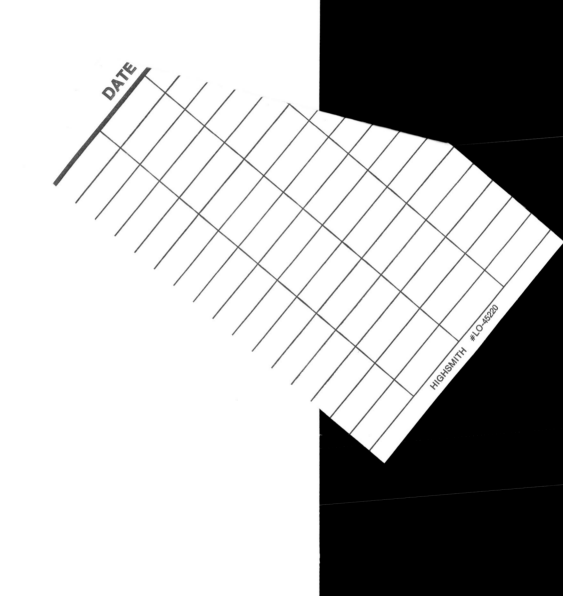

DATE

HIGHSMITH   #LO-45220